D1500741

PERSPECTIVES IN

individualized

LEARNING

ROBERT A. WEISGERBER

American Institutes for Research, Palo Alto

F. E. PEACOCK PUBLISHERS, INC.   Itasca, Illinois

Contents

Foreword

The art of progress
is to preserve order amid change,
and to preserve change amid order.
ALFRED NORTH WHITEHEAD

The tenor of our times is one of change. In every facet of society we are constantly reminded of the fact that the techniques and methods of the past no longer are apt to be unchallenged, even when they may have served quite adequately to meet past needs. Indeed, the current emphasis on change has brought with it a kind of jargon that is semantically loaded. For instance, the lexicon of "revolution," "overthrow," "upheaval," and similar words implies drastic change with *no* inherent guarantee that the new offers any improvement over the old. In contrast with "breakthrough," "advance," "innovation," and similar words we *assume* not only change but an inherent improvement. The use of these terms and the dynamics they represent are now as much a part of the educational system as they are in any other facet of our society.

It was fashionable, for quite a long time, to cite education as taking 50 years to assimilate a new development. Over the years numerous projects have been undertaken in order to disseminate educational information and to promote strategies for introducing change per se into what was viewed as essentially a static system.

Since the early 1960's, the momentum of change in education has been steadily increasing and today, partially in response to strong pressures from students, the whole framework of educational goals, curriculum, methods, and evaluation is undergoing "instant" revision . . . but *not* necessarily improvement.

In a trend that reflects our contemporary times, the emphasis is shifting from concern with the group norm toward concern for the individual, including his needs, his capabilities and his personal preferences. Though this trend is readily perceptible it is not equally clear just what *form* this individualization of teaching and learning should take, nor in what *contexts* it is most appropriately used. Interestingly enough, the very individuality of educators tends to make them view the subject of individualized learning from their unique perspectives. As a natural consequence there has been a proliferation of approaches.

ix

It is *not* the purpose of the companion books *Perspectives in Individualized Learning* and *Developmental Efforts in Individualized Learning* to provide an exhaustive coverage of all the efforts to individualize education that are under way today, for that would be as elusive a task as chasing change itself. Nor are they intended to answer the question of which approach is optimal, for that would be expected to vary with time and place, according to the educational purpose and within the constraints of locally available resources and personnel. Instead, these books are meant to provide some insight into the *process* of individualization through a selection of papers that represent both *principles and practice*.

Hopefully, the reader of *Perspectives in Individualized Learning* will develop a better understanding of some of the assumptions that underlie the concept of individualized learning, such as the determination of student need, specification of learning goals, and measurement of outcomes. The reader may also develop a better understanding of how these assumptions influence the functional roles of various components in the individualized setting, such as the teacher, technology, and facilities.

Developmental Efforts in Individualized Learning should provide the reader with an understanding of how the underlying assumptions and operational components are being applied in major developmental projects presently under way across the country. The reader will also become aware of the diversity of practice that presently characterizes individualized learning at the local school level and in higher education.

Papers have been grouped within each book to facilitate the reader's choice of which papers he reads and the order in which he reads them. Each group of papers has been prefaced with an overview page which relates each paper to the topic. In spite of this effort at grouping papers on a basis of their presumed commonality, the reader will no doubt discover that certain papers have relevance to more than one of the topical groupings. It is hoped that the overview page will be a shortcut by which the reader can readily select those papers which are most relevant to his individual interests.

Observers of the movement toward individualization in recent years will no doubt note that some of the leaders of the movement, some of the pioneering school districts, and some of the more widely published papers have not been featured in either book. This is neither an oversight nor a denial of their importance, for the work of men such as Frederic Burk, and Robert Anderson, to name two, and the pioneering of schools like Winnetka and Duluth have helped to lead the way in a very real sense. Instead, these books, to the extent that space permits, will try to provide a balance between some familiar authors and some relatively new ones. An attempt will be made to give recognition to modest experiments in local schools as well as to larger, better known projects. As a result of presenting a variety of views, the reader may better be able to recognize and adopt those evolving ideas and approaches that seem to be pertinent to his *own* individual needs.

As suggested by Alfred North Whitehead's statement, cited previously, commitment to change per se is not sufficient. For educational change to be an improvement rather than simply a replacement of the old routine, Whitehead suggests that the change should be orderly rather than chaotic. If, in the broadest sense, the experimental, analytic studies of researchers and the iterative, pragmatic tryouts of educators can be interrelated through these companion books (i.e., seen as parts of a larger process of evolution in learning), then a measure of order may be introduced to optimize the sweeping changes which are already under way in education.

Lest it be overlooked, the effect to be achieved through the symbiotic interplay of change and order, according to Whitehead, is *progress*. This progress, it seems to this writer, cannot be simply equated to the lowering of costs, to simplifying the tasks of educators, or to the regenerated school spirit that can result whenever there is appreciable break from routine. Rather, *progress should be measured by the extent to which the individualization of education can be demonstrated to have an observable and salutary effect on the learners themselves and on the process of learning.*

Acknowledgments

The companion books *Perspectives in Individualized Learning* and *Developmental Efforts in Individualized Learning* have resulted less from the vision of their editor than from the vision and leadership of John C. Flanagan. His conviction that learners should be recognized as individuals grows not from armchair reasoning but from decades of empiric research and development culminating in Project TALENT, a longitudinal study of 440,000 high school graduates who were the products of our educational system at the start of the sixties. His perceptiveness in recognizing that education's failure to meet the great diversity of needs in that student population was *not* an irreversible phenomenon led to his undertaking Project PLAN, described elsewhere in this book. In a very real sense, my association with John Flanagan in Project PLAN has educated *me* to the possibilities inherent in the individualization of education and to an awareness of the many diverse forms that individualization can take.

The editing of these books on an "off-duty" basis would have been immeasurably more difficult to achieve had not the organizational resources of the American Institutes for Research, particularly its library, been made available to me. Miss Laura Christopher and Mrs. Alice Grundy, Research Librarians, were most helpful. Similarly, the professional staff have been instrumental in providing me with intellectual inputs regarding the important parameters of individualized learning and in adding to my knowledge of persons and places active in the area. Thanks are due to Dr. William Shanner, Dr. Malcolm Danoff, Dr. Albert Chalupsky, Dr. H. J. A. Goodman, Dr. Richard Bell and Dr. Charles Bollman for their counsel.

In compiling this selection of readings a concerted effort was made to contact schools where work was reported to be under way, regardless of whether any written report had already emanated from those locations. Numerous suggestions were received in response to these inquiries and this led to further correspondence seeking specific summaries of local effort. Finally, authors of published articles, as well as selected speakers whose papers seemed relevant, were contacted. The size of the stack of correspondence which resulted attests to the number of educators around the country to whom I owe thanks for their cooperation and for the materials they sent. For those who consented to have their papers used I owe a double measure of gratitude. I regret that space limitations precluded my using more of them.

My wife, Adrienne, was truly my helpmate during the course of the manuscript preparation. She not only served as corresponding secretary but in more relaxed moments helped me keep a sense of proportion as the study in our house reached a state of constant overflow and disarray. Finally, she has shared with me the unique learning that has been ours to enjoy through long observation of two rather special individual learners . . . our children, Laraine and Scott, to whom these companion books are dedicated.

Part A.

Some Underlying Assumptions Concerning the Need for Individualized Learning

Introduction

When one considers whether there is a need for greater individualization of educational practices, there are, of course, a number of perspectives from which the question can be analyzed. One such viewpoint is that of the curriculum developer. Curriculum has all too often been thought of as a "logical" combination of courses, a kind of subject matter ladder on which the students climb, and, presumably, acquire a hierarchy of competencies. Of course, curriculum means much more than that. Tuckman, in the paper which constitutes Chapter 1, defines a number of postulates and propositions which must be considered if the curriculum is to be student centered rather than content centered.

A second viewpoint regarding the need for individualization is that of the learning theorist. While there is little question that success in learning is, in some degree, a function of instructional procedures, there has been far too little recognition of the reverse phenomenon, namely, that instructional procedures should be a function of learner variables. A preponderance of educational development efforts have been on the instructional side of the equation, addressed to the question of how teacher behavior can be upgraded to "do a more effective job." In contrast, relatively little has been established about ways that individual learners can meaningfully shape instructional practice to make it personally relevant, efficient and interesting. In Chapter 2, Robert Gagné reviews the research on learning. He offers interpretations of selected student-centered learning theories, ranging from stimulus-response theory to learning by discovery.

Chapter 3 is an excerpt from a monograph prepared by the Committee for Economic Development entitled *Innovation in Education: New Directions for the American School*. Representing the viewpoint of those who

2

look upon modern education as a critical component in the larger socio-economic system, this policy paper suggests that the schools need to review their priorities. The authors call for a shift away from the traditional school function (storing and transmitting information), and suggest instead an emphasis on the development of enabling skills to make feasible the pursuit of learning on a lifelong, individual basis. They further state that, because of the potential savings from the use of new staffing patterns in combination with new media and instructional technology, *individualization is not only economically feasible at the present time but is actually required* if schools are to accomplish their mission on an efficient basis.

In Chapter 4, Leslie J. Briggs examines the research findings of programmed instruction, an educational method which depends on individual study but differs in a number of ways from the practices associated with the term "individualized learning" as it is more generally used today. While programmed instruction has not been universally adopted in either its machine or workbook formats, there is no question that many of the *principles* which it engendered have become a "must" in the development of new educational methodologies.

Chapter 1. **CURRICULUM**

THE STUDENT-CENTERED CURRICULUM:
A CONCEPT IN CURRICULUM INNOVATION

Bruce W. Tuckman

The purpose of this paper is to describe a concept known as the *student-centered curriculum.*This curriculum concept is an emerging one, and this paper must be considered a working paper or draft of developing ideas, all of which are subject to continual refinement and revision. The student-centered curriculum concept will be described in terms of a series of postulates which provide a basic definition of what the student-centered curriculum is to be. From these postulates, propositions are then derived which describe the way the student-centered curriculum would be constructed and how it would operate. No attempt will be made to cite large amounts of literature in support of the postulates that are made. Some of the postulates can be supported empirically. Others represent some very basic assumptions about the nature of curriculum.

SOURCE: Reprinted from *Educational Technology,* Vol. 9, No. 10 (October, 1969), Englewood Cliffs, N.J., pp. 26-29, by permission of author and publisher.

Postulates

Postulate 1. A curriculum must be defined in terms of its goals as they apply to students. A curriculum must have a purpose. Its purpose ostensibly is to provide students with experiences that will lead them to attain certain desired end states. Pre-specification of these end states provides a guide for the direction of the instructional process as well as a basis for determining if the instructional process has been a success. Thus, a curriculum must be defined in terms of the educational goals of students.

It is considered reasonable to further assume that educational goals may be broken down into three broad areas, i.e., *(a)* occupational, *(b)* civic/ citizenship, and *(c)* personal/social.

Of maximum importance is the point that desired goals or end states are here posited as part of the basis for defining the curriculum.

Postulate 2. Occupational goals are, for a large majority of students, those requiring less than a bachelor's degree. This statement is more than a postulate. It is, in fact, a fact. At the present moment, approximately 20 percent of the young people in the United States obtain a bachelor's degree. The remaining 80 percent fall into one of the following categories: high school dropout, terminal high school graduate, two-year college dropout, two-year college terminal graduate, or four-year college dropout. Thus, for this large proportion of youth, ultimate goals in the occupational area must focus on occupations which require less than a bachelor's degree for entry.

Postulate 3. A curriculum must be defined in terms of the psychological structure (learning style), and educational experiences (what has already been learned) of students. It is necessary that the curriculum be defined and developed in such a way that the psychological structure of students is considered. That is to say, the curriculum must be structured in such a way as to be meaningful in terms of the way that people learn.

Secondly, learners do not come to any learning situation without having had prior experiences. In defining a curriculum which centers on students, it is necessary to consider the relevant prior learning experiences that students have had as they relate to the curriculum at every point. To this end, one must be sensitive to the issue of transfer of training.

Postulate 4. In terms of learning style, learning of the concrete must precede learning of the abstract. Jean Piaget, the eminent European developmental psychologist, has in the course of a 40-year career shown that children learn concrete operations before they learn abstract operations and that, moreover, abstract operations cannot be learned unless concrete operations are learned first.[1] Thus, the concrete learning style and materials which appeal to it must precede that of the abstract. Before the student can be expected to master some of the representational intricacies of subjects like algebra, he must in terms of Piaget's work first have mastered some very concrete principles such as those dealing with conservation of area and volume.

In general, younger children function more successfully in the concrete realm than in the abstract, with tendencies toward the abstract increasing with age. However, as a function of the experiences that a young person has had, it is entirely likely that he may develop into and through adolescence without ever completely reaching the stage of abstract operations. The extent to which development occurs beyond the concrete into the abstract is a function of the learning experiences that the youngster has already had.

Postulate 5. Learning can be maximized by controlling the sequence towards some goal and locating the student in that sequence. This postulate contends that learning is an experience which requires that the conditions under which it is likely to occur be controlled. The contention is that learning is not a haphazard occurrence.

To the extent that one can associate the conditions of learning with those that are relevant for a specific person, one should be able to produce learning. This position has been well documented by Robert M. Gagné, in his book *The Conditions of Learning.*[2]

Postulate 6. Learning can be made efficient by combining sequences that are psychologically similar. Any curriculum is going to include a multiplicity of goals. Following Postulate 5, any curriculum will also include a multiplicity of sequences. One can further structure the curriculum by grouping these sequences in some manner. Postulate 6 contends that the most efficient way to group them is in a way which takes into account the psychological characteristics of human beings. If one can identify a model which identifies the qualities of human behavior and human functioning across all domains of human activity, it is likely that such a model can be used to efficiently combine learning sequences.

Postulate 7. Learning is most meaningful when a person learns through interaction with his environment. Work such as that of Harvey, Hunt and Schroder,[3] and Anderson and Moore[4] provides strong evidence for the fact that interdependent conditions for learning are the most efficacious. In the interdependent learning model, the individual learns through interaction with his environment. This is in contrast with a unilateral model where some agent establishes external criteria and affects the behavior of individuals in terms of these criteria through the use of rewards and punishments. In the interdependent model, any rewards and punishments forthcoming would be a product of the interaction between the learner and the environment and would be intrinsic rather than extrinsic. Learning on this basis, however, requires that the environment be of such a nature as to result in the learning which is desired. The environment must be structured or "programmed" to maximize the occurrence of the desired outcomes.

Propositions

Proposition 1.   The curriculum must be vocationalized in order to: (a) meet a student's future employment needs, and (b) provide a concrete context for learning.   Since as many as 80 percent of today's young people will enter the work force with educational experiences at less than the bachelor's level, it is necessary that instructional activity be provided to help students master the skills and competencies that they will need for entry into the occupational world. To some extent, these experiences will be provided through industrial training programs; but, to a large extent, responsibility for this will fall to the public schools. Thus, the curriculum centered on students' needs must have a liberal sprinkling of educational experiences specifically relevant to the occupational needs of the large majority of youth. These experiences may revolve around a cluster concept of vocational education in order to provide students with the broadest possible experience.

A second reason for vocationalizing the curriculum is to take advantage of the postulate that concrete learning must precede abstract learning. The vocational context is a highly concrete one, within which previously considered abstract concepts may be more easily mastered by students, particularly those students whose experiences heretofore have provided a great opportunity for the mastery of concrete concepts. Individuals from somewhat disadvantaged backgrounds in particular will, by virtue of their biological need state and limited prior experience, be much more likely to learn in a concrete context even during their adolescent years than an abstract one. Thus, the vocational milieu is a way to make all education relevant in the sense of giving it the kind of referent that is meaningful to the learner. Teaching physics principles in an electronics laboratory or mathematic principles in a business course is a way to provide hitherto abstract notions with a highly concrete context, thus increasing the likelihood that mastery will occur.

Proposition 2.   Behavioral objective identification must precede curriculum development in order to identify goals and facilitate evaluation.   If the curriculum is to proceed from a delineation of goals, then the identification of goals must be the first step in the curriculum development process. Moreover, these goals must be identified and specified in behavioral terms in order to give them meaning to all who must follow in the process and contribute to the development of the curriculum. The place to begin is with goals, and behavioral objectives are a form of goal statement with enough specificity to make them usable by curriculum developers and evaluators alike.

Proposition 3. Behavioral objectives must be sequentially analyzed to provide sequences of learning experiences.   The behavioral objective is a good place to begin the process of identifying sequences of experience that will ultimately constitute the curriculum. Such sequences of experience are meaningful only in terms of what they add up to, that is, where they end up. In order to guarantee that such sequences end up where you want them to end up, one begins at the end point and works backwards.

Proposition 4. A model for combining sequences, and thus students in sequences, must be developed which is consistent with the psychology of human function and the three classes of goals.   A curriculum cannot consist of an infinite or near infinite series of disconnected sequences. Each sequence can take on additional meaning by being grouped and connected to other sequences which relate to it not only in terms of the goal object, but in terms of the nature of skill or competency or knowledge which the sequence is an attempt to facilitate. The practical requirements of a learning situation necessitate some form of packaging of the sequences. The form the packaging has taken thus far in our educational history has been by subject matter. However, subject matter is not inherent to the learning experiences nor to the learner. Perhaps it would be more meaningful to use some characteristics which are inherent in both the subject matter and the students who are to learn them as a basis of clustering learning experiences. Characteristics which are descriptive of human function and equally consistent with the three classes of goals—occupational, civic/citizenship, personal/social—should be maximally effective, since the curriculum is to be defined in terms of both of these kinds of characteristics.

Proposition 5. "Individualized" instruction can be approximated in groups, but these groups will be shifting rapidly in membership over time. Individuals will be simultaneously instructed when they are at the same point in the same sequence. This proposition argues against individualized instruction in the sense which we have come to think of it, namely, students working by themselves with relatively impersonal presentation devices or books, often linked to a computer to provide them with equally impersonal feedback. Many have argued against individualized instruction and opted for a major role for the teacher who can provide the "human element." If a curriculum were to be built around learning sequences, there is no necessary reason why each student should go through a sequence in isolation from all other students. Not only would isolation eliminate the opportunity for important social interaction, which is a desirable experience in its own right, but it would also reduce the efficiency with which learning sequences can be used in educational programming. At any point in time, it is entirely likely that within the large secondary school a number of students greater than one will be at roughly similar points in some of the same learning sequences.

However, these students will not constitute a group in the static and rigidified manner in which that term is presently used within the educational establishment. While they may exist as a group for a particular learning experience or sequence of experiences, for the following learning experience they may each find themselves as parts of other groups.

A computer will be useful for scheduling this kind of curriculum in that it requires the ultimate in modular scheduling. This curriculum would also necessitate the creation of an ungraded school since gradedness is not necessarily consistent with the sequences and learning experience that will be contained in the curriculum.

Proposition 6. Learning must be propagated through learning experiences, i.e., "hands on" experiences, rather than lecturing by the teacher. Materials must be prepared to allow students to learn through their environment. The environment must be structured to maximize the probability that the desired learning will take place. Based on the postulate that learning is maximized when one interacts with one's environment, it follows that in order to maximize learning, one would want to structure the environment in such a way that the probability of learning particular concepts or particular skills and competencies from interaction with a particular environment will be maximized. To this end, one concentrates not on writing lesson plans, but on writing experiential units, i.e., participation exercises which provide a vehicle for learning experiences to occur.

Conclusions

The student-centered curriculum ultimately will be built on the basis of the postulates and propositions described above. It will be a goal-oriented curriculum in that it will begin by a specification of goals broken down into the three goal areas identified. It will reflect the progression from concrete to abstract, using the vocationalizing experience as a context for concrete learning as well as a way of providing young people with occupationally-relevant experiences. It will be made up of a series of sequences which are analyzed from specified goals. These sequences will then be combined in terms of a psychological model.

Once the goals and the sequences are identified and combined, the next step undertaken will be to develop specific learning materials to achieve the goals that have been set forth. These materials will primarily be of a participatory nature, where the teacher's role will be to guide the participation so that desired end points may be reached.

At the same time that the curriculum is being constructed, it will be valuable for individuals to examine the physical and administrative structure of the educational system as we now know it. Any curriculum which is built based on the propositions and postulates described in this paper—that is, any truly student-centered curriculum—will require an administrative structure and perhaps a physical one which differs in many respects from that presently in existence in the majority of school districts in the United States. The student-centered curriculum would appear of necessity to require a non-graded school. It would do away with the traditional concept of ability grouping and tracking as it is presently practiced in most American secondary schools. It would require modular scheduling of the finest degree, and it would require a computer system for record keeping and sequence coordination. Teachers would have to be trained to function out of a framework other than the traditional subject matter framework, and to play a role in the classroom which is different from the instructional role the teacher presently plays. Rather than being the provider of information, the teacher will function within a student-centered curriculum as a guide and interactor.

A student-centered curriculum will make great use of multiple instructional strategies, allowing students to learn through interaction with their environment, utilizing all sensory modalities. Visual aids, as well as participation aids of all sorts, will be utilized.

Additional demands different from those presently in existence will be placed upon the guidance systems of the schools, whose activities will have to be closely coordinated with the student-centered curriculum. Guidance will no longer have the simple option of placing students in tracks and thus considering their developmental processes in good hands. Guidance will be continually needed as students proceed through a student-centered curriculum in order to help students to maximize themselves in terms of the choice process. At many steps along the way students will have to make choices between different sequences of activities. These choices will be aided by the use of a guidance system utilizing tests and interviews. However, the purpose of these tests and interviews will have to be to maximize the student's opportunities to learn and succeed in a student-centered curriculum, rather than to try to predict the degree to which the student can succeed—thus creating a self- and teacher-expectation, and irrevocably locking the student into a particular curriculum or program of study.

In conclusion, the advent of a student-centered curriculum, should it ever come to pass, would require some basic changes in the instructional system. Before one were to do something as dramatic as this, one would want to have great confidence in the postulates and propositions about which a curriculum is based, primarily by giving such a curriculum adequate tests on an experimental basis. At this point in time, it is necessary to discuss and consider what a student-centered curriculum is, what assumptions it makes, how it would be constructed, and how it would be implemented.

NOTES

[1] For a synthesis, see J. H. Flavell, *The Development Psychology of Jean Piaget* (New York: Van Nostrand Reinhold Co., 1963).

[2] R. M. Gagné, *The Conditions of Learning* (New York: Holt, Rinehart & Winston, Inc., 1965).

[3] O. J. Harvey, D. E. L. Hunt, and H. M. Schroder, *Conceptual Systems and Personality Organization* (New York: John Wiley & Sons, Inc., 1961).

[4] A. Anderson and O. K. Moore, "Autotelic Folk-Models," *Sociological Quarterly,* 1959, pp. 204-16. See also O. K. Moore, "Autotelic Responsive Environments and Exceptional Children," in O. J. Harvey (ed.), *Experience, Structure and Adaptability* (New York: Springer Publishing Co., Inc., 1966).

Chapter 2. LEARNING THEORY

LEARNING RESEARCH AND
ITS IMPLICATIONS FOR
INDEPENDENT LEARNING

Robert M. Gagné

It is abundantly apparent that one of the major threads of emphasis
running through the history of American education is a concern for the
capabilities of the individual student, and an associated tendency to place
upon him considerable responsibility for his own intellectual development.
The roots of this theme are to be found in the writings of English philoso-
phers, Locke and others, from whom our strong beliefs in individual liberty and responsibility are said to be derived. In practice, these beliefs
color our collective admiration for heroes like Abraham Lincoln, who
educated himself, as well as for many other self-made men, even including
the fictional heroes of Horatio Alger. There can be little doubt, too, that
the one-room schoolhouse of somewhat earlier times was a place in which
the individual student, under the guidance of a wise adult, pursued his
own learning in a largely individual manner. If he was apt and eager, he

SOURCE: Reprinted from G. J. Gleason (ed.), *The Theory and Nature of Independent
Learning* (Scranton, Pa.: International Textbook Co., 1967), by permission of author and
publisher.

could and did learn a great deal; if he was not so apt, the amount of his learning in a given space of time was much less.

Educational philosophy of somewhat more recent times has also emphasized individual responsibility for learning. When one reads, today, Dewey's *The Child and the Curriculum* (1902), it is entirely possible to find there, without any distortion, the idea that what the individual child needs to learn is whatever he has not already learned which will fill his needs and contribute to the meeting of his life goals. Throughout the years since this essay appeared, there have been those who believed that its message was primarily individual responsibility for learning, rather than the school's responsibility for fostering emotional adjustment.

In recent times, despite the overwhelming prevalence of the "classroom" as the model for education in most elementary and secondary schools, an increased emphasis on the centrality of the individual learner in the educational system can be noted. There is, for example, the nongraded school, whose characteristics at both the elementary level (Goodlad, 1965) and the secondary level (Brown, 1963) have been quite specifically described, and whose virtues are being proclaimed. Whatever its logistics may be, and these are not entirely standard, it is clear that an essential feature of the nongraded school is its dependence on the motivation, interest, and curiosity of the individual student, and the assumption of responsibility on his part for his own learning.

A second modern invention that has given impetus to the practice of individual learning is programmed instruction. This innovation is not a mere fad, and regardless of the variety of qualifications that are presently placed on its acceptance, it will not go away. It will continue to fulfill some functions that some teachers think are theirs, and that some book publishers think are theirs, and it will most probably persist into the indefinite future. Basically, the rationale of programmed instruction is simply this: Provide the individual learner with all the help you can give him (printed statements, pictures, directions, self-quizzes, or anything else), and let him undertake his own learning. But at any given point in time, the "help" that is provided by an instructional program must be given to the *individual*. This is necessary so that he will neither be held back in his learning, nor pushed forward before he has mastered some essential prerequisites. And so again it is the individual learner and the process of individual learning that receives the emphasis.

VIEWS OF LEARNING DERIVED FROM RESEARCH

If there are persisting educational trends stressing the importance of individual learning, are these compatible or incompatible with the models of the learning process derived from experimental studies of learning? If learning is individualized, and the responsibility for learning is placed on the individual student, is this the kind of educational arrangement that takes into account modern evidence about learning as a human activity, or does it perhaps ignore important parts of this evidence?

To answer these questions, it is necessary to consider two different models of the learning process. Experimental evidence about learning is typically gathered to answer rather specific questions—of a sort which are capable of puzzling some educators because of their very specificity. However, evidence about the learning process is seldom if ever applied to practical problems in this specific form. Instead, knowledge about learning is applied to a variety of educational situations by way of a "construct" or "model," which is a way of conceptualizing learning. For example, an investigator of verbal learning may with utterly serious purpose study the question of whether nonsense syllables of three letters each with a vowel in its middle are memorized more readily than nonsense syllables of three letters all of which are consonants. Obviously the results of any such investigation cannot be directly applied to an educational problem, no matter how firm are the "facts" it yields. The learning investigator knows that, of course. He is interested in finding out, not just these specific facts, but rather what sort of model of the learning process he is forced to adopt in order to account for all these facts.

Models of the learning process take various forms. Sometimes they are explicitly stated as theories, sometimes they are shown in diagrams, while sometimes they are not stated at all, but merely implied. At any rate, it is these models that must be considered when one attempts to answer questions regarding the practical implications of learning research.

What does learning research have to say about individual learning? In attempting to frame an answer to this question, I need to consider two different models of the learning process. Each of these has several subvarieties, but it is not of great importance to consider these here. The two models of learning may be called the *single-stage model,* and the *multi-stage model.* What needs to be considered, in the case of each, is what variables in the learning situation are of importance in evaluating the activities of the learner in relation to the events in his environment. In other words, what do the models require as *conditions of learning* (cf. Gagné, 1965)?

THE SINGLE-STAGE MODEL OF LEARNING

The single-stage model of the learning process has been around for quite some time. One might even say it has been "kicked around" for a good many years. It is the model of the "connection" between a stimulus and a response. Essentially, it is the model of the conditioned response of Pavlov (1927), as elaborated and applied to more general problems of learning by such theorists as Watson (1919). In only slightly different form, it is the model of Thorndike (1931), whose major theoretical accounts of the learning process were concerned with the conditions for establishment of the single connection (or association). For these older theorists, the problem of learning was in its essence a problem of how a stimulus came to be associated with, and therefore to elicit, a response.

I do not have the intention of setting up the single-stage model of these earlier writers as a straw man to be knocked down with the greatest of ease. As a matter of fact, the single-stage model has many admirable characteristics. One has only to read the introspectionistic maunderings of the British associationist psychologists whose models preceded it (cf. Mandler and Mandler, 1964), to have an immediate appreciation of its value for the scientific study of behavior. It is neat, simple, and carries its own immediate implications for the experimental operations needed in the study of learning. The single-stage model served scientific psychology well for many years, generated a tremendous amount of research on learning which is of lasting value, and spawned quite a number of elaborative models based upon it, such as those pertaining to the learning of motor skills, perceptual discriminations, and verbal behavior. Furthermore, this model persisted practically unscathed throughout the period of onslaught by Gestalt theory, which seems to have forged some fairly ineffective weapons against a fortress built of solid experimental evidence.

Theorists of a more recent vintage cannot be considered as being so firmly wedded to a single-stage model of learning, although they may have started with it. Russian investigators who followed Pavlov, for example, soon became keenly interested in what is called the "second signal system" (Razran, 1965), and thus, in effect, in a second stage added to the original model. Although Hull's (1943) efforts were heavily devoted to accounting for the factors affecting the strength of single connections, it is surely impossible to overlook his important papers on "adaptive behavior" (1937), and "knowledge and purpose" (1930). Skinner's initial concern with the single S-R connection (1938), which he called the reflex, came to be augmented by multi-stage models of learning such as those involved in chains (1934), and in verbal behavior (1957).

Returning to the single-stage model itself, it will perhaps be worthwhile to consider in summary form what were the conditions of learning according to such a model, and how these conditions were thought to be established, whether for experimental or practical purposes. What had to be done, according to this theory, in order to bring about learning? What did the experimenter (or by extension, the teacher) have to do in order to insure that learning would occur?

1. A stimulus must be presented. The agent for the learning process must present to the learner some form of stimulation on one or more particular occasions. Of course, it was recognized that on some occasions the accidental events provided by the environment presented the stimulus,

rather than a human agent, as for example when the dog's food dish happened to make a noise when being placed on the floor. But the principle was the same—the stimulus part of the connection to be learned must come from the environment.

2. A near contiguity in time must be made to occur between the stimulus and the response with which it was being associated. For the agent who was to be influential in learning, this was often a rather difficult thing to do, although not always. For example, it meant that the instructor must sometimes observe carefully when the learner was just about to do something, and then apply the stimulus. Certainly this description may be fairly applied to the means of training a rat to press a lever when a light is flashed.

3. A reward (or reinforcement) must be presented to the learner as a next step in the sequence of events. This again was to be provided by an external agent (or, as in the case of laboratory animals, by means of an environmental mechanism) as soon as possible following the correct response.

4. The learning sequence was to be repeated more than once, perhaps quite a number of times, in order to increase the strength of the connection. Again, the agent for learning needed to arrange a proper series of practice trials, in which the stimulus would be presented repeatedly at suitable time intervals.

On the whole, it can be seen that the operations needed for learning, according to the single-stage model, required careful planning and execution on the part of the human agent who was to induce the learning (that is, the experimenter, or the teacher). Stimuli had to be presented in a sequence which insured proper time relations with the response. Reinforcement had to be given, more or less immediately. And repetition of the situation had to be arranged. What did the learner have to do? Well, he had to be awake, of course, and attentive, and his nervous system had to be capable of processing the stimulation provided, and channeling it properly so that a response was made.

THE MULTI-STAGE MODEL OF LEARNING

One of the important pioneers with a multi-stage model of learning was Hunter (1913). Working with both animals and human children, he devised a number of experimental situations in which, as he argued, the learning that occurred could *not* be accounted for as a connection between a stimulus and a response. One of these was called "delayed reaction," the other "double alternation," and both are directly related to methods in use today. Hunter argued that the learner in each of these kinds of problem situations must be able to recall an internally stored cue, which he called a *representative process,* or a *symbolic process* (1924). For example, when an animal or human child was restrained from responding immediately to one of three positions shown as "correct" by means of a momentarily illuminated bulb, making an ultimately correct response required the animal to recall an internal representation of this position. (A human being might say to himself "on the left.") Similarly, the performance of a double alternation could not be under the control of an external stimulus; instead, the learner had to use a kind of internally aroused reversing process in order to continue responding correctly to right, right, left, left. In considering the history of learning theories, it is of interest to note that the necessity for a model including what is now generally called "mediation" was both recognized and demonstrated by Hunter a good many years ago.

The necessity for a multi-stage model of learning was also recognized by Hull, a somewhat more modern learning theorist. Hull (1930, 1935, 1937) pointed out that one could identify "knowledge" and "purpose" in the behavior of animals performing such tasks as finding their way through mazes. One could not, he believed, account for such behavior adequately simply by assuming the establishment of a chain of S-R connections, or conditioned reflexes. In fact, their behavior was capable of the kind of variability and adaptiveness which could not be accounted for by means of this simple model. Somehow, the animal was capable of representing to himself something about the goal he was eventually going to reach. Hull called this a "fractional anticipatory goal response," and it remained an important concept to be used in accounting for the learning of animals and men in both Hull's writings and those who followed him (cf. Miller, 1959). For present purposes, it is sufficient to note that the fractional anticipatory goal response did in fact represent a "mediational" or multi-stage model applicable to relatively simple learning tasks. Something in the animal's nervous system was reinstated as a representation of the external situation; something became a part of learning which did not come from the immediate stimulus situation in which the learner found himself.

Verbal Learning.   The learning of sequences and pairs of nonsense syllables is another field of learning research which operated for many years under a single-stage model. For example, the learning of sequences of words or nonsense syllables was accounted for in terms of a model which treated the initial word as a stimulus (or "S"), the next word in sequence as a response (or "R"), and the connection between them as a conditioned response. Elaborate and not entirely unsuccessful models (cf. Hull, *et al.,* 1940) were constructed to explain the phenomena of serial learning on the basis of these assumptions. For example, these models attempted to account for such phenomena as the greater difficulty of syllables in the middle of a list (Lepley, 1934), the effects on learning of distributed practice (Hovland, 1940), and the increased difficulty of learning lists containing similar members (cf. Gibson, 1940).

The learning of pairs of verbal associates was similarly accounted for, over a period of many years, in terms of a single-stage model. The first member of the pair was a stimulus, the second member a response, and the learned connection between them considered to have the properties of a conditioned response. E. J. Gibson's (1940) account of this model is surely one of the most systematic treatments, many of whose predictions have stood the test of time (Underwood, 1961).

The deficiencies of the single-stage model as an explanation for verbal learning, both serial and paired associate, were revealed over a period of relatively few years in which investigators began to take a very analytic view of such learning. It would be difficult to mention all of the sources of evidence that cast doubt upon the efficiency of this model. The major ones were probably the following:

1. It was found that what a learner had previously learned greatly affected the retention of what he had most recently learned (Underwood, 1957). A learner who had learned one list of nonsense syllables behaved quite differently from a learner who had never learned such a list. How well a verbal list was retained was found to depend to a very great extent on how many lists he had previously learned. In other words, it could not be assumed that a session of learning with one list was equivalent to a session with another list. Depending on his past learning, the learner brought something with him to the task that strongly affected how difficult the learning task turned out to be.

2. It was found that the stimulus term in verbal learning was not really what the learner responded to. A variety of experimental studies showed that the learner responded to a *functional* stimulus, which was not all the same as the *nominal* stimulus (Underwood, 1963; Underwood and Shulz, 1960). When presented with the nonsense word KUJ, the learner might respond only to a part of this word, such as K or J. It is but a step in reasoning to draw the inference that the learner is not treating the "stimulus word" as a stimulus at all. He is *coding* it, in accordance with some habits or predispositions he has previously acquired (Lawrence, 1963). The implication clearly is that the single-stage model doesn't fit. If the learner first performs some operation, or coding, on the stimulus term of a pair of verbal associates, then clearly that is another stage of the total learning process.

3. It was found that learning paired verbal associates was greatly affected by the familiarity of the *response* term (Underwood and Shulz, 1960). The degree to which the response term was familiar and pronounceable strongly affected the ease or difficulty of learning the associated verbal pair. This evidence suggested that paired associate learning was largely a matter of becoming familiar with the response term; a pair containing a response term like RUD was much more easily learned than a pair with a response term like ZYQ. Again, the evidence pointed to the

inadequacy of a single-stage model of learning. If pronouncing the response (or otherwise becoming familiar with it) had to be accomplished as well as acquiring an association with the stimulus, then clearly more than one stage of learning was involved. McGuire's (1961) Factors study of paired associate learning distinguished the three stages of (1) stimulus coding; (2) response familiarization; and (3) association.

4.   There are studies of verbal learning which deliberately introduce a coding process; in other words, studies of mediation (cf. Jenkins, 1963). For example, when a learner has acquired an association like BOP-KING, it becomes very easy for him to learn the new association BOP-QUEEN (Jenkins, 1963, p. 213). A single-stage model does not adequately account for the marked decrease in difficulty of this second task. Presumably, the second task is easy because the learner brings to the situation a previously acquired code. And this means that the learning has at least two stages, if not more. The learner supplies something himself out of his previous experience.

At the present time, most investigators of verbal learning would agree that a single-stage model is quite inadequate to account for this kind of behavioral change. At the very least, the model for verbal learning must contain three stages: first, a stimulus discrimination stage, second, a response familiarization stage, and third, a hook-up or association stage (cf. Wickens, 1964, pp. 85-86). Many people would add still another phase, which may be called stimulus coding.

Short-Term Memory.   Another source of evidence concerning the inadequacy of a single-stage learning theory is to be found in studies of the immediate storage of learned items, or what is called short-term memory. Typically, this important part of the learning process is investigated by a procedure somewhat as follows. The learner is told to remember a single verbal syllable or word, which is shown or said only once. Immediately, he has to begin another task, such as counting aloud backwards by intervals of three beginning with an arbitrarily chosen number like 241. After some particular number of seconds or minutes has elapsed, the experimenter asks the learner to recall the syllable or word originally given. Even though what has been learned is an extremely small "unit," forgetting can be measured, increasing regularly with the amount of time elapsing between learning and recall.

These are the basic findings in studies of the memory process. There are, however, still other results of considerable interest to the present discussion (cf. Melton, 1963). For one thing, it is found that a single syllable like QYN is not retained as well after one presentation as a syllable like NER, nor as well as a word like TOP. In fact, the *single* syllable QYN, pronounceable or not, is retained no better than *three* words. Why is it that a learner can as readily store three units, when they are words, as he can only one unit, when it is an unfamiliar syllable? The suggestion is that the learner *does something* to these units before they are stored. To use a term familiar by now, the units stored in memory are first *coded*.

When learners are given an increasing amount of time to receive the material to be stored, or additional repetitions (cf. Melton, 1963; Hellyer, 1962), retention improves. The suggestion is that the learner engages in rehearsal, as well as coding; or possibly, rehearsal is what brings about the coding. In any case, again the evidence shows that something is done to the stimulus by the learner before it can be stored. It is not simply "received." The process of memory storage requires a multi-stage model.

The Learning of Concepts.   Another field of learning that has yielded a strong evidence of the inadequacy of the single-stage model is concept learning. Studies in this field have been carried out with both animals and men. In some important respects, these studies are reminiscent of the earlier work of Hunter (1913), previously referred to.

Harlow (1949), found that monkeys who learned to solve successive discrimination problems acquired some retained capability which made it possible for them to solve new discrimination problems in very few trials. Furthermore, monkeys are able to solve "oddity" problems in which they have to choose the odd stimulus object from a set of three. At the end of such training, it seems not unreasonable to say of the monkeys that they have acquired and stored the concept "odd." They can recall this internal disposition when confronted with an entirely new problem, and solve it almost immediately. Such behavior cannot reasonably be accounted for on the basis of a single-stage learning theory. An experienced monkey is not simply learning to connect a new stimulus with a new response. Instead, the learning of the novel task is so rapid that one must infer a generalizable event supplied internally by the animal's nervous system as an additional stage in the total process. Other tasks used by Harlow (1959) appear to demand a similar set of conclusions regarding the learning model.

In concept learning with human children, Kendler and Kendler (1961) have also used learning situations in which the presence of two or more stages in learning must seemingly be inferred. When four-year-old children are required to "reverse" a learned discrimination (as to black and white cards), they perform as though they were learning a brand-new task. But when seven-year-olds are confronted with the same reversed task, they acquire it almost immediately. This age difference the Kendlers relate to the difference in verbal repertoire of learners in the two age groups. To solve a reversed discrimination in a single trial, a human learner must be able to represent to himself something like "reverse" or "opposite." Although one cannot tell whether he does exactly this, or whether he actually uses words, the effects are nevertheless clearly established. More than a single stage of learning appears to be definitely involved (cf. Kendler, 1964).

LEARNING AND THE MEDIATION PROCESS

From the early work of Hunter to modern research on concept learning, there is an ever-accumulating body of evidence showing that many varieties of human learning, and even most varieties, cannot be accounted for as "associations between stimuli and responses." Besides the fact that rather lowly animals can acquire, retain, and use what Hunter called a "representative process," there are the modern findings that the kind of learning that many people call "memorization" is really a rather complex affair involving several different stages. Even committing a single item to memory appears to be an event that is greatly influenced by processes internal to the learner.

In the face of this evidence, the conception of learning as a "stimulus-response association" is already an anachronism. The multi-stage model of learning must be accepted as applicable to most learning, if not all, and certainly to those forms of learning most relevant to the schools.

The importance of this general conclusion, however, lies not in the fact that the "dead horse" of S-R learning can no longer be beaten. Nor does it lie in the contention that those who have beaten it so long have finally triumphed. This is not at all the case, because explanations of behavior must still take fully into account both stimuli and responses. Furthermore, the conception of a connection (or association) between successive events remains a fundamental principle that almost surely must form a part of explanations of the learning process.

The importance of the multi-stage model of learning is that the emphasis on what must be explained shifts from the two ends of the total learning event to the middle. The process in the middle is now usually referred to as *mediation*. As mentioned previously, a process of mediation is now generally regarded as usually involved, if not always involved, in such fundamental varieties of learning as the memorizing of verbal associates and sequences. In addition, it must surely be a part of the process of learning concepts, acquiring principles, and problem solving (Gagné, 1965).

Mediation is an inferred process by means of which external stimuli are coded by the learner's nervous system before being functionally connected, or associated by learning, with responses. Obviously, the nature of the coding which takes place is dependent upon certain characteristics of the learner's nervous system. Coding is not determined solely by the stimulus situation, then. The coding may depend to some as yet undetermined degree upon inherited factors in the nervous system. But more importantly still, it is dependent upon previous learning which has put the nervous system into its present state. A simple example will serve to make this point. If a learner is faced with the task of learning the English equivalent of the French word *l'arbre,* he may be able to generate a coding response in the form of the English word, *arbor,* to provide the translation *tree.* But, of course, he will only be able to do this if he knows the English word *arbor,* and there are surely many individuals who do not know this word. As a consequence, the ease of learning *l'arbre—tree* is probably affected strongly by the availability of this or other codes, and these in turn are determined by what the individual has previously learned.

The importance of previously acquired mediational process for any given task of current learning has been emphasized in the studies of the present author and his associates (Gagné, 1962, Gagné, Mayor, Garstens, and Paradise, 1962). The learning of increasingly complex mathematical tasks was shown to depend upon the *previous mastery* of other contributory mathematical principles, in a hierarchical fashion. Evidence presented by these authors shows that the learning of any given task is successful to a high degree for those students who have mastered specific prerequisite tasks, and highly unsuccessful in those students who have not mastered the subordinate tasks. The learning of any given subject-matter, it is suggested, can be shown to depend upon the prior learning of other subject-matter. Thus the latter, previously learned capabilities, act as mediators of the learning of the new task.

It may be noted that the presence of mediation in learning introduces a distinct note of unpredictability into the total process. This is because the coding is, in the last analysis, idiosyncratic. The particular code provided by the learner's internal neural processes is *his* code, and not anyone else's. To be sure, if one has deliberately taught him a particular mediational unit previously, and it has been well learned, the probability is high that he will use it. In a similar way, one can more or less depend on learners' using codes which are known to be familiar words to most of the population, since they have been encountered so frequently in the past. The coding for the French word *la dame* can presumably be depended upon with high probability. Nevertheless, probability is not certainty, and one has to state that the particular mediation employed, dependent as it is upon previous learning, is fundamentally an individual matter.

It therefore seems true that, having admitted the necessity of a stimulus for learning, and a response for observing its effects, one must recognize that a highly important event in the process is contributed by the learner himself. The mediation which codes the stimulus situation, and provides the mechanism for connection with a response, is apparently *generated* by the learner. It does not come from the environment; it does not come (except in a most indirect sense) from a teacher; it does not come (except in special cases) as feedback from immediately preceding responses. It comes from the memory storage of the individual's nervous system.

THE NATURE OF CHANGE IN LEARNING

The multi-stage, or mediational, model of learning obviously implies something different from the single-stage model concerning the inferred nature of the change that takes place in learning. Whereas the latter model leads one to speak of the "strengthening of a connection," the former leads to the notion that the change is essentially the "discovery of the appropriate mediator." The basic event of learning is conceived as the generation by the learner, presumably by means of a search of his memory, of a mediational process which successfully leads to the desired performance.

Evidently, this brings us around to consideration of a popular though somewhat tarnished phrase, "learning by discovery." As the previous discussion will make plain, it seems evident that discovery is indeed an integral part of most kinds of learning, particularly of the kinds of greatest relevance to school subjects. Looked at from this point of view, there is nothing magical about discovery learning; in fact, it is practically a synonym for "learning." What is emphasized by the phrase, however, is that some essential event in learning must come from *inside* the learner himself. The new thing about a recently acquired capability is not the stimulus (which may have been seen before), and definitely not the response (which must have been learned previously), but the internally supplied mediator. The essential *change* is the use of this particular code, or mediator, in a sequence beginning with a particular stimulus and ending with a particular response.

The conditions needed for learning, this model implies, are those which make it possible for the individual to discover a mediating event which is recalled from his previous learning. Thus the answer of the multi-stage learning theorist to those who say "learning must involve discovery," is to say "of course!" But it is not very helpful to say "learning must involve discovery." Discovery is an inferred internal process, and a serious theorizer knows the rules and restrictions under which such a process can legitimately be invoked as an element in theory. A much more useful statement, however, would be the answer to the question, "How can one *promote* discovery in the learner?" Several hypotheses suggest themselves:

1. The learner who has previously acquired the greater number of "potential mediators" will learn more rapidly. If there are many possible codes from which the learner can choose, he will, on the average, acquire the new capability more rapidly than will a learner who has few codes from which to select. This proposition is, of course, quite consistent with the fact of the correlation of "intelligence" with achievement, since most intelligence tests may be said to measure the availability of verbal mediators. It has an additional meaning, also. It implies that a "store of facts," or perhaps more precisely, a "store of concepts" is going to be very helpful to a learner who sets out to learn new concepts and principles. The prediction is that "learning a store of facts" (which many students, and

some teachers, profess to abhor) is an important prerequisite to rapid learning of new and more elaborate facts and principles.

2.   A second way in which learning may be promoted is by means of what is known as "guidance" in discovery. Although not completely consistent, the evidence from a number of studies strongly suggests the efficacy of guidance as a means of bringing about effective learning (cf. Wittrock, 1966; Gagné, 1966). Guidance does not mean "telling the learner the answer." In terms of the present discussion, it means "hinting at a useful mediator." Thus, if the task of the student is to learn the English equivalent of *l'arbre,* a question like "What English word does it remind you of?" constitutes the application of guidance. To take another example, if the student were learning a procedure for simplifying fractions of the type 7/91, a question supplying guidance might be "Can the denominator be expressed another way?"

Again it is important to emphasize that the purpose of guidance is to *help the learner recall something he has previously learned.* He "discovers" it, to be sure; in the sense that he finds a useful mediator for a new learning task. But as an entity, this mediator must be there in the first place. The discovery is not really a matter of spontaneous generation of something brand new. What is new to the learner is this particular use of the mediator, this particular sequence of neural events in which it is placed for the first time. Conceived in this way, the process of discovery should be aided by suitable guidance, as the evidence suggests.

The change that takes place when learning occurs, according to a multistage view, is the novel arrangement of internally recalled mediators in a sequence beginning with an external stimulus situation and ending with an observable performance. The individual responds to external stimulation by coding it in a way which connects it with a set of responses not previously connected in just that way. A new sequence of internal neural events is thereby established. Does this new sequence have to be "strengthened"? Well, that depends on a number of factors, and is most probably a question of retaining rather than of learning. But the initial change is not one of gradually building up a connection—it is one of snapping into place an efficient mediating sequence.

INDIVIDUALIZED LEARNING

What are the implications of present-day learning theory for the promotion of learning, and for practices of instruction?

With regard to the process of learning, the following should be clear from the previous discussion. Modern learning theorists (and it is difficult to think of an exception) consider learning to be a change that takes place *inside the learner.* The change is not in the stimulus, or in its immediate effects. The change is not in the response, and it is only in a kind of figurative sense that theorists speak of "acquiring a new response." Learning is a change consisting of a rearrangement of internal neural processes.

One implication of this set of developments is that the straw man has disintegrated. Educational writers will need to become more precise in their targets, if they are aiming their darts against learning theorists, as they often seem to enjoy doing. It is no longer legitimate to castigate "rote learning" and applaud "meaningful learning," when it is agreed that almost all learning is in some sense meaningful (to the individual). It is no longer sensible to deplore "memorization" and acclaim "discovery learning" when it is generally recognized that most common forms of learning involve discovery. Nor is it particularly illuminating to praise "creative thinking" and lament "routine learning," when it has become clear that these two kinds of activities both partake of novel neural events, and thus in some important ways are not so very different. It seems very clear that educational plans and practices will be greatly improved when the cliché, "avoid rote memorization," is finally never heard of again.

A second implication of modern findings and the learning model that describes them is that this model can throw an uncomfortably piercing beam into some dark corners of complacency in education. Particularly, this model exposes the delusion that learning is in some manner or other an event of *social interaction*. There is nothing social about it, the mediational model says, except in a quite secondary sense. Learning is an *individual* act, a set of events which takes place entirely within the learner. In fact, it is a highly idiosyncratic event, and depends very much on the nature of the learner, particularly on his own past learning.

Many phrases in educational writing reflect the notion of learning as an event of social interaction, an "interpersonal encounter." Teaching is often referred to as something that is integrally involved in the learning process. The "teaching-learning process" is a phrase which often seems to imply that somehow these two entities are inseparable portions of a single type of event. Even "classroom learning" is sometimes used as though it defined a special variety of learning intimately bound up with the presence of other human beings in a social group. Actually, we know better than this, and if we do not, mediational theory will "learn" us better. Learning may take place in a social environment, but fundamentally it is a process that takes place *within the individual*.

Instruction and the Teacher. Am I saying that an implication of modern learning theory in some sense amounts to a disparagement of the teacher or of the activities of teaching? Most assuredly not. There are a number of purposes to teaching, all of them important and some of them highly satisfying. When the teacher is concerned with seeing that some particular achievement goal of the learner is realized, she is performing some eminently useful functions. Since this is not the subject of the present discussion, I shall only mention some of these functions here (cf. Gagné, 1965, p.284). In providing instruction, the teacher may be engaged in presenting the stimulus, with directing attention, with communicating a model of expected performance, with providing what we have called "learning guidance," with promoting transfer of learning, and with assessing the outcomes of learning. All of these are functions essential to the activity called instruction. Besides these, still other functions of tremendous importance to education are performed by the teacher, including particularly the enhancement of motivation and the imparting of values.

But learning takes place within the learner. One must not overlook the fact that learning can, and often does, take place in the absence of a teacher. The only *essential* part of an educational system is the learner, that is, the student. Dewey (1902, p. 40) said: "The case is of Child. It is his present powers which are to assert themselves; his present capacities which are to be exercised; his present attitudes which are to be realized." I see no reason to read into this statement any emphasis other than the intellectual one which seems to have been intended.

Some Hypotheses about Self-Instruction.   The learner is, then, in a fundamental sense responsible for his own learning. The practical question is, how much responsibility can the student take for his own instruction? If we set him free, will he know where to search for the proper stimuli, will he arrange his tools and his environment so as to receive the proper communications, will he recognize what his objectives are and be able to tell when he has reached them? These questions cannot be answered at the present time. Not only are there no results of experimental tests, there is not even any experience from which tentative conclusions can be drawn. Current practices are evidently optimal ones neither for individual learning nor for learner-controlled instruction.

The questions imply, as hypotheses, some conditions which might promote learning when its conditions are largely controlled by the learner. For example, they suggest that the following types of conditions would be of importance to individualized learning:

1.   The student needs to learn, as a general principle, that learning takes place inside his head, as a result of his own "thinking" activity.

2.   Outlines, indexes, reference lists, and other materials or devices need to be designed for maximum ease and efficiency of employment by the student in finding the stimuli ("learning materials") he needs.

3.   Concepts and principles to be learned must be communicated in a manner which is optimally effective. In many instances, this will be done by means of textbooks; and it is not known that these are designed as well as they might be for this purpose. Audio and visual modes of communication also need attention in this respect.

4.   Every stage of learning should begin with a statement that makes the objectives of learning clear to the learner. Such a statement probably also needs to remain readily available to the learner throughout a "lesson" or other unit to be learned.

5.   A means of appraisal should be provided to the learner which bears a direct and obvious relationship to the objectives of learning. By this means, the learner can check his own performance and obtain immediate feedback.

6.   Opportunities need to be provided for two activities of importance to the transfer of learning. The first of these is *discussion* of what has been recently learned with other people, whether teachers or students, for the purpose of refining, sharpening, and embellishing the mediational processes that have been acquired. The second is *application* of the acquired knowledge in specific practical situations.

Obviously, these propositions must be treated as hypotheses at the present time. Although various opinions may be expressed about them, we have little solid evidence to make us confident of their efficacy as means of promoting individualized learning. It is equally evident, though, that each one of them could be put into effect, and thus tested, for each refers fairly specifically to some definite procedures. The implication is this: Giving the learner responsibility for his own learning seems a feasible thing to do. The idea needs a good deal of research. In testing it experimentally, attention needs to be paid to a number of factors affecting the potentialities of instruction carried out by the learner under his own control.

REFERENCES

BROWN, B. F.   *The Nongraded High School.* Englewood Cliffs, N.J.: Prentice-Hall, Inc., 1963.

DEWEY, J.   *The Child and the Curriculum.* Chicago: University of Chicago Press, 1902.

GAGNÉ, R. M.   "The Acquisition of Knowledge," *Psychological Review,* Vol. 69 (1962), pp. 355-65.

GAGNÉ, R. M.   *The Conditions of Learning.* New York: Holt, Rinehart & Winston, Inc., 1965.

GAGNÉ, R. M.   "Varieties of Learning and the Concept of Discovery," in E. Keisler and L. M. Shulman (eds.), *Learning by Discovery.* Chicago: Rand McNally & Co., 1966.

GAGNÉ, R. M., MAYOR, J. R., GARSTENS, H. L., and PARADISE, N. E. "Factors in Acquiring Knowledge of a Mathematical Task," *Psychological Monographs,* Vol. 76, No. 526 (1962).

GIBSON, E. J. "A Systematic Application of the Concepts of Generalization and Differentiation to Verbal Learning," *Psychological Review*, Vol. 47 (1940), pp. 196-229.

GOODLAD, J. I. "Meeting Children Where They Are," *Saturday Review*, March 20, 1965, pp. 57-59, 72-74.

HARLOW, H. F. "The Formation of Learning Sets," *Psychological Review*, Vol. 56 (1949), pp. 51-65.

HARLOW, H. F. "The Development of Learning in the Rhesus Monkey," *American Scientist*, Vol. 47 (1959), pp. 459-79.

HELLYER, S. "Supplementary Report: Frequency of Stimulus Presentation and Short-term Decrement in Recall," *Journal of Experimental Psychology*, Vol. 64 (1962), p. 650.

HOVLAND, C. I. "Experimental Studies in Rote Learning Theory: VII. Distribution of Practice with Varying Lengths of List," *Journal of Experimental Psychology*, Vol. 27 (1940), pp. 271-84.

HULL, C. L. "Knowledge and Purpose as Habit Mechanisms," *Psychological Review*, Vol. 37 (1930), pp. 511-25.

HULL, C. L. "The Mechanism of the Assembly of Behavior Segments in Novel Combinations Suitable for Problem Solution," *Psychological Review*, Vol. 42 (1935), pp. 219-45.

HULL, C. L. "Mind, Mechanism, and Adaptive Behavior," *Psychological Review*, Vol. 44 (1937), pp. 1-32.

HULL, C. L. *Principles of Behavior*. New York: Appleton-Century-Crofts, 1943.

HULL, C. L., HOVLAND, C. I., ROSS, R. T., HALL, M., PERKINS, D. T., and FITCH, F. B. *Mathematics—Deductive Theory of Rote Learning*. New Haven, Conn.: Yale University Press, 1940.

HUNTER, W. S. "The Delayed Reaction in Animals and Children," *Animal Behaviour Monograph*, Vol. 2, No. 1 (1913).

HUNTER, W. S. "The Symbolic Process," *Psychological Review*, Vol. 31 (1924), pp. 478-97.

JENKINS, J. J. "Mediated Associations: Paradigms and Situations," in C. N. Cofer and B. S. Musgrave (eds.), *Verbal Behavior and Learning*. New York: McGraw-Hill Book Co., 1963, pp. 210-44.

KENDLER, H. H. "The Concept of the Concept," in A. W. Melton (ed.), *Categories of Human Learning*. New York: Academic Press, Inc., 1964, pp. 212-36.

KENDLER, H. H., and KENDLER, T. S. "Effect of Verbalization on Reversal Shifts in Children," *Science*, Vol. 141 (1961), pp. 1619-20.

LAWRENCE, D. H. "The Nature of a Stimulus: Some Relationships between Learning and Perception," in S. Koch (ed.), *Psychology: A Study of a Science*. Vol. 5. *The Process Areas, the Person, and Some Applied Fields: Their Place in Psychology and in Science*. New York: McGraw-Hill Book Co., 1963, pp. 179-212.

LEPLEY, W. M.   "Serial Reactions Considered as Conditioned Reactions," *Psychological Monographs,* Vol. 46, No. 205 (1934).

MCGUIRE, W. J.   "A Multiprocess Model for Paired-Associate Learning," *Journal of Experimental Psychology,* Vol. 62 (1961), pp. 335-47.

MANDLER, J. M., and MANDLER, G.   *Thinking: From Association to Gestalt.* New York: John Wiley & Sons, Inc., 1964.

MELTON, A. W.   "Implications of Short-term Memory for a General Theory of Memory," *Journal of Verbal Learning and Verbal Behavior,* Vol. 2 (1963), pp. 1-21.

MILLER, N. E.   "Liberalization of Basic S-R Concepts: Extensions to Conflict Behavior, Motivation and Social Learning," in S. Koch (ed.), *Psychology: A Study of a Science.* Vol. 2. *General Systematic Formulations, Learning, and Special Processes.* New York: McGraw-Hill Book Co., 1959, pp. 196-292.

PAVLOV, I. P.   *Conditioned Reflexes* (trans. by G. V. Anrep). London: Oxford University Press, Inc., 1927.

RAZRAN, G.   "Russian Psychologists' Psychology and American Experimental Psychology: A Historical and a Systematic Collation and a Look into the Future," *Psychological Bulletin,* Vol. 63 (1965), pp. 42-64.

SKINNER, B. F.   "The Extinction of Chained Reflexes," *Proceedings of the National Academy of Science,* Vol. 20 (1934), pp. 532-36.

SKINNER, B.F.   *The Behavior of Organisms; An Experimental Analysis.* New York: Appleton-Century-Crofts, 1938.

SKINNER, B. F.   *Verbal Behavior.* New York: Appleton-Century-Crofts, 1957.

THORNDIKE, E. L.   *Human Learning.* New York: Appleton-Century-Crofts, 1931.

UNDERWOOD, B. J.   "Interference and Forgetting," *Psychological Review,* Vol. 64 (1957), pp. 49-60.

UNDERWOOD, B. J.   "An Evaluation of the Gibson Theory of Verbal Learning," in C. N. Cofer (ed.), *Verbal Learning and Verbal Behavior.* New York: McGraw-Hill Book Co., 1961, pp. 197-216.

UNDERWOOD, B. J.   "Stimulus Selection in Verbal Learning," in C. N. Cofer and B. S. Musgrave (eds.), *Verbal Behavior and Learning.* New York: McGraw-Hill Book Co., 1963, pp. 33-48.

UNDERWOOD, B. J., and SHULZ, R. W.   *Meaningfulness and Verbal Learning.* Philadelphia: J. B. Lippincott Co., 1960.

WATSON, J. B.   *Psychology from the Standpoint of a Behaviorist.* Philadelphia: J. B. Lippincott Co., 1919.

WICKENS, D. D.   "The Centrality of Verbal Learning: Comments on Professor Underwood's Paper," in A. W. Melton (ed.), *Categories of Human Learning.* New York: Academic Press, Inc., 1964.

Wittrock, M. C.   "The Learning by Discovery Hypothesis," in E. Keisler and
    L. M. Shulman (eds.), *Learning by Discovery.* Chicago: Rand McNally & Co.,
    1966.

Chapter 3. ECONOMICS

INNOVATION IN EDUCATION

Committee for Economic Development

THE GOALS OF INSTRUCTION

It is not the task of the schools to provide final solutions for all problems, but rather to equip their students to face life's problems intelligently and effectively. The end result of competent instruction should be a desire and respect for knowledge and possession of the skills essential to getting and using knowledge. This means competence in verbal skills, especially the ability to read and write—to use language effectively in the identification and classification of facts and in the formation and communication of ideas. The quest for knowledge requires as well the skill of mathematical computation, the techniques of analysis and generalization, and the capacity for reasoning and a commitment to reasonableness.

It is more important to generate intellectual curiosity and a passion for knowledge, and to cultivate good habits of thought and inquiry, than to

SOURCE: Reprinted from *Innovation in Education: New Directions for the American School*, a statement on National Policy by the Research and Policy Committee, Committee for Economic Development. New York. July, 1968, by permission of publisher.

concentrate on learning countless detailed facts which may soon be forgotten or abandoned. This is particularly vital in a society such as ours, in which economic demands and the methods of industry and business change rapidly, and in which mobility in vocation and employment is widely accepted and practiced. To acquire basic intellectual and technical skills is of far more worth than simply to master a single specialized technique.

Knowledge and reason and their related skills must always lie at the center of the goals of instruction, but these goals refer also to the effective or emotional life of the individual and to his capacity for decision and action. The schools should be concerned with the relevance of reason and knowledge to personal and social values. They should enlarge the individual's social perspectives, sharpen his moral and artistic sensibilities, and strengthen his sense of responsibility and commitment to purpose.

To cultivate the creative talent of the individual is another basic task of the school. But the identification and cultivation of talent are difficult. They require instruction that avoids those classroom routines which tend to produce standardized effects upon the pupils. Fortunately, extensive research is now being done on creativity which should yield useful knowledge for future planning.

The Early Years

The schools have achieved their most obvious and unambiguous success in the area of the acquisition and communication of knowledge. This is not surprising. Most educational research has been in this area, and the methods and techniques of the schools are best adapted to this function of instruction.

But it is also here that the schools have experienced their most serious failures—notably the failure to bring the child to a successful mastery of the verbal skills essential to the further pursuit of learning. In countless cases this has its roots in the inability of children to learn effectively because of cultural deficiencies in their preschool and home environments.

Those who do not learn to read and write effectively are not only deficient in the basic tools for further learning. They are often lost from the mainstream of the educational process. They may develop resentments against social authority and formal education and become alienated from their teachers and school and from everything that school represents to them. Often they become dropouts with the risk of tragic failure.

If the efforts of the schools are to be fully effective, the children from many if not all segments of our society must receive regular educational services covering the early preschool years from at least the age of three.[1]

It is now known that far more can be learned at an earlier age than was formerly supposed, while the basic importance of acquiring the primary learning skills, especially reading and writing, in the beginning years is well established. The educational investment in the very early years yields the largest dividends in developing talent, skills, perceptivity, and creativity as well as in encouraging intellectual independence and self-discipline. The acquisition of these attributes by children in their early years will make them more receptive and effective learners later on, thus lightening the load now borne by the instructional staffs of the elementary and secondary schools and aiding them to teach more effectively and efficiently.

It is increasingly evident that our educational needs are not adequately satisfied by the schools as they are now organized. Whether the establishment of the large numbers of preschools that appear to be required should be accomplished under the present school establishments by adding preschooling to the traditional format, or outside of these systems, is a difficult question to answer. There are both advantages and drawbacks to either proposal. This Committee favors the development of a mixed "system" of preschooling, through the encouragement of both private and public preschools, with a place for nonprofit schools, supported both by public and private monies, that will serve as demonstration units.

> We believe that early schooling is probably desirable for all children and that it is a necessity for the children of culturally disadvantaged areas. We therefore recommend extensive experimental activity in preschooling, not only in the substance and processes of instruction but also in organization, administration, and finance. We urge the establishment of both public and private nursery schools, especially in the neighborhoods of the disadvantaged. There is room for much development in this direction by those industrial and business firms which employ large numbers of women, particularly by those firms that are establishing facilities in the ghetto areas.

Reform of the School Curriculum

Perhaps nothing has more dramatically demonstrated the possibility of improving the quality of education than recent curriculum reforms. Curriculum reform began with mathematics in 1951 and has spread to physics, biology, chemistry, elementary school science, English, modern foreign languages, geography, anthropology, economics, and other social sciences.

The relative success of the movement has been due in part to the fact that the curriculum projects have usually been under the direction of persons who are willing to break with educational custom and tradition. Most important, those projects have joined the efforts of highly competent subject-matter scholars and skilled teachers to those of specialists in educational theory and practice and technicians competent in the new technology.

The major curriculum projects have produced an updating and upgrading of course materials and have developed techniques for more effective teaching with those materials. They have also placed knowledge and the methods of obtaining and validating it at the center of the school's activities. In general they have made the classroom and laboratory more exciting and rewarding for both students and teachers.

There are three aspects of curriculum reform that give us special concern:

First: Some recent efforts to improve the curriculum have failed to produce materials that can be employed effectively in the context of the newer instructional systems, which depart radically from the traditional patterns of personnel organization, scheduling, group composition, individual progression, and school architecture. Curriculum improvement should keep pace with the new concepts of organization and method. It should recognize the value of multi-media, man-machine systems of instruction and make use of them when it is economical to do so.

Second: The curriculum materials and methods developed have been adopted by far too few schools. Thousands of children and youth are still being taught an outdated science by outdated methods, even though the materials are available for bringing their education up to date. Others are taught with improved materials, but by inadequately trained teachers using old methods and techniques that yield negative results because they are inappropriate for those materials.

Third: The curriculum study projects that are now under way should be the beginning of a continuing effort to reconstruct both the substance and methods of education from the ground up to insure that the schools keep in touch with the world in which their students live. There must be some guarantee that teachers and students have access to both up-to-date knowledge and improved techniques of instruction.

> Recognizing the improvement in the quality of instruction that already has resulted from the curriculum study projects of recent years, we recommend the continued funding of such projects by both public and private agencies. These studies should be extended to cover the entire spectrum of the school curriculum. The joint efforts of subject-matter scholars, education experts, and technicians are essential to the effective upgrading and updating of instructional materials and methods in all fields. Publishers and other producers of instructional materials

and manufacturers of educational equipment should assume a larger responsibility in this enterprise.

Re-examination of Goals

Both long-range educational purposes and the immediate goals of instruction must be continually re-examined and revised in light of changing conditions and new possibilities. The difficulty of this task issues from the uncertainties in current knowledge of human behavior and motivation, from the comparative inadequacies of contemporary learning theory, from failure to relate successfully means to ends in the educative process, and from the hard task of relating knowledge and the pursuit of knowledge to practical personal and social problems.

Whatever else may be set as a proper goal of education, it can at least be said that a school does not fully succeed unless it makes learning an interesting if not exciting experience; unless it effectively generates intellectual curiosity, a love of knowledge, and an open mind; unless it encourages a genuine incentive to create and the ability to think clearly; and unless it magnifies the self, establishes personal identity, and encourages individuality. The schools cannot expect to achieve ideal results. There are differences among both pupils and teachers, differences in their backgrounds and abilities and in their motivation and commitment. There are also limitations on the material resources that the nation can devote to schooling. Both failures and successes are to be expected, and there will always be variances in the level of the quality of different schools. But this does not mean that the schools should not set their standards high.

In stressing the value of knowledge, we are not proposing that the elementary and secondary schools be designed simply as preparatory to college and university education. Far from it. Although an increasing proportion of young people should seek university educations, many others should receive good vocational educations on the secondary level or should go on to technical schools or to vocationally oriented programs in community colleges. We believe that for the good of individuals as well as society, the secondary and post-secondary vocational and technical schools should be greatly strengthened. Jobs and income must be available to the youths who enter the labor force early. Technically trained manpower is essential for business and industry and for the general economic and social health.

INDIVIDUALIZED INSTRUCTION

We are especially concerned with the problem of equality of opportunity in education. In a free society, equality of educational opportunity is a basic ideal. However difficult it may be to achieve, it should always be kept as a civic goal. The individual's schooling is the best gateway to a satisfying, productive life, and full education is the best hope for a just society.

Whatever else is done to promote full educational opportunity, there must be a maximum effort to achieve more individualization in instruction. Only by this avenue is there hope for success with each individual— with the physically, mentally, or culturally disadvantaged—or with those who are especially gifted, who possess exceptional intellectual or artistic abilities.

By individualized instruction we do not mean a simple tutoring procedure. We mean instruction that is designed for the individual student rather than for an entire class. At times the individual will receive personal attention from the teacher. At other times he may be a member of a large group. At all times the school's resources are utilized to the best advantage of his intellectual growth. The differences among children require careful consideration if the learning experiences of the individual child are to be effective and rewarding. Individualized instruction is a good thing for all children; for the highly gifted and for the child of the ghetto and the slums it is essential.

We believe that it is now possible, in terms of both techniques and cost, to provide instruction that is effectively geared to the individual, to his learning capacities and interests, and to his personal problems. This can be accomplished if the schools take full advantage of the slowly growing body of competent learning theory, the possible uses of diversified grouping and scheduling, and the improved uses of instructional talent through the new staffing patterns that differentiate teaching personnel and their functions. These, when coupled with the wise exploitation of both the old and the new educational media, should provide invaluable instruments for bringing instruction directly to the individual student.

Emphasizing the individualization of instruction brings a new and personal dimension of education into the center of concern—the teacher's knowledge of the learner. Effective instruction requires more than knowing something to teach and having a practical grasp of good teaching methods. It requires a knowledge of the learner—his background, motives, interests, perspectives, and attitudes, his hopes and aspirations or his hopelessness and lack of aspiration. There is often little chance of success in instruction where the child as an individual person is not known to the teacher. This is a fact which must receive central attention in the reconstruction of teacher education.

The Organization of Instruction

The organization of instruction offers numerous possibilities for improving a school's effectiveness. The problem is to deploy staff time, energy, and talents more effectively than is now commonly the case. A flexible arrangement of student groups is required to provide more meaningful contacts with teachers and student peers than has been customary in the traditional classroom, and to permit a maximum of independence for those who are capable of pursuing their studies on an individual basis. This is especially important where the new media are enlisted for instructional purposes. The traditional grouping of students simply by age or years in school ignores the importance of treating every person in accordance with his individual needs and talents.

By team teaching, a technique of cooperative teaching that has already been widely employed, the special talents of teachers are combined to focus on major elements of the curriculum. Team teaching utilizes teachers in different functions in accordance with their own special abilities, interests, and education and in keeping with the variety of the curriculum and the needs of individual students. Through a flexible staffing pattern that uses teacher interns, aids, clerks, and media technicians, team teaching enhances the possibility for a school or school system to obtain the best returns on its investment.

The quality of education can be improved at relatively small additional costs where competent assistants of varying talents and preparation are employed to supervise routine and other matters both in and out of the classroom, thereby freeing the regular teacher for tasks which are more appropriate to his abilities. Communities can often provide competent and committed persons who cannot obtain full teacher certification, but whose talents are very valuable to the schools when utilized as assistants. These assistants should comprise a breadth of supportive talent in operating computers, projectors, and other media equipment and in performing routine clerical duties.

An Emerging Instruction Pattern

The traditional practice of placing approximately 30 or 40 students in a box-like classroom and staffing this unit with one teacher is under serious challenge in the modern school. Systems theorists have been examining this simple organizational pattern with increasing skepticism. There is now emerging a more efficient system with a comprehensive, flexible staffing pattern and with instructional system packages that permit greater personal contact between the teacher and the individual learner. While we do not suggest that there is an ultimate or final organization plan, there is a clearly discernible pattern common to many of the latest innovative developments across the nation.

In the new view, teaching and learning activities in schools can be classified under three categories: (1) lecturing, explaining, and demonstrating; (2) independent study and inquiry under supervision; and (3) discussion involving the teacher with small groups of students. An analysis of these categories can lead to a more sophisticated organizational plan for instruction than now generally obtains.

There is an increasing realization that too much teaching in traditional schools is devoted to the functions in the first category—i.e., mainly talking on the part of the teacher and listening on the part of the student.

Lecturing as carried on in the traditional manner is not usually an efficient use of the time of students and teachers. The lecturing, explaining, and demonstrating function of teaching can be produced in a studio and placed on films or video tapes. These can be available for selective use by the teacher on the basis of diagnoses of individual needs that become evident from the dialogue taking place between the teacher and small groups of three to eight students. The teacher can simply prescribe the lecture and delegate to an assistant the routine matter of showing the film or video tape before a small tutorial group of students.

In many advanced schools, the basic instructional unit has been increased from the customary 30 or so students to 90 or even 120 students. The group is housed in a large, open, carpeted area staffed with a team comprised of assistants, interns, and media technicians, who function in subcenters around a learning center containing various instructional resources. The certified teacher-to-pupil ratio is increased to 45 or 50 to one, with staff dollars deployed to employ assistants and to purchase audiovisual and other equipment and materials. Through the more efficient use of lecture and independent study activity, made possible in part by the new instructional techniques, there will be a decreased demand on the teacher's time. This, in turn, makes possible a closer and more personal relationship between teacher and student.

This emerging new pattern of organization for instruction should be developed more rapidly. At the current rate of change it will require decades to transform the classroom teaching system into this more open, adaptive, man-machine system.

> We recommend continued and more extensive experimentation in school organization to eliminate the regimentation of students that results from the conventional class units and lock-step method of advancement. We believe that the combination of differentiated staffs, team teaching, and variable student grouping, together with the use of instructional television and other audiovisual media, has much promise for individualizing instruction.

ADVANCED DESIGN FOR
AN ELEMENTARY SCHOOL

Utilizing Media Systems and Team Teaching
to achieve Individualized Instruction

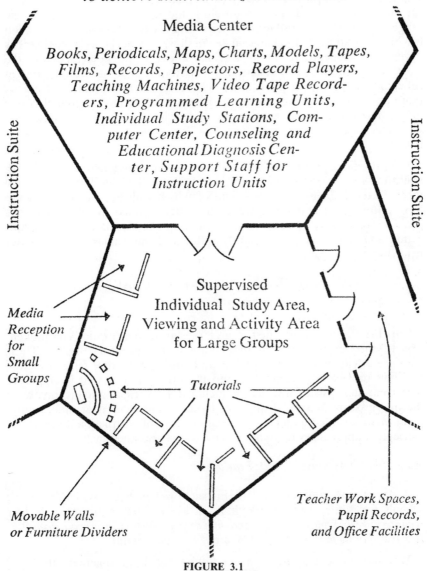

Media Center

Books, Periodicals, Maps, Charts, Models, Tapes,
Films, Records, Projectors, Record Players,
Teaching Machines, Video Tape Record-
ers, Programmed Learning Units,
Individual Study Stations, Com-
puter Center, Counseling and
Educational Diagnosis Cen-
ter, Support Staff for
Instruction Units

Instruction Suite

Instruction Suite

Supervised
Individual Study Area,
Viewing and Activity Area
for Large Groups

Media
Reception
for
Small
Groups

Tutorials

Teacher Work Spaces,
Pupil Records,
and Office Facilities

Movable Walls
or Furniture Dividers

FIGURE 3.1
THE FLOOR PLAN OF A TYPICAL LEARNING CENTER

THE USE OF THE NEW RESOURCES

Technology may be a powerful factor in the achievement of educational goals where the instructional program is planned by competent designers and the instruments are employed by properly prepared and skilled teachers. The use of advanced techniques in instruction can free teacher time for more intensive individual counseling and tutoring and can extend the range of the teacher's influence by enabling a closer relationship between teacher and student. Educational technology can serve as a vehicle for developing cooperation among teachers and can aid in overcoming the isolation of individual teachers and classrooms that has commonly resulted from traditional patterns of school organization and teaching. A more efficient deployment and specialized use of faculty personnel is one of the new instructional technologies and techniques. These are described in a special section entitled *"The New Resources for Learning: a Brief Guide."*

Educational equipment and methods may disclose new objectives in education that otherwise may have been ignored. The development of new means often influences the judgment of which ends are worth achieving. More effective teaching techniques may be expected to affect both the goals and substance of education, just as improved methods of communication and travel have importantly influenced our values as well as our behavior.

THE NEW RESOURCES FOR LEARNING:
A BRIEF GUIDE

This brief guide is intended to give the lay reader a quick comprehension of the developments in instructional or educational media. These embrace a wide variety of materials and equipment, from motion-picture film and projectors to computers and the programming that is employed with computer-assisted instruction. Included are various systems, involving the intermixture of several different kinds of audiovisual or other equipment. Also included under the general heading of instructional media are conceptual approaches to teaching, such as programmed instruction.

Audiovisual Materials and Equipment

A variety of materials to aid instruction has been available to the schools for some years, employing the use of such equipment as *tape recorders, record players, slide and filmstrip projectors, overhead projectors (for transparencies), motion-picture projectors, and radios.*

Whether these employ sight or sound, or both together, they are grouped as audiovisual materials. They are also frequently referred to as *conventional aids,* though the term is somewhat misleading. New uses for the equipment have been devised, sometimes in combination with other media or equipment. Meanwhile there has been considerable technical advancement in the design of equipment, resulting in easier and more flexible classroom use of audiovisual material, through cartridge loading, self-threading projectors, and remote push-button control.

Of particular note have been the advances in 8mm. film and projectors. Sound is increasingly used, giving 8mm. materials greater importance and impact. The introduction of the so-called *film loop* also has widened the uses of 8mm. materials. This device employs a repetitive film in a cartridge that rewinds itself and is simple to use. This has made for easy use in the classroom, and it has also facilitated the use of 8mm. for individual study. Film loops have proven especially useful for short *single-concept* films on a particular subject or demonstration, which students can see many times.

A similar development has taken place in *audio tape* with the introduction of the *cassette,* containing a repetitive loop of tape. This device is likewise easy to use and re-play.

The audiovisual field has been augmented in recent years by *television.* The TV set in the classroom can receive programs, either live or pre-recorded, from central broadcasting studios. Or it can be employed as an independent audiovisual unit through the means of *video tape.* Programs of all kinds can be recorded on tape and kept on hand in school libraries for use as needed, as in the case of motion-picture films. This frees teachers from the rigidities of scheduling imposed by central broadcasting, which is confined to the use of a limited number of channels at any given time.

Various video tape slave units for the re-playing of tapes through television sets are now on the market. As of the present, these slave units are several times more costly than motion-picture projectors, but there is a probability that less-expensive equipment may be offered in the relatively near future. Eventually students should be able to check out video tapes from the library for home use.

In the broadcast mode, dissemination of TV programming can be accomplished either through the use of ground stations or airborne equipment, or by means of closed circuit television (CCTV). Broadcasting for instructional use by educational institutions, either to the school or the home, is referred to as *instructional television* (ITV) to distinguish it from *educational television* (ETV), which serves a broader cultural and informational service to the general public.

Aside from its employment in classroom instruction, television has other uses in the educational process. Television is useful in the training of teachers, particularly in the improvement of teaching skills in conjunction with such techniques as *micro-teaching* by enabling the teacher to criticize his own performance on video tape. Television facilities in the school also provide a communication instrument between administrators and both staff and students.

Various instructional systems utilizing audiovisual and other equipment have been developed, the most familiar of these being the *language laboratory*. The purpose of the language laboratory is to develop listening and speaking skills in foreign languages. The system employs individual study *carrels* (booths) and the use of audio tape equipment and headphones in combination with other materials.

The *dial-access learning center,* which also employs carrels and headphones, makes it possible for the individual student to call up pre-programmed and recorded audio tapes, motion-picture films, or other visual resources. It also gives the student access to off-air and closed-circuit television programming. A limitation presently is the number of channels simultaneously available, a problem that will have to be solved before the system can reach its full potential.

Programmed Instruction

Programmed instruction is a self-tutoring technique of moving by convenient and sequentially arranged steps from old knowledge to new knowledge. With programmed instruction the individual can advance in the study of a subject at his own individual optimum rate.

The technique was originally developed in conjunction with so-called teaching machines, but the use of these devices is minimal. However, the principles of programmed instruction have been adapted widely to printed texts; they are essential in various modes of computer-assisted instruction.

Experimentation has established that programmed techniques can be effective in teaching logic, mathematics, and languages; improving the capacity to recognize distinctions and alternatives; teaching reasons and explanations as well as conditioning for correct responses; providing for student independence in the choice of subject matter and goals as well as in the determination of learning speed; and cultivating high learning motivation in the student.

Properly employed, programmed instruction can free the teacher from much routinized work and can contribute to the conditions necessary for the non-graded school that would overcome the present lock-step method of pupil advancement.

In certain uses, programmed instruction offers opportunities to increase greatly the effectiveness and efficiency of the learning process. Borrowing a case in point from higher education, a graduate school of business has cut the time required for students to master an accounting course from 19 hours to about 2 hours through the introduction of programmed instruction.

Individually prescribed instruction (IPI) is a system for the utilization of programmed instruction and other instructional materials. The student's point of entry in this system is through a placement test, on the basis of which the teacher prescribes a course on an appropriate level for the individual student. The student proceeds with a designated worksheet, which is checked by an aide who directs the student to other worksheets according to his performance. As the student progresses, he will move on to other levels.

Computer-assisted instruction (CAI) employs a central computer with electric typewriters, light pens, audio tape, and other equipment as terminals for the use of students. The system can be used in various modes of instruction, as for example, drill or practice, inquiry, tutorial instruction, or authorship.

In addition to its possible usefulness in furthering individualized instruction, the computer has the following advantages:

> It can provide conditions and capabilities for research on teaching under controlled conditions of individualized instruction.

> It can collect detailed records on student performance that help evaluate the effectiveness of both instructional materials and methods.

> It is useful in assisting teachers and authors in the development of instructional materials.

When employed in instruction, computers can provide remarkable versatility. Although research in this matter is in its early stages and the problem of specific objectives in education is complex and difficult, theoretically CAI can be employed for any subject matter that can be treated through the agency of books, films, or recordings.

It is important that central computers can be programmed for outlets widely distributed on a regional or even national basis. Teletypewriter equipment, which can be synchronized with both audio and visual instruments, can be connected with the central computer by the simple device of telephone lines.

NOTES

[1] On the basis of experience with the Head Start program for culturally deprived children, the per pupil cost of extending the program is estimated at close to $1,400 per child. Thus, if the program were to be extended so that it reached 80 per cent of the 2.5 million children between the ages of three and five of families within the poverty level it would cost about $2.8 billion.

Chapter 4. INSTRUCTIONAL METHODS

LEARNER VARIABLES AND EDUCATIONAL MEDIA

Leslie J. Briggs

Educators long have sought ways to adapt group methods of instruction in such ways that all children in the group progress at acceptable rates and reach satisfactory levels of achievement in reasonable amounts of time. It is not surprising that group teaching methods with some fixed set of materials normally fail to achieve the purpose. In both research and classroom practice, the attempt to find ways to meet individual needs by group methods tends to encounter confusion of three important parts of the problem: (a) *criteria*—how fast and how well the learner progresses; (b) the learning *variables*—why the child progresses or does not progress; and (c) the choice among *methods* for attempting to adapt group teaching to individual needs—branching instruction, parallel sets of material, grouping by ability, or diagnostic testing and remedial instruction.

SOURCE: Reprinted from Leslie J. Briggs, "Learner Variables and Educational Media," *Review of Educational Research*, April 1968, pp. 160-76, by permission of author and publisher. Copyright by American Educational Research Association.

If, somehow, attention could be focused first on the learning variables—why the person does or does not meet the criteria of progress—then insights might be gained into what the individual learner needs by way of instructional materials or media. We could then consider how this need can be met in spite of the necessity for group instruction. It is thus working backwards to ask first whether one should prefer to use ability grouping or branching programs, because one cannot know whether a branching program is the proper method for adapting to individual needs before he knows what the individual needs are. Branching is not the way to meet the need, for example, if the branching is a branching by words when the learner needs a picture.

In this chapter, therefore, no solutions will be found for *methods* of making group-presented media fill individual needs because we are still uncertain as to the needs of the learner. Various lines of research endeavor, however, conducted by group experiments (not experiments with individual learners), do throw some light on the problem. Interestingly enough, it is research with groups, using samples of actual instructional materials, which helps more than the individual treatments applied to one "subject" at a time in the learning laboratory. Apparently the variables used there are not the ones needed to solve the problem. More often than not, as will be seen, this group research employed programed instruction as the medium for research.

While no one learning variable (or characteristic of the learning program) can yet be said to outweigh all others in importance, the following issues do seem worthy of exploration when searching for the key characteristics of media and materials which may eventually bring about effective individual learning in either individual or group situations: sensory mode; IQ; special aptitudes; entering competencies; sequencing of instruction; and "programming variables" such as size of step, frequency of feedback, and variety of examples.

In the following portions of this chapter, research touching on the above points is summarized. When more such research has succeeded in identifying more fully the needs for learning by the individual, then progress later may be made in methods for adapting group media to individual needs in order to achieve the criteria. If such continued research succeeds in identifying the kind of program the individual learner needs, then it may be possible at some point in the future to employ computers for highly successful branching instruction—but probably not until then.

ABILITIES, PRIOR LEARNING, AND
SEQUENCING OF INSTRUCTION

In analyzing the task of finding formulas for "sum of *n* terms" in a number series, Gagné (1962) drew a hierarchical diagram of the subordinate skills, arranged in layers, and indicated the sequence in which the subordinate parts of the task should be taught. He theorized that the competencies so identified serve as mediators of positive transfer from lower level competencies to higher ones and that starting with the learning of the lowest levels, attaining each higher level depends on positive transfer, recall, and the effects of instruction in guiding thinking. At the very bottom of the hierarchy may be found relevant competencies supposedly learned earlier and basic abilities relevant to the learning of the task.

Gagné administered test items over each competency to ninth-grade boys. Each boy was tested first for the final task; if he failed, the test for the next lowest competency was given and so on down the hierarchy until the boy passed on a competency. At that point the testing stopped temporarily, and a learning program designed to teach the next highest competency (previously failed) was administered. Then the test items were given over the remaining levels. The results showed, first of all, that the boys exhibited wide individual differences in patterns on the tests, illustrating different entering competencies. There were no instances in which a person able to perform a higher level competency failed on a lower one. After completing the instructional portion for previously failed competencies, the boy was again tested, yielding scores on competencies both before and after administration of the learning program.

In reference to the abilities at the bottom of such hierarchies, Gagné theorized that if learning programs were of perfect effectiveness, everyone would pass all the component tests in the hierarchy, the variance would be zero, and all correlations of tests on the various competencies with basic abilities also would be zero. But if learning programs are not perfectly effective, the probability that a person will acquire each competency will be increased to the extent of his score on a test of the basic ability.

Gagné and Paradise (1961) dealt with sources of individual differences in rate of learning from a learning program. They suggested that differences in rate of learning observed among learners are due not to variations on some underlying general ability to learn fast, but rather to (a) the number and kinds of learning sets (competencies, knowledge) the learner brings to the situation, and, secondarily, to (b) his standing in respect to certain basic abilities relevant to the competencies to be acquired as they are identified in the theoretical hierarchy for the task and (c) his level of general intelligence. Reasons for failure to learn to perform a task after taking a learning program could be as follows: (a) some subordinate knowledge may have been left out of the learning program; (b) insufficient practice or some other program characteristic may have resulted in poor recall of a subordinate competency; or (c) the program may have been defective in guiding thinking required to induce the necessary integration of subordinate competencies.

Gagné and Paradise (1961, p. 3) hypothesized that a substantial amount of the variability during learning is attributable to the attainment or nonattainment of learning sets relevant to the final task the program is designed to teach. "Accordingly, as the learner progresses upwards in the hierarchy, his rate of learning should depend increasingly upon relevant abilities." In contrast, the correlation of general ability with rate of learning should remain constant as the learning progresses up the hierarchy. As contrasted to rate of achievement, the fact of achievement rather than nonachievement in a moderately ineffective learning program might depend increasingly on relevant abilities as one goes up the hierarchy, e.g., those of low ability "drop out" due to failure on some competencies while those of more ability continue to master competencies in spite of defects in the program.

The task of solving linear algebraic equations was selected to test some of the above hypotheses. A learning hierarchy was designed by a logical analysis procedure. The resulting hierarchy showed six levels of relevant competencies and, at the bottom, three specific relevant abilities.

The procedure employed in the study by Gagné and Paradise was as follows: First, basic ability tests were administered. Then the learning program was given, using eight booklets over eight class days. Then a performance test of solving equations was given, followed at once by a transfer test involving unfamiliar forms and unfamiliar symbols. On the next day, tests were given on each learning set in the hierarchy. Learning rate was recorded by having students draw a line on their program answer sheets on a signal given every three minutes.

As to overall achievement on the performance test and transfer tests, the results indicated that the program was only moderately effective.

As to transfer from learning of subordinate sets to higher ones in the hierarchy, students were scored as "pass" or "fail" on test items over each of the component capabilities. Patterns of pass-fail from lower skills to higher ones were then analyzed for each learner. The results for pairs of test items for adjacent levels in the hierarchy confirmed theoretical predictions on transfer from one competency to the next in proportions of instances ranging from 0.91 to 1.00.

On the relations between relevant abilities and learning sets, the results generally confirmed the prediction that rate of learning depends decreasingly on relevant abilities, whereas the achievement of the learning set depends increasingly on such abilities as one goes up the hierarchy. There was also evidence for the corollary assumption that since rate of learning comes to depend less on relevant basic abilities, as learning progresses up the hierarchy it does increasingly depend on achievement of successive subordinate competencies.

An implication of the findings is that as learning progresses, relevant abilities will correlate increasingly with achievement only for programs which are somewhat defective in mediating transfer from one level to the next.

Further data supporting the general theory of learning hierarchies and the implications for the sequencing of instruction were contained in reports by Gagné and others (1962, 1965) and Gagné and Bassler (1963).

INDIVIDUAL DIFFERENCES IN RATE OF LEARNING

Because of the factors identified above in determining rate of learning, it should be apparent that just pushing the learner through the program faster is not always a good way to improve learning. On the other hand, self-pacing by the learner is also no universal cure for slow learning. Gropper and Kress (1965) presented data to suggest that self-pacing can be nonadaptive to the needs of the learner. Some learners need to be speeded up and some need to be slowed down to improve the effectiveness and efficiency of learning. If a learner-determined rate is too fast, more errors occur, primarily because of low IQ. Many high IQ learners proceed slowly and inefficiently, while many low IQ learners go fast and ineffectively. But if the pace of presentation is increased for the total group, the error rate increases, and the achievement gap between the low IQ and the high IQ learners increases. It would appear, then, that experimental study of the individual learner's pace and learning record would be one way to proceed to adjust rate appropriately for each, while analysis of errors would be a way to improve mastery of needed subordinate competencies.

Suppes (1964) has reported that in computer-assisted instruction individual differences in rate are even larger than previously thought. He cited individual differences in learning rates for drill material paced in rate by the computer. For Russian-English word pairs Suppes found that the optimum size of unit for practice was typically the largest of several units employed. Thus when lists of Russian-English words were presented in different sizes of units as an application of the whole-part question, college students and junior high school students did better practicing a list of 108 items than a list of 6 when time for mastery of the total list was the criterion. The results, of course, might not be the same if English-Russian word pairs were employed. His general rule was that when learning is faster than forgetting the experimenter should show all 108 pairs on the first trial. But when forgetting is faster than learning, only one item should be presented; all exposure of a given pair should then be contiguous. The mathematics for in-between learning rates was given.

It would appear, then, that in the future branching in rate of presentation should become a new variable in research. Many media now employed for group instruction would need eventually to be adapted and employed for individually paced instruction. This may bring more improvement in use of films, for example, than working to improve the photography. Film material should be packaged more widely in smaller segments, with responding required, to capitalize fully on the stimulus advantages of this medium.

BRANCHING AS A MEANS OF
INDIVIDUALIZING INSTRUCTION

Crowder (1959) introduced a variation of programed instruction first identified as a "scrambled book" and later as "intrinsic" programing when machines replaced the books. The scrambled book, unlike other books, is not read in page sequence. The learner is given a paragraph or two of information followed by a multiple-choice question. If the learner chooses the correct alternative, he is directed to a page on which he is reminded of why he is right and then directed to another page having new material and another test question. If the learner chooses the wrong answer, he is directed to a page which tells him that he is wrong, with an explanation of why he is wrong, or he is given a hint and directed back to try again. Crowder has also developed electromechanical devices for presenting intrinsic programs (see review of autoinstructional devices by Briggs, 1960). These do the "page turning" for the learner, who needs only to push the coded buttons to be told what to do next. One such device was able to present short motion-picture sequences in addition to projecting pages of print. Later it was found by others that branching programs lend themselves to computerization.

Branching programs strike most people as eminently sensible. One could reasonably expect that branching programs should be superior to linear programs because they appear to provide the information the learner needs when he needs it without his being bothered by superfluous information. It is difficult, therefore, to understand why there is not more evidence showing branching to be superior to linear programs. Results from early experiments have not been especially encouraging (Campbell, 1963; Coulson and Silberman, 1961; Coulson and others, 1962; Roe, 1962). It may be that some of the early comparisons reflected the effects of inadequate techniques employed in making the decisions to branch ahead or to backtrack.

In recent years, equipment for the student station for computer-assisted instruction has been greatly improved. Early stations were limited to typewriter input and output. With the use of the cathode ray tube and light gun providing both printed and pictorial display and with the use of filmstrips, movies, and tape recorders in conjunction with the station, a greater range of instructional stimuli can be employed. Also, if accumulated historical data and series of responses made earlier in the program relevant to the next branching decision to be made can become the replacements for branching on the basis of a single test item, future results for branching programs might greatly surpass those for linear programs. Even so, it may be easier to achieve greater gains with computers for drill than for abstract, conceptual material.

In summary, early results would appear to suggest the need for basing branching on something other than the results of a single test item because of the (a) unreliability of a single item, (b) danger of failing to assess a competency in a relevant way in view of the next steps to be taken, and (c) possible adverse effects of making errors. At the present time, then, it is not entirely clear whether the somewhat disappointing results from comparison of linear with branching programs are due to inadequacy in evaluating the student's competence as a basis for branching decisions, to adverse effects of making errors, to removal of needed redundancy from branching programs, to inadequate basic programing, or to upsetting certain sequencing effects which need to remain unchanged, as in the basic linear program.

In general, improved equipment and techniques are needed in order to devise a multimedia capability which combines the response characteristics of programed instruction, the branching features of computers, and the stimulus advantages employed in film.

SIZE OF STEP

There is no standard definition of "size of step." In programed instruction it has referred variously to (a) how difficult a response is to make, (b) how large a reading segment is presented before a response is required, (c) how much progress toward the goal is represented by one frame, (d) how long it takes the learner to make a response, (e) whether or not the student responds correctly, and (f) how frequently reinforcement occurs.

At any rate, the theory of Skinner (1958) that small steps are needed, while adopted widely by linear programmers, has by no means gone unchallenged. Bruner (1963) has urged huge leaps, alternating on occasion with small steps. Scandura (1966) has questioned the relevance of learning theory as a basis for a theory of instruction and has chosen the principle rather than the S-R bond as the basic unit in meaningful learning (Scandura, 1967). Pressey (1967) objected to the fractionization of learning into small steps, preferring the larger, learner-determined, flexible size of step made possible by the technique of adjunct autoinstruction. Ausubel (1960) advocated the use of "advance organizers," introductory statements in the most general, abstract form, to serve as aids to cognitive structuring of subsequent material. Most motion pictures and television programs are apparently developed in the absence of any such concept as size of step.

Nevertheless, under a wide range of conditions, use of some form of explicit (overt or covert) responding has been shown to enhance the value of most media of instruction. Providing knowledge of results has had a similar effect, possibly more consistently for multiple-choice adjunct responding than for constructed responses (May, 1966, p. 134). This latter effect may be in part a function of size of step (difficulty of responding). New techniques are needed to permit the learner to adjust step size to his capabilities without suffering either many errors or tedious, unneeded redundancies. Recent evidence suggests that the neglected technique of adjunct autoinstruction needs wider user (Pressey, 1967).

PICTURES, SPOKEN WORDS, AND PRINTED WORDS

For learners who can read, few confident generalizations can be made as to whether the instructional media should display pictures, sounds, spoken words, or printed words. The review by Travers (1964) debunked the widely held notion that simultaneous visual and auditory stimuli, as in motion pictures or television, are consistently superior to one mode of sensory stimulation at a time. A more moot question is the issue of when to employ auditory and when to employ visual stimuli.

Cooper and Gaeth (1967) noted that historically the data regarding efficacy of auditory and visual materials have pointed to an interaction of modality with other factors, notably intelligence, reading ability, age, and difficulty of the material. These investigators employed five age-grade levels (grades 4, 5, 6, 10, and 12) of learners, two tasks of different degrees of meaningfulness (nonsense syllables and three-letter nouns), and two presentation modes (visual and auditory). All three main effects—grade, meaningfulness, and modality—were significant (.01 level). Performance for nouns was best with visual presentation in the fourth grade, while the auditory presentation was best at the twelfth grade. For the nonsense syllables, the visual presentation was consistently better than the auditory (e.g., no grade by modality interaction). The reported superiority of visual presentation for nouns in grades 4, 5, and 6 and inferiority in grades 10 and 12 is directly contrary to earlier findings by Day and Beach, as reported by Cooper and Gaeth. The investigators noted that while, in general, auditory stimuli are best for easy material and visual for difficult, the best presentation for new and difficult material is a function of the habit system of the learner as developed by personal experience. They concluded that at some point in language development of the person there ceases to be a functional distinction between the effectiveness of the two modalities, i.e., a well-educated adult may learn equally well by hearing or reading.

Rohwer and others (1967) presented 24 pairs of objects in the form of pictures of the objects or printed names of the objects to 96 third-and sixth-grade children. As each pair was presented, the experimenter spoke aloud one of four kinds of verbalization: (a) the names of the objects, (b) the names of the objects connected by a conjunction, (c) the names connected by a preposition, or (d) the names connected by a verb. For both older and younger subjects, pictorial materials produced more efficient learning than did the printed names, and verb connectors facilitated acquisition most, followed by prepositions, then conjunctions.

Snow, Tiffin, and Seibert (1965) reported that, while finding no main-effect difference in effectiveness between a training film and a live (lecture) presentation, among Ss with low prior knowledge those with an unfavorable attitude toward films learned better by live instruction. In terms of immediate recall, Ss characterized as active, self-assertive, self-assured, and independent learned better by live presentation. Those Ss characterized as passive, followers, dependent, and lacking in self-confidence learned slightly more by the film.

In a classroom situation, Westley and Severin (1965) reported (in agreement with a previous study they cited) that Ss seated farthest from the TV screen (up to 50 feet) learned best. Fargo and others (1967) reported mean scores on a picture vocabulary test to be no different by group TV administration than by the more time-consuming individual administration by an examiner.

James (1962) asked 503 basic airmen to express preferences for taking a lesson by reading or by lecture. A no-preference option was permitted. There were no performance differences associated with preference, but for the total sample learning by reading was superior to lecture (.05 level). Preference was unrelated to ability, but the superiority of reading was greater for high-ability airmen.

These few experiments lend little evidence arguing for increased use of auditory stimuli for the tasks and type of Ss employed. For high-ability students who are good readers, the reading mode is generally effective. For difficult material, reading permits a backtracking to check uncertain points in a more convenient fashion than backward scanning of a tape recorder. And often a lecturer cannot repeat on request an utterance of an earlier, inspired moment. It is suggested that audio is best for story-like material, for young children, and for poor readers. The new technique of speeded speech is effective and very economical in time for easy material. For young children or poor readers, pictures can, of course, be more effective than printed words. Advantages of both sound tracks and motion-picture presentations lie in presenting sounds a lecturer cannot produce effectively or efficiently for a group (as in language laboratories), in illustrating movements or scenes hard to find or hard to reproduce otherwise, and in serving a theoretical or microscopic function such as motion of molecules.

LEARNER CHARACTERISTICS AND PROGRAMED INSTRUCTION

As predicted by Schramm (1964), there is some recent indication that research in programed instruction is merging with the mainstream of educational research. In the earlier period, analytical studies in programed instruction tended to center on "treatments" studies of the esoteric "programing variables" such as size of step, mode of response, item sequence, and the like. Recently personality, intellectual, and cultural variables in the learner are coming to be studied in relation to programed instruction, and "systems" approaches and multimedia instruction have brought more examination of programed instruction as a "component" of instruction. Also the value of empirical methods of developing instructional materials, emphasized heavily by programmers, is coming to be thought of by many as the greatest permanent effect of the programed instruction movement.

One study relating a personality variable to a programing variable was conducted by Campeau (1965). Using a program on earth-sun relationships, she found that among fifth-grade girls, those scoring high on text anxiety did best with a program which provided feedback, while those low in anxiety did best with a program without feedback (.025 level of significance). No significant interaction was found for boys between these two variables.

Lublin (1965) reported that college students in introductory psychology scoring high on autonomy need achieved better than those with low need on programed instruction. Autonomy need was determined by score on the *Edwards Personal Preference Schedule (EPPS)* and was interpreted in terms of liking to work alone without interaction with a teacher. She also reported that for programs with no reinforcement or with variable ratio reinforcement, higher achievement resulted than for programs with continuous reinforcement.

Kight and Sassenrath (1966) reported that high-achievement motivated students performed better on three criteria than did students with low-achievement motivation. The criteria were time to complete the program, number of errors, and short-term retention score. High test-anxiety Ss worked faster and made fewer errors than low-anxiety students but failed to exhibit higher retention scores. This finding of lack of relationship between anxiety level and achievement is not in conflict with the findings by Campeau above, since Campeau's distinction was between programs with and without feedback, and significant results were obtained only for girls.

Doty and Doty (1964) reported that achievement through programed instruction appeared to be related to personality characteristics. They reported a nonsignificant correlation between achievement and learning from the program. Also, they reported a high positive correlation (0.71

for girls but 0.40 for both sexes) between grade point average and attitude toward programed instruction, but no significant correlation between achievement and attitude.

Fiks (1964) reported that attitude toward straight reading versus overt-response programs was dependent on the education of *Ss* and residence in cities or rural areas, although there were no treatment main effects relating to confirmation, response mode, or reading. For persons of low educational levels (all *Ss* were adults who spent 15 minutes with programs at a fair) attitude toward programs was more favorable if confirmation was provided. The reverse was the case for highly educated *Ss*. With covert responding, urban *Ss* liked programs less well than did rural *Ss*, but with written (overt) responses, urbanites liked programs more than rural *Ss*. Credence in the programs was reported as more closely related to achievement than was attitude.

Woodruff, Faltz, and Wagner (1966) correlated subscores on two personality tests *(EPPS* and *Gordon Personal Inventory)* with correct responses on program frames. Significant values were 0.53 for achievement motivation, 0.50 for cautiousness, 0.74 for original thinking, 0.81 for personal relations, and 0.81 for vigor. The correlation of IQ with frames correct was 0.75.

Turning from personality and attitudinal variables to intellectual variables in the learner, Buckland (1967) administered programs of three different response modes (written, thinking, reading) to *Ss* of high and low ability. Parallel tests were given immediately after learning and after 27 days. There were no significant differences among response mode treatments at either ability level on either test. But when retention was expressed as gains, there was a significant interaction; high-ability *Ss* employing written responses were superior to those employing reading, with covert responding falling in between; it was also found that low-ability *Ss* lost ground over the 27-day interval on all modes except that of reading.

Williams (1963), employing programs as review, compared results for *Ss* of high and low aptitude. Difference in achievement for these two aptitude groups was, in descending order, constructed response, multiple-choice, emphasis, then reading. Variability in achievement was least for constructed response. She concluded that aptitude makes the greatest difference in achievement for the less active modes of responding.

Woodruff, Faltz, and Wagner (1966) reported significant correlations for ninth-graders between ability measures (IQ, average grades for seventh and eighth grades, and grades in science for these two years) and number of frames correct on a program in electricity. For fourth- and fifth-graders, they reported similar high relationships between scores on a reading test and number of correct responses on a program in spelling.

Feldman (1965) assigned 144 *Ss* of high and low verbal ability to one of three programs differing in difficulty level or to corresponding texts of reading material created from the programs by printing in the blank terms so that programs and texts would consist of identical words. Two criteria were employed: a pre- and a post-test similar to items in the programs and a transfer test of items dissimilar to program items. Verbal ability, difficulty level, and format (program or text) were found to be unrelated to gain on the cloze test. But on the transfer test, Ss of high ability did better than those of low ability (.01), Ss of low ability did better from study by text than study by program (.05), and no differences were attributed to difficulty level. There was an interaction of ability with difficulty, suggesting that "challenging" materials were most effective. The investigator concluded that responding to programs interferes with organization of the material and that well prepared charts in a text can help overcome difficult wording.

Hershberger (1964) employed typographical cueing to distinguish core from enrichment materials in written texts and "adjunct" self-evaluation test questions interspersed among pages of reading material. Different groups received different combinations of conditions: terse or discursive text, simple or complex typographical cueing, and texts without questions as well as texts with questions. High-ability Ss benefited from either terseness or self-evaluation test items or from both used together. Low-ability Ss benefited from terseness only if it was accompanied by self-evaluation test items. The test items were a mixture of multiple-choice and constructed response items. For the sample as a whole, self-evaluation questions enhanced learning and retention of core content without detracting from enrichment content. Simple typographical cueing was more effective than complex cueing. The effects of simple cueing and self-test items were independent and additive.

The above experiment on "adjunct autoinstruction" is reported in this section dealing with programed instruction since some reviewers consider the adjunct method (using test items with prose material and immediate feedback) as a type of programed instruction. Pressey, however, considers the two methods to be independent and distinct. The only direct comparisons of overall effectiveness of the two methods were reported by Pressey (1967) and by Pressey and Kinzer (1964), both finding adjunct at least as effective and much more efficient, especially for terse texts. Hershberger inserted questions after each few pages of reading, depending on the terseness of the text. Frase (1967) found effective learning for certain materials and subjects by placing multiple-choice test questions after each 120 lines of reading.

Katz (1967) reported data suggesting that when different segments of material differ in difficulty for a task requiring formation of discrimination learning sets, high IQ Ss gradually improve regardless of whether successive practice sessions are arranged in order of increasing, decreasing, or unchanging difficulty. For low IQ *Ss*, however, performance is best with a *consistency* of problem type and problem difficulty. And after a six-month interval the high IQ *Ss* benefit more from additional practice than do the low IQ *Ss*.

Considerable research interest recently has been exhibited, especially in England, in comparing the effects of programed instruction as used by an individual for solitary study with effects from small-group utilization of programs. Early research comparing "paired" and "individual" learning from programs used linear programs. In two studies cited by Noble (1967), pairs did better than individuals. Noble also cited a study using intrinsic programs in which individuals performed better than groups of three. Noble further indicated that teachers in England ask about group use of an expensive device for displaying intrinsic programs as a possible economy move. Noble arranged eight weeks of learning by three groups of "fourth-form students in a mixed secondary modern school." The three groups were matched on four variables: age, sex, verbal and mathematics scores, and prior knowledge of trigonometry. Mean age was 15.3 years. Control groups had one child at a machine; experimental groups had two children working at each machine. Students chose their own work mates. Results indicated less learning by the pairs, although cost economy was achieved. There was no significant attitude difference, but there was a trend in favor of working alone.

A discussion paper by Crutchfield and Covington (1966) considered creativity as a learner variable in relation to use of programed instruction. They approached the linking of creativity and programs as an apparent paradox to be resolved, since features of programs appear to be antithetical to the requirements for creativity, and offered suggestions for the improvement of programs to enhance creativity. These suggestions included (a) keep the self-pacing, self-administering feature; (b) give choice of materials and paths; (c) use diagnostic and evaluative measures to change path when needed; (d) use more flexible kinds of feedback (see Bivens, 1964); (e) generate uncommon ideas; (f) lead students to evaluate their own ideas (see Johnson, Parrott, and Stratton, 1967); (g) reward deviant responses; (h) produce reasonable amounts of study work before it is criticized; (i) use actual problems to be solved in their entirety; (j) diversify content on a given topic; and (k) use large steps to create productive tension (see Pressey, 1967).

OVERVIEW AND NEEDED FUTURE RESEARCH

There is current interest among some educators and researchers in discovery of the *unique patterns* which may distinguish one student's style of learning from another's. The topic of personal cognitive style was not reviewed here because of time limitations. The reviewer hazards the conjecture, based on data such as the series of studies by Gagné and his associates cited earlier, that if one were to design media to adapt media programs rigorously to the individual learner's general ability, special aptitudes, and entering competencies, most of the variance would be accounted for, as compared to such variance as may reflect those characteristics meant by cognitive style.

This review generally has not covered comparative effectiveness studies, in which the merits of one medium are compared with another or with "conventional" instruction on the basis of criterion scores for some selected experimental lesson. Criticisms and recommendations for improving this type of study have been covered in previous reviews (Lumsdaine and May, 1965; Campeau, 1967). The review has been based on the assumption that just as one medium cannot be shown best across the board or even for one subject matter area, so also one cannot show that one medium is best for one type of student. Rather, a search was made for studies in which the achievement of learners with particular characteristics was compared with learners having other characteristics when particular media were programed in well defined ways. Said differently, one does not hope to find evidence for matching a medium with a person or subject matter area; instead one seeks to consider learner characteristics while analyzing tasks with respect to the optimum kind of stimuli and learning conditions (programing strategies) which can be provided by various media (Briggs and others, 1967; Gagné, 1965).

Learner variables examined include general and special ability, past specific achievement, personality variables, and demographic characteristics. Results for learners classified by these variables were related to media or programing characteristics including pacing, branching, size of step, and modality of stimulation (audio or visual). Results were not particularly clear-cut or consistent among similar studies. For example, one can find instances where students of low verbal ability learned better by reading than by constructed response programs and other instances where the reverse was reported. Such differences can arise because of use of a variety of learning tasks, variations in how skillfully the programing is done, or differences among subjects in amount of relevant prior learning.

Nevertheless, the advent of programed instruction has provided a stimulus and a vehicle for study of such person interactions with program style. A next step would be to take some "programing variable," such as size of step, defined in any one of several possible ways, and implement variations in size of step for several media for experimental lessons representing several kinds of learning. To date, such variables as size of step are studied mainly with programed instruction, while variables such as simplicity versus embellishment are studied by films. It would be desirable to attempt experimentally to introduce the same variable in several media and then to introduce matches with learner variables. There is thus some argument for complex interaction studies to assess interaction of person variable by media by programing feature by type of learning.

On the other hand, experiments which compare achievement, under defined instructional conditions, for subgroups of learners identified as high or low IQ do fail to account for other learner variables which may be operating. Thus intensive study of selected individuals learning from a wide variety of media for many kinds of learning objectives would be advisable. One problem in applying the results of such research might be difficulty in incorporating all of the kinds of differences found into manageable media packages. In short, one may find unique sources of variance by intensive study of individuals, but one may not be able to vary media programs for each unique person characteristic.

In the previous review cycle, Silberman (1962) commented that programed instruction has not been very much adapted to individual learners. The research which has taken place during the interval should provide a starting basis for making this needed improvement in practice in all media.

Some of the variables which have been studied with programed instruction, particularly the effort to sequence instruction in accordance with explicit analyses of the learning objectives into subordinate components, as in the research by Gagné, need to be extended into work with other media. In general the procedure of task analysis, empirical tryout by sequencing studies to validate or correct the task analysis, followed by further empirical revision, is a good interim model to follow until we have more refined theories of task taxonomies, learner variables, and media variables.

REFERENCES

AUSUBEL, DAVID P. "The Use of Advance Organizers in the Learning and Retention of Verbal Meaningful Material," *Journal of Educational Psychology,* Vol. 51 (October, 1960), pp. 267-72.

BIVENS, LYLE W. "Feedback Complexity and Self-Direction in Programmed Instruction," *Psychological Reports,* Vol. 14 (February, 1964), pp. 155-60.

BRIGGS, LESLIE J. "Teaching Machines," in GLEN FINCH(ed.), *Educational and Training Media: A Symposium.* Publication No. 789. Washington, D.C.: National Academy of Sciences—National Research Council, 1960, pp. 150-95.

BRIGGS, LESLIE J., and OTHERS. *Instructional Media: A Procedure for the Design of Multi-Media Instruction, a Critical Review of Research, and Suggestions for Future Research.* Monograph No. 2. Pittsburgh, Pa: American Institutes for Research, 1967, 176 pp.

BRUNER, JEROME S. "Needed: A Theory of Instruction," *Educational Leadership,* Vol. 20 (May, 1963), pp. 523-32.

BUCKLAND, P. R. "The Response in a Linear Program: Its Mode and Importance,"*Programmed Learning and Educational Technology,* Vol. 4 (February, 1967), pp. 47-51.

CAMPBELL, VINCENT N. "Bypassing as a Way of Adapting Self-Instruction Programs to Individual Differences," *Journal of Educational Psychology,* Vol. 54 (December, 1963), pp. 337-45.

CAMPEAU, PEGGIE L. *Level of Anxiety and Presence or Absence of Feedback in Programed Instruction.* U.S. Office of Education, NDEA Title VII Project No. 1155. Palo Alto, Calif.: American Institutes for Research, February, 1965, 25 pp. (Mimeo.)

CAMPEAU, PEGGIE L. "Selective Review of Literature on Audiovisual Media of Instruction," in LESLIE J. BRIGGS and OTHERS, *Instructional Media: A Procedure for the Design of Multi-Media Instruction, a Critical Review of Research, and Suggestions for Future Research.* Monograph No. 2. Pittsburgh, Pa.: American Institutes for Research, 1967, Chap. 5, pp. 99-142.

COOPER, J. C., JR., and GAETH, J. H. "Interactions of Modality with Age and with Meaningfulness in Verbal Learning," *Journal of Educational Psychology,* Vol. 58 (February, 1967), pp. 41-44.

COULSON, JOHN E., and SILBERMAN, HARRY F. "Automated Teaching and Individual Differences," *AV Communication Review,* Vol. 9 (January-February, 1961), pp. 5-15.

COULSON, JOHN E., and OTHERS. "Effects of Branching in a Computer Controlled Autoinstructional Device," *Journal of Applied Psychology,* Vol. 46 (December, 1962), pp. 389-92.

CROWDER, NORMAN A. "Automatic Tutoring by Means of Intrinsic Programming," in EUGENE GALANTER (ed.), *Automatic Teaching: The State of the Art.* New York: John Wiley & Sons, Inc., 1959, pp. 109-16.

CRUTCHFIELD, RICHARD S., and COVINGTON, MARTIN V. "Programed Instruction and Creativity," *Theory into Practice,* Vol. 5 (October, 1966), pp. 179-83.

DOTY, BARBARA A., and DOTY, LARRY A. "Programmed Instructional Effectiveness in Relation to Certain Student Characteristics," *Journal of Educational Psychology,* Vol. 55 (December, 1964), pp. 334-38.

FARGO, GEORGE A., and OTHERS. "Comparability of Group Television and Individual Administration of the Peabody Picture Vocabulary Test: Implications for Screening," *Journal of Educational Psychology,* Vol. 58 (June, 1967), pp. 137-40.

FELDMAN, MARGARET E. "Learning by Programed and Text Format at Three Levels of Difficulty," *Journal of Educational Psychology,* Vol. 56 (June, 1965), pp. 133-39.

FIKS, ALFRED I. "Some Treatment and Population Variables in Programed Instruction," *Journal of Educational Psychology*, Vol. 55 (June, 1964), pp. 152-58.

FRASE, LAWRENCE T. "Learning from Prose Material: Length of Passage, Knowledge of Results, and Position of Questions," *Journal of Educational Psychology*, Vol. 58 (October, 1967), pp. 266-72.

GAGNÉ, ROBERT M. "The Acquisition of Knowledge," *Psychological Review*, Vol. 69 (July, 1962), pp. 355-65.

GAGNÉ, ROBERT M. *The Conditions of Learning.* New York: Holt, Rinehart & Winston, Inc., 1965, 308 pp.

GAGNÉ, ROBERT M., and BASSLER, OTTO C. "Study of Retention of Some Topics of Elementary Nonmetric Geometry," *Journal of Educational Psychology*, Vol. 54 (June, 1963), pp. 123-31.

GAGNÉ, ROBERT M., and PARADISE, NOEL E. *Abilities and Learning Sets in Knowledge Acquisition.* Psychological Monographs: General and Applied, Vol. 75, No. 14 (Whole No. 518). Washington, D.C.: American Psychological Association, 1961, 23 pp.

GAGNÉ, ROBERT M., and OTHERS. *Factors in Acquiring Knowledge of a Mathematical Task.* Psychological Monographs: General and Applied, Vol. 76, No. 7 (Whole No. 526). Washington, D.C.: American Psychological Association, 1962, 21 pp.

GAGNÉ, ROBERT M., and OTHERS. "Some Factors in Learning Non-Metric Geometry." *Mathematical Learning.* (Ed. by Lloyd N. Morrisett and John Vinsonhaler.) Monographs of the Society for Research in Child Development, Vol. 30, No. 1 (Serial No. 99). Chicago: University of Chicago Press, 1965, pp. 42-49.

GROPPER, GEORGE L., and KRESS, GERARD C., JR. "Individualizing Instruction through Pacing Procedures," *AV Communication Review*, Vol. 13 (Summer, 1965), pp. 165-82.

HERSHBERGER, WAYNE. "Self-Evaluation Responding and Typographical Cueing: Techniques for Programing Self-Instructional Reading Materials," *Journal of Educational Psychology*, Vol. 55 (October, 1964), pp. 228-96.

JAMES, NEWTON E. "Personal Preference for Method as a Factor in Learning," *Journal of Educational Psychology*, Vol. 53 (February, 1962), pp. 43-47.

JOHNSON, DONALD M.; PARROTT, GEORGE R.; and STRATTON, R. PAUL. "Productive Thinking: Produce One Solution or Many," *Proceedings of the 75th Annual Convention of the American Psychological Association 1967.* Vol. 2. Washington, D.C.: American Psychological Association, 1967, pp. 299-300.

KATZ, PHYLLIS A. "Acquisition and Retention of Discrimination Learning Sets in Lower-Class Preschool Children," *Journal of Educational Psychology*, Vol. 58 (August, 1967), pp. 253-58.

KIGHT, HOWARD R., and SASSENRATH, JULIUS M. "Relation of Achievement

Motivation and Test Anxiety to Performance in Programed Instruction," *Journal of Educational Psychology,* Vol. 57 (February, 1966), pp. 14-17.

LUBLIN, SHIRLEY CURRAN. "Reinforcement Schedules, Scholastic Aptitude, Autonomy Need, and Achievement in a Programed Course," *Journal of Educational Psychology,* Vol. 56 (December, 1965), pp. 295-302.

LUMSDAINE, ARTHUR A., and MAY, MARK A. "Mass Communication and Educational Media," *Annual Review of Psychology.* (Ed. by Paul R. Farnsworth, Olga McNemar, and Quinn McNemar.) Vol. 16. Palo Alto, Calif.: Annual Reviews, 1965, pp. 475-534.

MAY, MARK A. *The Role of Student Response in Learning from the New Educational Media.* U.S. Office of Education, Project No. 5-0999, Contract No. OE-5-16-006. Hamden, Conn.: the author (72 Northlake Drive), August 1966, 149 pp. (Mimeo.)

NOBLE, GRANT. "A Study of the Differences between Paired and Individual Learning from a Branching Program," *Programmed Learning and Educational Technology,* Vol. 4 (April, 1967), pp. 108-12.

PRESSEY, SIDNEY L. "Re-Program Programing?" *Psychology in the Schools,* Vol. 4 (July, 1967), pp. 234-39.

PRESSEY, SIDNEY L., and KINZER, JOHN R. "Auto-Elucidation without Programing!" *Psychology in the Schools,* Vol. 1 (October, 1964), pp. 359-65.

ROE, ARNOLD. "A Comparison of Branching Methods for Programmed Learning," *Journal of Educational Research,* Vol. 55 (June-July, 1962), pp. 407-16.

ROHWER, WILLIAM D., JR., and OTHERS. "Pictorial and Verbal Factors in the Efficient Learning of Paired Associates," *Journal of Educational Psychology,* Vol. 58 (October, 1967), pp. 278-84.

SCANDURA, JOSEPH M. "Teaching—Technology or Theory," *American Educational Research Journal,* Vol. 3 (March, 1966), pp. 139-46.

SCANDURA, JOSEPH M. "The Basic Unit in Meaningful Learning—Association or Principle?" *Proceedings of the 75th Annual Convention of the American Psychological Association 1967.* Vol. 2. Washington, D.C.: American Psychological Association, 1967, pp. 275-76.

SCHRAMM, WILBUR S. *Research on Programed Instruction: An Annotated Bibliography.* Washington, D.C.: U.S. Government Printing Office, 1964, 114 pp.

SILBERMAN, HARRY F. "Self-Teaching Devices and Programmed Materials," *Review of Educational Research,* Vol. 32 (April, 1962), pp. 179-93.

SKINNER, B.F. "Teaching Machines," *Science,* Vol. 128 (October 24, 1958), pp. 969-77.

SNOW, RICHARD E.; TIFFIN, JOSEPH; and SEIBERT, WARREN F. "Individual Differences and Instructional Film Effects," *Journal of Educational Psychology,* Vol. 56 (December, 1965), pp. 315-26.

SUPPES, PATRICK. "Modern Learning Theory and the Elementary-School Curriculum," *American Educational Research Journal,* Vol. 1 (March, 1964), pp. 79-93.

TRAVERS, ROBERT M. W. (ed.). *Research and Theory Related to Audiovisual Information Transmission.* U.S. Office of Education, Interim Report, Contract No. 3-20-003. Salt Lake City: Bureau of Educational Research, University of Utah, July, 1964 (Offset) (Pagination by chapter).

WESTLEY, BRUCE H., and SEVERIN, WERNER J. "Viewer Location and Student Achievement," *AV Communication Review,* Vol. 13 (Fall, 1965), pp. 270-74.

WILLIAMS, JOANNA P. "Comparison of Several Response Modes in a Review Program," *Journal of Educational Psychology,* Vol. 54 (October, 1963), pp. 253-60.

WOODRUFF, ARNOLD BOND; FALTZ, CHARLES; and WAGNER, DIANE. "Effects of Learner Characteristics on Programed Learning Performance," *Psychology in the Schools,* Vol. 3 (January, 1966), pp. 72-77.

Part B.

Mental Abilities: A Possible Basis for Individualization

Introduction

Researchers, like teachers, have sought for years to develop techniques for identifying the mental abilities that are the enabling mechanisms for learning. They have also sought to develop reliable tests to assess these abilities in individuals; a precondition if instruction is to be more than intuitive.

One of the most prominent of these researchers is J. P. Guilford who, in Chapter 5, updates his theoretical model of mental abilities, developed through years of empirical study, and expands it to include those mental abilities which facilitate problem solving. His work continues at the University of Southern California.

Because of the importance of the Guilford "structure of the intellect" model as a potential base line for systematic development of learner-relevant instructional materials it has been the object of much study by educators. One of these studies, by Baker, Schutz, and Sullivan, is included as Chapter 6 in order to illustrate the difficulties that are attendant when a bridge is being built between theory and application. A reading of these two chapters relating to Guilford's theory should make it abundantly clear that the *science* of education supplants but as yet has not replaced the *art* of education.

Chapter 5. DEVELOPMENT OF A THEORY

INTELLIGENCE: 1965 MODEL

J. P. Guilford

Being the kind of person who prefers to accentuate the positive, I shall devote the following remarks entirely to new developments with respect to the subject of intelligence. I shall try quickly to bring you up to date with respect to progress in connection with explorations of intellectual abilities, and also some implications arising from this information. Not to belie the second part of my title, I do have a 1965 model to mention.

STATUS OF THE STRUCTURE OF INTELLECT

Structure-of-Intellect Model

The structure-of-intellect (SI) model, with its five operation categories intersecting with its four content categories, and these, in turn, intersecting with its six product categories, is the same in 1965 as it was when first

SOURCE: Reprinted from J. P. Guilford, "Intelligence: 1965 Model," *American Psychologist*, Vol. 21 (1966), pp. 20-26 by permission of the author and Robert R. Knapp, Publisher. Copyright 1966 by the American Psychological Association and reproduced by permission.

designed in 1958 (Guilford, 1959). To refresh your memories, a diagram of the model is given in Figure 5-1. In this respect there is no change or progress to report. The progress is mainly in terms of demonstration of many new intellectual abilities to occupy cells of the model, with only a very few movings of abilities within the model to give better logical fits to theory.

When efforts were first made in 1955 to organize the known intellectual abilities that had been segregated by factor analysis, 37 distinct abilities were recognized (Guilford, 1956). In 1958, there were 43 such abilities that could be placed within the model. From then on, the model has served as the heuristic source of hypotheses as to what new kinds of abilities for which to look. As of today, 80 abilities are believed to have been demonstrated and are placed within the model. Of the 120 cells of the model, five operations times four contents times six products, 75 cells are actually occupied. The discrepancy between 75 and 80 is that 3 cells have been found to contain 2 abilities each and 1 contains 3. The duplications within cells arise from distinctions among parallel visual, auditory, and kinesthetic, cognitive and memory abilities. More of such duplications are to be expected when appropriate investigations are made.

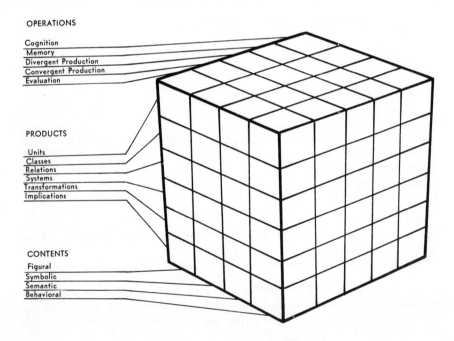

OPERATIONS

Cognition
Memory
Divergent Production
Convergent Production
Evaluation

PRODUCTS

Units
Classes
Relations
Systems
Transformations
Implications

CONTENTS

Figural
Symbolic
Semantic
Behavioral

FIGURE 5-1

MODEL OF THE STRUCTURE OF INTELLECT

To break down these figures more meaningfully, the numbers of demonstrated abilities in the various operation categories are of interest. The differences among operation categories with respect to numbers of known factors reflect the extents to which they have been investigated. Of the 24 theoretical cognitive cells (where cognition is confined by definition simply to comprehension or induction), all 24 are now occupied, with 2 cells having 2 abilities each and 1 having 3 abilities. In the latter instance, the 3 abilities are concerned with cognition of figural systems—visual-spatial orientation, kinesthetic-spatial orientation, and auditory systems (cognition of rhythms and melodies). One cell containing two abilities pertains to cognition of units, visual on the one hand and auditory (such as radio-code signals) on the other. The other cell containing two abilities pertains to symbolic units; the cognition of printed words on the one hand and the hearing of spoken words on the other.

Of 24 projected memory abilities, 12 have been demonstrated, one cell containing 2 abilities. The latter case includes memory for visual systems and memory for auditory systems. The main difference between cognition and memory abilities can be expressed very simply. Cognitive abilities pertain to how much you do know or can know at the time of testing, whereas memory abilities pertain to how much you can remember, given a standard exposure to information. Six memory abilities are currently under investigation in the Aptitudes Research Project (ARP) at the University of Southern California, with the chance of demonstrating some new ones. By the time this paper appears in print, there may be 15 demonstrated memory factors.[1]

In the area of divergent production, which is believed to contain some of the most directly relevant intellectual abilities for creative thinking and creative production, 16 of the 24 potential abilities have been investigated and demonstrated, in both adult and ninth-grade populations; also 6 of them at the sixth-grade level. Lauritzen (1963) has demonstrated a like number at the fifth-grade level. At the present time, 6 additional hypothesized divergent-production abilities are under investigation in the behavioral-content area, by the ARP.

One of the least explored operation areas is that of convergent production. Ten of the 24 possible convergent-production abilities have been demonstrated, with 2 more of them being currently under study in an analysis of classification abilities cutting across three operation categories.

Two recently completed analyses aimed at evaluative abilities have brought the number of known factors in the evaluation category to 13, and they have added a great deal to the understanding of this particular class of abilities (Hoepfner, Guilford, & Merrifield, 1964; Nihira, Guilford, Hoepfner, & Merrifield, 1964).

Behavioral-Cognition Abilities: Of special note in recent developments is the demonstration of six cognitive abilities for dealing with behavioral information. This is the area marked off years ago by E. L. Thorndike (1920) as "social intelligence." Spearman (1927) was speaking about the same aptitude area under the heading of "psychological relations."

In the 1958 version of the SI model, an entire section involving 30 abilities was hypothesized for this area, with the belief that among the things that we can know, remember, and evaluate, and about which we can do productive thinking, is information about the behavior of other individuals and about ourselves. The major step was in bringing such areas of experience within the general concept of information. The abilities to be expected in this area were thought to be systematically parallel to abilities already found in other information areas—figural, symbolic, and semantic. There were no known abilities found by factor analysis to support such a hypothesis.

According to SI theory, there should be six abilities in the cognition column for dealing with behavioral information. In the ARP, we proceeded to build tests for each of the six hypothesized abilities, for cognition of: behavioral units, classes, relations, systems, transformations, and implications. With a decision to stay within the context of printed tests as much as possible, the cue information used was in the form of photographs and line drawings of expressions involving the face, hands, arms, head, legs, and combinations of these body parts, also cartoons and cartoon strips, and photographed scenes involving people in pairs and triplets. In three tests, vocalized sound stimuli were also used. We stayed away from tests involving verbalizations on the part of the examinee, but used verbal statements pregnant with social or behavioral meanings as item material in some tests.

With an average of four such tests for each expected factor, the factor analysis demonstrated the six predicted factors, clearly segregated from figural and semantic abilities, with most of the new tests leading on factors where expected (O'Sullivan, Guilford, & deMille, 1965). So far as basic research is concerned, it appears that the large area of social intelligence has been successfully entered. Further work is naturally needed to determine the general significance of these abilities, as measured. We are now in the process of constructing tests for a parallel analysis of abilities predicted in the operational category of divergent production where behavioral information is concerned. Such abilities should be of considerable importance where any person has special need for creative approaches in dealing with others.

SOME RELATED PROBLEMS

Age and Differentiation of Abilities

Because of the Garrett hypothesis there is considerable interest in knowing whether as much differentiation of abilities occurs for children as for adults. Most of our own recent information has come from the testing of senior high school students, for whom the expected differentiations have always thus far appeared, when test batteries have been adequate to check on the hypothesized factors. I have mentioned the fact that ninth-grade students show the usual differentiations among the divergent-production abilities. The same kinds of differentiations are found at the same level for other categories of abilities as well. There is a little less assurance of clear separations at the sixth-grade level, but our experiences have been very limited at that level.

From other sources, it can be noted that some of the factors have been found differentiated at the age of 6 (McCartin, 1963), also at the mental ages 4 and 2, in retarded as well as in normal children (Meyers, Dingman, Orpet, Sitkei, & Watts, 1964). From still other sources (Stott & Ball, 1963), there are suggestions of a number of the SI abilities being detected for preschool and infant populations down to the age of 1. At this time it would appear that when children have reached the level of maturity at which appropriate tests for a factor can be administered and individual differences in scores can be obtained, the factors should be found differentiated. There is thus little to support the Garrett view that factors of intelligence come into being by differentiation from a single, comprehensive ability like Spearman's g.

This is not so strange, when we consider that the four kinds of information—figural symbolic, semantic, and behavioral—come into the child's sphere of experience at different times, and development in coping with them progresses at different rates. Figural and behavioral information are encountered almost from birth whereas semantic information begins to come later, and symbolic information much later. The early differentiations of abilities must mean that the brain develops naturally different ways of processing the various products of information, as it develops different mechanisms for the five kinds of operations.

Predictive Validity in Mathematics

The ARP has always had a firm commitment to do basic research on the differentiable aptitudes, realizing that the number of investigators who undertake to solve such problems is exceedingly small. We have done one major study devoted to predictive validity, however, in which the criterion was achievement in ninth-grade mathematics (Guilford, Hoepfner, & Petersen, 1965). The study was somewhat premature, since it was realized that some of the potentially relevant SI abilities had not yet been demonstrated, nor were there tests for such hypothesized abilities. But, on the basis of what factors were known, the objective was to determine how well achievement could be predicted from factor tests, singly and in combination, as compared with three traditional academic-aptitude tests and also in combination with them.

Predictions of scores from specially prepared achievement tests in general mathematics and algebra were as good from combinations of factor-test scores as those from standard aptitude tests, or better, with multiple correlations ranging from .5 to .8. The factor tests also added significantly to prediction obtainable from standard aptitude tests in the case of algebra. Discrimination between successful algebra students (above the median in achievement) and successful general-mathematics students could be made with errors of only 10%, using a weighted combination of factor tests.

PSYCHOLOGICAL THEORY

The finding of differentiated abilities in the area of intelligence is largely a taxonomic exercise. The outcome is in the form of basic concepts as to kinds of ability, answering the question "What?" Further steps need to be taken in order to answer the questions "How?" and "Why?" The SI theory is a step in these directions, and inferences from that theory lead further toward the goal of general psychological theory.

Role of Information

Of the 15 categories of the structure of intellect, 10 pertain to information, indicating the relative importance of kinds of information in the economy of intellectual functioning. This has suggested the view that we should regard the organism as a processor of information. A general informational approach to psychological theory is not unique, by any means. The increasing tendency to talk about input and output in place of stimulus and response is very noticeable. It is desirable, then, that we have some systematic categories of information, if we are to have an informational psychology.

Information, of the type with which we deal in psychology, I have defined as that which the organism discriminates. Discrimination is along the lines of the content and product categories, but of course discriminations also occur within each of these categories. The emphasis upon discrimination is in line with the concept of information in the field of communication engineering, but from that point on there is considerable divergence, for by "information" the engineer means *uncertainty,* whereas the psychologist's information must be in terms of reduction of uncertainty, or in terms of probabilities approaching *certainty.* There is not time to go into these issues here.

Principle of Association

Another noteworthy innovation derived from SI theory is the proposal

(Guilford, 1961) that we now interpret the ancient and respected concept of association in terms of the six products of information, giving us much more discriminative meaning and extending the possibilities for explanatory effectiveness. This suggestion will be very unpopular, for associationism has been a cornerstone for most psychological theory. The proposal is for a refinement and extension of a concept, not for complete replacement. But it does imply that what is learned and remembered is in the form of acquired products of information rather than stimulus-response connections. And it calls for the reinterpretation of habits or skills also in terms of products of information, largely systems, many of which become units.

Psychoepistemology and Psycho-logic

By his clinical-genetic approach, Piaget has demonstrated efforts working toward the goal of an epistemology empirically derived. I propose that the 24 cells derived from intersecting content and product categories in the SI model can furnish one such an epistemology. The mention of 24 categories, of course, ignores the distinct possibility that there will be more when we see how far auditory, kinesthetic, and perhaps tactual areas of information extend the number. Piaget's efforts have been directed more toward particular concepts, although generalizing somewhat in dealing with classes and relations as generic categories of information. He has by no means covered the whole range of 24 categories.

Piaget also places a great deal of emphasis upon the relation of psychology to modern logic (Inhelder & Piaget, 1964). On the one hand, he emphasizes the principle that the individual's development is in the direction of formal logic in his thinking. On the other hand, he intimates that the application of formal logic should be the goal of the theoretical psychologist and he suggests that as a step in the direction of that goal we need a psycho-logic (Piaget, 1953). The six product categories are proposed as the basis for such a psycho-logic. Although not chosen with formal logic in mind, the names of the product categories are in fairly good correspondence with concepts of formal logic. Whether formal logic is now adequate for supplying the models for theory in connection with the six products remains to be seen.

A MODEL FOR PROBLEM SOLVING

My title promises a 1965 model, so here it is: an operational model for problem solving in general. Since most behavior readily involves a bit of problem-solving activity, the model could also have applications over wide areas of behavior. Although emphasizing SI concepts, the model also takes into account many of the new findings and new thinking from other sources. The model is represented in Figure 5-2.

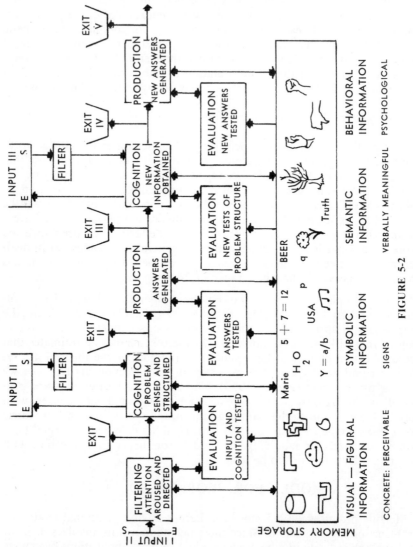

FIGURE 5-2

MODEL FOR PROBLEM SOLVING

The typical, traditional model for problem solving, since John Dewey (1910), has been a linear time series running through steps such as: seeing the problem, analyzing or structuring the problem, generating solutions, and judging and selecting one of the solutions. Things look more complicated now with respect to problem solving as well as with respect to intelligence. Cybernetics and the computer-simulator people have seen to that.

The occasion for a problem-solving episode begins with a certain input, mostly through the sense avenues, of course, represented at Input I in the model. The E and S stand for environmental and somatic sources of input, respectively. The somatic source may include both motivational and emotional components, from within the brain as well as from internal receptors. A filtering step determines which input goes further and has any appreciable consequences in behavior. Note that the memory storage underlies and potentially affects all steps, beginning with the filtering operation. "Filtering" is a new and more operational name for "attention." Evaluation is another operation that has to be taken into account at all steps along the way, for the organism is perpetually self-checking and self-correcting. Evaluation is not left to the final stage of problem solving, as commonly supposed in traditional models.

Awareness that a problem exists and identification or structuring of the problem are cognitive operations. During these operations there is dependence upon memory storage and there is evaluation of cognized information. In the effort to cognize the problem, there may be a seeking for new input information, as at Input II in the model. Filtering of this input also occurs, as well as evaluation.

With the problem reasonably well structured, there is a search for answers, or for information from which answers can be constructed, in memory storage, with the ubiquitous interplay with evaluation. If a solution is accepted, there is an exit from this problem-solving episode at Exit III. Exit I would be a dodging of the problem. Exit II would be a giving up or perhaps a result of distraction before the productive operation got started.

If no good solutions are found to the problem, and if there are doubts about its proper interpretation, a new major cycle begins as shown at the second cognition block. For reinterpretation of the problem, new input may be sought, with steps similar to those already outlined. A number of these major cycles may go on, in what has often been described as trial-and-error behavior. Within each major cycle there are subsidiary loops in the flow of events, each of which might be followed by a number of similar loops. The looping phenomena follow cybernetic principles, with feedback information involved, and evaluation.

The relation of this model to the SI model is fairly obvious. The operation categories have been given prominent roles except that no distinction is shown between divergent and convergent production, both of these kinds of operation being subsumed under the plain heading of "production." Which kind of productive activity occurs will depend upon the kind of search model that is set up consequent to cognition of the problem structure. If the structuring is complete and if enough information is available and is used, the production should be convergent; if there is not enough information for determination of the answer or if the problem is incompletely structured, the production is likely to be divergent.

The information categories are represented by the objects illustrated in memory storage. The four kinds of content are segregated for illustrative purposes. Various examples of products can be found if one looks for them—figural units and systems; symbolic units, relations, and an implication; and units of semantic and behavioral information. Transformations, being changes, are not easily represented in pictorial form, but a modification of either equation would be an example, or an inversion or rotation of any of the figures would be others.

It should be said that the model in Figure 5-2 is a very general or generic one, and not designed to fit necessarily any particular episode of problem solving. But the basic kinds of operation are there. Modifications would be needed to suit the particular case.

FUTURE DEVELOPMENTS

As indicated earlier, under way and near conclusion is an analysis of symbolic memory abilities. In the test-development stages are an analytical study involving nine abilities dealing with classes in which relations of classification abilities to attainment of concepts will be investigated, and a study of divergent-production abilities in the area of behavioral information. In the stage of planning are analyses of figural-memory and figural-evaluation abilities, also transformation abilities across operation categories. The manuscript for a book on the nature of human intelligence, its development and its decline, is in progress (Guilford, 1967). This effort will include the integration of intelligence into general psychological theory, thus giving intelligence a thorough psychological-theoretical foundation, which it has never had. Another book is planned, which will summarize the findings from the ARP, in preparation for which some reworking of old data will be carried out. As to other future developments, these are very much in the laps of the gods.

NOTES

[1] I cannot pass by the opportunity to express a deep appreciation for liberal support to the Project from the Personnel and Training Branch, Office of Naval Research; the Cooperative Research Program, United States Office of

Education; and the National Science Foundation. I should also like to pay tribute to the many graduate students who have collaborated in this effort.

REFERENCES

DEWEY, J. *How We Think*. Boston: D. C. Heath & Co., 1910.

GUILFORD, J. P. "Les dimensions de l'intellect," in H. Laugier (ed.), *L'analyse factorielle et ses applications*. Paris: Centre Nationale de la Recherche Scientifique, 1956, pp. 53-74.

GUILFORD, J. P. "Three Faces of Intellect," *American Psychologist*, Vol. 14 (1959), pp. 469-79.

GUILFORD, J. P. "Factorial Angles to Psychology," *Psychological Review*, Vol. 68 (1961), pp. 1-20.

GUILFORD, J. P. *The Nature of Human Intelligence*. New York: McGraw-Hill Book Co., 1967.

GUILFORD, J. P., HOEPFNER, R., and PETERSEN, H. "Predicting Achievement in Ninth-Grade Mathematics from Measures of Intellectual-Aptitude Factors," *Educational and Psychological Measurement*, Vol. 25 (1965), pp. 659-82.

HOEPFNER, R., GUILFORD, J. P., and MERRIFIELD, P. R. "A Factor Analysis of the Symbolic-Evaluation Abilities," Report No. 33, 1964, University of Southern California, Psychological Laboratory, Los Angeles.

INHELDER, B., and PIAGET, J. *The Early Growth of Logic in the Child*. New York: Harper & Row, Publishers, 1964.

LAURITZEN, E. S. "Semantic Divergent Thinking Factors among Elementary School Children." Unpublished doctoral dissertation, University of California, Los Angeles, 1963.

MCCARTIN, ROSE A. "An Exploration at First Grade of Six Hypotheses in the Semantic Domain." Unpublished doctoral dissertation, University of Southern California, 1963.

MCNEMAR, Q. "Lost: Our Intelligence? Why?" *American Psychologist*, Vol. 19 (1964), pp. 871-82.

MEYERS, C. E., DINGMAN, H. F., ORPET, R. E., SITKEI, E. G., and WATTS, C. A. "Four Ability-Factor Hypotheses at Three Preliterate Levels in Normal and Retarded Children," *Monographs of the Society for Research in Child Development*, Vol. 29, No. 5 (1964).

NIHIRA, K., GUILFORD, J. P., HOEPFNER, R., and MERRIFIELD, P. R. "A Factor Analysis of the Semantic-Evaluation Abilities," Report No. 32, 1964, University of Southern California, Los Angeles.

O'SULLIVAN, MAUREEN, GUILFORD, J. P., and DEMILLE, R. "Measurement of Social Intelligence," Report No. 34, 1965, University of Southern California, Los Angeles.

PIAGET, J. *Logic and Psychology.* Manchester, England: Manchester University Press, 1953.

SPEARMAN, C. *Abilities of Man.* New York: The Macmillan Co., 1927.

STOTT, L. H., and BALL, RACHEL S. *Evaluation of Infant and Preschool Mental Tests.* Detroit: Merrill-Palmer Institute, 1963.

THORNDIKE, E. L. "Intelligence and Its Uses," *Harpers,* Vol. 140 (1920), pp. 227-35.

Chapter 6. APPLICATION OF GUILFORD'S THEORY

AN APPLICATION OF GUILFORD'S STRUCTURE OF INTELLECT TO PROGRAMMED INSTRUCTION

Robert L. Baker
Richard E. Schutz
Howard J. Sullivan

I.   INTRODUCTION

A.   *Problem*

A critical problem in the development of an educational technology involves identification of the learner abilities that are relevant to any given instructional objective. When the relationship between the relevant

SOURCE: Reprinted from *Final Report*, Project No. 1142, Grant No. OEG 7-12-0030-232, Office of Education, Bureau of Research, U.S. Department of Health, Education, and Welfare, February, 1968, by permission of the author.

learner variables and achievement is known, a knowledge of the individual learner's status with respect to the variables can be used to predict and hopefully to control his achievement of the instructional objective.

Since most learning is mediated by words (Bloom, 1963), verbal intelligence is typically the ability that shows the highest correlation with school achievement. However, initial studies (Schutz and Baker, 1963; Getzels and Jackson, 1962) suggest that verbal intelligence might not be such a critical variable in programmed instruction. It appears that learner variables must be treated at a more refined level than "verbal intelligence" if useful specifications are to be derived.

The most significant breakthrough in the identification of discrete mental abilities has been made by Guilford (1956). Employing the mathematical model of factor analysis, he and his associates have attempted to analyze the nature of man's intellect. Reacting against the omnibus nature of single score measures of intelligence Guilford has elaborated a cubical model of the intellect which reflects the factorial interaction of the three broad bases by which the factors can be classified (Guilford, 1959, 1960, 1967). The first basis for classification is according to the kind of process or operation, e.g., cognition, memory, thinking, or evaluation. The second is according to the kind of material or content involved, e.g., figural, symbolic, or semantic. The third basis concerns the product; that is, when a certain kind of *operation* is applied to a certain kind of *content,* as many as six kinds of *products* may be involved—units, elements, etc. Representation by means of a cube simply reflects that each specific factor or ability can be described in terms of operation, content, and product.

The fact that Guilford's work has successfully challenged the concept of a "one unanalyzed intelligence" is well accepted (Jensen, 1963; Torrance, 1962; Getzels and Jackson, 1962). The implications of his model for educational practice are yet unclear. The educational application of the model awaits the empirical specification of the factorial abilities that play a significant role in each type of pupil behavior. This specification must go beyond simple correlational studies dealing with gross educational outcomes. What is required is the precise identification of the unique learner characteristics and their interaction with practice and task variables in common learnings (Stolurow, 1961). Gross correlational studies have actually served to obscure the functional relationships involved. For example, as Bloom (1963) points out, the student who is especially good in visualization may respond well to learning procedures which give him an opportunity to use his spatial talent. However, the low correlation between spatial talent and verbal product has provided a misguided rationale for eliminating figural-spatial stimulus materials altogether.

The fact that non-verbal tests have relatively low r's with verbal performance should not deter efforts to determine the role that specific non-verbal abilities might play as vehicles for later verbal performance. Supportive of this challenge is the interesting hypothesis (Ferguson, 1956) that the factors derived from Guilford's model are a consequence of the principles of transfer. This implies that past experience has much to do not only with achievement, but with the development of the abilities themselves (Piaget, 1964). It further suggests that presently developed abilities might be used to develop other abilities and serve as vehicles for shaping more advanced classes of behavior.

Just as Guilford's model of the intellect provides a strong basis for assessing learner characteristics relevant to a specific learning task, it also provides a basis for direct suggestions for the types of stimulus materials which are consistent with the learner characteristics. Experimental studies have been inconclusive with respect to the variables that influence the effectiveness of visual presentation. These studies (Vernon, 1954; Swanson, 1956; Swanson, Lumsdaine, and Aukes, 1956; Sheffield, 1957, 1961; Sheffield, Margolius, and Hoehn, 1961) have been limited to the presence or absence of certain kinds of stimulus material, and have not attempted to control, isolate, or manipulate the influencing variables. The findings do, however, indicate that certain general aspects may have important implications when preparing stimulus materials.

B.   Objectives

Identifying the relevant learner characteristics and matching these characteristics with appropriate instructional stimulus materials could or should optimize the efficiency of self-instructional programming procedures and permit the generalization of a psychometric model to the solution of specified instructional problems.

Specifically, the objectives of the project were to determine:

1.   The comparative effectiveness of symbolic and semantic content-based linear programs for teaching the rules of logic to eighth-grade students.

2.   The relationship between intellectual abilities as measured by selected tests available in Guilford's compendium of aptitude tests and achievement in each of the two program variations.

3.   The efficiency of matching pupils with the instructional program variation on which they have the highest predicted success using ability factor raw scores to generate average z-score performances for the two Guilford content areas—symbolic and semantic.

II. METHODS

A. Preparation of Instructional Materials

The general research strategy followed was to develop two variations of a self-instructional program on the basis of cues provided by the content dimension of Guilford's model. Therefore, two versions of a previously prepared basic logic program were developed, each differing with respect to type of stimulus content, but identical with respect to the development of logic concepts. The decision to use logic as the subject area was based on three considerations:

1. It provides an excellent set of terminal behaviors that are highly amenable to the development of semantic and symbolic program variations.

2. It can be introduced into all schools at any time during the year without difficulty.

3. The background necessary for programmed entry is of a more general nature and can be assumed to be a part of most student repertoires as a function of a general development of learning skills.

A self-instructional program (1962) on logic originally developed and used by researchers at System Development Corporation was selected for modification. The base program was first revised and tried out prior to completing the experimental modifications. Two variations of the 404 frame logic program were developed, field tested, and revised for use in the study. The programs are identical with the exception of stimulus content. The semantic variation includes no symbols and the symbolic variation includes symbols wherever words can be replaced. Criterion tests for the two variations sample identical substantive content and differ only with respect to the stimulus content used. In addition, 17 mastery, or what might be called unit review tests, were constructed to conform to a behavioral analysis of the program. Two variations were developed, one set of semantic mastery tests and one set of symbolic tests. To aid in analyzing the effects of certain feedback strategies, two types of answer sheets were developed. One type of answer sheet was chemically pretreated so that the subject would receive immediate knowledge of the correctness of his test response. The other answer sheet made no provision for immediate feedback.

B. Preparation of the Guilford Aptitude Tests

The ability factor measures used are adaptations of tests from Guilford's compendium of aptitude tests (1959, p. 47; 1967). Selection was based upon an interpretation of program objectives in terms of Guilford's structure of the intellect. To avoid tampering with the factorial purity of the various tests, modifications were restricted to rewriting the directions and adjusting test length.

Twelve tests were selected that saturated the *cognitive* dimension as it relates to the *product* and *content* dimensions. In addition, tests were selected that represented the memory, convergent thinking, and evaluation dimensions as they relate to the product and content dimensions. The tests were made available to the Classroom Learning Laboratory by Professors J. P. Guilford and R. Hoepfner of the University of Southern California. The list of tests and their trigram definitions are shown in Table 6-1.

TABLE 6-1

Aptitude Tests Employed, by Dimension
and Trigram Symbols

Operation (Product)	Content Dimension	
	S-Symbolic	M-Semantic
C-Cognitive		
U-(Units)	Omelet	Wide Range Vocabulary
C-(Classes)	Number Relations	Verbal Classification
R-(Relationships)	Word Relations	Verbal Analogies
S-(Systems)	Circle Reasoning	Math Aptitude
N-Convergent Thinking		
R-(Relationships)	Object Number	Sentence Completion
E-Evaluation		
U-(Units)	Finding A's	Sentensense

C. Sample

420 eighth-grade students from a large metropolitan elementary school district were made available for the project. The several studies covered a period of three semesters and two calendar years. Over 30 classes have been involved in the design since its beginning.

D. Experiments

Four studies have been completed to date. They are described in the order in which they were conducted.

1. *Study One.* The comparative effectiveness of two logic program variations was determined by randomly assigning 160 eighth-grade students to one of four cells in a 2 × 2 factorial design. The two levels of the first factor relate to the symbolic and semantic instructional program variations. The other factor consists of two levels related to the feedback mechanisms employed. In one case, chemically pretreated answer sheets were used by the student for the 17 unit mastery tests that were interspersed throughout the program. Students assigned to cells in the other level received no chemical feedback, but were able to compare their responses to the key following the testing situation. The criterion variable was a 55 item logic test. Those students working with the symbolic program took the test using symbols, while those working through the semantic variation of the logic program were administered the test that used words. The logic criterion test was given immediately following the program and readministered two weeks later.

2. *Study Two.*   The relationship between intellectual abilities as measured by the 12 Guilford tests selected and achievement in each of the two program variations was based on data obtained from Study One. Regression analyses of the criterion predictors were made for each program variation treatment.

The compendium of 12 tests was administered to the Study One experimental groups prior to the time that they worked through the logic program. Data obtained from these tests were entered in a regression analysis that used the 55 item logic criterion test as the dependent variable.

3. *Study Three.*   Based on the results of the regression analyses students were matched with the program variation on which they would have the highest predicted success. That is, if a student's performance on the Guilford tests representing the *semantic* dimension was superior to his performance on the *symbolic* tests, it was hypothesized that he would be better assigned to the semantic-based program variation. The actual assignment of a student to either the symbolic or semantic variation of the program was based on his average standard score on the six symbolic referenced aptitude tests as compared to his average standard score on the six semantic referenced tests. If, for example, the student showed a standard score of −1.00 on his performance to the six symbolic tests and

+ 1.00 on the semantic tests, he was assigned to receive the semantic program variation.

The 12 Guilford tests were administered to 180 eighth-grade students. Four weeks later, they were assigned on the basis of their test performances. Ninety students were drawn randomly from the pool of 180 and were assigned randomly to the symbolic and semantic treatment groups. The remaining 90 students were assigned on the basis of predicted success. The results were analyzed in a 2 × 2 factorial analysis of variance.

4. *Study Four.* Data representing measures of 33 variables were collected for each student participating in Study Three and punched into IBM cards. A product moment intercorrelation matrix was prepared and a principal components analysis was performed. Components with eigenvalues greater than unity were rotated to simple structure using normalized varimax procedures. All statistical computations were performed using a CDC 3400 computer.

The 33 variables identified for inclusion in the factor analysis were the logic program criterion test, 17 *en route* unit mastery tests, 12 Guilford aptitude tests, sex, and instructional program variation form. The analysis was completed to determine the contribution, if any, of Guilford's tests to those factors with primary loadings represented by achievement variables.

III. RESULTS

A. *Study One.* The Differential Effectiveness of Symbolic and Semantic-Based Linear Programs for Teaching the Rules of Logic to Eighth-Grade Students.

To avoid logistical problems 10 eighth-grade classes were assigned randomly as intact units to the chemical feedback and delayed feedback groups. The two program variations were then assigned randomly within each class. The results of the analysis indicate no differences in treatment effects and no interaction. As a matter of fact, random assignment of the two programs yielded almost identical criterion mean scores, 30.74 and 31.10 for the semantic and symbolic forms respectively. Table 6-2 shows the descriptive statistics and resulting *F*-values. Based on Study One data, KR-20 reliability coefficients of .91 and .90 were computed for the semantic and symbolic forms of the logic criterion test respectively.

B. *Study Two.* Relationship between Intellectual Ability and Achievement in Each of the Two Logic Program Variations.

Two regression analyses using the 12 Guilford tests as predictors and the two 55 item logic criterion tests as the criterion variables yielded two distinct patterns. The predictors with the highest correlation with the semantic and symbolic program performances are in both cases tests related to semantic content. The best predictors of symbolic program performance

TABLE 6-2

Descriptive Statistics and F-Values for Logic Criterion
Test Mean Scores, by Program Variation and Feedback Method

		Program Variation				
		Semantic			Symbolic	
Feedback	N	Mn.	S.D.	N	Mn.	S.D.
Chemical	40	29.35	10.16	40	31.55	10.29
Delay	40	32.13	11.42	40	30.75	10.19

F_{1-156} (Program Variation) = .06 ns

F_{1-156} (Feedback Method) = .32 ns

F_{1-156} (Program x Feedback) = 1.41 ns

are the Vocabulary Completion and Verbal Analogies tests. Both have r values of .50 with the logic criterion test and both represent the semantic content dimension in Guilford's structure of intellect.

The best predictor of semantic program performance is the Verbal Classifications test, showing $r = .63$ with the criterion test. Table 6-3 shows the product moment correlation coefficients between the Guilford tests and the logic criterion test score by instructional program content form. Also shown in the table are the proportions of total variance contributed to the regression by the Guilford Tests and the proportion of explained variance contributed by each. Further inspection of Table 6-3 yields a point of interest. That is, once the variance contributed by the primary variable has been extracted, the proportion of unique variance explained by the remaining tests does not conform to the reported zero order correlation coefficient between the tests and program performance. For example, the Verbal Classifications test contributes 68 percent of the total variance explained by all of the tests, while the Vocabulary Completion test, with a r of .60, contributes only 2 percent unique variance to the total explained variance. The same two tests reverse their order of contribution to performance on the symbolic form of the instructional materials.

The correlation between the two factor tests is .69 which demonstrates that they share a great deal of common variance. Multiple correlation

TABLE 6-3

Correlation Coefficients Between Guilford Tests
and Program Variation Criterion Scores, and
Proportion of Unique Variance Contributed to the Regression by the Tests

Test	Trigram Code	Proportion of Variance Contributed					
		Semantic Program			Symbolic Program		
		r	Total	Explained	r	Total	Explained
Semantic (M)							
1. Vocabulary Completion	(MNR)	60	01	02	50	25	58
2. Wide Range Vocabulary	(MCU)	34	00	00	38	00	00
3. Math Aptitude Test	(MCS)	44	00	00	39	00	00
4. Sentensense	(MEU)	50	00	00	42	00	00
5. Verbal Analogies	(MCR)	59	09	16	50	09	21
6. Verbal Classification	(MCC)	63	40	68	38	01	02
Symbolic (S)							
7. Finding A's	(SEU)	26	00	00	16	00	00
8. Letter Series	(SNR)	44	01	02	39	00	00
9. Circle Reasoning	(SCS)	42	04	07	37	02	05
10. Omelet	(SCU)	51	00	00	38	01	02
11. Number Relations	(SCC)	59	02	03	35	00	00
12. Word Relations	(SCR)	57	01	02	45	05	12
Total Battery		R = 76	58	100	R = 66	43	100

coefficients between the predictors and logic performance are .76 and .66 for the semantic and symbolic instructional forms respectively.

The differential pattern of contributed variance by the tests is best seen in Table 6-4. Table 6-4 shows the proportion of variance contributed by the tests as they are organized into various combinations representing the several homogeneous functions. Note that two proportions for each entry are entered in the table, one relating to the percentage of *total* variance and the other relating to the percentage of total *explained* variance. The data suggest that differential performance on the two forms of the logic program cannot be explained in terms of the content dimension of Guilford's model, since, in both cases, the semantic tests contribute the overwhelming proportion to the total *and* explained variances. Further inspection suggests that the performance differential may be explained in terms of an interaction between the *operations* and *product* dimensions. Tests representing the *cognition operation* and *classes product* contribute heavily to the variance related to the semantic form of the instructional program; whereas, tests from the *convergent thinking* operations and *relationship* product contributed most heavily to the symbolic form of the logic program. It should be noted that the contribution of the various tests to the symbolic form are somewhat more complex. Dotted lines have been drawn around those proportions that are not primary but do have significance in terms of the overall interpretations. These data suggest that tests loaded on the factors represented in the "convergent thinking *operation* - semantic *content* - relationship *product*" cell have greater utility for predicting performance on the symbolic logic program. Tests representing the "cognitive *operation* - semantic *content* - classes *product*" cell are most predictive of the performance of those using the semantic instructional form.

C. *Study Three.* Matching Pupils with the Logic Program Variation on Which They Have the Highest Predicted Success.

Data analyzed in the first two studies suggest strongly that assignment to the two program variations on the basis of performance on tests sampling the *content* dimension of Guilford's compendium might not be as efficient as other combinations. At this stage of the project, it was decided to complete Study Three as outlined in the original proposal. Matching pupils with the program variation on which they have the highest "predicted" success was accomplished by computing two standard scores each for all of the students in this part of the study. One standard score relates to the combination of semantic content aptitude tests, the other relates to the combination of symbolic content tests. On the basis of comparing each individual's two standard scores, assignments were made to the program variation that conformed to their highest standard score. From a pool of 144 students, 72 were drawn randomly and assigned to the program variation on which they had the highest standard score. The remaining 72 were assigned randomly to the two program variations.

TABLE 6-4

Proportion of Variance Contributed to the Regression
by Guilford's Tests, by Ability Categories

	Proportion of Variance			
	Semantic Variation		Symbolic Variation	
Aptitude Dimensions	% of Total	% of Explained	% of Total	% of Explained
Operation				
Cognition	56	96	18	42
Convergent Thinking	02	04	25	58
Evaluation	00	00	00	00
Content				
Semantic	50	86	35	81
Symbolic	08	14	08	19
Product				
Units	00	00	01	02
Classes	42	71	01	02
Relationships	12	22	39	91
Systems	04	07	02	05
Operation x Content				
Cognition - Semantic	49	84	10	23
Cognition - Symbolic	07	12	08	19
Convergent - Semantic	01	02	25	58
Convergent - Symbolic	01	02	00	00
Operation x Product				
Cognition - Units	00	00	01	02
Cognition - Classes	42	71	01	02
Cognition - Relationship	10	18	14	33
Cognition - Systems	04	07	02	05
Convergent - Units	--	--	--	--
Convergent - Classes	--	--	--	--
Convergent - Relationship	01	02	25	58
Convergent - Systems	--	--	--	--

Table 6-5 shows the results of this analysis. The *F*-value 1.74 for assignment method was not statistically significant. Thus, assigning pupils to a program variation on the basis of highest "predicted" success has no differential influence on performance. The program variation *F*-value .26 was again indication of the equivalence of the two program forms.

The statistically significant interaction may be explained by two related points. First, there is a high correlation between the semantic aptitude test scores and performance on both logic program variations. Second, the system used to determine "predicted" success was based upon the relationship between each student's two standard scores. Thus, those assigned to the symbolic program variation were the students who in general had relatively depressed semantic aptitude test performance by comparison.

Based on the several analyses completed to date, and subsequent to the first part of Study Three, two classes of 28 high school freshman English majors were used for a preliminary study of the predictive efficiency of other test combinations. They were administered two tests chosen from the Guilford compendium on the basis of maximum effectiveness in explaining variance associated with the two logic program variations. As pointed out previously, the "convergent thinking *operation* - semantic *content* - relationship *product*" cell seems to have the highest degree of relevancy to performance on the *symbolic* program variation. The aptitude test with the

TABLE 6-5

Descriptive Statistics and F-Values for Comparison of Logic Criterion Test Mean Scores for Assignment Method (Content) and Program Variation

| Assignment Method | Program Variation | | | | | |
| | Semantic | | | Symbolic | | |
	N	Mn.	S.D.	N	Mn.	S.D.
Predicted	36	30.17	10.59	36	27.32	9.89
Random	36	31.05	11.46	36	32.38	10.14

F_{1-143} (Assignment Method)   = 1.74 ns

F_{1-143} (Program Variation)   = .26 ns

F (Assignment x Program) = 4.10 P $<$.05

highest factor loading and highest correlation with success ($r = .50$) on the symbolic program variation is Vocabulary Completion. For the semantic program variation, the "cognitive *operation* - semantic *content* - class *product*" cell has the greatest relevance. The Verbal Classification test is representative of this factor ($r = .63$). Note that in both cases the content dimension is *semantic*. Since all of the data point to the fact that symbolic ability is overshadowed by semantic ability as a predictor of success irrespective of the stimulus content of the instructional materials, this new assignment strategy seems to hold greater promise.

On the basis of comparing the standard scores of the two tests for each of the students, 28 randomly chosen freshman students were assigned to the logic program variation on the basis of the highest prediction. The remaining 28 students were assigned randomly to the program variations. The results of this analysis are shown in Table 6-6.

The *F*-value 2.13 is significant beyond the .05 level of confidence. It is obvious that assignment on the basis of predicted success is potentially quite useful. The fact that the mean difference between these two groups is not dramatic, although statistically significant, is undoubtedly a function of the high intercorrelation between the Vocabulary Completion and Verbal Classification tests. Although they are reported to have reasonable

TABLE 6-6

Descriptive Statistics and Resulting F-Values for the Comparison of Logic Criterion Test Mean Scores for Assignment Method (Operation x Product) and Program Variation

Assignment Method	Program Variation					
	Semantic			Symbolic		
	N	Mn.	S.D.	N	Mn.	S.D.
Predicted	14	36.25	10.69	14	37.16	11.04
Random	14	32.10	11.15	14	33.20	11.64

F_{1-55} (Program Variation) = 1.25 ns

F_{1-55} (Assignment Method) = 2.13 P < .05

F_{1-55} (Program and Assignment) = .27 ns

TABLE 6-7

Correlation Matrix for Guilford's Aptitude Tests and the
Logic Instructional Program Criterion Tests

Top Half – Semantic Criterion Test Plus Predictors N=110

Bottom Half – Symbolic Criterion Test Plus Predictors

	1*	2*	3*	4*	5	6	7*	8	9	10*	11*	12	13
1	—	31	53	39	60	48	62	63	56	54	57	69	60
2	16	—	30	24	27	30	46	22	19	21	35	31	26
3	27	12	—	43	39	54	48	60	47	61	54	60	44
4	32	03	48	—	19	33	45	38	22	43	43	39	43
5	58	37	17	08	—	30	43	41	44	33	46	42	34
6	39	18	35	39	35	—	46	49	45	61	49	55	44
7	40	28	34	28	41	35	—	38	41	49	62	52	51
8	58	09	45	35	30	42	41	—	58	58	48	64	50
9	52	17	31	22	51	37	29	38	—	54	53	52	59
10	44	13	45	30	39	64	32	47	41	—	59	56	59
11	42	22	46	42	26	44	43	37	36	45	—	55	57
12	43	27	32	17	38	38	28	35	30	36	39	—	63
13	50	16	39	37	38	39	38	42	50	35	45	38	—

N = 110

* Tests from the symbolic content structure

Tests

1. Voc. Compl.
2. Finding A's
3. Letter Series
4. Circle Reas.
5. Wide Range Voc.
6. Math. Apt.
7. Omelet
8. Sentensense
9. Verb. Anal.
10. Number Rel.
11. Word Rel.
12. Verb. Classif.
13. Logic Criterion

TABLE 6-8

Factors and Principal Loadings

Factor I Achievement		Factor II General Intelligence	
Test O	.84	Voc. Completion (MNR)	.79
Test N	.84	Wide Range Vo. (MCU)	.70
Test P	.83	No. Relations (SCC)	.66
Test M	.82	Verbal Classif. (MCC)	.66
Test L	.79	Sentensense (MEU)	.66
Logic Criterion	.69	Verbal Analogies (MCR)	.64
Test I	.64	Math. Aptitude (MCS)	.60
Test J	.60	Omelet (SCU)	.54
Test Q	.58	Letter Series (SNR)	.52
Test K	.57	Logic Criterion	.42
Test H	.54	Test F	.37
Test F	.46	Circle Reasoning (SCS)	.37
Test D	.40		
Sentensense (MEU)	.35		
Test C	.34		

Factor III Exemplar Discrimination		Factor IV Clerical	
Test B	.74	Finding A's	.73
Test A	.57	Sex	-.67
Test C	.46	Omelet	.44
Sex	-.45		

Factor V (?)		Factor VI (?)	
Semantic Form	.89	Immediate Feedback	.82
Test D	-.42	Circle Reasoning (SCS)	.46
Circle Reason	-.31		

Factor VII Symbolic Representation		Factor VIII Practical Judgment	
Test G	.68	Test Q	.57
Test E	.64	Test H	.51
Test C	.51	Test K	.41
Letter Series (SNR)	.48		
Word Relation (SCR)	.39		
Test J	.34		
Math. Aptitude (MCS)	.34		
Test I	.32		
Test B	.30		

factorial purity, the data obtained in this project recorded zero-order correlation coefficients of .69 and .43 between the two tests on the semantic and symbolic analyses respectively. This is evidence that they are tapping quite a bit of common variance. Table 6-7 shows the correlations between all variables for both the semantic and symbolic program analyses.

D.   *Study Four.*   Factor Analysis of Aptitude Test Scores, Logic Criterion Test Scores, and Related Variables.

In an attempt to ferret out some interpretable underlying structure the factor analysis described as Study Four in the previous section was completed. Although the analysis of data related to this study is not complete, there are several points that can be made. First of all, the analysis yielded seven interpretable factors with eigenvalues greater than unity. Interestingly, there is very little factorial complexity amongst the variables included in the analysis.

Table 6-8 shows the factors and variable loadings of .30 and greater. The two dominant factors are labeled *achievement* and *general intelligence.* Twelve of the 17 mastery tests from the logic program and the logic criterion test have loading above .30 on Factor 1. Sentensense is the only Guilford test to have a loading on the factor. Surprisingly, 10 of the 12 Guilford tests have significant loadings on Factor 2. Along with the 10 tests were the criterion tests and one of the logic program mastery tests. The remainder of the factors, although interpretable, shed little in the way of immediate light on the potential contribution of Guilford's model to the development of instructional strategies.

IV.   CONCLUSIONS

This document actually constitutes a progress report, since the studies done to date are highly suggestive of other directions that might profitably be taken. Too, the kinds of statements that can be made now must be considered tentative, since the instructional situations employed in this project do not represent the whole spectrum of instructional situations to which Guilford's model might be applicable. Certainly from the data gathered and analyzed to date, there are a few points that should be made.

1.   The stimulus content dimension as defined by Guilford's tests may not be critical from an instructional point of view. Although the general factor has validity in a psychometric context, its value in offering procedural cues for developing teaching strategies may be limited.

2.   The limitation of the utility of the content dimension is undoubtedly related to the fact than an analysis of most any instructional objective yields a considerable number of verbal aspects. For example, the terminal objectives of both variations of the logic program

suggest a set of verbal skills. Since the symbols in the symbolic variation of the program are still related to specified verbal manipulations, a great deal of verbal mediation is necessary to handle efficiently the symbols in the logic program.

3. Related to the point above, the data strongly suggest that further efforts at determining the instructional utility of Guilford's model might better be aimed at analyses of objectives and learning tasks in terms of the *products* demanded and the *operations* involved.

4. The data from this project reflect considerable magnitude of inter-correlations among the Guilford tests. This may be a function of the high degree of verbal skill (reading or texting) necessary to respond to the tests. But the specific variance associated with each test should be quite useful in determining more precise recipes of abilities related to various types of tasks. They should also be useful for identifying differential recipes for varying stages of learning.

5. Use of Guilford's model to aid in the prediction of differential performance on instructional tasks has considerable potential. That is, given certain specified instructional alternatives, the model should have utility in helping to make decisions as to which alternative is the most effective.

6. Use of Guilford's model to suggest design aspects of the alternatives themselves, either the description of instructional objectives or the specifications of instruction, is not supported by these data. Literal translation of the dimensions related to his broad principles into instructional language and strategies is not warranted.

REFERENCES

Bloom, B. S.   "Testing Cognitive Ability and Achievement," in N. L. Gage (ed.), *Handbook of Research on Teaching.* Chicago: Rand McNally & Co., 1963, Chap. 8.

Ferguson, G. A.   "On Learning and Human Ability," *Canadian Journal of Psychology,* Vol. 8 (1956), pp. 95-112.

Getzels, J. W., and Jackson, P. W.   *Creativity and Intelligence.* New York: John Wiley & Sons, Inc., 1962.

Guilford, J. P.   "The Structure of Intellect," *Psychological Bulletin,* Vol. 53, No. 4 (1956), pp. 267-93.

Guilford, J. P.   "Three Faces of Intellect," *The American Psychologist,* Vol. 14, No. 8 (1959), pp. 469-79.

Guilford, J. P.   *The Nature of Human Intelligence.* New York: McGraw-Hill Book Co., 1967.

GUILFORD, J. P., and MERRIFIELD, P. R. *The Structure of Intellect Model: Its Uses and Implications.* Report of the Psychological Laboratory No. 24, Los Angeles: University of Southern California, 1960.

JENSEN, A. "Learning Ability in Retarded, Average, and Gifted Children," *Merrill-Palmer Quarterly,* Vol. 9, No. 2 (1963), pp. 168-73.

PIAGET, J. *Origins of Intelligence.* New York: International Universities Press, 1964.

SCHUTZ, R. E., BAKER, R. L., and GERLACH, V. "Teaching Capitalization with a Programmed Text," *AV Communication Review,* Vol.10 (1962), pp. 359-62.

SCHUTZ, R. E., and BAKER, R. L. *Adaptation of Measurement Procedures to Promote the Efficiency of Self-Instruction.* Progress report to U.S. Office of Education, NDEA Title VII, Grant No. 7-12-0030-160.0, Tempe: Arizona State University, 1963.

SHEFFIELD, F. D. *Perceptual Mediation in the Learning of Organizable Sequences: Theory and Experiment.* Air Force Personnel and Training Research Center, Maintenance Laboratory, Technical Memorandum ML-TM-57-14, September, 1957.

SHEFFIELD, F. D., MARGOLIUS, G. J., and HOEHN, A. J. "Experiments on Perceptual Mediation in the Learning of Organizable Sequences," in A. A. Lumsdaine (ed.), *Student Response in Programmed Instruction: A Symposium.* Washington D.C.: National Academy of Sciences—National Research Council, Publ. No. 943, 1961, Chap. 8.

SHEFFIELD, F. D. "Theoretical Considerations in the Learning of Complex Sequential Tasks from Demonstration and Practice," in A. A. Lumsdaine (ed.), *Student Response in Programmed Instruction: A Symposium.* Washington D.C.: National Academy of Sciences—National Research Council, Publ. No. 943, 1961, Chap. 2.

SPAULDING, S. "Communication Potential of Pictorial Illustrations," *AV Communication Review,* Vol. 4 (1956), pp. 31-46.

STOLUROW, L. M. *Teaching by Machine.* Washington D.C.: U.S. Government Printing Office, 1961.

SWANSON, R. A. *The Relative Effectiveness of Training Aids Designed for Use in Mobile Training Detachments.* Lackland Air Force Base, Texas: Air Force Personnel and Training Research Center, Research Report AFPTRC-TN-56-2, January, 1956.

SWANSON, R. A., LUMSDAINE, A. A., and AUKES, L. E. "Two Studies in Evaluation of Maintenance Training Devices," in G. Finch and F. Cameron (eds.), *Symposium on Air Force Human Engineering, Personnel, and Training Research.* Washington D.C.: National Academy of Sciences, Publication No. 455, 1956, pp. 267-75.

Symbolic Logic. Education and Training Staff, Research and Technology Division, System Development Corporation, Santa Monica, Calif., 1962.

TORRANCE, E. P.   *Guiding Creative Talent.* Englewood Cliffs, N.J.: Prentice-Hall, Inc., 1962.

VERNON, M. D.   "The Instruction of Children by Pictorial Illustration," *British Journal of Educational Psychology,* Vol. 24 (1954), pp. 171-79.

Part C.

Individual Differences: Do They Make A Difference?

Introduction

There are very few modern teachers who, given a group of youngsters, would not recognize numerous differences among them and try to teach accordingly. When they do, they often make intuitive judgments about the students' abilities, interests and prior experiences. Unfortunately, after instruction, they make further intuitive judgments about whether their differential teaching efforts had the intended effect on the learners.

A number of researchers have tried to accommodate these differences systematically and intriguing and sometime contradictory findings have been reported. For the most part, when efforts are made to replicate studies which have found significant relationships between specific aptitudes and specific instructional methods, the results have been disappointing. In some instances these studies have been handicapped by the absence of precision in data collection and reduction. In other instances the results could not be generalized beyond the subject matter or student population tested.

In spite of what currently appears to be a muddled situation (due at least in part to the overlap in meaning that occurs between terms which describe human abilities and personality traits) it must be recognized that there is every *logical* reason to believe that individual differences *do* exist and *can* be compensated for in educational practice. It may well be that more careful research will point the way, or it may be that the solution will come in a heuristic way from the large-scale individualized learning projects described in the companion book, *Developmental Efforts in Individualized Learning*. In the meantime, those who face the practical problem of matching instructional practices to individual differences might well heed the counsel of the authors in this book, for they have critically interpreted much of the work that has gone on to date.

In Chapter 7, which follows, William R. Powell reviews and analyzes the various ways that individual differences have been studied, summarizes some of the important findings, and relates the "state-of-the-art" to the mastery of a fundamental learning skill . . . reading.

In Chapter 8, by Elaine Wolfe (*née* Vilscek), the reading/individualized learning relationship is discussed in depth. This is appropriate, for probably in no other scholastic area has individualization been a goal for so long. She suggests that teacher-assigned independent reading "projects" are being replaced or subsumed within comprehensive learning systems in which the diagnosis of the learner's reading skills and needs are no longer the sole responsibility of the classroom teacher.

Chapter 7. THE BACKGROUND OF INDIVIDUAL DIFFERENCES

THE NATURE OF INDIVIDUAL DIFFERENCES

William R. Powell

The concern for individual differences in reading behavior stems from the pervasive fact that some children are found to be successful while others are not. To fully understand why these two categories of children "differ," the related variables which influence the reading-learning process need to be identified and investigated further. Such inquiry may suggest better techniques for controlling and modifying these influencing factors. Therefore, an examination of individual differences in reading performance leads into a network of relationships and causes of differential achievement and their implications for instructional programming.

Differences between and within individuals are the primary focus of this chapter. Many factors affecting individual differences obviously could be identified and explored at length; however, only those traits which have

SOURCE: This paper was delivered at the Ninth Perspectives in Reading Conference, International Reading Association, Seattle, Washington; May 2-3, 1967. It appeared in slightly different form in *Organizing for Individual Differences* (Newark, Del.: International Reading Association, 1968). Reprinted with permission of William R. Powell and the International Reading Association.

presumed effect on reading achievement will be given particular attention here. The many approaches and plans which attempt to account for and channel these differences into instructional schemes remain outside the purpose and scope of this discussion. . . .

Any survey of individual differences must be inevitably be incomplete. As more information about the topic accumulates, new methodology for further research is discovered, thus making further inquiry necessary. This phenomenon is well illustrated by the change in the titles of two recent reviews of the psychological literature in this field. In the 1960 edition of the *Annual Review of Psychology,* the topic was entitled "Individual Differences" *(8)* The next review, five years later, used the label "Human Abilities" *(9)* to describe the same subject. If we can assume this is not the game of changing labels on an old product just to make it marketable, this shift in nomenclature might indicate a new focus on the same problem.

One of the most serious problems facing a student in this area is the lack of structure in it. Apparently, a cohesive, unified framework underlying the topic does not exist. Therefore, the organization of the material that follows represents the idiosyncratic nature of both the topic and the author. First, we will discuss what appears to be some of the sources of difficulty behind this lack of cohesiveness; give reference to the causes of individual differences; present the four major characteristics which permeate any discussion of the subject, and then, in turn, identify and discuss a few of the important dimensions of individual differences which can affect reading instruction.

SOURCES OF DIFFICULTY

One explanation for the diversity and diffusion (confusion??) surrounding the topic, individual differences, lies in the imperfection of the two main sources which have supplied most of the information about it. First of all, historically, the genesis of individual differences resides in psychological measurement and test theory and in various multivariate statistical methods, particularly factor analysis. The recent literature gives the impression of being very enamored of factorial techniques which move toward the further distillation of abilities, traits, and other related variables. While factor analysis does hold some hope of revealing a hierarchical structure of some of the "bits" that other statistical nets are ensnaring, it suffers from incompleteness, or it might be more accurate to say, it suffers from the difficulty of interpretation. A key question in factorial problems is: "When have we segmented and specified the constructs sufficiently?" or in other less esoteric terms, "When have we cut the pie into the right number of pieces, knowing that further slicing will produce just useless crumbs?"

The basic concept in psychological measurement and test theory which provides the foundation for exploring individual differences is the concept of dimensionality. The assumption is made that differences between pupils can be measured in terms of identifiable abilities, traits, or dimensions. A given score on a reading test is presumed to indicate how far a youngster is above or below the norm established for a selected reference group. Tyler *(24)* contends that "in this system the *uniqueness* of the individual is defined by his *combination* of measurements along all possible dimensions. A person is represented by a point in n-dimensional space." From this point of view, an individual is the sum of his multidimensional traits, while the differences between and within an individual are due to the variation on these many coordinate, but not identical, dimensions. While this concept undoubtedly has furthered our understanding about individual differences, it has simultaneously clouded our perspective concerning the use of discontinuous traits, i.e., non-dimensional qualities such as preferences, in the study of differences between individuals. Instructional programs attempting to give serious attention to individual differences must provide for the discontinuous traits, as well as the continuous ones, of the individual.

The second source of difficulty in the delineation of individual differences centers around the identification and isolation of the most significant traits or abilities for study. If a single criterion could be identified for selection, the task would be greatly simplified. Regrettably, this is not possible, nor do there appear to be any signs which would support the idea that it will be possible to do so in the near future. What happens in practice is that a researcher selects for study those variables which are related to his area of expertise. Thus, the neurologist seeks specific brain lesions as the cause of differential performance; the medical practitioner—physical and metabolic explanations; the vision specialist—ocular defects and dominance; the psychiatrist—personality aberrations; etc. Quite practically, the type of variables of concern to a researcher or to a school administrator may vary markedly due to the setting of the investigation or the expected application of the findings. A person who is concerned with individual differences in terms of planning and implementing a program for an entire school district might logically place more importance on a different set of factors than a person who is planning a program for a single classroom, a gifted group, or a remedial class. The optimist continues to hope that one of these days in the development of prediction formulas, we will be able to select and weight the various factors of significance; but, alas, even this solution implies judgments on the part of the investigator, and thereby any selection will be influenced by a person's area of special interest.

Probably the greatest source of difficulty in the analysis of individual differences lies in the problem alluded to earlier; namely, the diverse character of the field, and the apparent fact that the variables pertinent to reading behavior do not fit any generalizable additive model. To have such a model, it would have to run like this: a given amount of skill "A" requires a designated amount of skill "B," whereas if skill "A" is absent, no amount of skill "B" will be sufficient to compensate for it. Separate components of reading performance interact, instead of serving as an either-or function in an adaptive organism. (Fortunately!) Many children are reading today because compensation for missing or deficient skills, somehow, can be made.

ETIOLOGY OF INDIVIDUAL DIFFERENCES

It would serve no useful purpose in this chapter to enter into the polemics surrounding the causes of individual differences. It should be sufficient at this juncture to enumerate and define the two most fundamental causes generally listed by authors in the psychological literature and to indicate some of the current directions in this area.

Since the days of Galton, psychologists have pitted heredity against environment in a pseudo-issue which has settled down into what is today known as the interactionist theory of the regulation of human development *(1, 15)*. This theory states that the genetic factors depend upon the stimulation from the environment and that the environmental factors depend upon certain genetic mechanisms for full actualization. This issue is sometimes labeled the "nature-nurture" controversy. Both heredity and environment set limits for an individual. Heredity sets the absolute limits as to what it is possible for one to do or to become, while the environment sets the limits as to what one actually does with the inborn equipment that he receives through biological inheritance.

Recent advancements in a relatively new field, molecular biology, have begun the process of breaking the "genetic code" of an individual, and these advancements are providing the stimulus for new avenues of research into many of the dominant traits that are inherited. Refined experimental techniques used in investigations conducted with twins *(25)* and other siblings raises new questions about the relationship between intelligence, socioeconomic sub-populations, personality, etc. On the environmental side, the recent inauguration of stimulation programs, such as Head Start, the Neighborhood Youth Projects, etc., may provide some of the necessary missing data as to how much and in what ways stimulation through education and training can assist in the developmental growth of an individual.

CHARACTERISTICS OF INDIVIDUAL DIFFERENCES

Although the literature concerned with individual differences is highly fragmented, four basic concepts tend to implicitly characterize this diverse area. Any programmatic attempt to improve reading instruction is confronted with the situation of having to deal with these latent characteristics. The four characteristics which typically affect individual differences are: normality, variation, covariation, and velocity.

Virtually all measures of traits and abilities, whether they be physiological or psychological or any combination of traits, show the characteristic of *normality*. In any measurement of large groups of individuals the results tend to be distributed according to the phenomenon of normal probability as characterized by the bell-shaped curve. The distribution is bilaterally symmetrical on each side of the mean with just as many individuals above the average as below it. In Figure 7-1 the normality is indicated by the shape of the curve and the even numbers represented on each side of the mean.

Everyone knows that living things vary. Two trees are never exactly alike. Not all puppies born to the same dog in the same litter are exactly alike. Individuals are not different in this attribute (excepting identical twins, but environment soon modifies even this)! *Variations* are the deviations among the members of any species of living organisms. On any given measure, the observed scores of individuals tend to disperse or spread themselves out along a continuum. This range or distribution is illustrated in Figure 7-1 below by the line X_1 X_2. If a heterogeneously grouped classroom is measured on the same selected factor, such as average reading ability, the range of average reading ability, "that is, the spread [of scores] from the best reader to the poorest reader—is usually two-thirds of the chronological age of the usual child in that classroom" *(7)*. Teachers with heterogeneous classes have to find a way to meet this wide range of differences if they are to provide effective instruction. However, the difficulties in attempting to adjust instruction to this range of differences is closely related to the problems of assessment. When one moves from the original criterion selected for the purpose of separating a group of individuals (in this illustration—average reading ability), the scores of the individuals in each separate group tend to disperse again on any other criteria which might be chosen for specific development, such as vocabulary, comprehension, or more specific skills such as syllabication or

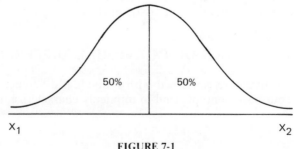

FIGURE 7-1
NORMAL PROBABILITY CURVE

tracing sequences. The fact that persons possess intra-individual, as well as inter-individual, variation restricts the amount of reduction possible for heterogeneous groups to a maximum of 20 to 25 percent. We can reduce the range or amount of individual variation, excepting on the original factor, by only one-fourth to one-fifth of the initial spread *(1,6)*. This means that if we were to make a profile analysis of the specific reading skills of a group of youngsters, after grouping them initially on average reading ability, the intra-individual test patterns would reveal wide discrepancies (up to 75-80 percent) between different areas or types of competencies. The phenomenon of intra-individual variation in reading abilities is, in fact, so common that it is surprising how little it has been utilized or even investigated.

Not only do traits and abilities vary, but they also *covary*. Separate reading abilities do not develop along discrete parallel continuums, but instead they interact and are interrelated to the other reading skills. In the development of reading behavior, a child's word perception skills normally grow in a close relationship with his comprehension skills. This is undoubtedly true of the highly specific skills within an area such as word perception, etc. Covariation is a positive sign, and it is only when selected reading skills do not covary in their usual relationship that difficulty is encountered. It is when normally covarying abilities become discrepant, difficulty arises. When such cases occur, a differential diagnosis is necessary to discover where, specifically, the reader is having difficulty. The problem is that we do not know what the usual covariation relationship of specific reading skills is or should be.

Within the range of normal development, abilities are not stationary, although admittedly they can enter into an abeyant state. Children grow, develop, mature, and learn, but each at a different rate of *velocity*. The term velocity implies direction. Pupils' rate of change in a given direction not only differs but fluctuates. Each child has his own built-in velocity system; and even with youngsters who apparently have the same rate, their cycling process (rate of fluctuation) often operates on a different calibrated scale. One child's learning rate plateaus for a period of time, while the other child's learning ascent moves forward, only to level off at a different stage. Both children could have the same generic learning ratio, but the teacher perceives a notably different style of learning.

DIMENSIONS OF INDIVIDUAL DIFFERENCES

The term "difference" inherently implies a comparison with some type of criterion or standard. Typically, two types of standards are considered for comparison purposes. One type lies outside the individual. Often this type of difference is expressed in terms of some other persons or some previously defined hypothetically average person. These differences are *inter-individual*. The second type of difference is considered in terms of the individual himself and thus is an *intra-individual* difference. One teacher expressed this type of difference well when she said, "The child is a whiz at calling words, but he cannot tell me a thing about what he has read." Intra-individual differences often deal with constructs which may also be described in both inter- and intra-individual terms: "The child has the word pronunciation ability of a seventh grader, but he comprehends at the second grade level."

Whether to compare a skill internally or externally can be decided best in terms of the type of educational decision to be made. Perhaps too often the classroom teacher has a tendency to limit his observations and concern to the realm of inter-individual differences. Typically, the focus on intra-individual differences is attended to only when a child has been singled out for more intensive evaluation. Far too frequently, plans for instruction are based on the differences between individuals and neglect to account for the differences within individuals. Ideally, both types of differences should be given equal consideration in planning for more efficient and effective educational programs for children.

The dimensions of individual differences which have direct influence on reading growth are legion. The discussion that follows will focus on those dimensions which represent the major variables that previous investigations have indicated to have a relationship with reading performance: chronological age, growth age, sex differences, intelligence, cognitive abilities, cognitive style, interests, and cultural background. Some of these dimensions are distinctly inter-individual differences; others represent both types of differences.

Chronological Age

Chronological age is considered to be a unitary inter-individual difference. This dimension of individual differences has been traditionally, and basically still is, the standard basis for school admission and promotion policies. The implications from such policies have applied, unfortunately, even to the level of instructional materials to which children are exposed during the school year.

As our knowledge from research has accumulated about rates of growth, maturation, and learning, it has become more widely recognized that chronological age is woefully insufficient to serve as the single criterion for school admission. Regrettably, the legal structure imposed on the educational enterprise has not yet acknowledged this fact completely. However, Vernon *(26)* implies that at present, this is the only stable and accurate assessment which is acceptable to society, as all other arrangements tend to arouse intense controversy.

Comments are frequently made using age as the referent, when in reality what is implicitly meant is ability, interest, aptitudes, etc., of the average child of a specific age. In spite of all the inherent difficulty in the criterion of age as calculated from the calendar, it has the strong practical appeal of simplicity. Chronological age can be easily and accurately determined, is readily understood by all, and is subject to a very stable rate of change (26). In our culture, the greatest asset of chronological age is probably that it is extolled with the popular virtue of being democratic, non-prejudicial, and equalitarian.

Growth Ages

In evaluating the total growth of a child, many different ages can be determined—not just chronological age. Relying principally upon physiological and anatomical growth factors, Olson (20) developed the concept of organismic age. He averaged the seven qualities of weight, height, dentition, carpal development (measurement of wrist bones), grip, mental age, and reading age into a composite score which he contended represented the central age of the organism. It is readily apparent that this procedure of Olson's is heavily weighted in favor of the physical characteristics of an individual's growth pattern. Five of his seven factors are physical measurements. Whether just adding a few psychological measures to several aspects of physical growth raises our predictability of educational achievement is severely open to question. In fact, other investigations (5) have challenged this concept. The adding of physical factors to mental age alone will raise a multiple correlation coefficient for predicting reading achievement only a negligible amount. The difficulties in obtaining and integrating such data would hardly be worth the effort, that is, if prediction is of primary concern.

A similar type of approach of combining various factors, only this time with the emphasis being more on the psychological factors, is now being experimented with in various parts of the country. This approach produces an emotional age or behavior age and may indicate whether a child is under- or over-placed in his school setting (16). Such an approach, and any others like it, are challenging the use of chronological age as the major determinant of individual differences in school placement.

Sex Differences

Sex is distinctly an inter-individual difference. Differential performance between the sexes, especially in reading, have been reported with consistent regularity. Three hypotheses have been offered to explain this phenomenon—a maturational-based theory, an identification hypothesis, and a conjecture based on the evolutionary character of man.

The classic explanation for the sex differences in reading is based on the fact that boys have slower maturation rates than girls. By inference, it is suggested that this difference affects the reading achievement of boys. While this differential growth rate does exist between the species' gender, this theory does not account for the existence of the greater differences within a particular sex in achievement than the differences between the sexes in reading performance.

The second hypothesis offered to explain the sex differential in reading achievement is expressed in terms of sex-typed behavior and sex-role identification. Boys in our society are taught to view feminine pursuits with disdain as indicated by a youngster's remark when told to do some of the housework, "Aw, gee, Mom—that's sissy work." If boys perceive of reading in a similar manner, then reading becomes inappropriate for them. Cultural patterns encourage certain types of sex-linked activity. Our culture encourages boys to seek out roles which exemplify that mythical "All-American boy"—and that role does not emphasize reading in the idealized model. Further complications arise when a culture does not provide ample opportunities for identification with appropriate models at home and at school. It is suggested that our culture suffers in providing such models. The cultural limits of such a view are supported by the Preston (21) study which indicated that in Germany the boys typically are better readers than girls. As added injury, one recent investigation indicates that the teachers' marks (grades) are biased in favor of the girls over the boys (2). Should a male youngster select a sex role rationale for his difficulty, he likely will find much corroborative evidence in the classroom.

Bannatyne (3) suggests a third hypothesis for the differential achievement between the sexes. He explains these deviations as a function of an evolutionary difference based on survival value. Bannatyne speculates that men of greater visuo-spatial ability (the ability to manipulate objects and their interrelationships intelligently in three-dimensional space) tended to survive and reproduce. Those that did not have this ability risked the possibility of extinction. The strong visuo-spatial male was more adroit at throwing spears, shooting arrows, and avoiding his adversaries than those of low ability in this area. In contrast, the female to be successful in family rearing needed to be able to manipulate the members of the family group. This manipulation required excellence in communication or verbal skills. The spatially able tend to utilize both visual fields and both hemispheres of the brain. The verbally able, in Western languages particularly, utilize the right half of the body, especially the right visual field which is controlled by the left hemisphere. Thus, Bannatyne suggests the evolutionary changes in man have biased the male toward greater interhemispheric integration and females to left hemispheric dominance with a resultant advantage in verbal skills.

While the first and the third hypotheses explaining the sex differences in reading may be tenable (they have not been proved or disproved), it is the second theory which provides some possibility of giving the educator clues as to variables he can change. Social determinants are far more malleable than genetic determinants.

Intelligence

This dimension of individual differences has variously been labeled as intelligence, capacity, potential, and expectancy. It is often invoked to indicate the differences *between* children in terms of their maximum expectancies—both in rate of learning and in level of achievement at a point in time. While there is, and can be, some theoretical discussion as to the degree of "thingness" that should be attached to the term intelligence, it is nonetheless of practical value in aiding in the determination of realistic goals or expectancies for children.

Two methods are commonly used in expressing intelligence. The first method utilizes a quotient or ratio figure to obtain what is commonly called "an IQ score." This procedure provides a measure of differences between persons of the same chronological age. Chronological age is treated as a constant. While this method does identify the broad concepts like "superior" or "retarded" rather well, this type of information may not be the most propitious basis for the day-by-day decision-making process necessary in the classroom. A second method of expressing differences in intelligence is through the concept of mental age. The use of this approach provides a comparison of differences without regard to a fixed chronological age. By this mental age method, the standard becomes the typical performance of an "average" child with a given chronological age and gives some indication of level of functioning. This approach provides the teacher with a technique for judging the appropriateness of instruction for a given child. While this second method has the advantage of setting theoretical expectancies for achievement, it ignores several other important traits of the individual.

A distinct disadvantage of this dimension of individual differences by either method described above is that it tends to lead to a false assumption that intelligence is a singular trait; and thereby, the concern should be with inter-individual deviations. Actually, intelligence is composed of many components or cognitive abilities and is subject to inter- and intra-individual differences.

Cognitive Abilities

One of the more persistent sources of confusion in the field of psychological measurement has resulted from the failure to define the relation between specific mental abilities and general intelligence. Scores on separate components of intelligence tests are usually substantially correlated; yet the existence of persons who show much greater competence in one area than another has long been noted. Earlier in the century, Thurstone *(23)* declared that IQ was not a homogeneous trait. He thought intelligence could better be defined as a cluster of primary abilities, and an individual's intellectual assessment could better be illustrated by a profile of scores rather than by the designation of a single score. Guilford's *(13)* more recent work supports and expands Thurstone's original conception. Guilford believes there are many underlying dimensions which contribute in varying degrees to a wide variety of intellectual skills and that these factors can be identified and classified. Such identification and classification would lead to notable intra-individual differences in intelligence.

Teachers in the course of their classroom experience come across many children with discrepant abilities. Though it is more typical to find the cognitive abilities of children developing at a fairly even rate, it is not unusual to discover youngsters with a high mathematical ability or a very favorable artistic aptitude being afflicted with an apparent "block" when it comes to printed verbal material. Other discrepancies could easily be identified. Any person who has ever administered a WISC or a Stanford-Binet test to children can easily identify cases where pupils achieve a highly similar total score, but yet an analysis of the items passed and failed reveals that the similar score was achieved through markedly different abilities. Seemingly different intellectual abilities were functioning to achieve the global summary score.

Cognitive Styles

Recent investigations by students of cognitive style have been concerned with the problem of determining what type of orientation toward the environment facilitates the cognitive processes and what type does not. To avoid misunderstanding between the areas of cognitive abilities and cognitive style, one distinction will be offered. Researchers in the area of cognitive abilities are attempting to discover a minimum number of functions to account for the covariation of mental abilities while the students of cognitive style are attempting to study the processes underlying the primary mental abilities.

Witkin *et al. (28)* found individuals are of two types in their orientation to the environment. One approach is field-independent; the other is field-dependent. The field-independent oriented persons are basically free from irrelevant and distracted perception. The field-dependent oriented individuals are impulsive and cannot separate an item from its context; thus, they have a low ability to discriminate. Kagan *et al. (18)*, using different terms for the same categories (field-independent—analytical; field-dependent—relational), found essentially the same type of behavior. An analytically styled person is objective and more able to control his environment, but a

relational-styled individ"
ronment in a global wa)
tween reading behavior an
ing was verified by another
disability *(22)*. Teachers of rea
ers if they would train children to

Enough evidence is available to su
differ in their approach to learning expe
any one of several different types. Each ty
effectively when taught by methods which
proach into account. This dimension of cog
variable that needs to be accounted for in ma
ual differences.

Interests

A brief conversation with the children in virtually any classroom will
quickly reveal a variety of interests in both range and kind. Normally, the
older the children, the greater the range of interests, because interests can
develop commensurate only with the quantity and quality of experience.
Without experience, there cannot be interests. Tyler *(24)* makes a major
point of encouraging the use of interests as one of the features in planning for individual differences.

Too often in the reading situation all of the children are exposed continuously to the same diet of material. Olson *(20)* declares that the solution to the diversity of interests is through "self-selection." In this approach the teacher permits the children to seek and select their own reading materials. Olson and other advocates of this system contend this approach will also result in children reading at their instructional level.
However, Fleming's *(10)* recent study casts doubt on the efficacy of a
system of self-selection. Using a fifth-grade population, Fleming explored
the relationship between pupils' reading levels and their choices. Low
positive correlations were found, but they hardly give strong practical
support to a system of attending to individual differences on the basis of
self-selection.

Cultural Background

It is no secret that the educational system is built around the middle-
class values and is usually run by middle-class teachers and administrators; nor do we need to apologize for this fact. Perhaps what we do need
to do, though, is follow Plato's admonition to "examine thyself." An *a
priori* assumption of many teachers is that the classrooms are composed of
persons being socialized into the society of which he, the teacher, is a
member. He anticipates among the youngsters a similarity of extra- and

pre-school experience and a comparability of these experiences with a rather amorphous national norm. In many instances, these assumptions may be justified, but there are many significant exceptions. Sometimes the entire class is quite consistently different in background from the teacher and the "average class"; other times only specific individuals differ markedly.

Among the many factors influencing the development of the child, one must recognize the effect of the child's environment, the people with whom he associates, the sounds and words that he hears, and the places he has been and seen. The extent to which the child experiences these things will be primarily determined by the home and family of which he is a member. The home environment in turn is greatly influenced by the social class status, economic level, and cultural background of its members. Not only will socioeconomic class often determine the child's aggressions, motivations, and interests, but "studies repeatedly show that the home is the single most important influence on the intellectual and emotional development of children" (4). Other studies have quite clearly indicated that the relationship between socioeconomic class and achievement is higher than the correlation between intelligence and achievement (11). Vilscek (27), in 1964, replicated the early mental age studies of the 1930's (12, 19), but added the dimension of socioeconomic class. Her findings reinforced the previous studies, but indicated the functional relationship between socioeconomic and mental age: the lower the mental age, the higher the socioeconomic level must be for children to be successful, initially, in learning to read; and conversely, the lower the socioeconomic level, the higher the mental age needs to be. The concept of "cumulative deficit" could have been a corollary derived from findings such as these.

Other critical areas which may be affected by cultural variations are: amount of language experience, dialect, multilingualism, proportions of verbal to non-verbal expression of ideas, experience with abstractions, interests, and factors involved in motivation, such as types of reinforcement, values and attitudes to school, and the effectiveness of immediate and deferred reinforcement. The implications of studies in these areas for instruction remain to be developed in practical environments.

Reading Achievement

Differences in reading behavior are affected by all the characteristics of individual differences: normality, variation, covariation, and velocity. Typical reading differences in a heterogeneous classroom could be similar to the diagram represented in Figure 7-2. If we assume Figure 7-2 represents a typical third-grade classroom, we see that only 12 of the 30 pupils read "at grade level," and 9 pupils read above and below grade level. This describes only the normality and variation of the class members; still each pupil has reading skills which covary and an individual velocity system which must be considered.

It is precisely situations like this one that necessitate a discussion of the practical administrative matters considered in this perspectives study. Decisions must be made constantly by school administrators and teachers as to how to cope with these variables.

If the professional literature is any indication, the principal concern in reading and its related areas has been with factors of how one child differs from another. A more significant, and less explored, area is the way an individual reader differs within himself. The most generally used concept of intra-individual differences in reading is the "expectancy level discrepancy." This discrepancy is closely related to the common comment that a person is not "reading up to his capacity." More formally, it is a measure of the difference between the current level of reading achievement and the inferred potential (with corrections for measurement errors). Many important instructional decisions can and should be based on an analysis of this type of discrepancy. For example, if a youngster's performance level is much below his class, though quite in keeping with his potential level, the teacher may seek simply to maintain the potential-achievement relationship while modifying the surroundings. If the potential-achievement discrepancy is significantly large, the teacher must plan for decreasing this difference by bringing achievement more in harmony with potential. This type of analysis concerning level and potential is of general classroom importance.

Empirical data are not abundant on the variation of intra-individual differences in specific reading skills. Yet the downfall of many a grouping plan in reading rests on the disregard of deviations in skill within the

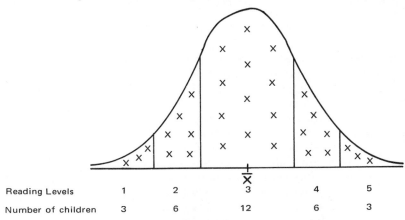

Reading Levels	1	2	3	4	5
Number of children	3	6	12	6	3

FIGURE 7-2 *

EXAMPLE OF THE RANGE AND GRADE LEVEL EXPECTANCIES IN
A TYPICAL THIRD-GRADE CLASSROOM

*Acknowledgment is made to Professor Dale E. Bennett of the University of Illinois for the design of this figure and for other valuable suggestions.

readers themselves. When divisions are made on the basis of a generic score, the variations between and among pupils on specific reading skills redistribute themselves after the initial grouping. Any grouping pattern is subject to the covariation of skills, and the instruction within a given pattern should attend to those differences.

The phenomenon of intra-individual variability in specific reading skills is in fact so common that it is surprising how little it has been investigated. Harris *(14)* infers that there are different patterns of manifested reading behavior. He discusses the word-caller, the context reader, and the slow rate type and indicates the discrepancies between skills which identify each of these patterns. It is my contention that there are several types, or more accurately, there are several *syndromes of reading behavior* which can be characterized and described. Like in the psychiatric literature where syndromes of psychoses are classified and characterized by signs and symptoms, it should be possible by careful study and analysis to do likewise with the various signs and symptoms of reading behavior. The recognizable complexes of highly related signs and symptoms of reading behavior can be clustered to form identifiable syndromes of reading ability or disability. Likely, such an investigation would uncover several specific reading syndromes which overlap and form a central core syndrome (like the medical syndrome of stress). Naturally, this central syndrome of reading behavior would have to be described and characterized, too. Investigations in the area of intra-individual differences of specific reading skills could offer new perspectives to reading instruction as well as to different programmatic approaches to cope with these differences.

CONCLUDING STATEMENT

It was the purpose of this chapter to attempt to explore and to structure certain concepts about the nature of individual differences with particular reference to the teaching of reading. How reading might be organized for instructional purposes is in the pages that follow. However, any administrative scheme for organizing reading instruction should attempt to account for, in as far as it is feasible, the four major characteristics of individual differences: normality, variation, covariation, and velocity. In addition to the usual attention to inter-individual differences in reading, intra-individual differences need more emphasis, especially in the dimensions of the cognitive abilities, the cognitive styles, and the specific reading skill development of the individual. Current grouping practices tend to focus more on the inter-individual differences and the dimensionality aspect of psychological measurement. As more attention is given to the differences within an individual including his non-continuous traits, then a program which contends to "meet individual differences" will give substance and meaning to the cliche.

REFERENCES

1. ANASTASI, ANNE. *Differential Psychology.* New York: The Macmillan Co., 1958, pp. 68, 320.

2. ARNOLD, RICHARD D. "The Relationship of Teachers' Sex to Assigned Marks and Tested Achievement among Upper Elementary Grade Boys and Girls." Unpublished doctoral thesis, University of Minnesota, 1966.

3. BANNATYNE, ALEX D. "Verbal and Spatial Abilities and Reading." Paper presented to the First International Reading Association Congress, Paris, France, August, 1966.

4. BLOOM, BENJAMIN, DAVIS, ALLISON, and HESS, ROBERT. *Compensatory Education for Cultural Deprivation.* Chicago: Holt, Rinehart, & Winston, Inc., 1965, p. 69.

5. BLOOMERS, PAUL, KNIEF, LOTUS M., and STROUD, J. B. "The Organismic Age Concept," *Journal of Educational Psychology,* Vol. XLVI (1955), pp. 142-50.

6. COOK, WALTER W. *Grouping and Promotion in the Elementary School.* Minneapolis: University of Minnesota Press, 1941, p. 33.

7. CLYMER, THEODORE. "Criteria for Grouping for Reading Instruction," in Helen M. Robinson (ed.), *Reading Instruction in Various Patterns of Grouping.* Supplementary Educational Monographs, No. 89. Chicago: University of Chicago Press, 1959, p. 43.

8. DU BOIS, PHILIP H. "Individual Differences," *Annual Review of Psychology,* Vol. XI (1960), pp. 225-53.

9. FERGUSON, GEORGE A. "Human Abilities," *Annual Review of Psychology,* Vol. XVI (1965), pp. 39-62.

10. FLEMING, JAMES T. "Children's Perception of Difficulty in Reading Materials." Paper read at the American Educational Research Association, New York City, February, 1967.

11. FRIERSON, EDWARD C. "Determining Needs," *Education,* Vol. LXXXV (April, 1965), p. 462.

12. GATES, ARTHUR I. "The Necessary Mental Age for Beginning Reading," *Elementary School Journal,* Vol. XXXVII (1937), pp. 497-508.

13. GUILFORD, J. P. "The Structure of Intellect," *Psychological Bulletin,* Vol. LIII (1956), pp. 267-93.

14. HARRIS, ALBERT J. *How to Increase Reading Ability.* New York: David McKay Co., Inc., 1961, pp. 180-84.

15. HUNT, J. MCVICKERS. *Intelligence and Education.* New York: The Ronald Press Company, 1961.

16. ILG, FRANCES L., and AMES, LOUISE BATES. *School Readiness: Behavior Tests Used at the Gesell Institute.* New York: Harper & Row, Publishers, 1965.

17. KAGAN, JEROME. "Reflection-Impulsivity and Reading Ability in Primary Grade Children," *Child Development,* Vol. XXXVI (1965), pp. 609-28.

18. KAGAN, JEROME, MOSS, HOWARD A., and SIGEL, IRVING E. "Psychological Significance of Styles of Conceptualization," in "Basic Cognitive Processes in Children," *Monograph of the Society for Research in Child Development,* Vol. XXVIII (1963), pp. 73-114.

19. MORPHETT, MABEL V., and WASHBURNE, CARLETON. "When Should Children Begin to Read," *Elementary School Journal,* Vol. XXIX (1931), pp. 496-503.

20. OLSON, WILLARD C. *Child Development.* Boston: D. C. Heath Company, 1959, pp. 3-7.

21. PRESTON, RALPH C. "A Comparative Study of the Reading Achievement of German and American Children," in J. A. Figurel (ed.), *Changing Concepts of Reading Instruction.* New York: Scholastic Magazines, 1961, pp. 109-12.

22. SANTOSTEFANO, SEBASTIANO, RUTLEDGE, LOUIS, and RANDALL, DAVID. "Cognitive Styles and Reading Disability," *Psychology in the Schools,* Vol. 2 (1965), pp. 57-62.

23. THURSTONE, L. L. "Primary Mental Abilities," *Psychometric Monograph,* Vol. I (1938).

24. TYLER, LEONA E. "Toward a Workable Psychology of Individuality," *The American Psychologist,* Vol. XIV (1959), pp. 75-81.

25. VANDENBERG, STEVEN G. "Innate Abilities: One or Many." Paper read at the American Educational Research Association, New York City, February, 1967.

26. VERNON, PHILIP E. "Education and the Psychology of Individual Differences," *Harvard Educational Review,* Vol. XXVIII (1958), pp. 91-104.

27. VILSCEK, ELAINE C. "An Analysis of the Effect of Mental Age Levels and Socio-Economic Levels on Reading Achievement in First Grade." Unpublished doctoral thesis, University of Pittsburgh, 1964.

28. WITKIN, HERMAN A., *et al. Psychological Differentiation.* New York: John Wiley & Sons, Inc., 1962.

Chapter 8. INDIVIDUAL DIFFERENCES AND READING

INDIVIDUAL INSTRUCTION

Elaine Wolfe

The demand for instructional diversity is more prominent today than ever before in the history of American reading instruction. Merely counting the number of times the term "individualized instruction" appears in the literature would be overwhelming. Is it probable that educators have deluded themselves into believing that the concept of "individualized instruction in reading" is desirable, is understood, and could be operational within the realm of public education? Is individualized instruction a myth, a misconception, a mirage, or an inevitable educational innovation?

Procedures related to individualized instruction are creative innovations that are less easily institutionalized than lockstep routine or systematized disorganization. Jules Henry *(23),* one of the contemporary educational critics, states,

SOURCE: Reprinted from *Organizing for Individual Differences* (Newark, Del.: International Reading Association, 1968), pp. 47-68, with permission of Elaine Vilscek Wolfe and the International Reading Association.

Schools cannot handle variety, for as an institution dealing with masses of children it can manage only on the assumption of a homogeneous mass. Homogeneity is therefore accomplished by defining the children in a certain way and by handling all situations uniformly.

Few educators today would accept Henry's dim perspective. The endorsement of a need for individualized instruction in reading would be nearly unanimous. Yet, as one observes behaviors of teachers and pupils, it is evident that "individualized instruction" is a concept more often verbalized than understood or applied. At one extreme are classrooms in which unique pupil responses, within some type of systematized uniformity, are the only evidence of instructional differentiation. While at the opposite end of the continuum one may observe pupils working solely within a segmented computerized environment. Consequently, longitudinal studies and surveys yield evidence that pupils who achieve are the "surviving fittest" *(17, 33)*.

The impact of technology, the findings in educational behavioral research, the integrity of educators, the present magnitude of federal educational appropriations, and other factors will inevitably affect instructional diversification. In further exploring the topic "individualized instruction," the following will be considered:

1. The evolving concept of individualized instruction
2. Individualized reading goals
3. Evaluation for individualized instruction and learning
4. Individually prescribed instruction
5. Related factors affecting instructional diversification
6. Individualizing instruction and learning within various approaches to reading and within various administrative provisions.

THE EVOLVING CONCEPT OF INDIVIDUALIZED INSTRUCTION

If there is an instructional characteristic common to the Dame Schools of the 17th century and to the Responsive Environment Schools of the 20th century, it is that children learn in an individualized setting. Nila Banton Smith *(25)* describes practices of the Dame School:

There was no particular philosophy or psychology which guided Dame School practice. The pupils who came to the Dame were at different stages of development and small in number, and there was no particular need for attempting to mold them into one achievement level for "mass production" purposes.

Differences do exist, similarly, among children of the 20th century whether they are within nongraded or graded instructional units. Appropriate pacing per pupil in learning to read is a major concern in accommodating masses of children. These concerns about meeting pupils' needs evolved over the years and contributed to changing concepts of "individualized instruction."

Between 1910 and 1950, individualized learning and instruction were expected as adjustments were made in curricular or classroom organization. The Winnetka and Dalton Plans are examples of curricular adjustments through which a child might progress at his own rate toward goals common to all pupils. Instructional practices reflected the philosophy that expectations and goals for pupils were common but could be individually reached in different lengths of time *(25)*. Even in the "sixties" the residue of this theory is voiced in a demand for "equal educational experiences for all," when, in fact, the word *equal* cannot be rationally substituted for the word *appropriate*.

Educators of the "fifties and sixties" have extended concepts of accommodating learning in reading. The term *reading instruction* now comprehensively refers to teaching pupils to read as well as to directing or simulating an environment in which pupils learn to read through independent insights. As a result, the terms that represent an approach to and accommodations for pupils' needs and potentials in reading have been used synonymously to reflect totally different considerations. Included are labels such as individualized instruction in reading, individualized reading, individualized reading instruction, the individualized approach, individualizing reading instruction, personalized reading, individually prescribed instruction, and instructional diversification.

The chaotic effects of language semantics are evident as the term *individualized reading* is defined by Strang and subsequently by Lazar. Strang *(27)* concludes that "individualized reading" is a specific method of teaching reading. Lazar *(19)* states:

> Individualized reading is a way of thinking about reading—an attitude toward the place of reading in the total curriculum, toward the materials and methods used, and toward the child's developmental needs. It is not a single method or technique but a broader way of thinking about reading which involves newer concepts with class organization, materials, and the approach to the individual child.

These and other synonymous labels are confusing when one attempts to summarize and evaluate the related conflicting research findings.

For purposes of clarification in this paper, two distinctions between terminology are presented to the reader:

1. A descriptive label for a *learning approach in reading*

2. Descriptive labels of *accommodations for pupil differences within various learning approaches and within various administrative provisions.*

The term *individualized approach* will be used, exclusively, in referring to the first distinction. The terms *individualized instruction and learning, individually prescribed instruction,* and *diversifying instruction* will be employed as indicated in the second point of clarification.

INDIVIDUALIZED READING GOALS

Educators are becoming increasingly aware of the utility of well-designed blueprints of desirable instructional outcomes in the language arts. Foremost among published materials that represent a design for classifying learning goals are the *Taxonomy of Educational Objectives: Handbook I Cognitive Domain (5)* and the *Taxonomy of Educational Objectives: Handbook II: Affective Domain (18).* Two major classifications of educational objectives are designated in the taxonomies, those encompassing the products and processes of knowing (cognitive domain) and those encompassing some personalized emotional response (affective domain). More specifically, objectives that reflect the acquisition of knowledge, understandings, habits, skills, and abilities are within the scope of the cognitive domain. Cultural-literary-aesthetic appreciations, values, and attitudes are classified within the affective domain. Such classifications of goals are of significance when attempting to formulate complete inventories of learning outcomes in reading.

Supported by school funds, funds from the U.S. Office of Education, or funds from the national foundations, educators have undertaken the task of compiling reasonably complete listings of desirable outcomes for pupils in the communicative arts. Such a project, sponsored by the Ford Foundation and directed by J. Steele Gow, was initiated in Pittsburgh in 1960. One facet of this Curriculum Continuity Demonstration Project in Pittsburgh involved the compiling of progressions of outcomes for potentially college-bound students, K-12, in reading and other language arts areas. The total language curriculum committee included teachers and supervisory personnel from the Pittsburgh Public Schools as well as University of Pittsburgh faculty from the departments of education, English, speech, and linguistics. Learning goals for pupils were listed under three major headings: understandings and knowledges, habits and skills, and attitudes and appreciations. The committee proposed and isolated five subcategories of knowledges and behaviors in reading. The subcategories were referred to as learning streams and were labeled *Thought Processes, Literary Appreciations, Study Skills, Mechanics,* and *History and Function of Language.*

Specifics were included under each learning stream and some attempts were made to sequence them *(30)*.

The listings of pupil-learning outcomes, prepared by the Curriculum Continuity Demonstration Project committee, were reevaluated and refined to serve as pupil goal guidelines in the U.S.O.E. Project, *A Comparison of the Basal and the Coordinated Language Experience Approaches in the First Grade Reading Instruction (31)*. Interrelationships between language outcomes were designated. The five learning streams, originally suggested, were redefined as seven channels of language transfer and were labeled as *Perceptual-Conceptual Development, Physiological Aspects, Mechanics, Functional Linguistics, Comprehension, Study Techniques,* and *Aesthetic Appreciations.* Definitions for the seven channels of language transfer, as quoted in the U.S.O.E. Cooperative Research Project No. 2729 Report, follow:

1. *Perceptual-Conceptual Development*—processes through which children learn to interpret and express everything sensed. Growth in this area is cloaked by past and present experiences and values; reflects cultural, psychological, and biological influences; and is principally characterized by kind and degree of arousal of meaning.

2. *Physiological Aspects*—processes generally labeled as or associated with visual acuity, auditory acuity, kinesthetic acuity, posture, and visual manifestations of nonvocal dramatization.

3. *Mechanics*—processes that require use of one or more of the senses. Motor coordination, production of speech sounds, and other physiological aspects dictate the degree to which any child may or should be expected to master mechanics.

4. *Functional Linguistics*—those processes, overt and conceivably abstract, that necessitate understanding and application of linguistic symbolism and structure. Abstractly labeling or generalizing perceptions would serve as an example. Other factors of functional linguistics might include recognition and generation of sentence patterning; awareness of pitch, pause, juncture; or attention to dialectic or colloquial profiles.

5. *Comprehension*—growth in specific types of abilities including unit and global considerations. Specific areas to be considered include vocabulary, main ideas, following directions, creative interpretation, critical evaluation, etc.

6. *Study Techniques*—processes established so that learning through all six acts of language can be most effective. Study techniques may include ordering steps in perceiving, knowing how to utilize the

differential between a speaker's rate and the author's rate, reference methods, ways to convey information to others, etc.

7.   *Aesthetic and Cultural Appreciations*—processes that directly reflect growth in a pupil's sensitivity to beauty and to his literary heritage. Learning in this channel will be overtly manifested through pupil personality development, stimulation and breadth of interests, and discriminative tastes.

A design, such as one of those described for classifying complete sets of goals for pupils in reading, might serve as a grid within which a pupil's individual profile of variability could be observed and charted. But, considerations of an individualized profile of a pupil's goals in reading will be controlled by answers to three basic questions related to educational philosophy and child psychology:

1.   Do pupils possess an innate goal-patterning potential activated by need and gauged by maturation when learning to read?

2.   Should children be exposed to some hierarchy of instructional sequencing while learning to read through directed or discovery techniques?

3.   Can a pupil's patterning potential be predicted or consistently observed, and what effects would this possibility have on instructional sequencing in reading?

Conflicting answers to these questions are voiced in the literature. Some are based on research studies while others are the products of speculation. Indirectly, too, these views are reflected in the instructional provisions set for individualizing reading instruction. For example, use of self-directive, corrective kits such as the SRA Reading Laboratories would imply an affirmative response to the second question of sequencing in learning to read.

A positive endorsement of a child's innate goal-patterning potential is reflected in studies by Willard Olson *(21)*. The terms "self-seeking," "self-selection," and "pacing" were an outgrowth of his studies of child behavior. These terms imply that each pupil, propelled by motivating forces, will seek reading experiences congruent with his levels of maturation and interest. Characteristically, through such innate behavioral responses, the child is in fact patterning his own sequential progress and reaching individualized learning goals. According to Olson, the answer to question one would be "yes."

John Carroll *(9)* makes a dual recommendation about a child's patterning or his teacher's setting of learning sequences in reading. In part, Carroll supports Olson's conclusions as he compares relationships in reading and oral language, thusly:

One major mystery is the fact that through an experience in which the child is presented with a tremendous variety of language utterances, not sequenced, ordered, or programmed in any particular way, not even "taught" in the usual sense, the child is nevertheless able somehow to acquire the complex patterns of his language that linguists attempt to describe in terms of the phonology, the syntax, and the semantics of that language.

Accordingly, Carroll recommends the process of native language learning as "ideal" and questions:

Could reading perhaps be acquired through conditions and experiences analogous to those by which the child acquires his native language, rather than by the slow, careful teaching processes which we have thought necessary?

He further states:

When presented with a rather diverse set of stimuli, it is natural for the learner to pick out those which are easiest for him to learn and perhaps it is beyond the capability of any programmer to predict exactly what these will be.

Yet, for years children have learned to read when sequences were presented or controlled. Levels of readiness and interest tempered the child's successes in learning to read. In defense of these facts, Carroll's final recommendation remains:

The proper strategy, from this analysis, is to present a rich diet of reading materials at every stage, but as a parallel tactic also to call the child's attention to particular items or patterns, in a systematic way, so as to facilitate his own developmental progress through spiraling levels of complexity.

Thus, through contrasting the kinds of learning periods, controlled sequencing versus natural patterning, John Carroll contends that pupil progress in reading will be more adequately facilitated.

Of current significance in answering the question of how children acquire linguistic skills are studies by behaviorists such as Omar K. Moore *(12)*. One aspect of Moore's work involves the creation of new educational devices that permit the learner to explore freely, to be paced at a self-determined rate, and to discover independently various relationships within a structure. The child is allowed to set his own pace, explore, and respond within a prepared environment programmed into the device. Moore's work also extends to an examination of the effects of prepared school and class curricular environments on a pupil's learning at the laboratory school in Hamden, Connecticut.

The question of scientifically reliable procedures for predicting a child's innate learning patterning in reading remains, hopefully, to be answered in the future. A step toward answering this question was proposed by Holmes and Singer in their study of the substrata factor theory of reading. Singer *(24)* states:

> The major developmental hypothesis of the substrata factor theory of reading states that as an individual learns to read, he sequentially develops a hierarchically organized mental structure of interrelated neuropsychological subsystems. . . .

Singer further indicates that subskills spiral toward a major skill and that these subsystems can be organized, reorganized, or mobilized. The fact that some readers achieve at higher levels may in part be attributed to a better integration or organization of subsystems. In a critical evaluation of the Substrata Factor Theory, Plessas *(22)* raised a number of questions that deserve attention. Among them are questions about the validity of test measures of pupil performance and questions about the rationale for considering reading products rather than the processes themselves. Plessas states:

> At this time there is no evidence to indicate that scores on a reading test reflect a high order of reasoning or intellectual skills in reading. Perhaps correct responses are actually a product of incomplete knowledge or partial guessing.

Quite obviously, individualized learning goals for pupils represent an educational ideal even though the procedures for goal anticipation, setting, and accomplishment remain questionable. Regardless of theoretical views related to this problem, teachers should become acquainted with the total goal perspectus in reading. A teacher cannot begin to encourage or accommodate for pupil differences and variability in reading unless she recognizes the total possible scope of maturity in reading.

EVALUATION FOR INDIVIDUALIZED INSTRUCTION AND LEARNING

Learning in reading can only be individualized if teachers employ instruments and procedure for determining a child's possible and current performance levels. Appraising a pupil's attitudes toward reading is as important as appraising his reading habits and skills. Yet, determining such a profile is useless unless teachers examine results, evaluate them, and subsequently make judgments related to individualized learning. Evaluations are important before the child is exposed to individualized instruction but are just as crucial as instruction and learning continue.

A teacher's judgments about a pupil's needs and accomplishments in reading should be based on an examination of standardized test results as well as results obtained through informal appraisal procedures. Both allow a means of measuring and evaluating how a pupil is progressing toward designated learning goals. This information should guide the teacher in initially structuring a learning environment and subsequently restructuring that environment in accord with findings from continuous evaluations.

If the information gathered about pupils is to be of value in individualizing instruction or learning, the measurement must be appropriate per pupil. Standardized and informal appraisal should be challenging to a student but not overwhelming. The degree to which present measurement instruments are appropriate for assessing reading potentials and achievements of pupils who have had diverse cultural, social, and educational experiences is often questioned. One of the many related questions is whether we are validly measuring uniqueness and breadth of pupils' reading vocabularies in standardized testing.

The instruments and techniques for appraisal in reading are being revised and improved. Numerous standardized and informal measures, currently available, deserve consideration by teachers. Leo Fay (11) classified the types of standardized reading tests according to their function in yielding information about what the pupil can read, how he reads, and how well he may learn to read. Respectively, the three categories of types of standardized reading tests included survey tests, diagnostic tests, and tests of reading potential. Fay describes survey tests as power tests for measuring general levels of comprehension and vocabulary, diagnostic tests as measures of strengths and weaknesses in specific reading skills, and tests of reading potential as measures of a pupil's expected level or readiness for learning. Comprehensive annotated lists of these tests appear in books and periodicals related to reading instruction.

Additional information about standardized reading tests at primary grade levels has been and is currently being evaluated in the cooperative research projects on beginning reading instruction. One experimental provision required of each cooperating project center was that selected group reading readiness tests, group reading achievement tests, and various individual tests be administered to participating pupils (7). In some instances longitudinal test data were gathered as pupils progressed for three years under varying experimental instructional conditions. Item analyses of responses to these tests by pupils who represented diverse social, intellectual, cultural, racial, and educational experiences could yield scientific implications for future test revision and construction.

To gain individual insights into pupils' reading behaviors, resourceful teachers maintain a balance between standardized and informal appraisal procedures. Informal appraisal procedures may include recording observations of pupil performance, using group or individual informing reading inventories, assigning individualized learning demonstration tasks to students, and eliciting pupils' indications of reading interests. Informal techniques, too, are important prior to and during reading instruction.

Charts, checklists, and anecdotal summaries serve as formats for recording observed behavior in reading. Individual pupil performance or attitudes in applying word recognition techniques, in employing study skills, in linguistic applications, in comprehending, and in demonstrating literary tastes can be noted and evaluated. As such subjective judgments are made, the evaluator should be guided by the criteria representing desirable progressive performance levels. Two of the problems in this type of informal evaluation are determining the consistency of a behavioral pattern and finding the time to record and analyze numerous observations per pupil.

Group and individual reading inventories such as those recommended by Betts *(4)*, Strang *(27)*, and Botel *(8)* are clues to grade level of pupils' reading performance. Betts and Strang suggest percentages of proficiency as criteria for assuming the level at which a student is instructed and the level at which he is able to read independently. A pupil's specific interest or lack of interest in selections that comprise the inventory will affect his level of performance on such inventories. Tests of phonics mastery, word mastery, and word recognition are separate features of the Botel Reading Inventory.

A third procedure for supplementing information about pupils is assigning individualized learning demonstration tasks to them. For example, an individualized demonstration of a pupil's skills in comprehending might be warranted. Such an assessment can be made with reading paragraphs graduated in difficulty levels. Each paragraph should be followed by a task related to a specific comprehension skill. A pupil could be asked to demonstrate skill in stating a comparison, finding a nonsense detail, or evaluating plausibility in the selection. Any number of comprehension specifics could be assessed separately. Specific demonstration tasks should be assigned at a pupil's general instructional level as indicated by the Betts, Strang, or other inventories.

There are many ways teachers can find out what a student's interests are in reading. Kinds of materials pupils self-select are often testimonies of reading preferences. Using a technique that will result in a ranked order of pupil preferences is often advisable. Such a procedure could involve asking each pupil to create a modernistic collage of interests. To represent interests, pupils are asked to cut assorted forms and shapes from construction paper. The construction paper form or shape representing the subsequent degrees of interest should be scaled down in size. Each interest area may be labeled as forms and shapes are arranged on the collage. This activity also serves as a demonstration of a pupil's originality and associations.

A different kind of measurement can occur in computer-assisted instruction. The criterion test, as it is often called, is a go/no-go test that indicates whether a student is ready to progress to the subsequent study unit. As described by Coulson and Cogswell *(10)*, these diagnostic items yield information about the mastery of subskills the program is designed to teach. If the program contains branching elements, test diagnostic items may also reflect which remedial branch the student requires. Idealistically, the investigators predict that computerized pupil diagnosis and data processing will be possible and economically practical in schools of the next decade. Much research on the role of computer-assisted diagnosis and data processing in reading remains to be initiated.

INDIVIDUALLY PRESCRIBED INSTRUCTION

The term "individually prescribed instruction" implies that each child's learning environment will be set, maintained, or modified in accord with his assessed progress toward individualized reading goals. To think of individually prescribed instruction as only tutorial in type would be completely unrealistic and impractical for the education of large numbers of children. The gap between population growth and teacher supply is presently apparent when elementary class sizes number in the forties.

As a function of similarities in pupils' interests, goals, and needs at a common period of time, instruction can be prescribed and individualized justifiably for groups or pairs of pupils. There are occasions, though, when a teacher must work with a pupil entirely on an individual basis. But, sharing literature, feelings, and ideas with peers is essential in the process of learning to read. Discovering knowledge or acquiring a desirable common reading habit, skill, or attitude can be operational within group instruction for pupils at varying age, ability, interest, and reading levels. Examples of contrasts in a group approach to individually prescribed instruction for acquiring a reading understanding, commonly needed by pupils, are charted below.

PUPIL UNDERSTANDING

Exaggeration is sometimes a device for creating humor in a story.

MATERIALS

Humorous caricatures.

Tradebooks that are varied in interest level and grade level.

CONTRASTING APPROACHES

1. Teacher Prescribed, Initiated, and Directed

Show the children a set of caricatures. Encourage the pupils to generalize that some figures are funny because they depict an element of exaggeration. Then, give each child a preselected tradebook in accord with his reading interests and independent reading levels. Ask each to read a designated page in his book (predetermined by the teacher) that is humorous. Suggest that each pupil note whether the humor is apparent or is created with exaggerations or some other device. Give the pupils an opportunity to share their findings.

2.   Teacher Prescribed, Pupil Initiated and Self-paced

Set the learning environment by making numerous carica-tures and varied trade books available to the children. Permit pupils to self-select and pace themselves in these materials when they demonstrate an interest in humorous selections. Af-ter observing pupils using these materials, encourage each child to individually share his findings. Ask types of questions that elicit insights about the effect of exaggeration in producing humor.

In both of these approaches, learning was a function of prescriptive instruction, but the teacher's techniques of controlling and directing the learning environment differed. The time at which the prescription is ful-filled in the first approach is set by the teacher in accord with her evalua-tions of the pupil's need for the specific understanding. The timeliness of prescriptive instruction in the subsequent contrasting approach is deter-mined by the child through his own goal-patterning potential.

Decisions made by the teacher related to her role in management of a learning environment are a critical part of individually prescribed instruc-tion. The kinds of materials a teacher has in her classroom as well as her instructional philosophies will affect her decision making, and subse-quently, the prescription. When programmed materials, for example, are used by pupils, the teacher has made an initial prescription. This prescrip-tion is extended, hopefully, as a child works through programmed materi-als in reading. The program author's proficiency in anticipating the pu-pil's subsequent learning sequence and his probable changing needs will affect the adequacy of the programmed prescription.

An extensive study entitled "The Individually Prescribed Instruction Project" is now underway at one of the public school laboratories of the Learning Research and Development Center, University of Pittsburgh (13). The research study, under the direction of John Bolvin, involves individually prescribed instruction in reading, math, and science. Partici-pating teachers and the research center personnel have cooperatively stated instructional objectives in behavioral terms. These objectives have been sequenced in view of student performance criteria. Instructional materials for reading, as well as math and science, that support the accomplishment of an objective were selected from those available commercially or were prepared by teachers and the research center personnel.

Pupil evaluations in this project are continuous and include general placement tests, periodic pretesting of specifics, and periodic post-testing of specifics. Teachers are taught how to examine pupil data, make evaluations, and subsequently write instructional prescriptions for groups and individual pupils. An evaluation staff, under the direction of Richard Cox and Mauritz Lindvall, supervises the collection of pupil data, the processing of pupil data, and the evaluation of curriculum materials and tests.

Since the initiation of the Individually Prescribed Instruction Project in 1964, many interesting observations have been made. The school plant itself is an architectural ideal. Collapsible paneled walls permit for large group, team type, teaching-learning experiences. Each classroom also contains a glass anteroom for small group or individual pupil study. The anteroom allows teachers to observe while managing instruction in the main classroom or vice versa.

Major instructional emphasis in reading is placed on knowledge, habits, skills, and abilities that can be behaviorally defined and measured. A portion of the prescriptive instruction seems related to use of work-type pages of material extracted from commercial sources or prepared by teaching and research personnel. Findings related to an analysis of prescriptions written by teachers are currently reported by Bolvin *(6)*. Bolvin states that for writing prescriptions the following data are provided to teachers about children: *(a)* background information such as age, family, and past achievement; *(b)* placement profiles; and *(c)* pretest profiles. From an analysis of teachers' prescriptions the investigator concluded the following:

1. Pretest information was the most useful single type of data.

2. The prescriptions reflect teacher estimates and evaluations based on data available.

3. Prescriptions, typically, include the teacher's speculation about necessary degrees of practice and review for concept mastery.

A scientific evaluation of the feasibility and management of individually prescribed instruction within various learning approaches—such as, the basal approach, individualized approach, linguistic approach, language experience approach, and others—is, without doubt, a massive proposal. Concurrently, too, individually prescribed instruction within any one of the learning approaches must be tested within various public school administrative provisions, such as the Joplin Plan, Cross Grade Grouping, Team Teaching, the Nongraded School, Departmentalized Classes, and others. Reasonably controlled guidelines toward such a dual endeavor remain yet to be completely theoretically conceived and absolutely empirically sound.

Related Factors Affecting Instructional Diversification

Issues and factors that affect instructional diversification remain, are changed, or are generated in a continuous but compounding fashion. Four of the many factors affecting the degree of probable individualized instruction are suggested through these questions:

1. What probable effects will technological developments have on reading instruction?

2. How will class size and school plant have to be modified to affect instructional diversification?

3. Do teachers possess competencies essential for accurate and discerning individualization of instruction? Can teacher limitations be resolved through in-service education?

4. What kinds of instructional materials are available to support extended concepts of individualized instruction?

An emerging educational phenomenon now unleashed by technological developments in our nation is commonly called the "computer." The far-reaching potential of this instrument could be an important factor affecting individualized instruction. As described by Patrick Suppes (28), computer-based teaching systems will be available in a variety of student-operated instructional devices at a reasonable cost in public education. The fact that presently 30 to 40 students or classrooms can each work at a different task simultaneously makes computerized instruction economically feasible.

These flexible instruments have the capacity to store, analyze, and organize masses of data that will enable the researcher to learn about individual students as they are in the process of learning. Current computers described by Suppes reflect three types of learning systems. The first is a Drill-and-Practice System that may supplement the teacher's role. Exercise at various levels of difficulty can be selected for a pupil by the instrument in accord with stored information about his past performance. A second type of learning system, the Tutorial System, replaces the teacher in the main task of aiding a pupil to develop skill in the application of a concept. Computers now have the potential for assessing the validity of a pupil's stated inferences about material presented through the machine. The third learning system, the Dialogue System, might even be able to accommodate the natural language of the student respondent and allow him to conduct a dialog. Research in this area is now directed toward the problems of speech recognition by the machine (28).

Atkinson and Hansen *(2)* describe proposed research on computer-assisted instruction in initial reading. The Stanford project involved 100 first graders for the 1966-1967 school year. The investigators proposed that 100 first graders would receive the major portion of their reading instruction under computer control. The Stanford Computer-Assisted Instructional System has the potential for presenting completely different sets of materials and instructional prescriptions for 16 students simultaneously. Thus, branching and self-pacing are featured within a predetermined, minute instructional sequence. The computer evaluates each pupil's responses and makes a decision about what to present next. All computer options must be preanticipated and written by the curricular programmer as detailed lists of commands for the computer. In the Stanford Project, 200 lessons were designed and read into the machine for the first year by a curriculum writing team. Consequently, pupil results at the close of one year will be affected by the adequacy of the prepared curriculum. Whether the program can appropriately anticipate and provide pupil diversity will attest to its adequacy.

Any comment except one of hope for improving procedures in individualizing instruction, with computers as one of the tools, would be premature at present. Computers can offer vicarious experiences but should never be a complete substitute for direct experiences. The sensations a pupil has in sharing ideas with a computer are not the sensations he has in sharing ideas with his teacher and his peers.

If our speculations about computer-assisted instruction become a reality, class size and school plant will come under completely reversed situations. Reducing class size will not be as critical, and the school plant may appear more like a manufacturing plant for educational production. Reasonably, it will be some time before the problems and mechanics of computer assistance are resolved. In the meantime, teachers are confronted with the tasks of individual assessment and prescriptive instructions.

It is a safe assumption at present that a reduction in class size could facilitate more accurate pupil goal setting, more frequent pupil evaluation, and better-designed instructional prescriptions. Charts of births, birth rates, and the total U.S. population between 1910 and 1970, prepared in the U.S. Department of Health, Education, and Welfare, are evidence that in 1972 there will be 15 percent fewer children in first grade than there are today *(32)*. Teachers could reasonably expect class size reduced on an average of about five pupils per class unit. If the rate of teacher preparation continues to rise and the school economy permits, teacher-pupil ratios may even be smaller as first graders of 1972 move up through the grades. Whether this population decline will continue for first grades in subsequent years remains to be seen. Problems of school plant and space will concurrently be resolved in relationship to class size. Pupils function much more adequately in individualized instructional settings when there are fewer in the class and the school plant is reasonably modified to accommodate large group, small group, paired-pupil, and individual instruction.

Fewer pupils by 1972, more adequately prepared preservice teachers, and continued in-service for teachers would lend a fantastic boost to instructional diversification for pupils. The March issue of *The Reading Teacher*, 1966, is related to the need for continued in-service education. Austin *(3)*, Aaron *(1)*, Kasdon *(16)*, Jan-Tausch *(15)*, and Niles *(20)* either substantiate the present inadequacies of reading teachers, suggest areas of needs, and/or present suggested solutions. During the past two years, the current magnitude of federal appropriations for higher education, including teacher education, has amounted in excess of $640,000,000. This figure does not include programs such as Upward Bound and Head Start *(14)*. With a continuation of funds and through sincere in-service teacher interest, progress toward teaching teachers about individualizing instruction can occur.

However, merely preparing teachers to better understand instructional diversification without improved instructional materials would produce a compounding educational effect. Various types of audio-visual-kinesthetic materials are available or are being prepared. Some of these can be called auto-instructional materials since they include means for pupil-response, registering, and checking at multi-achievement levels. Self-pacing is also permitted as pupils pursue prescribed instructional goals. Available materials that contain auto-instructional features include reading laboratory kits, representing high interest selections of varying difficulty; workbook materials with self-directive, self-corrective features; and audiovisual machines for controlled practice on rate of comprehension. Programmed materials, tradebooks of high interest and varying levels of difficulty, records, films, filmstrips, and many other kinds of materials should be used to support the concept of individualized instruction. Care is recommended in the selection of such materials on the basis of quality. At present the purchase of materials that lend to instructional diversification has been possible, as never before, through federal educational funds *(29)*.

INDIVIDUALIZING INSTRUCTION AND LEARNING WITHIN VARIOUS APPROACHES TO READING AND WITHIN VARIOUS ADMINISTRATIVE PROVISIONS

Perhaps a distinction can be made about the philosophies and learning psychology operant within various approaches to reading and within various administrative provisions. Individualized learning appears to be facilitated at or along a continuum. At one end of the continuum the teacher prescribes, initiates, and paces learning, while at the other extreme the teacher supervises or prescribes the environment in which the child self-seeks, selects, and self-paces his learning. Figure 8-1 charts some learning approaches to reading and some materials and illustrates the principle of an individualized instructional continuum.

In examining the chart, one should remember that the extent to which a pupil gains insight while learning may vary within teacher prescribed, teacher initiated, and teacher paced instruction; and within teacher prescribed, pupil initiated, self-paced instruction. Determining the degree to which a teacher should initiate and pace a pupil in learning, as contrasted with the degree to which he is self-motivated and can self-pace learning, is

FIGURE 8-1

INDIVIDUALIZED INSTRUCTION

TEACHER PRESCRIBED   TEACHER PRESCRIBED
TEACHER INITIATED, AND   PUPIL INITIATED, SELF-
TEACHER-PACED INSTRUCTION   PACED INSTRUCTION

APPROACHES

Basal Approach
Phonetic Approaches
Linguistic Approaches

◄——————————— Individualized Approach

◄——————————— Language Experience Approach

MATERIALS

Self-Directive, Corrective

Programed ————————————►

---

perhaps one key to individualizing instruction. The teacher's role and the child's role in instruction might also change in accord with the kind of understanding, habit, skill, attitude, or appreciation the child is acquiring. Similarities and differences in learning tasks that lend to a natural transfer or reinforcement of learning are also important considerations.

The arrows on the chart are presented to illustrate variations in interpreting and setting the conceptual framework of an approach or material. In classifying the approaches and materials, attention is directed to basic underlying philosophies and designs. When unsupplemented or employed in a singular fashion, the basal, phonetic, and linguistic approaches are largely implemented by the teacher. She initiates and paces instruction in accord with a set of directions that accompany the specific basal, phonetic, or linguistic materials.

The individualized approach and language experience approach are placed at the far right of the continuum to illustrate that some advocates of these approaches perceive learning as primarily pupil initiated and self-paced. Arrows deflecting toward the left of the continuum indicate that other investigators have conceived variations of language experience and individualized approaches as tempered by a watchful teacher who takes a more active role when deemed necessary or appropriate.

When the approaches on the chart or others are employed in combinations, they can be placed all along the instructional continuum. For example, teachers using combination basal and language experience approaches to facilitate a pupil's learning may be simultaneously managing instruction at both ends of the continuum. If we could isolate the approach, the combination of approaches, or spaced rotation of approaches per child, learning might be more easily facilitated and instruction more appropriately individualized. We would, then, necessarily assume that a teacher would know how to consistently employ an approach or would know when and how to shift from one approach or combination of approaches to another according to pupil needs. Is this, in fact, a reasonable assumption in view of varied teachers' potential versatilities and competencies? Certainly a more scientific exploration of how pupils learn best and how individual teachers can facilitate learning best is warranted.

The task of classifying instructional materials is less complicated. The present complexion of the instructional materials on the chart determine their position. This placement changes as the materials themselves are modified. For example, self-directive-corrective materials, such as the SRA Reading Laboratories, hold a mid-position since to a degree they can be pupil initiated and some self-pacing is recommended. Programmed materials by their very nature set the learning sequence even though the child may pace himself within this lockstep pattern.

In this paper, individualized instruction has been treated as an instructional provision within various approaches rather than as an administrative provision separately. Approaches and combinations, such as the basal approach, language experience approach, individualized approach, and phonetic approach, are employed within nongraded, team teaching, cross-graded, and other administrative organizations.

Administrative attention to approaches, to procedures, and to materials is nevertheless crucial in curricular planning. Basic philosophies and policies should be stated before planning ways to individualize instruction. But, regardless of approach, material, or administrative provisions, the teacher who sparks the interest of each child in learning and meets his needs through individualizing instruction can truly be called "master of his trade."

REFERENCES

1. AARON, IRA, "In-Service Help on Word Analysis Techniques," *The Reading Teacher*, Vol. XIX (1966), pp. 410-14.

2. ATKINSON, RICHARD, and HANSEN, DUNCAN. "Computer-assisted Instruction in Initial Reading: The Stanford Project," *Reading Research Quarterly*, 1966, pp. 5-26.

3. AUSTIN, MARY. "In-Service Reading Programs," *The Reading Teacher*, Vol. XIX (1966), pp. 406-09.

4. BETTS, EMMETT. "Informal Inventories," *Handbook on Corrective Reading for the American Adventure Series*. New York: Harper & Row Publishers, 1952.

5. BLOOM, BENJAMIN (Ed.) *Taxonomy of Educational Objectives: Handbook I: Cognitive Domain*. New York: David McKay and Co., 1956.

6. BOLVIN, JOHN. "An Analysis of Teacher Performance as a Step in Curriculum Evaluation," *Paper Abstracts* (1967 Annual Meeting of the American Educational Research Association), p. 104.

7. BOND, GUY, and DYKSTRA, ROBERT. *Coordinating Center for First Grade Reading Instruction Programs* (Final Report of Project Instruction Programs, Final Report of Project No. X-001), Office of Education, U.S. Department of Health, Education, and Welfare, 1967.

8. BOTEL, MORTON. *Guide to the Botel Reading Inventory*. Chicago: Follett Publishing Co., 1961.

9. CARROLL, JOHN. "Some Neglected Relationships in Reading and Language Learning," *Elementary English*, Vol. XLIII (1966), p. 577.

10. COULSON, JOHN, and COGSWELL, JOHN. "Effects of Individualized Instruction on Testing," *Journal of Educational Measurement*, Vol. II (1965), pp. 59-64.

11. FAY, LEO. "Formal Materials for Evaluating Growth in Reading Skills,"

Individualizing Instruction in Reading (A Report of the Twentieth Annual Conference and Course on Reading), University of Pittsburgh, 1964, pp. 43-48.

12. GLASER, ROBERT. "The Responsive Environments Project," *Learning R & D Center Publication,* University of Pittsburgh, 1966, pp. 12-13.

13. GLASER, ROBERT. "The Individually Prescribed Instruction Project," *Learning R & D Center Publications,* University of Pittsburgh, 1966, p. 4.

14. HOWE, HAROLD. "Growth and Growing Pains," *Saturday Review,* Dec. 1966, pp. 68-70.

15. JAN-TAUSCH, JAMES. "The Team Approach to In-Service Education," *The Reading Teacher,* Vol. XIX (1966), pp. 418-23.

16. KASDON, LAWRENCE. "In-Service Education in a New Key," *The Reading Teacher,* Vol. XIX (1966), pp. 415-17.

17. KOWITZ, GERALD, and ARMSTRONG, CHARLES. "Patterns of Academic Development," *Journal of Educational Measurement,* Vol. II (1965), pp. 207-12.

18. KRATHWOHL, DAVID, BLOOM, BENJAMIN, and MASIA, BERTRAM. *Taxonomy of Educational Objectives: Handbook II: Affective Domain.* New York: David McKay Co., 1964.

19. LAZER, MAY. "Individualized Reading: A Dynamic Approach," *The Reading Teacher,* Vol. XI (1957), pp. 75-83.

20. NILES, OLIVE. "Systemwide In-Service Programs in Reading," *The Reading Teacher,* Vol. XIX (1966), pp. 426-28.

21. OLSON, WILLARD. "Seeking, Self-Selection, and Pacing in the Use of Books by Children," *The Packet.* Boston: D. C. Heath Co. (Spring 1952), pp. 3-10.

22. PLESSAS, GUY. "Substrata Factor Theory of Reading: Some Questions," *Reading and Inquiry* (Proceedings of the Annual Convention of the International Reading Association), Vol. 10 (1965), pp. 322-24.

23. SCHRAG, PETER. "Education's Romantic Critics," *Saturday Review,* February 1967, p. 81.

24. SINGER, HARRY. "A Developmental Model for Speed of Reading in Grades Three Through Six," *Reading Research Quarterly,* Vol. I (1965), pp. 29-49.

25. SMITH, NILA BANTON. *Reading Instruction for Today's Children.* Englewood Cliffs, N.J.: Prentice Hall, Inc., 1963, pp. 130-33.

26. STRANG, RUTH. "Controversial Programs and Procedures in Reading," *School Review,* Vol. XLIX (1961), pp. 413-28.

27. STRANG, RUTH. *Diagnostic Teaching of Reading.* New York: McGraw-Hill Book Co., 1964.

28. SUPPES, PATRICK. "Plug-In Instruction," *Saturday Review,* July 1966, pp. 25-30.

29. VILSCEK, ELAINE. "Self-Directive, Corrective Materials," *Individualizing Instruction in Reading* (A Report of the Twentieth Annual Conference and Course on Reading), 1964, pp. 77-84.

30. VILSCEK, ELAINE. "Coordinating the Language Arts in the Primary Grades," *Reading and the Related Arts* (A Report of the Twenty-First Annual Conference and Course on Reading), 1965, p. 129.

31. VILSCEK, ELAINE, and CLELAND, DONALD. *A Comparison of the Basal and the Coordinated Language Experience Approaches in the First Grade Reading Instruction* (Cooperative Research Project Report No. 2729), Office of Education, U.S. Department of Health, Education, and Welfare, 1964, pp. 16-18.

32. WOODRING, PAUL. "There'll Be Fewer Little Noises," *Saturday Review,* March 1967, pp. 54-55.

33. WRIGHT, BETTY. *Educating for Diversity.* New York: John Day Co., 1965, p. 29.

Part D.

**Individual Differences: How
Should They Be Measured
and Accommodated**

Introduction

Two perplexing tasks confront the educator who desires to match an individual learner with an appropriate set of learning experiences. First, the student's developed ability levels, current interests, and long range goals must be assessed accurately and efficiently. Second, the characteristics of the learning materials must be known (for instance, their difficulty level determined), especially as these characteristics relate to the learner variables to which they are being matched. Thus a reader who is (measurably) below expected grade level in reading proficiency must have appropriate (known difficulty) materials to read.

The complexity of this multidimensional problem conjures up the specter of infinite combinations of materials being required to meet the great variety of individuals who comprise the learning population. Obviously, generic rather than specific characteristics must be relied on in most instances. It is probable that quantum gains in learning cannot be accomplished by an overattentiveness to minute details in either the description of the materials or in the assessment of individual readiness. This is the case largely because we are still far from knowing just *which* characteristics are the salient ones to employ when prescribing learning experiences for individual youngsters and we have not even reached a really *functional* knowledge of the causal relationships between learner interest and the ability to achieve.

In Chapter 9, Samuel Messick discusses the measurement problem in individual differences and gives special attention to relationships between cognitive style and the learner's affective state.

In Chapter 10, James G. Holland takes issue with some of the present practices, values and assumptions that are employed when instructional methods are "matched" to individual differences. As a starting point, he recommends a complete reexamination of the goals of individualization. He concedes that students' entering behavior will certainly be different; however, he argues that efforts to vary learning experiences in order to accommodate for learner differences typically depends on the appropriateness and completeness of both diagnostic and criterion testing procedures, and these may be open to question. He suggests a new look at *divergent learner goals* to arrive at a basis for differential instruction. In other words, he suggests that alternative learning materials be designed to *enhance* differences rather than *minimize* them.

In Chapter 11, Lee J. Cronbach suggests several approaches by which instructional methods can be adapted to provide for individual differences among learners. He offers no guarantees or promises of early success but is nevertheless hopeful that "the school can be fitted to the individual" in the years ahead. It is quite probable that his suggested approaches will fundamentally influence the direction of research on aptitude-treatment interaction for some time to come.

It is true that most of the research to date does not indicate that learning styles (i.e., aptitudes for learning by different kinds of instructional method) make an important difference in how much or how well something is learned. Nevertheless, research is continuing at the American Institutes for Research, Stanford University, and many other sites. As a result we may learn that certain traits, such as curiosity, could link together behavior patterns in meaningful ways and explain some of the inconsistencies in the learning style research to date.

Chapter 9. MEASUREMENT OF COGNITIVE STYLE AND AFFECTIVE REACTIONS

THE CRITERION PROBLEM IN THE EVALUATION OF INSTRUCTION: ASSESSING POSSIBLE, NOT JUST INTENDED OUTCOMES

Samuel Messick

This paper[1] will discuss two major classes of criterion variables that should be taken into account in the evaluation of instruction—namely, cognitive styles and affective reactions. I emphasize these two types of variables because of the kinds of questions I think should be asked in evaluation studies—questions that stem from particular views about the diversity of human performance and about the role of values in educational research.

SOURCE: Reprinted from M. C. Wittrock and D. Wiley, *The Evaluation of Instruction: Issues and Problems* (New York: Holt, Rinehart & Winston, Inc., 1970), by permission of the author and publisher.

INDIVIDUAL DIFFERENCES IN RESPONSE TO
EDUCATIONAL TREATMENTS

Traditional questions in education and psychology have frequently spawned answers that are either downright wrong, in that they summarize findings "on the average" in situations where a hypothetical "average person" doesn't exist, or else are seriously lacking in generality, in that they fail to take account of the multiplicity of human differences and their interactions with environmental circumstances.

Consider the kind of "horse race" question typical of much educational research of past decades: Is textbook A better than textbook B? Is teacher A better than teacher B? Or, more generally, is treatment A better than treatment B? Such questions are usually resolved empirically by comparing average gains in specific achievement for students receiving treatment A with average gains for students receiving treatment B. But suppose treatment A is better for certain kinds of students and treatment B better for other kinds of students. Depending upon the mix of students in the two groups, the two treatments might exhibit negligible differences on the average when they actually produce wildly different effects upon individuals. A completely different evaluation of the treatments might have resulted if some other questions had been asked, such as "Do these treatments interact with personality and cognitive characteristics of the students or with factors in their educational history or family background to produce differential effects upon achievement? Do certain student characteristics correlate with gains in achievement differently in one treatment than in the other?"

From the vantage point of differential psychology, it would appear that educational researchers frequently fail to take proper account of consistent individual differences. They tend to assess treatment effects on the average, presuming that variations in performance around the average are unstable fluctuations rather than expressions of stable personal characteristics. Developmental psychologists, on the other hand, survey essentially the same arena with their own limited purview. They not only frequently make the same assumption about individual variation but the obverse one about environmental variation as well. They seek to uncover general laws of learning and cognition for the generic human being—at best a small number of different laws for assorted idealized types of individuals—and to map the course of mental development *on the average,* where now the average is taken over all the differential educational experiences and environmental impacts that might interact with current psychological status to moderate change.

To evaluate educational treatments in terms of their effects upon individual students requires not only the assessment of variables directly related to the specific goals of the treatment, such as achievement level, but also the assessment of those personal and environmental variables that may moderate the learning. Similarly, to understand how a cognitive or personality characteristic develops from one time to another, i.e., to formulate the psychology of its development over a fixed period, may require not only information about individual differences in the trait in relation to other traits at the two times, but also information about the educational treatments and environmental variations accompanying the change and perhaps even information about the course of the trait's previous development and about the personal, social, and environmental factors associated with prior growth.

If concerns about personal characteristics and concerns about social and environmental characteristics were systematically combined with concerns about the effects of educational treatments, a conceptual framework for educational and psychological research would result from which questions about interactions among these components would flow naturally—questions such as "What dimensions of educational experience are associated with growth on dimensions of cognitive functioning or with changes in attitude or affective involvement, and what social and environmental factors moderate these effects?" The need for such a multivariate interactional approach derives from the view that we are dealing in education and psychology with a complicated *system* composed of differentiated subsystems and that even in research on presumably circumscribed issues it is important to recognize the interrelatedness of personal, social, environmental, and educational factors. In such a system it is possible that compensating tradeoffs among variables will occur under different conditions to produce similar effects and that particular outcomes will frequently be multiply determined and sometimes overdetermined. This is not to say that overall main effects due to specific educational treatments will not occur or that no personal characteristics will prove to be general over situations, but rather that interactions between treatment variables and personal or environmental factors are likely and should be systematically appraised in evaluating treatment effects.

The major thrust of this approach is that evaluations of the significance of changes in performance or attitude over a given time period as a presumed function of a specific instructional program should take into account other changes in human characteristics also transpiring during the same period and other environmental influences active at the same time. Educational growth should not be viewed as independent of human growth, and the effects of instructional experiences should not be viewed as independent of other life experiences.

These multiple influences upon behavior should not only be considered at the grand level of systems analysis, but at much simpler levels as well—such as in developing and evaluating a measure of academic achievement—where we sometimes forget that even specific responses are frequently complexly determined and buffeted by many environmental influences. Consider a researcher who attempts to assess quantitative reasoning in a lower class, culturally disadvantaged child by inquiring, "If you had seven apples and I asked you for two, how many would you have left?" The answer comes quickly and triumphantly—"Seven!" Hopefully, of course, we would never use such loose phrasing in any of *our* questions, but it serves to illustrate the point. We often fail to appreciate the extent to which the respondent's affect will be engaged by the content of the question and the extent to which personal, social, and economic factors will focus his attention upon problems quite different from the ones we thought we had posed.

When the efficacy of instruction is evaluated in such a multivariate framework, cognitive styles and affective reactions assume particular interest in three ways: (1) as personal characteristics that may interact with treatment variables to moderate learning, retention, and transfer; (2) as dispositions to be monitored to detect any possibly undesirable side effects of instruction; and (3) as qualities to be fostered either directly as specific objectives of the instructional program or indirectly as by-products of other efforts. This latter possibility of fostering stylistic and affective qualities appears to be consonant with general educational aims as far as affects are concerned, for who would dispute the desirability of developing positive attitudes toward school or learning or subject matter or self? But with respect to cognitive styles there is much less consensus, for we are not sure whether to emphasize particular styles or flexibility in the use of multiple styles, nor are we sure what the options are for changing styles. This problem will be discussed in more detail later after we have had an opportunity to consider the nature of cognitive styles and some reasons why individual differences in characteristic modes of cognition are relevant to educational practice.

THE ROLE OF VALUES IN THE SCIENCE OF EDUCATION

To suggest that cognitive styles and affects might serve as additional criteria in the evaluation of instruction is of course to make a value judgment. But value judgments abound in the evaluation process, as its name implies, and appear to be made with hesitancy only at the end of the enterprise when a decision about the worth of the program is required. Value judgments are usually made explicitly when the specific goals of the instructional program are outlined and when particular standards of excellence are accepted for judging success; but they are also made, usually implicitly, when criterion instruments are selected to assess the intended outcomes, when additional criterion measures are chosen to appraise side effects, when particular teaching methods or media or materials are scrutinized during the course of instruction, when certain types of transactions between the student and other persons are observed[2]—in short, whenever a subset of the possible alternatives is marked for special attention. The selection of a subset from the range of possibilities implies priorities, that some things are more important to assess than others. But it is not enough to label such decisions "value judgments" and then proceed with the assessment. If it were, evaluation would be a straightforward affair indeed: We could specify the goals of the instructional program as we intend them and select criterion measures to assess those outcomes that seem directly relevant to the stated objectives. This is what Scriven has called "estimation of goal achievement" in contradistinction to evaluation proper. All appraisal in this case is relative to the stated goals, and the concern is with how well the program achieves its intended objectives. In addition, however, we should inquire to what extent the objectives are worth achieving and, in general, should endeavor to include in the evaluation process provisions for evaluating the value judgments, especially the goals.[3]

An important step in this direction is to exhibit concern about *possible* outcomes and not just *intended* outcomes. Evaluation comprises two major functions—one is to ascertain the nature and size of the effects of the treatment and the other is to decide whether the observed effects attain acceptable standards of excellence. These two components have been termed "description" and "judgment" by Stake.[4] The point here is that the descriptive phase of evaluation should be as complete as our art and resources can make it. In this instance the evaluation specialist should be, in Bruner's words, a "diviner and delineator of the possible"—he should "provide the full range of alternatives to challenge society to choice."[5] This attempt to describe the full range of possible effects of instruction is an important prerequisite for the judgmental phase of evaluation, since it might unearth alternatives that ought to be weighed in reaching the final appraisal. As Henry Dyer has emphasized, "Evaluating the *side* effects of an educational program may be even more important than evaluating its intended effects." Dyer also pointed out that such broad assessment of the possible effects of an educational program should contribute to an evaluation of the goals of the program. Inverting the customary prescription that one must determine the objectives of instruction before one can develop measures of instructional outcomes, Dyer suggested that it may not be possible to decide what the objectives ought to be until one has first measured the outcomes.[6]

In practice, of course, evaluation studies rarely approach completeness. We in fact include in any feasible assessment program only a selection of criterion variables—those that reflect our current view of priorities (or our attempt to represent several diverse viewpoints). But again it is not enough just to admit that practical considerations force us to be selective. If we are to develop a science of evaluation, we should endeavor to justify these value judgments on rational grounds not only in terms of the specific objectives of the instructional program in question but in terms of goals of education in American society that transcend the particular course.[7] In this exercise it is important not only to explicate the separate value judgments implicit in the choice of each criterion variable, but also to consider interrelations among them. Values rarely exist in isolation. They are typically part of organized frameworks called ideologies that provide characteristic ways of thinking about man and society. In considering the assortment of variables to be assessed in a particular evaluation study and the goals that the instruction might potentially serve, we should inquire to what extent do the possible outcomes reflect divergent value systems that "need to be reconciled or compromised and to what extent do they represent simply different frames of reference for compatible goals."[8]

Incidentally, the particular teaching methods chosen for use in an instructional program should also be evaluated for their compatibility with multiple goals and values. It sometimes happens that even though two goals are reasonably compatible, the method of instruction selected tends to foster one aim and hinder the other. Wallach, for example, has expressed concern that modern methods of teaching, especially those using programmed materials and teaching machines, so emphasize accuracy of responding that the student is likely to acquire a generalized intolerance of error, with a consequent decline in his originality of thinking. Some other method or combination of methods might be used instead that would develop facility in the analysis of logical implications, as desired, but would not at the same time diminish fluency in the generation of conceptual possibilities.[9]

Since educational values derive from broader systems of social values, it is appropriate to evaluate goals and criteria for instruction not only in terms of specific educational implications but also in terms of more general social implications. The suggestion in the present instance that cognitive styles and affective reactions be used as criterion variables in the evaluation of instruction, for example, should be upheld in precisely such terms, but a consideration of the educational and social implications of these dimensions must await a more detailed discussion of the nature of the variables themselves.

COGNITION, AFFECT, AND PERSONALITY

In recent years several dimensions of individual differences in the performance of cognitive tasks have been isolated that appear to reflect consistencies in the manner or form of cognition, as distinct from the content of cognition or the level of skill displayed in the cognitive performance.[10] These dimensions have been conceptualized as *cognitive styles,* which represent a person's typical modes of perceiving, remembering, thinking, and problem solving. Some examples of these dimensions are:

1. *Field Independence versus Field Dependence.* "An analytical, in

contrast to a global, way of perceiving (which) entails a tendency to experience items as discrete from their backgrounds and reflects ability to
overcome the influence of an embedding context." [11]

2. *Scanning.* A dimension of individual differences in the extensive-
ness and intensity of attention deployment, leading to individual variations in the vividness of experience and the span of awareness.[12]

3. *Breadth of Categorizing.* Consistent preferences for broad inclu-
siveness, as opposed to narrow exclusiveness, in establishing the acceptable
range for specified categories.[13]

4. *Conceptualizing Styles.* Individual differences in the tendency to
categorize perceived similarities and differences among stimuli in terms of
many differentiated concepts, which is a dimension called *conceptual differentiation*,[14] as well as consistencies in the utilization of particular conceptualizing approaches as bases for forming concepts (such as the routine
use in concept formation of thematic or functional relations among stimuli as opposed to the analysis of descriptive attributes or the inference of
class membership).[15]

5. *Cognitive Complexity versus Simplicity.* Individual differences in
the tendency to construe the world, and particularly the world of social
behavior, in a multidimensional and discriminating way.[16]

6. *Reflectiveness versus Impulsivity.* Individual consistencies in the
speed with which hypotheses are selected and information processed, with
impulsive subjects tending to offer the first answer that occurs to them,
even though it is frequently incorrect, and reflective subjects tending to
ponder various possibilities before deciding.[17]

7. *Leveling versus Sharpening.* Reliable individual variations in assimilation in memory. Subjects at the leveling extreme tend to blur similar
memories and to merge perceived objects or events with similar but not
identical events recalled from previous experience. Sharpeners, at the
other extreme, are less prone to confuse similar objects and, by contrast,
may even judge the present to be less similar to the past than is actually
the case.[18]

8. *Constricted versus Flexible Control.* Individual differences in susceptibility to distraction and cognitive interference.[19]

9. *Tolerance for Incongruous or Unrealistic Experiences.* A dimension
of differential willingness to accept perceptions at variance with conventional experience.[20]

Stylistic consistencies have also been observed in the differential tendencies of individuals to err by omission or by commission on memory
tasks.[21] In addition, several dimensions deriving from the work of
Thurstone, Cattell, and Guilford, although usually considered to fall

within the purview of intellectual abilities, also reflect such potential exemplars of style or mode of cognition as speed, flexibility, divergence, convergence, and fluency.

Cognitive styles, for the most part, are information-processing habits. They are characteristic modes of operation which, although not necessarily completely independent of content, tend to function across a variety of content areas. Before considering some possible implications of cognitive styles for educational practice, let me discuss one of them in more detail to give you some feeling for their generality and breadth of operation. For these purposes, the dimension of analytic vs. global attitude offers the best example, since it has been extensively studied in various forms for over twenty years, primarily by H. A. Witkin and his colleagues but also in other laboratories around the globe.

Witkin's early work emphasized individual differences in the characteristic ways in which people perceive both the world and themselves. One of the test situations used was a tilted room in which the subject, seated in a tilted chair, must adjust his body to the true upright. Reliable individual differences were found in the ability to do this; i.e., some individuals were reliably more susceptible than others to the influence of the surrounding tilted room. In another test, the subject was seated in a completely dark room and confronted with a luminous rod surrounded by a luminous picture frame; his task was to set the rod to the true vertical position while the frame was set aslant. Again, reliable individual differences were found in the ability to do this, and a substantial correlation was noted between the two tests: the subject who had difficulty withstanding the influence of the surrounding room while adjusting his body to the upright also had difficulty withstanding the influence of the surrounding frame while adjusting the rod to the upright. These individual differences were initially conceptualized in terms of a differential reliance upon visual cues obtained from the external field as opposed to kinesthetic cues obtained from the subject's own body.

This interpretation of field vs. body orientation was extended to a more general dimension of perceptual analysis, however, when it was found that subjects who had difficulty overcoming the influence of the tilted room and the tilted frame also had difficulty overcoming the influence of superimposed complex designs when asked to find hidden simple forms in an embedded-figures test. This extended conception of the dimension was now termed "field dependence vs. field independence": the perception of relatively field-dependent subjects is dominated by the overall organization of the field, whereas relatively field-independent subjects readily perceive elements as discrete from their backgrounds. Sex differences have been repeatedly obtained on the measures of this dimension, with females being relatively more field dependent and males relatively more field independent.[22]

Since many correlates for these perceptual scores have been subsequently uncovered in several areas of intellectual and personality functioning, field-independence vs. field dependence is now viewed as the perceptual component of a broader dimension of *articulated vs. global cognitive style*. For example, when the possible relation of field independence to intelligence was investigated, substantial correlations were obtained with some subtests of the Wechsler intelligence scales but not with others. The subtests of the Wechsler scales cluster into three major factors—a verbal dimension composed of the Vocabulary, Information, and Comprehension subtests; an attention-concentration dimension composed of the Digit Span, Arithmetic, and Coding subtests; and an analytic dimension, composed of the Block Design, Object Assembly, and Picture Completion subtests. The measures of field independence were found to correlate substantially with the dimension of analytic intelligence but not with the other two. Thus field-independent subjects exhibited a marked advantage on analytical intelligence tasks, but they could not be characterized as being superior in verbal intelligence or, in a meaningful way, as being superior in general intelligence.[23]

Children with a relatively articulated mode of cognitive functioning have also been found to have relatively articulated body concepts, as inferred from figure drawings; i.e., when asked to draw human figures, these children display more realistic body proportions, more details, and more sex and role characteristics than children with a relatively global mode of functioning. Global subjects also tend to lack a developed sense of separate identity, as reflected in their relative reliance upon others for guidance and support, the relative instability of their self-view, their suggestibility, and their susceptibility to social influence in forming and maintaining attitudes and judgments.[24]

Developmental studies have indicated that mode of cognitive functioning becomes progressively more articulated, and perception more field independent, with age up to late adolescence. At the same time, however, a child's relative level of articulation vis-à-vis his peers is quite stable. From age 10 to 14, the test-retest reliability of the perceptual index score of field independence was .64 for a group of 30 boys and .88 for a group of 30 girls, and from age 14 to 17 it was .87 for the boys and .94 for the girls.[25]

In an effort to uncover the possible origins of this cognitive style, Witkin and his colleagues studied patterns of maternal child-rearing practices and mother-child relations. On the basis of interview data, the mothers were classified into two groups: those who fostered the child's differentiation from herself and who helped him develop a sense of separate identity, and those who did not. In general, this classification of the mothers was found to be significantly related to the performance scores of the children, with the children of the mothers judged to have fostered differentiation being more field independent and cognitively articulated.[26]

Differences have been noted in the type of defense mechanisms likely to be adopted by subjects at the two extremes of articulated and global cognitive style when confronted by conflict and stress. Articulated subjects are more likely to utilize specialized defenses, such as intellectualization and isolation, and global subjects are more likely to utilize primitive defenses, such as denial and repression. No general relation has been found, however, between the degree of articulation of the cognitive style and the degree of personal adjustment or psychopathology. Rather, as with the defenses, when psychological disturbances occur, there are differences in the kinds of pathology that are likely to develop at the two extremes of the style. Psychopathology in articulated persons is more likely to involve problems of overcontrol, overideation, and isolation; in severe pathological states, delusions are more likely to develop. Pathology in global persons, on the other hand, is more likely to involve problems of dependence, with symptoms such as alcoholism, obesity, ulcers, and asthma; in severe states hallucinations are more likely to develop.[27] Such findings highlight the fact that styles of intellectual and perceptual functioning are part of the total personality and are intimately interwoven with affective, temperamental, and motivational structures. In some cases for example, "The general style of thinking may be considered a matrix . . . that determines the *shape* or *form* of symptom, defense mechanism, and adaptive trait." [28] In other cases the form-determining matrix may not be a mode of cognition but perhaps a type of temperament or character structure or neurosis—the cognitive style would then be more derivative and would reflect but one component of a broader personality structure that permeates several areas of psychological functioning.

Although in most of this discussion one probably gets the impression that articulated, field-independent subjects have the advantage over their field-dependent peers, situations do exist where a more dependent reliance upon the external field, and particularly a reliance upon social stimuli for guidance and support, pays off in the accrual of incidental information. Field-dependent subjects have been found to be significantly better than field-independent subjects, for example, in their memory for faces and social words, even though their incidental memory for nonsocial stimuli is not generally superior.[29] The fact that certain types of problem situations and certain types of subject matter favor field-dependent subjects over field-independent subjects and vice versa (just as other types of problems might favor broad categorizers over narrow categorizers or levelers over sharpeners, and vice versa) is extremely important, since it highlights the relativity of value of the opposing extremes of each cognitive style. Unlike conventional ability dimensions, one end of these stylistic dimensions is not uniformly more adaptive than the other.

The perceptual and intellectual consistencies just discussed have been interpreted in stylistic terms, which implies, for example, that an individual spontaneously and habitually applies his particular degree of analytic or articulated field approach to a wide variety of situations. Even though a relatively global individual may appear typically global in most situations, however, when confronted with a situation that patently demands analysis, it is conceivable that he might be able to analyze with acceptable skill. Yet in the measurement of this cognitive style, it is usually presumed that subjects who characteristically display an analytic approach will in fact perform better on tasks requiring analysis (such as finding a simple figure in a complicated one) than will subjects who characteristically display a more global approach. Accordingly, most measures of analytic attitude are cast in an ability or maximum performance framework: if a subject does well at the task, he is assumed to have performed analytically and if he does poorly, he is assumed to have performed more globally (or to be inadequately applying an unfamiliar, atypical analytic approach). In order to buttress the stylistic interpretation, it would be of interest to relate such maximum performance scores to measures of the spontaneous tendency to articulate the field in a task that ostensibly does not demand analysis.

In one attempt to develop such a task, subjects were required to learn to identify by name (a nonsense syllable) ten complex visual designs, each consisting of a large dominant figure, composed of elements, against a patterned background. In learning to identify these designs, the subject does not have to articulate the component parts, although the instructions do encourage analysis. The subjects are then told that each design was a member of a family of similar designs and that the names they had learned were family names. They are now presented with variations of the original designs (such as the element alone, the form alone, and the form composed of different elements) and asked to identify them in terms of the appropriate family name. In this strategy of test design, it was assumed that subjects who spontaneously articulated the designs during the learning process would be able to identify more variations than subjects who learned to identify the designs in a more global fashion. The total number of variations correctly identified, however, did not turn out to correlate significantly with the embedded-figures test. But this was because individuals differed consistently not only in the degree to which they articulated the original designs but in the type of figural component articulated, and the articulation of only one of these components was associated with embedded-figures performance. A factor analysis of variation scores uncovered two major dimensions representing two distinct modes of stimulus analysis, one emphasizing the articulation of discrete elements and the other of figural forms. A third mode reflecting the utilization of background information was substantially correlated with the other two. A significant relation was obtained between embedded-figures performance and the element articulation factor but not the form articulation factor.

Although on the one hand element and form articulation are distinct dimensions of stimulus analysis and exhibit different personality correlates, on the other hand they are significantly correlated with each other and combine, along with the background information factor, to form a second-order dimension.[30]

These findings underscore the fact that the generality of the articulated vs. global cognitive style appears at a higher-order level in the factor-analytic sense. Another illustration of this point occurs in a study that attempted to extend Thurstone's perceptual closure factors into the verbal and semantic domains. Thurstone's factor of flexibility of perceptual closure, which is measured by tests like embedded figures, deals with the ability to break one closure in order to perceive a different one and thereby depends upon the capacity to analyze a highly organized perceptual field. Thurstone's factor of speed of perceptual closure deals with the ability to assemble discrete parts into an integrated, meaningful whole and thereby reflects the capacity to structure a relatively unorganized perceptual field.[31] The concept of an articulated mode of perception implies facility in both analysis and structuring,[32] thereby requiring that the two closure factors be correlated, which usually tends to be the case. When several experimental closure tests were constructed using single words and meaningful discourse at the stimulus fields, factors were also uncovered for both speed and flexibility of verbal closure and for both speed and flexibility of semantic closure, in addition to the two perceptual closure factors. The concept of a general articulated vs. global cognitive style requires that all of these closure factors be mutually intercorrelated, which also tends to be the case, although the level of correlation is certainly not uniform. Indeed, some limitation on the generality of the style appeared in a second-order factor analysis, which revealed two relatively independent articulation dimensions, one involving the analysis and structuring of figural materials and the other the analysis and structuring of symbolic materials. In addition, a separate second-order factor of general analytical reasoning was also obtained.[33]

Studies of other cognitive styles, particularly scanning and breadth of categorizing, have revealed a similar range of involvement in areas of personality and psychopathology. Silverman, for example, found that paranoid schizophrenics exhibited significantly more extensive scanning behavior and utilized significantly narrower categories than nonparanoid schizophrenics.[34] Gardner and Long reported that extreme scanning was marginally related to ratings of isolation, projection, and generalized delay on the Rorschach.[35] This latter finding that scanning behavior tends to be associated with two different defense mechanisms suggests the possibility that extensive scanning may serve different purposes under different circumstances or, perhaps, that there may be two distinct types of scanning. The association with isolation, which is a preferred defense mechanism of obsessives, suggests that the scanning may occur in the service of information seeking, as reflected in the obsessive's concern with exactness to offset doubt and uncertainty. The association with projection, which is a preferred defense mechanism of paranoids, suggests that the scanning may occur in the service of signal detection, particularly danger-signal detection, as reflected in the paranoid's concern with accuracy to offset suspicion and distrust. Some current research now in progress at Educational Testing Service attempts to differentiate empirically between these two possible types of scanning. This is being done using perceptual search tasks in which the subject is required to locate stimuli (signals) embedded in meaningfully organized visual fields, e.g., to locate faces camouflaged in pictorial scenes or four-letter words embedded in sentences. Upon completion of the search task, the stimulus materials are removed, and the subject is then asked specific questions about the content of the scenes or the meaning of the set of sentences. Subjects who incidentally take in information about the field in the process of scanning can thus be differentiated from those whose concern is apparently limited to detecting the signals.

With this brief characterization of cognitive styles in mind, let us now consider some of their possible implications for educational practice and evaluation. To begin with, cognitive styles, by embracing both perceptual and intellectual domains and by their frequent implication in personality and social functioning, promise to provide a more complete and effective characterization of the student than could be obtained from intellectual tests alone. These stylistic dimensions offer us new types of process variables to appraise that extend the assessment of mental performance beyond the crystallized notion of achievement levels to a concern with patterns of cognitive functioning. These stylistic characteristics should have relevance, although direct research evidence is admittedly very scanty, not only for the course of individual learning in various subject matter areas, but also for the nature of teacher-pupil interactions and of social behavior in the classroom.

Thus, cognitive styles, by virtue of their widespread operation, appear to be particularly important dimensions to assess in the evaluation of instruction. Yet, the very pervasiveness that underscores their importance at the same time interferes with the measurement of other important personal characteristics, such as dimensions of specific aptitude. This is because cognitive styles operate in testing situations as well and frequently interact with test formats and test conditions to influence the examinee's score. Consider, for example, the possibility that the five-alternative multiple-choice form of quantitative aptitude tests may favor subjects who prefer broad categories on category-width measures. Quick, rough approximations to the quantitative items might appropriately be judged by these subjects to be "close enough" to a given alternative, whereas "narrow range" subjects may require more time-consuming exact solutions before answering. Significant correlations between category preferences and quantitative aptitude tests have indeed been found, but the level of the correlation turns out to vary widely as a function of the spacing of alternatives on multiple-choice forms of the quantitative items. Scores for breadth of categorizing were found to be substantially correlated with quantitative aptitude scores derived from a multiple-choice form having widely-spaced alternatives, marginally correlated with scores on a free-response quantitative test, and negligibly correlated with scores derived from a narrowly-spaced form. This suggests that wide spacing of alternatives enhances and narrow spacing disrupts the "approximation" strategy that broad categorizers tend to employ on multiple-choice quantitative tests.[36] Such findings suggest that we should consider the "fairness" of our aptitude and achievement tests not only for different cultures and different sexes, but for individuals having different stylistic propensities. Thus, it is quite possible that cognitive styles are already being reflected in standard evaluation devices, but their operation under these circumstances is not being assessed for evaluation purposes but serves to contaminate the interpretation of other measures.

Information about cognitive styles offers several possibilities for instructional practice, but choices among them depend upon the results of much needed empirical research. For example, as soon as we are able to assess the cognitive styles of students, we have the possibility of placing them in classrooms in specified ways, perhaps in homogeneous groupings or perhaps in particular mixes or combinations. At this point it is by no means clear which particular placements will foster learning for individuals, just as it is by no means clear that homogeneous ability grouping is uniformly beneficial. Similarly, if we can assess the cognitive styles of students, we could also assess the cognitive styles of teachers and consider the possibility of assigning teachers to students to obtain particular combinations of styles that would optimally foster learning. We could also consider selecting particular teaching methods that would be especially appropriate for certain cognitive styles and certain subject matters. As yet, of course, there is very little research to guide us on these points. But in even considering the possibility of matching the student to the teacher or the teaching method and remembering that with our present assignment procedures some students are in effect so matched while others are not, we should ponder what the criterion of success in this enterprise should be. Should it be the maximal learning of content skills and information?

Consider as a possibility that, in the sciences at least, students with an articulated field approach, and perhaps reflective students as well, might learn better with an inductive or "discovery" method of teaching, since it would probably capitalize upon their propensities for analysis and careful consideration of alternatives. More global and more impulsive students, on the other hand, might learn content information better with a directed method of teaching in which rules and principles are specified rather than induced. Consider the likelihood, however, that in our efforts to optimize the learning of subject matter we may so solidify the global child's cognitive style that he may never learn to discover anything in this entire school career. This possibility suggests that teaching to produce maximal learning of subject matter is not enough. We should also be concerned with the student's manner of thinking. One possibility here is that we should attempt to foster alternative modes of cognition and multiple stylistic approaches to problem solving.

Such a goal will not be easily attained, however, since there are many cognitive and personality dimensions that could interact with properties of teaching methods to produce negligible or adverse results. It makes a difference, for example, when and to whom and to what subject matter an inferential discovery method of teaching is applied. Kagan warns us, as an instance, that "Impulsive children are apt to settle on the wrong conclusion in the inferential method and become vulnerable to developing feelings of inadequacy. . . . Since these impulsively derived hypotheses are apt to be incorrect, the impulsive child encounters a series of humiliating failures and eventually withdraws involvement from school tasks." [37]

The success of attempts to develop multiple modes of cognition in the individual will depend to a large extent upon the degree to which cognitive styles are malleable. Cognitive styles, as usually conceived, are habits that are spontaneously applied without conscious choice in a wide variety of situations. The possibility being considered here is that through manipulation of educational experience we might convert cognitive *styles* into cognitive *strategies,* by which I mean to imply a conscious choice among alternative modes of perceiving, remembering, thinking, and problem solving as a function of the conditions of particular situations. If the cognitive styles are relatively mutable, such efforts at change and multiple development might be feasible at all levels of the educational sequence. If the cognitive styles, or at least some of them, are relatively immutable, it may be necessary to focus attention on the early years and attempt to foster multiple modes of cognition before particular styles crystallize and become predominant. This latter possibility of predominant cognitive styles may be inevitable, regardless of our educational efforts, but we might at least be able to increase somewhat the power of alternative cognitive modes in the hierarchy, thereby reducing to some extent the preemptiveness of habitual thought. As always, however, we must also consider and evaluate the potential dangers in such an enterprise: our efforts to foster multiple modes of cognition in a child may prevent him from soaring in the unfettered application of his preferred style in a particular field.

I have not discussed affective variables at length because most educators, at least when pressed, affirm the importance of enhancing curiosity and of implanting in the student massive and enduring positive affects toward learning and subject matter. Most of us would agree, therefore, that even when an instructional program does not attempt to enhance positive attitudes directly, these variables should still be monitored if possible in the evaluation of the program to guard against unintended decreases in interest or involvement. In the measurement of these affective reactions, however, it seems to me unfortunate that evaluation studies rely so heavily upon the engineering model, which relates inputs and outputs, for there is a marked tendency to assess student achievement and attitudes only at the beginning and the end of the course. As Scriven has emphasized, the medical model is the appropriate paradigm for educational research,[38] and one derivative from that model should be an explicit attempt in evaluating a program to take account of the student's attitudes and feelings about the course of the treatment and not just the end result.

I wish to close by underscoring the importance of affect for learning and hence the importance of assessing affect in the evaluation of instruction. This point has been elegantly summarized by John Barth in his novel, *The Sot-Weed Factor:*

> ... of the three usual motives for learning things—necessity, ambition, and curiosity—simple curiosity was the worthiest of development, it being the "purest" (in that the value of what it drives us to learn is terminal rather than instrumental), the most conducive to exhaustive and continuing rather than cursory or limited study, and the likeliest to render pleasant the labor of learning. ... this sport of teaching and learning should never become associated with certain hours or particular places, lest student and teacher alike ... fall into the vulgar habit of turning off their alertness, as it were, except at those times and in those places, and thus make by implication a pernicious distinction between learning and other sorts of natural human behavior.[39]

NOTES

[1] This paper was originally presented at the Symposium on Problems in the Evaluation of Instruction, Research and Development Center for the Study of Evaluation, University of California at Los Angeles, December 1967.

[2] R. E. Stake, "The Countenance of Educational Evaluation," *Teachers College Record,* Vol. 68 (1967), pp. 523-40.

[3] M. Scriven, "The Methodology of Evaluation," *American Educational Research Association Monograph Series on Curriculum Evaluation,* No. 1.

[4] Stake, *op. cit.*

[5] J. S. Bruner, *Toward a Theory of Instruction*. Cambridge, Mass.: Harvard University Press, 1966.

[6] H. S. Dyer, "The Discovery and Development of Educational Goals," *Proceedings of the 1966 Invitational Conference on Testing Problems* (Princeton, N.J.: Educational Testing Service, 1967), pp. 12-24.

[7] Scriven, *op. cit.*

[8] *Proposal for a Research and Development Center for Measurement and Evaluation in Education* (Princeton, N.J.: Educational Testing Service, 1965).

[9] M. A. Wallach, "Creativity and the Expression of Possibilities," in J. Kagan (ed.), *Creativity and Learning* (Boston: Houghton Mifflin Co., 1967), pp. 36-57.

[10] L. L. Thurstone, "A Factorial Study of Perception," *Psychometric Monograph No. 4* (Chicago: University of Chicago Press, 1944); H. A. Witkin, H. B. Lewis, M. Hertzman, K. Machover, P. B. Meissner, and S. Wapner, *Personality through Perception* (New York: Harper Bros., 1954); H. A. Witkin, R. B. Dyk, H. F. Faterson, D. R. Goodenough, and S. A. Karp, *Psychological Differentiation* (New York: John Wiley & Sons, Inc., 1962); R. W. Gardner, P. S. Holzman, G. S. Klein, H. B. Linton, and D. Spence, "Cognitive Control: A Study of Individual Consistencies in Cognitive Behavior," *Psychological Issues,* Vol. 1 (1959), Monograph 4; R. W. Gardner, D. N. Jackson, and S. Messick, "Personality Organization in Cognitive Controls and Intellectual Abilities," *Psychological Issues,* Vol. 2 (1960), Monograph 8.

[11] H. A. Witkin *et al., op. cit.*

[12] P. S. Holzman, "Scanning: A Principle of Reality Contact," *Perceptual and Motor Skills,* Vol. 23 (1966), pp. 835-44; H. J. Schlesinger, "Cognitive Attitudes in Relation to Susceptibility to Interference," *Journal of Personality,* Vol. 22 (1954), pp. 354-74; R. W. Gardner and R. I. Long, "Control, Defense, and Centration Effect: A Study of Scanning Behavior," *British Journal of Psychology,* Vol. 53 (1962), pp. 129-40.

[13] T. F. Pettigrew, "The Measurement and Correlates of Category Width as a Cognitive Variable," *Journal of Personality,* Vol. 26 (1958), pp. 532-44; J. S. Bruner and H. Tajfel, "Cognitive Risk and Environmental Change," *Journal of Abnormal and Social Psychology,* Vol. 62 (1961), pp. 231-41; N. Kogan and M. A. Wallach, *Risk Taking* (New York: Holt, Rinehart & Winston, Inc., 1964).

[14] R. W. Gardner and R. A. Schoen, "Differentiation and Abstraction in Concept Formation," *Psychological Monographs,* Vol. 76, No. 41 (1962); S. Messick and N. Kogan, "Differentiation and Compartmentalization in Object-sorting Measures of Categorizing Style," *Perceptual and Motor Skills,* Vol. 16 (1963), pp. 47-51.

[15] J. Kagan, H. A. Moss, and I. E. Sigel, "Conceptual Style and the Use of Affect Labels," *Merrill-Palmer Quarterly,* Vol. 6 (1960), pp. 261-78; J. Kagan, H. A. Moss, and I. E. Sigel, "Psychological Significance of Styles of Conceptualization," in J. C. Wright and J. Kagan (eds.), "Basic Cognitive Processes in

Children," *Monographs of the Society for Research in Child Development,* Vol. 28, No. 2 (1963), pp. 73-112.

[16] G. A. Kelly, *The Psychology of Personal Constructs,* Vol. 1 (New York: W. W. Norton & Co., Inc., 1955); J. Bieri, "Complexity-Simplicity as a Personality Variable in Cognitive and Preferential Behavior," in D. W. Fiske and S. R. Maddi (eds.), *Functions of Varied Experience* (Homewood, Ill.: The Dorsey Press, 1961); J. Bieri, A. L. Atkins, B. Scott, R. L. Leaman, H. Miller, and T. Tripodi, *Clinical and Social Judgment: The Discrimination of Behavioral Information* (New York: John Wiley & Sons, Inc., 1966); W. A. Scott, "Conceptualizing and Measuring Structural Properties of Cognition," in O. J. Harvey (ed.), *Motivation and Social Interaction* (New York: The Ronald Press Co., 1963). See also the closely related work on abstractness-concreteness of conceptual systems: O. J. Harvey, D. E. Hunt, and H. M. Schroder, *Conceptual Systems and Personality Organization* (New York: John Wiley & Sons, Inc., 1961).

[17] J. Kagan, B. L. Rosman, D. Day, J. Albert, and W. Phillips, "Information Processing in the Child: Significance of Analytic and Reflective Attitudes," *Psychological Monographs,* Vol. 78 (Whole No. 58) (1964); J. Kagan, "Reflection-Impulsivity and Reading Ability in Primary Grade Children," *Child Development,* Vol. 36 (1965), pp. 609-28.

[18] P. S. Holzman, "The Relation of Assimilation Tendencies in Visual, Auditory, and Kinesthetic Time-Error to Cognitive Attitudes of Leveling and Sharpening," *Journal of Personality,* Vol. 22 (1954), pp. 375-94; P. S. Holzman and G. S. Klein, "Cognitive System-Principles of Leveling and Sharpening: Individual Differences in Assimilation Effects in Visual Time-Error," *Journal of Psychology,* Vol. 37 (1954), pp. 105-22; R. W. Gardner, *et al., op. cit.,* 1959.

[19] G. S. Klein, "Need and Regulation," in M. R. Jones (ed.), *Nebraska Symposium on Motivation* (Lincoln: University of Nebraska Press, 1954), pp. 225-74; R. W. Gardner, *et al., op. cit.,* 1959.

[20] G. S. Klein, R. W. Gardner, and H. J. Schlesinger, "Tolerance for Unrealistic Experiences: A Study of the Generality of a Cognitive Control," *British Journal of Psychology,* Vol. 53 (1962), pp. 41-55.

[21] V. McKenna, *Stylistic Factors in Learning and Retention* (Princeton, N.J.: Educational Testing Service, Research Bulletin 68-28, 1968).

[22] H. A. Witkin *et al., op. cit.,* 1954.

[23] D. R. Goodenough and S. A. Karp, "Field Dependence and Intellectual Functioning," *Journal of Abnormal and Social Psychology,* Vol. 63 (1961), pp. 241-46; H. A. Witkin, *et al., op. cit.,* 1962.

[24] H. A. Witkin *et al., op. cit.,* 1962; H. B. Linton and E. Graham, "Personality Correlates of Persuasibility," in I. L. Janis *et al., Personality and Persuasibility* (New Haven, Conn.: Yale University Press, 1959).

[25] H. A. Witkin *et al., op. cit.,* 1962; H. A. Witkin, D. R. Goodenough, and S. A. Karp, "Stability of Cognitive Style from Childhood to Young Adulthood," *Journal of Personality and Social Psychology,* Vol. 7 (1967), pp. 291-300.

[26] R. B. Dyk and H. A. Witkin, "Family Experience Related to the Development of Differentiation in Children," *Child Development,* Vol. 36 (1965), pp. 21-55.

[27] H. A. Witkin, "Psychological Differentiation and Forms of Pathology," *Journal of Abnormal Psychology,* Vol. 70 (1965), pp. 317-36.

[28] D. Shapiro, *Neurotic Styles* (New York: Basic Books, Inc., Publishers, 1965).

[29] S. Messick and F. Damarin, "Cognitive Styles and Memory for Faces," *Journal of Abnormal and Social Psychology,* Vol. 69 (1964), pp. 313-18; D. Fitzgibbons, L. Goldberger, and M. Eagle, "Field Dependence and Memory for Incidental Material," *Perceptual and Motor Skills,* Vol. 21 (1965), pp. 743-49.

[30] S. Messick and F. J. Fritzky, "Dimensions of Analytic Attitude in Cognition and Personality," *Journal of Personality,* Vol. 31 (1963), pp. 346-70; S. Messick, *Cognitive Interference and Flexible Control* (Princeton, N.J.: Educational Testing Service Research Bulletin, in preparation).

[31] L. L. Thurstone, *op. cit.,* 1944.

[32] R. B. Dyk and H. A. Witkin, *op. cit.,* 1965.

[33] S. Messick and J. W. French, "Dimensions of Closure in Cognition and Personality," Paper delivered at the American Psychological Association meetings, Washington, D.C., 1967.

[34] J. Silverman, "Scanning-Control Mechanism and 'Cognitive Filtering' in Paranoid and Nonparanoid Schizophrenia," *Journal of Consulting Psychology,* Vol. 28 (1964), pp. 385-93.

[35] R. W. Gardner and R. I. Long, *op. cit.,* 1962.

[36] S. Messick and N. Kogan, "Category Width and Quantitative Aptitude," *Perceptual and Motor Skills,* Vol. 20 (1965), pp. 493-97.

[37] J. Kagan, "Personality and the Learning Process," in J. Kagan (ed.), *Creativity and Learning* (Boston: Houghton Mifflin Co., 1967), pp. 153-63; J. Kagan, L. Pearson, and L. Welch, "Conceptual Impulsivity and Inductive Reasoning," *Child Development,* Vol. 37 (1966), pp. 583-94.

[38] M. Scriven, "Student Values as Educational Objectives," *Proceedings of the 1965 Invitational Conference on Testing Problems* (Princeton, N.J.: Educational Testing Service, 1966), pp. 33-49.

[39] J. Barth, *The Sot-Weed Factor* (New York: Grosset & Dunlap, Inc., 1964), p. 17.

Chapter 10. EMPHASIZING DIFFERENCES AND GOAL RELEVANCE

THE MISPLACED ADAPTATION TO INDIVIDUAL DIFFERENCES

James G. Holland

Today there is a great deal of interest in an educational technology which stresses adaptation to individual differences. It is feared that programming and the increased processing of masses in the name of education will obliterate all divergence and individuality by making the student a mere replica of the *standard* student defined in *our* behavorial objectives. Emphasis on systems, such as Individually Prescribed Instruction or Computer Assisted Instruction, that adapt to differences is often taken as an answer to this problem. I suggest that it is *not* an answer. The fear of deadly uniformity is as great with so-called individualized instruction as without it. To adjust to individual differences in most IPI and CAI systems, continual small modifications of teaching-sequence are made as the result of repeated measures of individual differences. And, although this

SOURCE: Presented as a part of a symposium at the 1969 convention of the American Psychological Association. Reprinted by permission of the author.

procedure is taken as "obviously" worthy, I suggest on the one hand, that there are little compelling data to support its "obvious" merit and on the other, that no one, as yet, has resolved a basic dilemma between the cost in efficiency (in terms of time and effort) and the *demands* of test theory for validity and reliability of tests.

First consider the question of cost efficiency versus reliability of testing. While the rationale for the design of teaching and testing items in IPI and CAI is not often clearly stated and perhaps not universally agreed upon, it seems that generally the rationale for teaching sequences draws directly on that of programmed instruction. For example, Suppes (1966) acknowledges that teaching material in CAI is based on the rationale of programmed instruction. To be sure, many programmers are very lax in program design and rely on testing to keep those individuals, whom we may consider to be failures of the program, working on additional material until mastery. Generally there is agreement that the teaching elements are supposed to follow good programming principles. Ideally the experiences given individually are arranged in a gradual progression. In the case of individualization, the effort is to uniquely tailor the particular progression to the individual to accommodate to his learning rate or his past experience. Individual teaching items, when functioning as teaching items, are expected to require appropriate behavior before the student reaches a correct answer; thus a low black-out ratio (Holland, 1967) is required. And, if functioning as teaching items, they must be able to elicit the behavior to be learned; thus they must have a low error rate. The teaching item does not trap the student into errors or diagnose his difficulties, rather it evokes the desired behavior so that it may be reinforced and established. But individualization requires another type of item. It requires test items which serve a diagnostic function. Such items serve to differentially predict. They are designed to recommend different things for different individuals. Considerations in test design should be brought to bear on the design of diagnostic material for individualization. First, to be useful as a diagnostic item, an item must discriminate among individuals. They must perform differently on it. Some must answer correctly; others must be in error. A low error rate item does not differentiate individuals. Thus a good diagnostic item meets criteria incompatible with those met by a good teaching item. There is, then, an *incompatibility* between teaching items and diagnostic items, or at least there is an incompatibility between teaching and diagnostic functions.

To be useful as a diagnostic test, a test must have validity and reliability. Of special importance to us is the relationship between reliability and test length. In general, the shorter the test, the poorer its reliability and validity.

A test enabling one to make a good decision normally requires a reasonable number of items. This problem is openly recognized in the development of IPI. Lindvall and Cox (1969), writing placement tests in IPI note that they require five to ten items for each behavioral objective. Often, especially in CAI, a heavy predictive burden is placed on a single multiple choice item. Consider an item from the Stanford CAI reading program (Atkinson, 1968).

In an item presented by Atkinson (1968) as a typical one from the Stanford CAI reading program the child is shown the letter "r" to the left of an empty cell, and the letters "an" above the cell, and four alternative words listed below ("rat," "bat," "fan," "ran"). The student's response is to touch one of the words. If the correct word is touched, the next mainline item is presented. If an incorrect alternative is touched, an item is presented which requires either choosing the appropriate final consonant (if "rat" was touched) or the appropriate initial consonant (if "fan" was touched) or each of the corrective items in turn (if "bat" was touched). After the corrective item or items the original mainline item is repeated.

In its diagnostic function, the mainline item which initiates the branching has severe limitations as a four-alternative item. There is a twenty-five percent opportunity to be correct by chance, and each alternative provides a different course of action. The reliability of such an item (though nowhere stated) must be low. But the consequence is small also; the student receives one or two items and then repeats the missed item. This brings us to the other component of the dilemma of individualization—the size of the consequence. The size of the decision so far as the student is concerned may vary greatly. How many items must a student do as a function of failing the diagnostic unit? or how much time must he spend? In traditional testing, consequences are often large; a child is given an intelligence test to determine whether he should be in a school for the retarded, a student takes the college boards to determine whether he will profit from college. With such large decisions, it would be a waste to use even a single diagnostic item—even one of perfect reliability— to spare half the students only a single unnecessary teaching item. Moreover, single diagnostic items are seldom very reliable. Thus, the basic technological problem to be worked out for individualization is one of a type of cost efficiency for the student based on the cost in time of the diagnostic material and the resulting savings in the decisions.

A small decision, as frequently made in the constantly adjusting sequence of a CAI program, cannot justify a lengthy diagnosis, but the short tests are unreliable and the estimate of cost efficiency must take into account the false positives and false negatives. The more finely grained the adjustment the worse the dilemma, with single test items being unreliable, and, even if they could be reliable, requiring at least two-item consequence to simply break even.

The present great stress on individualization takes considerably more student time in testing to find the teaching items they don't need than the items themselves would have taken. In an IPI system, a student may spend as much as two-fifths of his time taking tests. With this much testing, the results might be reliable (although reliability and validity information is seldom provided), but the consequences seem insufficient to justify so much testing (as compared, for example, with a once-a-year placement test).

Individualization, to escape this dilemma, will require development of measures of cost effectiveness corrected for empirically determined reliabilities. It seems unlikely that many of the more well-known programs would fare well against opposite criteria of this type.

But there is yet a more serious failure of individualization to live up to its press. Today, adjustment for individuality needs to produce greater diversity, rather than less. Programs branch on past achievement, on learning rate, on latency in answering items, but they do not branch on desired terminal behavior. Educational objectives are set by an educational establishment and create a homogeneous middle class. In Skinner's *Walden Two* (1948), a visiting critic argues against behavioral design in society by objecting to the uniformity he imagines to be a natural consequence of such designs. He is answered by *Walden Two*'s founder, Frazier, that creation of such uniformity would be bad behavioral engineering. It seems that there are few Fraziers in today's world of behavioral technology. And the demands of blacks, of radical students, and others are often for the pursuit of different objectives. To sell individualization as a panacea for these problems is a sham. Branching should be on the basis of different desired outcomes rather than on different entering behavior.

REFERENCES

ATKINSON, R. C. "Computerized Instruction and the Learning Process," *American Psychologist*, Vol. 23 (1968), pp. 225-39.

HOLLAND, J. G. "A Quantitative Measure for Programmed Instruction," *American Educational Research Journal*, Vol. 4 (1967), pp. 87-101.

LINDVALL, C. M., and COX, R. C. "The Role of Evaluation in Programs for Individualized Instruction," in *Educational Evaluation: New Roles, New Means*. 68th Yearbook, NSSE, Part II. Chicago: University of Chicago Press, 1969, pp. 156-88.

SKINNER, B. F. *Walden Two*. New York: The Macmillan Co. 1948.

SUPPES, P. "The Uses of Computers in Education," *Scientific American*, Vol. 215 (1966), pp. 206-21.

Chapter 11. ADAPTING INSTRUCTIONAL METHODS

HOW CAN INSTRUCTION BE ADAPTED TO INDIVIDUAL DIFFERENCES?

Lee J. Cronbach

Adapting education to the individual has meant many things in educational discussions; these tend to be jumbled together, perhaps because this topic has never been subjected to logical or philosophical analysis. I shall use the rubrics in Table 11-1 to distinguish methods of adaptation and thereby to structure this discussion. In due time I shall amplify each of these and examine the social and pedagogical concepts on which it rests.

Two preliminary remarks are called for. First, these adaptations are by no means mutually exclusive; they can combine in various patterns, and no doubt all of them have a place in the ideal educational system. Second, it is category 3b that is most interesting for this discussion since all the other devices alter administrative arrangements rather than instructional technique. This is the approach that calls for a new psychological theory

SOURCE: Reprinted from Lee J. Cronbach, "How Can Instruction Be Adapted to Individual Differences," in Robert M. Gagné (ed.), *Learning and Individual Differences* Columbus, Ohio: Charles Merrill Publishing Co., 1967), by permission of author and publisher.

TABLE 11-1

PATTERNS OF EDUCATIONAL ADAPTATION TO INDIVIDUAL DIFFERENCES

Educational goals	Instructional treatment	Possible modifications to meet individual needs
Fixed	Fixed	1a. Alter duration of schooling by sequential selection.
		1b. Train to criterion on any skill or topic, hence alter duration of instruction.
Options	Fixed within an option	2a. Determine for each student his prospective adult role and provide a curriculum preparing for that role.
Fixed within a course or program	Alternatives provided	3a. Provide remedial adjuncts to fixed "main track" instruction.
		3b. Teach different pupils by different methods.

of aptitude. An aptitude, in this context, is a complex of personal characteristics that accounts for an individual's end state after a particular educational treatment, i.e., that determines what he learns, how much he learns, or how rapidly he learns. I presume that an individual has greater aptitude for learning, say, to multiply from one method of teaching than from another method that is equally good on the average. Aptitude, pragmatically, includes whatever promotes the pupil's survival in a particular educational environment, and it may have as much to do with styles of thought and personality variables as with the abilities covered in conventional tests.

ADAPTATION WITHIN A PREDETERMINED PROGRAM

It was in the early years of this century that individual differences became a primary topic in educational theory. Until that time, there was largely a fixed curriculum starting with the common branches of knowledge, and proceeding through an academic high school program and a college liberal arts program. Individual differences were taken into account chiefly by eliminating students. Less successful students (and those from poorer families) dropped out all along the way.

When ability tests became available they were used by schools—to put it bluntly—to decide which pupils should be allowed to drop by the wayside or to vegetate in an undemanding "slow" classroom, and which should proceed briskly, be indoctrinated with high aspirations, and go on to higher education. Those mental tests have prospered which show predictive validity for success in the predetermined curriculum.

The social theory behind 1a, the selection system, is that every child "should go as far in school as his abilities warrant." This assumes a point of diminishing returns in education, reached early by some persons, late by others. Such an assumption supports a periodic weeding-out of the less responsive pupils.

There is some logic to the opposite position: that certain common learnings should be attained, that everyone should stay in school until he masters them, and hence that we should train to criterion on the central educational outcomes. Such a procedure has never been followed in any pure form, since it would extend the education of some youngsters until they are oldsters. But it is clearly more humane than the Procrustean keep-pace-or-fall-out policy, and in modified form it is widely practiced. We saw it in the old policy of keeping a child in the first grade until he could read his primer, and we see it in today's non-graded primary unit that some children complete in two years and some in four. It appears in the claim that linear programmed instruction brings all learners to criterion on its fixed content, each at his own rate. Homogeneous grouping likewise has been premised on adjusting the pace of instruction, with some sections spending time on the more fundamental subskills and others going ahead. Adjusting pace or time implies changing the amount of exercise given to a particular connection, to use the appropriately Thorndikean terminology.

The most interesting psychological point about this approach is that it invokes a construct of "rate of learning." This concept is distinctly arguable. Woodrow (1946), you may recall, spent twenty years compiling evidence that rate of learning is entirely inconsistent from one task to another, and that there is no justification for identifying mental test score with ability to learn. His position is in harmony with the interpretations of John Anderson (1939) and Humphreys (1960). While the evidence does not support the idea of a general capacity to learn, sophisticated studies can perhaps salvage the concept of ability to learn as distinct from past learning.

My working hypothesis is that, when several intellectual tasks are to be learned under much the same instructional conditions, there will indeed be some individual consistency in time needed to reach the criterion. If the several tasks all lie in the same field—foreign language, say, or mathematics—the consistency will be much stronger. Research steps in the right direction have been taken by several studies in Gulliksen's laboratory (Allison, 1960; Stake, 1961; Duncanson, 1964; see also Jensen, 1962, and Mackay and Vernon, 1963). I shall not be satisfied, however, until we get data on learning rates under instructional conditions; present studies have invariably measured learning rates under conditions of practice unguided save for knowledge of results. My hypothesis implies that the person's learning rate will vary, depending on the nature of the instruction; I therefore expect that adapting instructional *technique* will in the long run be more important than merely altering the duration of exposure.

ADAPTATION BY MATCHING GOALS TO THE INDIVIDUAL

When the high school began to serve all youngsters—that is, when the nation began fifty years ago to regard dropouts as undesirable rather than as good riddance—the influx of unselected students called for a radical alteration of program. In Thorndike's laboratory, Margaret Cobb (1922) found, for example, that there is considerable risk of failure if a pupil with a mental age below 15-6 enrolls in high school algebra. Extrapolating, she wrote: "Probably in 90 cases out of 100, it is unwise to guide the average or less intelligent than average child into the present academic high school . . . He should be encouraged to try some other type of training" (p. 549). Consequent to such thinking, schools introduced vocational and homemaking curricula, and new courses were designed. The course in algebra, for example, was replaced for the less able student by a course in general mathematics. This solution is more than a decision about education; it is a decision about the role the individual is to play as an adult.

There are dangers, however, in setting differentiated goals. Differentiation of mathematics courses meant that the discipline of mathematics was kept an arcane possession of a selected class, while the lower classes were drilled on formulas useful to shopkeepers. Today the theme in mathematics teaching (and similarly in other subjects) is to give every pupil an understanding of the same basic discipline, even though some pupils go farther and deeper. Cobb had carefully qualified her report as applying to algebra as customarily taught, but the educational profession lost sight of the qualification and for thirty years ignored the possibility that algebra can be taught by a considerable variety of techniques. In startling contrast to the easy way out that reserved algebra to bright adolescents, there are now many primary-grade curricula teaching what is unmistakably algebra.

Goals are also modified when the student is allowed to select his major field of study or to choose among elective courses. This is, of course, necessary and will continue. The only comment pertinent in this discussion is to note the rather small success of differential aptitude tests in predicting which academic subjects the person will learn most easily (McNemar, 1964). We haven't the faintest evidence, for example, what constitutes mathematical aptitude, save for the obvious fact that a person who has mastered one mathematical fact or process has an advantage in learning the next process in a hierarchy. According to most studies, the complex of abilities the British call *v:ed* makes for success in all fields of academic work. Two rationalizations for this fact are available. Concepts in the end require a verbal or at least a symbolic form, and hence call for verbal skills. Secondly, our academic subjects are all taught by much the same verbal abstract methods. This second condition is not obviously necessary, and we can hope to reduce the dependence of success on the *v:ed* complex.

ADAPTATION BY ERASING INDIVIDUAL DIFFERENCES

Most tactics the school uses are intended to minimize the nuisance of individual differences so that it can go on teaching the same unaltered course. This is true also of remedial instruction, which adds onto the common program rather than redesigning it. Remedial work takes it for granted that the classroom work is largely a fixed program. Many a pupil needs help that the standard program does not give him, and supplementary instruction is therefore provided, with the intention of repairing the gaps in skill and putting him back on the pace. That is to say, remedial instruction attempts to erase individual differences.

Some remedial treatments are developed by breaking the subject matter into component processes, classifying the pupil's errors, and providing special explanations or drill. Under the Thorndikean view of every multiplication combination as a separate bond, the diagnostic process was to take an inventory of combinations mastered and not mastered and then to direct practice to the weak bonds. We see similar thinking today, considerably elaborated, in Gagné's (1962) discussion of hierarchies of information and skill. It takes still another form in branched programmed instruction, where there is a continuous diagnosis of misconceptions or gaps in recall, and an appropriate remedial loop follows each significant error. It is also seen in the assignment of a short linear program covering a single topic or subskill for independent study when the teacher finds a pupil weak in that respect. This type of hole-patching is not very interesting psychologically, and its value may be quite limited.

What is monitored in a branched program is subject-matter mastery, in the narrowest sense. The programs check on the learner's ability to give the response as taught. But education is aiming at transferable responses, both cognitive and affective. Unless these broader outcomes are monitored the program may do harm rather than good. It ought to be possible to teach a historical unit on the years 1856-1861 and ask questions at these various levels, among others: (1) Does the student know the facts about what Lincoln did that Buchanan didn't? (2) Has the student arrived at a sensible opinion about the responsibilities of an elected leader in dealing with a controversial matter? (3) Can the student give a fair-minded evaluation of partisan comments, both contemporary and retrospective? Since each of these is an objective of teaching history, a poor performance on any one of these outcomes would call for remediation; three distinct remedial loops would be needed. I doubt that anyone has been designing remedial loops for the important transfer outcomes. To recognize multiple outcomes, moreover, we will need new program structures allowing for multidimensional monitoring and branching.

The "compensatory education" now being proposed for young disadvantaged children is remedial. It is hoped that appropriate stimulation will develop the intellectual skills and attitudes that constitute normal readiness for primary school. There is knowledge about readiness for reading and its development on which these activities can draw. Also needed is a theory, presently lacking, about the process of information intake and study. Recent observations on encoding, mediation, and use of feedback are carrying us in the right direction (Bloom, Davis and Hess, 1965, pp. 45-48).

A distinction needs to be made regarding the scale of adaptation. Branched programming is a microadaptation; a new decision is made every few minutes. The decision to put a six-year-old into lessons that generate reading readiness, instead of giving him a primer, is a microadaptation; the decision prescribes several weeks of treatment. The choice of scale merits a good deal of thought. The finer scale is more responsive, but not necessarily superior, since each microdecision is made with less information. Microdecisions keep such a multiplicity of treatments in play that it becomes impossible to evaluate every branching rule with care. Macrotreatments, being fewer, can be designed on the basis of theory and can be empirically validated.

ADAPTATION BY ALTERING INSTRUCTIONAL METHOD

The teacher adapts instructional method to the individual on both the micro and macro scales. He barely acknowledges the comment one pupil makes in class discussion, and stops to praise a lesser contribution from another who (he thinks) needs special encouragement. He turns away one pupil who asks for help—"You can find the answer by yourself if you keep at it"—and walks the length of the classroom to offer help to another, because he has decided to encourage independence of the former pupil and to minimize frustration of the latter. On the larger scale, he not only allows options for a term paper, but may custom-tailor a project for the student with special abilities or limitations.

The significant thing about these adaptations is their informality. The teacher picks up some cues from the pupil's test record and his daily work, and other cues from rather casual observation of his social interactions. The teacher forms an impression of the pupil from the cues, usually without an explicit chain of reasoning. He proceeds on the basis of the impression to alter the instruction; the adaptation too is intuitive, without any explicit theory. No doubt the decisions tend to be beneficial, but there is reason to think that intuitive adaptations of this kind will be inefficient and occasionally may be harmful.

When we encourage a teacher to adapt in this way to individual differences, we are asking him to function as a clinician. Clinical procedures are advantageous under certain circumstances. The reading specialist or speech specialist is a clinician who selects from a wide repertoire of instructional methods. But to guide his adaptations he has been taught an explicit theory of the subject matter, worked out through a generation or more of careful observation, whereas theories are not available for most school subject matter. Diagnosis in reading and speech is aided by special tests, such as the *Illinois Test of Psycholinguistic Abilities* (McCarthy and Kirk, 1961) which charts an elaborate profile of encoding and decoding skills; no such formal devices are in regular classroom use. The selection of exercises for a clinical case is guided by the transmitted experience of previous clinicians, but the classroom teacher has no such dependable guide.

It is very likely that teachers overdifferentiate. I know no research on impressionistic adaptation of instruction, but something can be learned from studies in which counselors have been asked to predict a student's grade average. Various biases appear in the estimates, but the most significant finding (Cronbach, 1955, pp. 182-183) is that the counselors overdifferentiate; they tend to expect too much from the persons who tested high, and too little from those who tested low. A regression line is an actuarial formula that starts with the group average and ranks differential information as a correction factor, giving the latter just as much weight as it deserves. The greater the accuracy and pertinence of the differential information, the greater its weight. The judges in the study cited gave considerably more weight to differential information than the regression formula did. Certain reasonable assumptions, entered into a decision-theoretic model, lead us to the conclusion that the poorer the differential information, the less the teacher should depart from the treatment that works best on the average (Cronbach, 1955, p. 181; Cronbach and Gleser, 1965, p. 62). Modifying treatments too much produces a worse result than treating everyone alike.

To systematize the process of adaptation, and hence reduce error, calls for a theory whose propositions would state the conditions of instruction best for pupils of certain types, both conditions and types being described in terms of fairly broad dimensions (cf. Jensen, 1962). I doubt that we can develop a separate rationale for each area and level of the curriculum, but I have hopes for the more general theory applicable at many levels and in many areas. Such a theory deals with aptitude-treatment interactions.

Aptitude information is not useful in adapting instruction unless the aptitude and treatment interact—more specifically, unless the regression line relating aptitude to payoff under one treatment crosses the regression

line for the competing treatment (Cronbach and Gleser, 1965). An aptitude measure that validly predicts success within both treatments may
have no value in deciding which treatment to give Johnny. If two treatments are about equally good on the average, the decision about Johnny
requires a predictor that correlates with payoff under one treatment and
does not correlate under the other treatment (or, what is less likely, that
correlates negatively with payoff under the second treatment). This implies
that general ability is likely to be a poor basis for differentiating instruction, because it correlates with success in most instruction.

I doubt that the dimensions manipulated in conventional studies of
learning are the ones most likely to be important in instruction. In instruction the stimulus material develops progressively, whereas in the practice
conditions of the conventional experiment the stimuli remain essentially
unchanged from trial to trial. Educational content has a meaningful structure; hence, a learner can reach the point of judging his own response
without external feedback, indeed, of judging a response before he utters
it. Variables having to do with logical organization and with dependency
on the teacher should loom considerably larger in research on instruction
than they have in past research on learning.

There are many hints of interactions in the literature, but I am not able
to synthesize these findings. Few variables have been given the concen-
trated attention that produces consistent findings. When there are two or
more studies involving more or less the same aptitude and treatment dimensions, they not uncommonly disagree. I shall confine myself to some
remarks on three types of variables.

General Ability. Of all individual differences, the one that comes first
to the educator's mind is general mental ability. We naturally think that
teaching very bright students calls for methods unlike those that fit average students. I do not believe, however, that there are any well-established
interactions of instructional method with mental age, within any age
group.

One reason is that a truly general aptitude would correlate with performance no matter what the instructional method. The attainment score
under any of the treatments should show an uptrend with increase in
aptitude; while there may be some difference in slope, from treatment to
treatment the differential effect will be small. Early in the work on programmed instruction, it was thought that linear, small-step programs
would succeed with everyone, so that the regression of attainment on
ability would have essentially a zero slope. Such a horizontal regression
would be likely to cross the upsloping line for a conventional treatment.
Stolurow (1964) reports one such interaction: learning from a set of irreg-
ularly-sequenced exercises correlated with general ability, but when the
same exercises were formed into a well-sequenced program, the correlation vanished. The sequence, Stolurow says, does for the poorer students

what the good ones can do for themselves. Results with quite the opposite implications are reported by Schramm (1964, p. 33), however. When regular classwork in English was compared with the programmed *English 2600*, the abler students achieved better with the program, and the below-average students suffered from the change. Other studies of programmed instruction only confuse the picture further.

Puzzlement of a different sort is introduced by the Osler studies (Osler and Fivel, 1961; Osler and Trautman, 1961). These studies used the usual concept-attainment procedures. Older children tend to do better. Within an age group, the brighter children did conspicuously better than average children when the concept was presented by means of simple, schematic stimuli. Common sense leads us to think that bright children ought to be better able to handle complex stimuli, but when meaningful stimuli were used, the bright children were very much handicapped, and indeed, did slightly worse than average children. We cannot generalize that lessons for brighter children ought to use simplified stimuli, but we can at least hesitate before offering them lessons richer in detail. What is especially noticeable in the Osler studies is that some of the results are more strongly related to IQ than to MA; that is to say, the difference between MA and CA tells more about the child's process of concept attainment than his ability level does.

Something rather similar is implied in the study of G. L. Anderson (1941). He studied about 300 fourth-graders taught arithmetic by either a meaning or a drill method for an entire year. Outcomes were projected onto two pretests, one of general ability and one of past arithmetic achievement. The Johnson-Neyman method (Johnson and Neyman, 1936) which Anderson applied not only established the presence of an interaction of method with individual differences for ten outcome measures (out of eleven investigated), but also divided the pretest space into regions where each method was superior. Anderson presents a number of charts showing those dividing lines, in a space defined by the ability test and the compass arithmetic pretest. I have made a composite in Figure 11-1. Since the two scales have nearly the same standard deviations it has not been necessary to put a metric onto my figure. Each line on the chart is the dividing line for one of Anderson's post-test scores; the persons below and to the right tended to achieve better under the meaning method than under the drill method. Where the line is nearly horizontal, the interaction was determined almost entirely by the arithmetic test; where the line is nearly vertical, the mental test is the significant predictor of differential success. Where the line makes a 45° angle with the horizontal, the significant differential information is the difference between the two scores. Most lines are in about this position. Hence the person who has "overachieved" in the past will profit most from the drill method, and the underachiever, whose mental test standing places him higher than his past achievement, does best under the meaning method. For only one of the outcome measures did the mental test considered alone give a noteworthy interaction. Too often psychologists have tried to find correlates of the mental test score and to use the mental test score as a basis for adapting instruction. This study turns attention to the difference between the mental test score

FIGURE 11-1

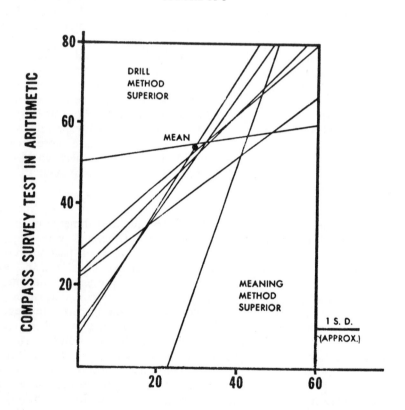

MINNEAPOLIS SCHOOL ABILITY TEST

Pretest patterns favorable to learning from drill or meaningful instruction. Each line is a "line of nonsignificance" determined by Anderson for one class of elementary school children and its control group, using the Johnson-Neyman method. This is best interpreted as showing the location where the regression plane for the Neyman method intersects the regression plane for the drill method. In each comparison, pupils below or to the right of the line tended to do better on the Johnson-Neyman method than the drill method, while those above or to the left of the line tended to do better on the drill method.

and that on other variables. Anderson's study implies that the difference can be valid for selecting an educational treatment when the mental test itself is not.

Modes of Presentation. Though we might uncover interactions by hit-and-miss exploration in which results under one instructional treatment after another are projected onto a mass of differential information, another experimental strategy is more promising. I suggest that we set out to invent interactions. Specifically, *we ought to take a differential variable we think promising and design alternative treatments to interact with that variable.* Until the present time, the differential psychologist has let the institution tell him the treatments for which he is predicting success, and he has designed tests or batteries to make that prediction. I suggest that we now let the institution specify only the criterion—not the treatment—and that the psychologist select an aptitude variable and design treatments expected to interact with it.

One place to begin is with the abilities that have emerged repeatedly in factor analysis. We can accept the position of Ferguson (1954) and Gagné (1960) that spatial ability, for example, ought to transfer to the mastery of tasks calling for spatial transformations of data. As I said earlier, spatial tests have had very little power to predict learning, but this may be because instruction is so largely verbal. Demonstrative geometry remains in the school curriculum not to teach theorems about triangles but to develop understanding of and skill in proof. Other mathematical and logical systems provide equally vigorous illustrations of proof. Suppose, then, that we develop a mathematics course calling for reasoning about figures, with maximum demand placed on spatial abilities. We develop a second course calling for reasoning about, say, number theory. Pupils high on suitable spatial measures would take one course, those high on certain numerical or logical measures would take the other. With ingenuity, we might create a third course, equally good as mathematics, for pupils weak on both of these aptitudes and high on a third. Here we would begin to capitalize on the principle that guides military classification: if you define distinct tasks and sort persons on differential aptitudes rather than general aptitude, a far larger proportion of the population turns out to be successful. A proposal like this was outlined by Gagné (1960), when he suggested that the addition of signed numbers be taught to eighth-graders using either spatial, verbal, or symbolic concepts. Primary abilities, he surmised, would differentially predict success in the three treatments. To the best of my knowledge his study has not been carried out.

Constructive versus Defensive Motivation. The interaction that is most thoroughly documented at present involves attitudes having to do with confidence, willingness to risk failure, and motivation for self-directed achievement. J. W. Atkinson (1964) reviews many studies of need for achievement and motive to avoid failure (or anxiety). For the sake of brevity I shall speak of the student high on achievement motivation and low on anxiety as "constructively" motivated and the one with the opposite pattern as "defensively" motivated, setting aside the intermediate patterns which generally give intermediate results. This person variable interacts with perceived risk or difficulty, a treatment variable. The constructives show their best persistence when led to think they are dealing with problems where there is moderate risk. The defensives are most persistent when led to think the chance of success is very low (Feather, 1961). Consistent with this, Kogan and Wallach (1964, p. 192) find defensives rigid when in difficulty, and unwilling to withdraw from a blind alley. Given simple instructions to get to work and to do a task, constructives achieve well; adding pressure lowers their score (Atkinson and Reitman, 1956). The same pressure—a cash prize, pacing, and stern supervision—improves the work of the defensives. Telling the low-anxious student that he has done poorly improves his work, while favorable comment improves the work of the defensives (Mandler and Sarason, 1952). These studies are of enhancement of performance through short-term treatment, and do not bear directly on learning from instruction. Three other studies were conducted in the classroom.

Atkinson and O'Connor (1963) find that homogeneous grouping enhances the school learning of constructives, and has no appreciable effect on defensives. A larger study by Grimes and Allinsmith (1961) compared primary reading achievement under a structured phonics program with achievement under a less structured whole-word approach. Self-rated anxiety and rated compulsivity were used as differential variables, with the results in Table 11-2.

TABLE 11-2

MEAN OVER- OR UNDER-ACHIEVEMENT[a] OF PUPILS OF VARIOUS TYPES UNDER TWO METHODS OF INSTRUCTION (GRIMES & ALLINSMITH, 1961)

Compulsiveness Anxiety	High High	High Low	Low High	Low Low
Structured Instruction	1.24	.42	.08	.08
Loosely Structured Instruction	−.22	.16	−.68	−.14

[a] Expressed in years of overachievement, using regression of achievement test on IQ to define expectation.

While the structured treatment produced better results for all groups, there was a marked interaction; structure was particularly helpful to the defensive pupils in the left column. Unfortunately, this was not a well controlled study, and one cannot say which of many differences between the structured and unstructured classes produced the results.

These studies give considerable support to the hypothesis that defensive pupils will learn most if the teacher spells out short-term goals, gives a maximum of explanation and guidance, arranges feedback at short intervals to keep the pupil from getting off the track—in general, if the teacher maximizes opportunity for dependence. The constructives, on the other hand, should face moderately difficult tasks where intermediate goals are not too explicit; feedback should be provided at intervals, for the purpose of teaching them to judge themselves rather than for motivational support. Perhaps these are the pupils most apt to profit by a shift from didactic teaching to learning by discovery.

There is one study not consistent with my hypothesis. Flanders (see Amidon and Flanders, 1961; Flanders, 1965) compared a "direct" style of teaching geometry by lecturing and criticism with an "indirect" style in which the teacher praises and draws out the students. The published data are not very complete, but there is a highly significant tendency for dependent students to do best under the indirect treatment. Independent students do equally well under either treatment. In a counterpart experiment in social studies, there was no interaction. Another treatment variable, clarity of short-term goals, was also studied, but produced no significant effects. This seems to suggest that dependent students should *not* be kept on the track by spelling out goals and applying prompt corrective feedback, but Flanders' final conclusion (1965, p. 99) is that there is no interaction. I note also that it is quite possible that Flanders made his indirect teacher supportive and his direct teacher unsympathetic and antagonistic. I would expect the dependent student to respond to supportive, warmly-toned direct teaching.

If further research confirms such hypotheses as the foregoing, wisdom will be required in educational applications. If defensives learn fastest under conditions of dependency, we probably want to arrange strongly supporting conditions for the schoolwork we take most seriously. But it would be shortsighted to restrict these pupils so that they remain defensive. Some part of the school program ought to be designed to increase their self-assurance; only this will release their full potential (Sears and Hilgard, 1964). A similar comment is to be made about verbal ability. It is all very well to put across a particular subject by a method that makes few demands on verbal ability, but it would be a disaster to keep the low-verbal child in a verbally impoverished environment. We have two coordinate problems: capitalizing on the existing aptitude pattern and modifying that pattern. The school need not deal with both at the same moment, but neither should be neglected.

My conception of strategy for adapting instruction has much in common with Cooley's (1964) proposal for "programmed experiences" in guidance. He suggests that students can be diagnosed quasi-mechanically with the aid of a computer, which can use empirically validated rules to suggest activities appropriate to the student's interests and abilities. It might, for example, list books on careers the student should consider, or recommend a second course in algebra.

It seems likely to me that even with the sort of multivariate testing a computer can provide, we will have to build up adaptations slowly, on the basis of only a few differential variables. While in principle a unique instructional diet could be matched to the student's idiosyncratic intellectual metabolism, nothing is to be gained by introducing unvalidated modifications. And it will be a long time before we have adequately validated rules of adaptation that take into account even a half-dozen differential variables. As I see it, our greatest hope for fitting the school to the individual lies in the development of theory that finally marries the differential and experimental approaches to learning.

REFERENCES

ALLISON, R. B.   "Learning Parameters and Human Abilities," unpublished doctoral dissertation, Princeton University, 1960.

AMIDON, E., and FLANDERS, N. A.   "The Effects of Direct and Indirect Teacher Influence on Dependent-prone Students Learning Geometry," *Journal of Educational Psychology,* Vol. 52 (1961), pp. 286-329.

ANDERSON, G. L.   "A Comparison of the Outcomes of Instruction under Two Theories of Learning," unpublished doctoral dissertation, University of Minnesota, 1941.

ANDERSON, J. E.   "The Limitations of Infant and Preschool Tests in the Measurement of Intelligence," *Journal of Psychology,* Vol. 8 (1939), pp. 351-79.

ATKINSON, J. W.   *The Psychology of Motivation.* Princeton, N.J.: D. Van Nostrand Co., Inc., 1964.

ATKINSON, J. W., and O'CONNOR, P.   "Effects of Ability Grouping in Schools Related to Individual Differences in Achievement-related Motivation," final report. Office of Education Cooperative Research Program, Project 1283, University of Michigan, 1963. Available in microfilm from Photoduplication Center, Library of Congress, Washington, D. C.

ATKINSON, J. W., and REITMAN, W.   "Performance as a Function of Motive Strength and Expectancy of Goal Attainment," *Journal of Abnormal and Social Psychology,* Vol. 53 (1956), pp. 361-66.

BLOOM, B. S., DAVIS, A., and HESS, R.   *Compensatory Education for Cultural Deprivation.* New York: Holt, Rinehart & Winston, Inc., 1965.

COBB, MARGARET V.   "The Limits Set to Educational Achievement by Limited Intelligence," *Journal of Educational Psychology,* Vol. 13 (1922), pp. 546-55.

COOLEY, W. W.   "A Computer-measurement System for Guidance," *Harvard Educational Review,* 1964.

CRONBACH, L. J. "Processes Affecting Scores on 'Understanding of Others' and 'Assumed Similarity,' " *Psychological Bulletin,* Vol. 52 (1955), pp. 177-94.

CRONBACH, L. J., and GLESER, G. C. *Psychological Tests and Personnel Decisions.* 2d. ed. Urbana: University of Illinois Press, 1965.

DUNCANSON, J. P. "Intelligence and the Ability to Learn," unpublished doctoral dissertation, Princeton University, 1964.

FEATHER, N. "The Relationship of Persistence at a Task to Expectation of Success and Achievement Related Motives," *Journal of Abnormal and Social Psychology,* Vol. 63 (1961), pp. 552-61.

FERGUSON, G. A. "On Learning and Human Ability," *Canadian Journal of Psychology,* Vol. 2 (1954), pp. 95-112.

FLANDERS, N. A. "Teacher Influence, Pupil Attitudes, and Achievement," Cooperative Research Monograph No. 12, Washington: U.S. Office of Education, 1965.

GAGNÉ, R. M. "Ability Differences in the Learning of Concepts Governing Directed Numbers," in *Research Problems in Mathematics Education.* Cooperative Research Monographs, No. 3, 1960, pp. 112-13.

GAGNÉ, R. M. "The Acquisition of Knowledge," *Psychological Review,* Vol. 4 (1962), pp. 355-65.

GRIMES, J. W., and ALLINSMITH, W. "Compulsivity, Anxiety, and School Achievement," *Merrill-Palmer Quarterly,* Vol. 7 (1961), pp. 248-71.

HUMPHREYS, L. G. "Some Investigations of the Simplex," *Psychometrika,* Vol. 25 (1960), pp. 313-23.

JENSEN, A. R. "Reinforcement Psychology and Individual Differences," *California Journal of Educational Research,* Vol. 4 (1962), pp. 174-78.

JOHNSON, P. O., and NEYMAN, J. "Tests of Certain Linear Hypotheses and Their Application to Some Educational Problems," *Statistical Research Memorandum,* University of London ,Vol. 1 (1936), pp. 57-93.

KOGAN, N., and WALLACH, M. *Risk Taking.* New York: Holt, Rinehart & Winston, Inc., 1964.

MACKAY, G. W. S., and VERNON, P. E. "The Measurement of Learning Ability," *British Journal of Educational Psychology,* Vol. 33 (1963), p. 177.

MANDLER, G., and SARASON, S. B. "A Study of Anxiety and Learning," *Journal of Abnormal and Social Psychology,* Vol. 47 (1952), pp. 166-73.

MCCARTHY, J., and KIRK, S. A. *Illinois Test of Psycholinguistic Abilities.* Urbana: Urbana Institute for Research on Exceptional Children, 1961.

MCNEMAR, Q. "Lost: Our Intelligence. Why?" *American Psychologist,* Vol. 12 (1964), pp. 871-82.

OSLER, SONIA F., and FIVEL, MYRNA W. "Concept Attainment. I. The Role of Age and Intelligence in Concept Attainment by Induction," *Journal of Experimental Psychology,* Vol. 62 (1961), pp. 1-8.

OSLER, SONIA F., and TRAUTMAN, GRACE E. "Concept Attainment. II. Effect of Stimulus Complexity upon Concept Attainment at Two Levels of Intelligence," *Journal of Experimental Psychology,* Vol. 62 (1961), pp. 9-13.

SCHRAMM, W. *Four Case Studies of Programmed Instruction.* New York: Fund for the Advancement of Education, 1964.

SEARS, PAULINE S., and HILGARD, E. R. "The Teacher's Role in the Motivation of the Learner," *63rd Yearbook, National Society for the Study of Education,* Part 1, pp. 182-209 (1964).

STAKE, R. E. "Learning Parameters, Aptitudes, and Achievements," *Psychometric Monographs,* No. 9 (1961).

STOLUROW, L. M. "Social Impact of Programmed Instruction: Aptitudes and Abilities Revisited," in J. P. DeCecco (ed.), *Educational Technology.* New York: Holt, Rinehart & Winston, Inc., 1964, pp. 348-55.

WOODROW, H. A. "The Ability to Learn." *Psychological Review,* Vol. 53 (1946), pp. 147-58.

Part E.

Educational Objectives: The Key To What Is To Be Learned

Introduction

There are many moments in life where serendipity plays its part and we learn by sheer accident or by trial and error. The intent of education is purposeful rather than accidental, however, and so it is essential that both the process and content in an educational program be clearly understood by the learner so that he can relate them meaningfully to his own long range goals.

In recent years the process of defining content elements and relating them to the learner has been simplified by the technique of specifying educational objectives. (The term educational objectives is used here rather than instructional objectives or learning objectives simply because it has a more inclusive connotation.)

Just as educational objectives help to define elements of subject-matter content they also make it possible for both learner and educator to have a common understanding of how and under what conditions mastery is to be demonstrated.

In other words, the educational objective is simply the statement of a measurable behavior; one which the learner recognizes as a competency to be mastered through practice in relevant activities. The teacher also will be guided by the educational objective for it alerts her to ways she should provide the student with personalized assistance and with an appropriate learning environment, including materials, equipment and facilities.

Before educational objectives can be mastered they must, of course, be developed. In Chapter 12, Newton S. Metfessel, William B. Michael, and Donald A. Kirsner tell how new objectives can be formulated according to a hierarchy of educational objectives previously established in the cognitive and affective domains.

In Chapter 13, Joseph R. Jenkins and Stanley L. Deno describe a set of developmental procedures to ensure that newly written educational objectives communicate clearly to the learner the prescribed task, the context or parameter of the task, and the criterion behavior by which the task will be judged.

To the extent that objectives are developed in a coherent fashion across grades and subject matters it becomes quite possible to involve the student to a greater degree in selecting and managing his own behavior. For example, objectives might be selected for study because they relate particularly well to a learner's long-range career goals. From the school's point of view, the use of objectives allows a more precise knowledge of the individual's past educational experiences. They also enable the teacher and student to "contract" for increments of learning (often called units or modules) to be mastered by certain dates, with the contracts adjusted for different students' rates of progress.

The reader who is interested in pursuing in depth the study of educational objectives and their many forms may well want to familiarize himself with the work undertaken in the Project for Research on Objective-Based Evaluation (PROBE), at the Center for the Study of Evaluation, University of California at Los Angeles.

Chapter 12. **DEVELOPING OBJECTIVES ACCORDING TO COGNITIVE AND AFFECTIVE TAXONOMIES**

INSTRUMENTATION OF BLOOM'S AND KRATHWOHL'S TAXONOMIES FOR THE WRITING OF EDUCATIONAL OBJECTIVES

Newton S. Metfessel, William B. Michael and Donald A. Kirsner

During the past six or eight years an increased amount of attention has been given to the statement of educational objectives in behavioral terms both to facilitate the evaluation of educational programs and to improve the validity of the measures and scales utilized in the evaluation process (Metfessel and Michael, 1967; Michael and Metfessel, 1967). Although set

SOURCE: Reprinted from a mimeographed version supplied by the senior author. A slightly modified version is included in *Psychology in the Schools*, Vol. 6 (3), 1969, pp. 227-31, Psychology Press, Inc. Reprinted by permission of the author and publisher.

up as a programmed learning text, Mager's (1962) *Preparing Instructional Objectives* has been one of the most useful guides to teachers and specialists in curriculum who have sought help in stating the desired outcomes of instruction in behavioral language—in describing the kinds of specific and relatively terminal behaviors which the learner will be capable of exhibiting subsequent to his exposure to a program of instruction. Another useful source has been the volume edited by Lindvall (1964) who, in collaboration with Nardozza and Felton (Lindvall, Nardozza, and Felton, 1964) not only prepared his own chapter concerned with the importance of specific objectives in curricular development, but also enlisted the aid of several distinguished educators (e.g., Krathwohl, 1964; Tyler, 1964) with specialized interests in evaluation. Such efforts have essentially involved a fusion of curriculum design with the evaluation process in that curricular planning is described in terms of behavioral objectives that are necessary for the construction of valid tests and scales. The taxonomies provide the required model necessary to furnish meaningful evidence regarding the attainment of desired behavioral changes.

Although Krathwohl (1964) related the taxonomy of educational objectives in both the cognitive (Bloom, Englehart, Furst, Hill, and Krathwohl, 1956) and the affective (Krathwohl, Bloom, and Masia, 1964) domains to curriculum building, he was able to present only a limited number of concrete illustrations, some of which Mager would probably challenge because of their relative lack of specificity. Admittedly, Krathwohl has made an important and helpful start in relating objectives to a meaningful and rather well-known conceptual framework. However, the writers believe that there exists a need for an instrumentation of the taxonomy of educational objectives within both the cognitive and affective domains— that is, a more clear-cut description of how the taxonomy can be implemented in the school setting. The approach utilized was the development of *behaviorally oriented* infinitives which, when combined with given objects, would form a basis for meaningful, cohesive, and operational statements.

PURPOSE

Thus, the essential purpose of this paper was to show how specific behavioral objectives can be formulated within the hierarchy of the major levels and sublevels of the taxonomies of educational objectives as set forth by Bloom *et al.* (1956) and Krathwohl *et al.* (1964). Such a framework should furnish a helpful base around which behavioral statements of objectives can be formulated.

Definition

An educational objective consists of a description of the behaviors of an individual (the learner or examinee) in relation to his processing information embodied in subject matter—that is, what the learner must be capable of doing with certain characteristics or properties of subject matter. The behavioral component, which may be described as a process involved at an appropriate level of the taxonomic classification, is usually expressed in the form of a noun "ability" or an adjective "able" followed by an infinitive such as the "ability to do" or "able to do." The second component of the objective, which consists of the specific content often found in the formal learning experience (e.g., in the curricular or instructional unit), constitutes a direct object of the verb or infinitive form. The terms "subject matter" or "content" are used in a fairly broad sense, as their level of specificity is highly variable, depending upon the characteristics of the curricular unit.

INSTRUMENTATION

To facilitate the formulation of statements of specific behavioral objectives within the framework of Bloom's taxonomy, the writers have included a table made up of three columns. The first column contains the taxonomic classification identified by both code number and terminology employed in Bloom's (1956) taxonomy. The entries in the second column consist of appropriate infinitives which the teacher or curriculum worker may consult to achieve a precise or preferred wording of the behavior or activity desired. In the third column somewhat general terms relative to subject-matter properties are stated. These direct objects, which may be expanded upon to furnish specificity at a desired level, may be permuted with one or more of the infinitive forms to yield the basic structure of an educational objective—activity (process) followed by content (subject-matter property). At the discretion of the reader the words "ability" or "able" can be inserted in front of each of the infinitives.

Although within a given major process level or sublevel of the taxonomy each infinitive cannot in all instances be meaningfully or idiomatically paired with every direct object listed, many useful permutations of infinitives and direct objects that furnish entirely readable statements are possible. Certainly use of these tables should lead to a substantial gain in the clarity and speed with which teachers and curriculum specialists, as well as those involved in construction of achievement tests, may state curricular objectives. The writers have found that these tables have been of considerable help to their students, as well as to personnel in public schools who are concerned with writing objectives prior to curriculum development, constructing test items, or to carrying out evaluation studies. Slight modifications can be made with the entries to meet the requirements of specific learning situations.

INSTRUMENTATION: AFFECTIVE DOMAIN

The instrumentation of the Affective Domain is the same as that of the Cognitive Domain, to wit, the selection of behaviorally oriented infinitives

TABLE 12-1

Instrumentation of the Taxonomy of
Educational Objectives:
Cognitive Domain

Taxonomy Classification	Examples of Infinitives	KEY WORDS	Examples of Direct Objects
1.00 Knowledge			
1.10 Knowledge of Specifics			
1.11 Knowledge of Terminology	to define, to distinguish, to acquire, to identify, to recall, to recognize		vocabularly, terms, terminology, meaning(s), definitions, referents, elements
1.12 Knowledge of Specific Facts	to recall, to recognize, to acquire, to identify		facts, factual information, (sources), (names), (dates), (events), (persons), (places), (time periods), properties, examples, phenomena
1.20 Knowledge of Ways and Means of Dealing with Specifics			
1.21 Knowledge of Conventions	to recall, to identify, to recognize, to acquire		form(s), conventions, uses, usage, rules, ways, devices, symbols, representations, style(s), format(s)
1.22 Knowledge of Trends, Sequences	to recall, to recognize, to acquire, to identify		action(s), processes, movement(s), continuity, development(s), trend(s), sequence(s), causes, relationship(s), forces, influences
1.23 Knowledge of Classifications and Categories	to recall, to recognize, to acquire, to identify		area(s), type(s), feature(s), class(es), set(s), division(s), arrangement(s), classification(s), category/categories
1.24 Knowledge of Criteria	to recall, to recognize, to acquire, to identify		criteria, basics, elements
1.25 Knowledge of Methodology	to recall, to recognize, to acquire, to identify		methods, techniques, approaches, uses, procedures, treatments
1.30 Knowledge of the Universals and Abstractions in a Field			
1.31 Knowledge of Principles, Generalizations	to recall, to recognize, to acquire, to identify		principle(s), generalization(s), proposition(s), fundamentals, laws, principal elements, implication(s)

TABLE 12-1 *Continued*

Taxonomy Classification	Examples of Infinitives KEY WORDS	Examples of Direct Objects
1.32 Knowledge of Theories and Structures	to recall, to recognize, to acquire, to identify	theories, bases, inter-relations, structure(s), organization(s), formulation(s)
2.00 Comprehension		
2.10 Translation	to translate, to transform, to give in own words, to illustrate, to prepare, to read, to represent, to change, to rephrase, to restate	meaning(s), sample(s), definitions, abstractions, representations, words, phrases
2.20 Interpretation	to interpret, to reorder, to rearrange, to differentiate, to distinguish, to make, to draw, to explain, to demonstrate	relevancies, relation-ships, essentials, aspects, new view(s), qualifications, conclusions, methods, theories, abstractions
2.30 Extrapolation	to estimate, to infer, to conclude, to predict, to differentiate, to determine, to extend, to interpolate, to extrapolate, to fill in, to draw	consequences, implications, conclusions, factors, ramifications, meanings, corollaries, effects, probabilities
3.00 Application	to apply, to generalize, to relate, to choose, to develop, to organize, to use, to employ, to transfer, to restructure, to classify	principles, laws, conclusions, effects, methods, theories, abstractions, situations, generalizations, processes, phenomena, procedures
4.00 Analysis		
4.10 Analysis of Elements	to distinguish, to detect, to identify, to classify, to discriminate, to recognize, to categorize, to deduce	elements, hypothesis/hypotheses, conclusions, assumptions, statements (of fact), statements (of intent), arguments, particulars
4.20 Analysis of Relationships	to analyze, to contrast, to compare, to distinguish, to deduce	relationships, inter-relations, relevance, relevancies, themes, evidence, fallacies, arguments, cause-effect(s), consistency/consistencies, parts, ideas, assumptions
4.30 Analysis of Organizational Principles	to analyze, to distinguish, to detect, to deduce	form(s), pattern(s), purpose(s), point(s) of view(s), techniques, bias(es), structure(s), theme(s), arrangement(s), organization(s)

TABLE 12-1 *Continued*

Taxonomy Classification	Examples of Infinitives	KEY WORDS Examples of Direct Objects
5.00 Synthesis		
5.10 Production of a Unique Communication	to write, to tell, to relate, to produce, to constitute, to transmit, to originate, to modify, to document	structure(s), pattern(s), product(s), performance(s), design(s), work(s), communications, effort(s), specifics, composition(s)
5.20 Production of a Plan, or Proposed Set of Operations	to propose, to plan, to produce, to design, to modify, to specify	plan(s), objectives, specification(s), schematic(s), operations, way(s), solution(s), means
5.30 Derivation of a Set of Abstract Relations	to produce, to derive, to develop, to combine, to organize, to synthesize, to classify, to deduce, to develop, to formulate, to modify	phenomena, taxonomies, concept(s), scheme(s), theories, relationships, abstractions, generalizations, hypothesis/hypotheses, perceptions, ways, discoveries
6.00 Evaluation		
6.10 Judgments in Terms of Internal Evidence	to judge, to argue, to validate, to assess, to decide	accuracy/accuracies, consistency/consistencies, fallacies, reliability, flaws, errors, precision, exactness
6.20 Judgments in Terms of External Criteria	to judge, to argue, to consider, to compare, to contrast, to standardize, to appraise	ends, means, efficiency, economy/economies, utility, alternatives, courses of action, standards, theories, generalizations

TABLE 12-2

Instrumentation of the Taxonomy of
Educational Objectives:
Affective Domain

Taxonomy Classification	Examples of Infinitives	Examples of Direct Objects
	KEY WORDS	
1.0 Receiving		
1.1 Awareness	to differentiate, to separate, to set apart, to share	sights, sounds, events, designs, arrangements
1.2 Willingness to Receive	to accumulate, to select, to combine, to accept	models, examples, shapes, sizes, meters, cadences
1.3 Controlled or Selected Attention	to select, to posturally respond to, to listen (for), to control	alternatives, answers, rhythms, nuances
2.0 Responding		
2.1 Acquiescence in Responding	to comply (with), to follow, to commend, to approve	directions, instructions, laws, policies, demonstrations
2.2 Willingness to Respond	to volunteer, to discuss, to practice, to play	instruments, games, dramatic works, charades, burlesques
2.3 Satisfaction in Response	to applaud, to acclaim, to spend leisure time in, to augment	speeches, plays, presentations, writings
3.0 Valuing		
3.1 Acceptance of a Value	to increase measured proficiency in, to increase numbers of, to relinquish, to specify	group membership(s), artistic production(s), musical productions, personal friendships
3.2 Preference for a Value	to assist, to subsidize, to help, to support	artists, projects, viewpoints, arguments
3.3 Commitment	to deny, to protest, to debate, to argue	deceptions, irrelevancies, abdications, irrationalities
4.0 Organization		
4.1 Conceptualization of a Value	to discuss, to theorize (on), to abstract, to compare	parameters, codes, standards, goals
4.2 Organization of a Value System	to balance, to organize, to define, to formulate	systems, approaches, criteria, limits
5.0 Characterization by Value or Value Complex		
5.1 Generalized Set	to revise, to change, to complete, to require	plans, behavior, methods, effort(s)
5.2 Characterization	to be rated high by peers in, to be rated high by superiors in, to be rated high by subordinates in	humanitarianism, ethics, integrity, maturity
	and	
	to avoid, to manage, to resolve, to resist	extravagance(s), excesses, conflicts, exorbitancy/exorbitancies

combined with selected direct objects. As in the case of the Cognitive Domain, these are to be conceptualized as examples for the stimulation of other infinitives and objects and, more important, meaningful objectives in a total framework.

EPILOGUE

... They had been discussing didactics and transitions and the student asked his tutor, "Master, what is needed to change the world?" And the sage pondered, then replied, "A proper definition of things."

Attributed to Confucius

Fifth Century, B.C.

... And the Texan who claimed he has the best six-gun shot in the West would take those who challenged him to the side of an immense barn and fire aimlessly. He would find where his bullets had landed and then draw targets with his bullet in the bull's-eye every time!

Moral: He aimed at nothing so he couldn't miss!

REFERENCES

BLOOM, B. S. (ed.), ENGLEHART, M. D., FURST, E. J., HILL, W. H., and KRATH-WOHL, D. R.   *A Taxonomy of Educational Objectives: Handbook I, The Cognitive Domain.* New York: Longmans, Green & Co., 1956.

KRATHWOHL, D. R.   "The Taxonomy of Educational Objectives—Its Use in Curriculum Building," in C. M. Lindvall (ed.), *Defining Educational Objectives.* Pittsburgh: University of Pittsburgh Press, 1964, pp. 19-36.

KRATHWOHL, D. R., BLOOM, B. S., and MASIA, B.   *A Taxonomy of Educational Objectives: Handbook II, The Affective Domain.* New York: David MacKay Co., 1964.

LINDVALL, C. M. (ed.).   *Defining Educational Objectives.* Pittsburgh: University of Pittsburgh Press, 1964.

LINDVALL, C. M., NARDOZZA, S., and FELTON, M.   "The Importance of Specific Objectives in Curriculum Development," in C. M. Lindvall (ed.), *Defining Educational Objectives.* Pittsburgh: University of Pittsburgh Press, 1964, pp. 10-18.

MAGER, R. F.   *Preparing Instructional Objectives.* Palo Alto, Calif.: Fearon Publishers, 1962.

METFESSEL, N. S., and MICHAEL, W. B.   "A Paradigm Involving Multiple Criterion Measures for the Evaluation of the Effectiveness of School Programs," *Educational and Psychological Measurement,* Vol. 27, Part II (1967), pp. 931-43.

MICHAEL, W. B., and METFESSEL, N. S.   "A Paradigm for Developing Valid Measurable Objectives in the Evaluation of Educational Programs in Colleges and Universities," *Educational and Psychological Measurement,* Vol. 27 (1967), pp. 373-83.

TYLER, R. W.   "Some Persistent Questions on the Defining of Objectives," in C. M. Lindvall (ed.), *Defining Educational Objectives.* Pittsburgh: University of Pittsburgh Press, 1964, pp. 77-83.

Chapter 13. **DEVELOPING OBJECTIVES ACCORDING TO CRITICAL COMPONENTS**

ON THE CRITICAL COMPONENTS OF INSTRUCTIONAL OBJECTIVES

Joseph R. Jenkins and Stanley L. Deno

The purpose of this paper[1] is to develop a formal description of an instructional objective based on several prior analyses of instructional objectives which were recently reviewed by Gagné (1965). A second and related purpose is to develop a succinct statement of the critical components of an objective which would be useful to curriculum designers, teacher educators, and students of education when they either attempt to write instructional objectives or analyze instructional objectives written by others.

Curriculum developers and educational psychologists have generally agreed that it is necessary to specify and state instructional objectives prior to constructing curriculum materials. According to Gagné (1965), the

SOURCE: Reprinted from *Psychology in the Schools,* Vol. 5, No. 4 (1968), Psychology Press, Inc., pp. 296-302, by permission of author and publisher.

careful statement of an instructional objective in terms of specific observable human behavior reveals to the curriculum designer the terminal behavior desired, allows measurement of student success, allows for an implementation of the conditions necessary for establishing the behavior, and finally, reveals to the learner the contingencies of reinforcement. Although a number of writers have extolled the virtues of a behaviorally stated objective, there is as yet no useful formal description which would facilitate the systematic analysis or writing of an instructional objective by most educators.

A primary concern in the development of any formal description and analytic instrument is simplicity and generality. The description and analysis should be general enough that it is applicable to objectives from such disparate subject matters as art and zoology. To achieve this generality the present authors assumed that the formal statement of any well-written objective regardless of content contains certain identifiable critical components, and that once specified these components will serve as a basis for constructing or analyzing instructional objectives.

A by-product advantage of such a general analysis might be that people who are neither curriculum designers nor subject-matter specialists could reliably and effectively describe and analyze objectives. That is to say, in order to analyze the *formal statement* of a curriculum objective in a subject matter such as nuclear physics, one would not need to be a nuclear physicist. Such a notion, of course, does not suggest that the inclusion of a particular objective in any curriculum would not depend on the curriculum designer or subject-matter specialist—in this case, the nuclear physicist.

A review of the writings of Miller (1961), Mager (1962), Gagné (1965), and Taber, Glaser, and Schaefer (1965) indicates that while there is some variability in the number of components in instructional objectives as identified by these writers, the following three components are agreed upon by all:

1.   A description of the kind of behavior which the learner is expected to perform; that is, an *action word* or verb.

2.   A description of the important conditions under which the behavior will be expected to occur; that is, a *context* (or signal) for the action.

3.   A description of how well the learner must perform to have his behavior accepted; that is, a *criterion* for tabulating that the behavior has occurred.

Let us first examine and describe each of the aforementioned components in some detail.

Action Word.   Task analysts have made strong appeals that the kind of action described in an instructional objective be classified as specific *ob-*

servable human behavior. In response to this appeal the behavioristically oriented curriculum developer begins with the question, "What will the learner be doing when he is demonstrating that he has achieved the objective?" In so doing, he presumably designates what *observable* data must obtain in order to make the inference that learning has occurred. An action word's candidacy for usage in an instructional objective is to be determined, in part, by the extent to which the term denotes observable behavior. The position is taken that selection of appropriate language labels for student performance ought to be facilitated as educators agree upon the observability of events implied by various verbs. While it may at first seem obvious that certain words label observable events and others do not, a recent study by the present authors suggests that such is not the case. A brief description of that investigation is relevant here.

In an attempt to gather normative data on the judged observability of a set of verbs frequently employed in instructional objectives, a scale of observability was developed based upon the action words recommended by several behavioristic curriculum developers. The clear cases (polar extremes) of observability have been frequently pointed to in the writing of Miller, Gagné, and Mager. Clear case observability is evidenced by terms such as "to underline" or "to point to" while clear case unobservability is implied by terms such as "to know," "to understand," and "to appreciate." Employing a scale which used as polar extremes the clear cases, the authors attempted to determine whether the terms frequently used in instructional objectives are judged as clearly observable, or clearly unobservable.

Inspection of the verbs' rated observability revealed that, to a striking degree, few verbs are judged to refer to strictly observable or unobservable events, but fall at some intermediate position with respect to observability.[2] If one wished to write behavioral objectives or, for that matter, analyze written objectives in terms of their observability, it would be possible to use the tables developed from the above study as a basis for comparing or selecting words that reflect various degrees of observability.

Context or Signal.   Since inferences regarding learning usually depend on the activity of the learner *in context,* the circumstances which surround that activity must be described. Taber, Glaser, and Schaefer (1965) describe this component as the "conditions under which the designated behavior is expected to occur"; Miller labels this the "indicator or signal which is to be the discriminative stimulus for the behavior"; and Gagné describes it as "words denoting the stimulus situation which initiates the performance."

As previously suggested, the action verb component of an instructional objective may vary in terms of judged observability. Similarly, a differentiation between levels of generality of the context or signal can be made.

For example, the context "when given the following set of addition problems: $2 + 2 = \ldots , 2 + 3 = \ldots , 3 + 5 = \ldots$, and the direction 'write
the sums of the above set of addition problems in the blank space' " is a
more specific context than "when given single digit addition problems."
The more general context of the latter implies that any of a class of problems may be given to the student for him to act upon (although it is not
entirely clear whether those problems will be in the form of mathematical
sentences or in columns with a plus sign beside each number and a line
below).

While the first more specific type of context is open to less interpretation it does not suggest what inference should be drawn about the pupil's
capability with respect to *a general class* of problems. Characteristic of the
more specific context is that it includes the actual test question or test
items. The more general context, on the other hand, can serve as the basis
for generating a class of specific problems on which, presumably, the
learner ought to be able to perform.

The distinction between general and specific context is made here because curriculum developers in requiring "*specific* observable human behavior," in an instructional objective, oftentimes confuse the observability
of the action verb with the nature of the context involved (specific or
general). If the context is specific then the objective will appear to be more
specific (and, perhaps to some, more behavioral or observable) since this
component of the objective has been described in greater detail.

In some cases a distinction between the generality and specificity of
context may be determined simply by whether, in stating the direction to
be given to the students, the directions are placed in quotes. While such a
criterion may seem, at first, to be trivial or unnecessary, the history of
standardized testing shows that variability in the spoken directions of test
givers substantially contributes to lower test reliability.

Criterion. The final component of a behavioral objective upon which
there is general agreement is that of the criterion of acceptable performance. An examination of both the literature dealing with instructional
objectives and available curriculum objectives reveals that there are generally two types of criteria employed by most curriculum writers. The first of
these is established by explicitly stating the correct answer to a given
objective or problem. For example, in the objective "when given the problem: $5 + 2 = \ldots$, the student writes 7 in the blank," the criterion for an
acceptable response is explicitly given as "7." Anyone attempting to score
pupil achievement on the objective would be able to do so because the
problem and its acceptable answer "7" is explicitly stated. Clearly, this
type of criterion would be useful to teacher aids, who may not be subject-
matter specialists.

The second type of criterion frequently occurring is that which indicates some percentage or proportion of correct responding on the part of the student. This second type of criterion is exemplified in the objective "counts orally from one to ten at least six out of seven times correctly." That the student counts from one to ten once correctly may be unsatisfactory for some. To have his response accepted the student is required to perform correctly six or seven times. Another example of this type might be, "when given a multiple choice examination on the nature of plastics the student will answer 90 per cent of the questions correctly." Again a proportionality of total responding is specified as an accepted level of performance.

It is easy to ignore the often made recommendation that a criterion be explicitly stated by saying that the criterion is nearly always implied in a stated objective. Nevertheless, the criterion that is oftentimes obviously implied is not always the criterion that is employed in an instructional situation (Deno & Jenkins, 1967).

To determine whether the preceding breakdown and description of the components of instructional objectives could be applied to pre-planned curriculum objectives, the authors developed the following instrument based on the above description and distributed it to a group of twelve in-service teachers.

A Critical Component Analysis of Instructional Objectives

Several frequently cited educators (Miller, Gagné, Mager) have agreed that well-stated behavioral objectives should include at least the following characteristics:

1. A specification of the kind of behavior which the learner is expected to perform, that is the *action word* or verb.

2. A description of the important conditions under which the behavior will be expected to occur, that is the *signal* or *context* for the action.

3. A description of a criterion of how well the learner must perform to have his behavior accepted, that is a *criterion* for tabulating that the behavior has occurred.

To begin with we will concern ourselves with only the 2nd and 3rd components, the signal and the criterion for acceptability.

Context

First, let us determine if a given objective includes the statement of context (A) or if the writer of the objective has neglected this component (B). Below are examples of two objectives with:

Contexts Stated

A. 1. *Given the direction,* "write the states of the union that come
into physical contact with the Mississippi River," the student writes
all of the states.

2. *Presented with pairs of numbers connected by an addition sign*
(+), writes the number that is the sum of the pair.

(context underlined)

Below are examples of two objectives with:

Contexts Not Stated

B. 1. Performs an "overhand smash."

2. Constructs a collage.

(A statement of the conditions under which the behavior should
occur is absent.)

Specificity of the Objective

A second related classification of behavioral objectives involves an objective's degree of specificity. An objective may be either specific (C) or
general (D) depending on whether the test condition is explicitly included
in the statement. A specific context includes the actual test item, while a
general context does not. Below are examples of two objectives with:

Specific Context

C. 1. Presented with the statement "Regroup the following numbers:

$65 = 60 +$ ___ $= 50 +$ ___

$168 =$ ___ $+ 68 =$ ___ $+ 78$,"

writes the numbers in the blanks that complete each operation.

(Test included)

2. When directed to:

"Write five examples of organisms that are included in the class
mammal,"

writes the names of five mammals.

(Test included)

Consider the following objective:

When directed "check those consonants that are voiced,"

ta

da

pa

ba

ka

ga

checks da, ba, ga.

This last objective would be classified as specific since the actual test item is included. However, had the objective read:

When directed to check those consonants that are voiced

ta

da

pa

ba

ka

ga

checks da, ba, ga,

the objective would be classified as general because the test item is *not* explicitly stated. In the objective, as it was initially written, the quotes indicate that the actual direction is stated.

General Context
(Test not included)

D. 1. When given *several states of the union* — and told to write their capital cities, writes their capitols.

2. When presented with *a series of names,* writes the names in alphabetical order.

(Underlined phrases are general descriptions, not specific test items.)

An examination of examples in A (1., 2.) and B (1., 2.) in terms of the specific-general classification may be helpful.

Look back to each of those examples now and try to determine which you would classify as general and which you would classify as specific.

According to the definition only example A-1. is specific since only this objective explicitly states the test.

By now you may have discovered a rule of thumb to aid your classification. The rules state "a *signal* must be stated *explicitly* if the objective can be classified as specific. If no *signal* or context is stated the objective is necessarily general." This cannot be interpreted to mean that if a signal is present the objective is specific, only that one requirement for an objective to be specific is that a signal must be present.

Criterion

The final classification concerns the presence or absence of an explicitly stated criterion. For the purposes of our classification we will consider two kinds of criteria: answer stated and percentage of correct responses. Let us look at some examples.

E.   1.   Counts orally from one to ten.

2.   Counts orally from one to ten by saying aloud, "one, two, three, four, five, six, seven, eight, nine, ten."

3.   Counts orally from one to ten at least six out of seven times.

Each of the above three objectives is a general objective in that the test is not explicitly stated. This is especially easy to determine since none of the three contains a signal which is a necessary requisite for a specific instructional objective.

Before determining whether the above objectives contain a stated criterion, remember that the criterion may be stated as either the correct answer or as a percentage of correct responses. Which of the above three objectives fit this rule?

Obviously, E-1 does not fall within the category since neither the correct answer is stated, nor is there a statement of percentage of correct responses. Consequently, E-1 falls into the category of *criterion not stated*.

However, E-2 fits the rule because the correct answer is explicitly stated. Objective E-3 also fits the rule because a statement of percentage of correct responses is contained. Consequently, both E-2 and E-3 fall into the category of *criterion stated*.

Consider three more objectives:

F.   1.   When given the problem "5 + 2 = ___," writes 7 in the blank.

2.   When given the problem "5 + 2 = ___," writes the correct answer in the blank.

3.   When given the problem "5 + 2 = ___," writes the correct answer in the blank nine times out of ten.

All three objectives (F-1, F-2, and F-3) are specific objectives since all contain the test conditions. However, only F-1 and F-3 contain criterion components. It is noteworthy that the criterion component in F-1 and F-3 is different. F-1 contains a criterion component because the answer is *explicitly* stated (7), while F-3 contains a criterion component because a percentage of correct responses is stated (nine times out of ten).

Consider two more examples:

G. 1.   When presented with five laboratory slides, writes the correct name for the muscle tissue for four out of the five slides.

     2.   When presented with five addition problems, writes the correct answers to them.

Both objectives are general since neither contain the test. However, G-1 contains a criterion statement, while G-2 does not. It is tempting to argue that a criterion is implied in G-2, that is, that *all* five problems must be answered correctly even though *all* is not explicitly stated. The fact is that the criterion used to score pupil achievement is often not the criterion that *is implied;* consequently, we require an explicit statement of the criterion.

Now with a sheet marked CLASSIFICATION OF CRITICAL COMPONENTS you should be able to classify objectives on the basis of the following categories:

1.   Signal: stated - not stated

2.   Specific - General

3.   Criterion: stated - not stated

For practice, rate the following objectives:

Obj. 1.   Given a set of pictures, names the animals contained in the picture. Now check your rating with the correct answer. You should have checked the following columns: signal-stated, general, criterion-not stated.

Obj. 2.   When presented with the following multiplication problems, 5 × 2 = *10,* 6 × 12 = *72,* and 2 × 100 = *200,* writes the *underlined* answers. You should have checked the following columns: signal-stated, specific, and criterion-stated.

Obj. 3.   Given the direction, "place all instances of positive reinforcement in pile A and all instances of negative reinforcement in pile B," classifies all instances correctly.

You should have checked the columns: signal-stated, general, and criterion-stated. Since the instances of positive and negative reinforcement are neither included nor referenced the objective is general. This instance contains a criterion statement because "classifies *all* instances correctly" is a statement of the percentage of correct responses required, in this case 100%.

A Note on the Action Word

Clearly, the problem with the action word component is not to determine whether or not an objective contains such a component. Rather, concern about the action component usually centers on the extent to which a verb labels observable behavior. Clear case observability is evidenced by terms such as "to underline," and "to point to," while clear case unobservability is implied by words such as "to know," "to understand," and "to appreciate." Terms such as "to identify," "to demonstrate," and "to complete" are judged to refer to events not directly observable but to events that are not as non-specifiable as "to understand" and "to know." Should you desire to analyze an objective's action word in the above manner you may refer to the Tables of Observability developed by Deno and Jenkins (1967).

CLASSIFICATION OF CRITICAL COMPONENTS

Objective Number	Signal Stated	Signal Not Stated	Specific	General	Criterion Stated	Criterion No Stated
1						
2						
3						

After the teachers had studied the preceding passage,[3] they were presented with 64 objectives sampled from a widely cited experimental curriculum. The results of this investigation indicated that the teachers could reliably rate objectives consistent with the technique provided them. Two or more judges disagreed on only 6 out of a possible 192 classifications (i.e., three binary choices on each of 64 objectives). Again, this research is reported in detail by Deno and Jenkins (1967).

SUMMARY

The purpose of this paper was to develop a description and a technique for analyzing the critical components of behavioral objectives.

It is most important to note at this time the above description of the components of behavioral objectives is made neither prescriptively nor evaluatively. Rather than engage in the polemics surrounding the use of instructional objectives the present study was undertaken to provide an analytic description of curriculum objectives which could be both reliably and meaningfully used. In this sense, then, it is more appropriate to refer to this formal description and the ancillary instructional passage as an analysis rather than an evaluation.

It might be reasonable to conclude, however, that should one wish to reliably communicate the objectives of a curriculum, the more specific the context, observable the behavior, and carefully stated the criterion, the more likely are people to agree that a desired objective has been achieved. On the other hand, as an objective becomes more specific and "behavioral" it becomes less inclusive. This increased specificity, then, produces objectives which may seem superficial or educationally trivial. It may be the case, then, that an increase in the reliability of communication may be purchased at the risk of sacrificing linguistic and substantive sophistication in curriculum objectives.

NOTES

[1] This research was conducted for Research for Better Schools, Inc., Philadelphia, Pa.

[2] A complete discussion of the non-categorical nature of the ratings along with the observability norms, their rationale and a detailed description of their collection may be found in the report of this work (Deno & Jenkins, 1967).

[3] The above passage has been slightly revised in that practice examples from various subject matters have replaced some practice examples in mathematics.

REFERENCES

DENO, S. L., and JENKINS, J. R. "Evaluating Preplanned Curriculum Objectives," Project Report, Research for Better Schools, Inc., Philadelphia, 1967.

GAGNÉ, R. M. "Analysis of Instructional Objectives," in R. Glaser (ed.), *Teaching Machines and Programmed Learning, II: Data and Directions*. Washington D.C.: National Educational Association, 1965.

MAGER, R. F. *Preparing Objectives for Programmed Instruction*. San Francisco: Fearon Publishers, Inc., 1962.

MILLER, R. B. "The Newer Roles of the Industrial Psychologist," in B. Von Gilmer (ed.), *Industrial Psychology*. New York: McGraw-Hill Book Co., 1961, pp. 353-80.

TABER, J. I., GLASER, R., and SCHAEFER, H. H. *Learning and Programmed Instruction*. Reading, Mass.: Addison-Wesley Publishing Co., Inc., 1965.

Part F.

**Evaluation: The Key
To Improving The
Learning Environment**

Introduction

When individualized learning is introduced into a school it is natural and appropriate that it should be observed with interest by all those directly associated with the school. Of course, the parents, faculty, administrators, and students will all formulate their own ideas of the new program's success or failure, and sometimes their views may be divergent. One of the reasons for this divergence may be that each group is evaluating a different aspect of the program. Or, it might be that no real evaluation was going on at all—it may simply have been that divergent views about success resulted from the generation of unsubstantiated opinions.

In Chapter 14, Gabriel Della-Piana, Michael Hogben, and Daniel Anderson present a plan for evaluation of one kind of program component, the new *learning materials*. In the example used, the evaluated materials constituted a programmed reading series but the authors suggest that their evaluation procedure is applicable to other materials as well.

In Chapter 15, Paul Richard and Robert Sund report on a project which adapted a set of existing instructional materials to enable their use for individualized learning. The reader will note that Richard and Sund were interested in eliciting *student reactions* to the materials and in comparing *performance data* between experimental and control groups. It is important to keep in mind that students' reactions on a questionnaire are *not* substitutes for performance data but must be supplementary to those data. Of course, students' reactions can be obtained unobstrusively (by use of the critical incident technique or some other method for systematically observing behavior) and this is probably preferable to the use of direct questionnaire methods.

Another kind of evaluation concerns the impact of a new *program* in achieving overall school goals. In Chapter 16, Charles L. Jenks describes a plan for broad programmatic evaluation as it was developed for use in a small school district.

Chapter 14. PROGRAM IMPROVEMENT BY SYSTEMATIC COMPARISON

A SCHEME FOR MAXIMIZING
PROGRAM EFFECTIVENESS

Gabriel M. Della-Piana, Michael Hogben and
Daniel R. Anderson

The purpose of this article is to present and describe a sequential evaluation procedure, intended for use with comparative studies in a natural (non-laboratory) setting. This evaluation procedure has been effectively applied to determine the relative efficiency of programed reading materials as compared with standard (non-programed) materials in a research study supported in part by the Granite School District Exemplary Center for Reading Instruction in Salt Lake City, funded under Title III. However, it is our belief that the paradigm presented is applicable to the majority of instructional programs.

Basically, the procedure involves comparative evaluations conducted in a sequential fashion, with criterion data gathered more than once

SOURCE: Reprinted from *Educational Product Report*, Vol. 2, No. 6 (1969), pp. 6-9, by permission of the author and publisher.

throughout the period of experimentation. This strategy makes it possible either to terminate the evaluation at an early stage if the time-cost has not been justified in effectiveness criteria or to continue evaluation through the stages which lead to program improvement. The sequential nature of the strategy allows the evaluator to constantly modify both the materials and the relevant behaviors of those using them so as to maximize the likelihood of improving their instructional effectiveness. In addition, it reduces the possibility that the final results will be liable to ambiguous interpretation.

In the accompanying flow chart, it can be seen that criterion data was collected twice throughout the school year period; however, the extension to more collection points is readily apparent (Figure 14-1).

FIGURE 14-1

FLOW CHART ILLUSTRATING INSTRUCTIONAL SYSTEM EVALUATION PARADIGM

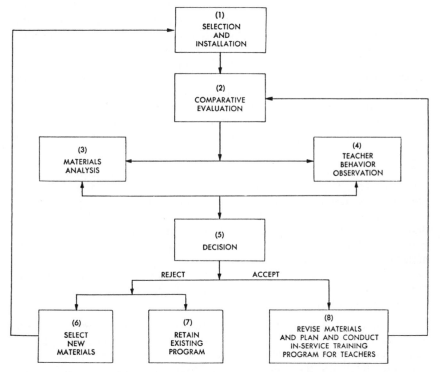

1. MATERIALS SELECTION AND INSTALLATION

a) *Materials Selection.* Initial selection of an instructional program to be evaluated must be based on potential value of the program for the purposes of the relevant institution. For example, in our study of reading programs we chose to evaluate the effectiveness of the McGraw-Hill *Programed Reading Series*. There were two major reasons for this choice: (1) administrators of the school district sponsoring the work were interested in individualizing reading instruction, and (2) they felt that a programed series would relieve the teacher from some tasks and give her more opportunity for diagnosis and prescription. Also, the achievement data on the program available from the publisher and others looked favorable. The initial costs were a problem but by the use of transparencies the workbooks were made non-consumable and thus less costly.

b) Materials Installation. Prior to the actual installation of the selected materials several problems demand serious consideration from the experimenter. First, how shall the classes constituting the experimental and control groups be selected? Ideally, one should select these groups so that they are representative of all student populations to which the experimenter wishes to generalize the results of his experimental effort. Thus, the experimenter should see that both groups contain proportionate sample components of grade levels, measured ability levels, sex, etc. In addition, because one wishes to generalize not only to other students, but also to other teachers, it is crucial that both samples be nearly equivalent with respect to whatever teacher characteristics, sex, years of experience, class size, or other variables are deemed likely to cause the ambiguous interpretation of the experimental results. A base measure of achievement must also be obtained prior to or concurrent with the installation of the new materials. Such measures are collected from both control and experimental groups.

The experimenter is also faced with the problem of acquainting the teachers selected as the experimental group with the new materials. Attitudes of these teachers towards the programed materials may profitably be examined during this acquaintance process. For example, it may be found that a particular teacher expresses extremely antagonistic feelings, for one reason or another, towards programed materials. Assignment of the new materials to this teacher thus may result in an experimentally confounding event which may not be subject to control through counterbalancing techniques, and consequently may increase the ambiguity with which the final results may be interpreted.

Prior to the first comparative evaluation of the new materials, instruments must be developed with which to judge the experimental teachers' behaviors. Of particular interest here is the extent to which the teacher maintains fidelity to the procedures required by the teacher's guide for the programed materials. For example, a rating scale for assessing teacher use of programed reading materials might be developed to include the following: sound-symbol preparation (referring to the m-sound, n-sound, etc., providing periodic reviews and using sound-symbol and alphabet cards), words discrimination (pointing out and providing experience in noting similarities and differences in "like" words such as pin, pan, pen, etc.), word formation (filling in missing parts of words), dictation at least twice a week, student self-pacing (no holding back the faster students and no forcing the slower ones to cover material which they can't master), check on mastery (80 percent or better before being allowed to go on), and appropriate tutoring if necessary before going on to the next unit.

Control classes should also be observed, at least until the first comparative evaluation is made, in order to control the likelihood of a "Hawthorne effect" resulting from attention focused only on experimental group performance.

2. COMPARATIVE EVALUATION

Comparisons are made between gains on criterion variables earned by both groups after a suitable period of instruction. It is recommended that post data be gathered on more than one occasion before a decision concerning the relative efficiency of the programed materials is made. For example, assume that post data is collected in both December and in May. Consider the September-December comparison. If the experimental groups' gains are at least equal to, or better than those of the control group, this provides an indication that the new materials are worthy of further consideration and development. On the other hand, should the control group score significantly better on most measures, this does not necessarily indicate that the new materials be abandoned. Given the initial investment in both time and effort on the experimenter's part, and the relative newness of the materials as far as the experimental teachers are concerned, it would seem that further analysis be attempted before a decision is made to accept or reject the new materials—hence, the recommendation that post data be collected on more than one occasion during the school year and ultimately for more than one year.

In our programed reading study, this first stage evaluation—the comparative evaluation—yielded, in part, the following information. *Programed Reading* gains in silent reading vocabulary and comprehension were significantly better than control classes for students with middle and high beginning-of-the-year total readiness scores. However, no significant differences between treatments were found on vocabulary and comprehension for the low readiness pupils. *Programed Reading* also was significantly better on *Gilmore Oral Reading Rate and Comprehension* measures but not on *Oral Reading Accuracy*. These results then suggested that the program was justified in terms of effectiveness and at the same time pointed up the areas where comparative gains of the new program were not significant. These weak outcome areas then provided the focus for the next stages of the evaluation.

It should be noted here that since the *program* was the unit to be evaluated rather than the pupil, it was possible to give some time-consuming individual tests (e.g., the *Gilmore Oral Reading Test*) to a small sample of pupils in each class and still effectively assess the comparative effectiveness of the programs.

Regarding further analysis, there are at least two sources of variance which can contribute to the results observed during the first comparative evaluation. An investigation of these sources will provide information suggesting modifications which can be introduced into the program prior to the final evaluation. These two sources of variance are effectiveness of materials and teacher behavior.

3. MATERIALS ANALYSIS

Adequate evaluation must include a comparison of the efficiency of the new materials across various sublevels of student abilities. For instance, it was apparent in our example that the new materials produced significantly greater gain in all groups except those having lower ability scores. Developmental efforts may then be directed towards improvement of materials for this specific group. Some specific recommendations for adequate analysis using programed materials in reading include the following steps:

a) A developmental record must be kept. Thus if reading errors are not recorded at the end of each book in the series, one cannot tell which of the early errors drop off later and which of the early successes occur as errors later.

b) Supplementary methods or materials not prescribed by the teacher's guide should not be used for this stage of the evaluation. If the leanest instructional program possible is desired (all fat or excess exercises to be carved out) one must not add instructional material whenever an error occurs. After all, the error may disappear in later stages of instruction without extra-program treatment.

c) For the experimental period, all words and skills tested at the end of the first book in the series must be tested at the end of each book until they occur correctly in two end-of-book tests in succession. Otherwise a skill not adequately taught may drop off without being identified. As these tests are not typically included with the program they must be developed for the evaluation project.

d) To adequately guide later development of supplementary material, not only the type of reading error should be recorded but what appears to be the determinant of the error. Thus, it is helpful to know not only that there were frequent repetitions in oral reading, but also that they occurred primarily as a result of word recognition problems rather than poor phrasing and consequent rereading for a "sensible" phrasing.

4.   TEACHER BEHAVIOR OBSERVATION

The extent to which the experimental teacher maintains fidelity to program specifications may be found to be a significant variable contributing to observed results. During this phase of the study, teachers should not be forced into rigid conformity in using the materials. In our reading study, some limited data showed that the teacher who deviated most from the program specifications obtained the highest for the low ability children at a sacrifice to high ability children.

The development of adequate in-service training programs is largely dependent upon this information on teacher behavior. But appropriate observation schedules for teaching behavior must be developed and systematically used. There are two major sources for categories to be included in the observation schedules. The first source is the teacher's guide recommendations for teaching behavior. It was concerning this kind of teacher behavior that the study reported that teachers with least fidelity to the prescribed program obtained greatest gains for low ability pupils at a sacrifice to higher ability pupils. The second source of categories for the teacher observation schedule is a theoretical model of significant teacher behaviors. For example, one might include teacher's use of "verbal positive contingent reinforcement." If teachers with greatest gains give more frequent positive contingent reinforcement than lower-gain teachers, there are obvious implications for in-service training.

But the leap from such data to the development of in-service training programs is not always so direct. Consider the case of the teacher with greatest gains for low ability pupils. One implication of these results would be to introduce a teacher aide into the class to do the things this teacher did with low ability pupils with time she "stole" from the high ability pupils. But an alternative implication would be to attempt to automate some of the things this teacher did for low ability pupils so as to give her more time for the rest of the class.

Thus the primary importance of evaluation during stages 1 and 2 is to suggest the focus for studies of either the materials or the teacher's behaviors or both to be carried out in stages 3 and 4 of the evaluation procedure. Final decisions should usually be made after the completion of stage 4. However, it is conceivable that the evaluator may wish to extend his analysis, in some cases withholding a decision for a period of more than a school year.

If the decision is made to implement the new program, several other tasks still face the experimenter. He must first compile and integrate the suggested material modifications for the following year, and he must prepare an in-service training program to compensate for those deficiencies revealed by the evaluation. A detailed analysis in these areas during the previous year of experimentation will greatly facilitate the execution of these tasks.

Perhaps we shall see the day when a publisher installs and monitors an instructional system until it is operating effectively and even provides a maintenance contract similar to the installation and maintenance services for an air conditioning system or a computer. Meanwhile evaluation staffs of school districts, private research corporations, or university-based evaluators will provide these services for installation and revision of instructional systems to maximize their effectiveness.

Chapter 15. PROGRAM PREFERENCE FROM THE STUDENTS' POINT OF VIEW

INDIVIDUALIZED INSTRUCTION IN BIOLOGY

Paul Richard and Robert B. Sund

The advent of flexible scheduling and a volume of new educational aids has increased the feasibility of using individualized instruction in science classes. Because of this, the staff at Colorado State College Science Education Department and Laboratory School began two projects in the summer of 1966 to investigate various approaches to individualizing biology and earth science.[1] The ideal approach would have been to design materials, texts, and audio-visual aids specifically for individualized instruction. This would have meant the production of many unique materials. However, the time and cost involved in such a production were beyond our capabilities. It was, therefore, decided to adapt presently produced materials to individualized instruction.

Individualizing can be organized along two general patterns: The continuous progress plan, or the individualized unit approach. The continuous

SOURCE: Reprinted from *The American Biology Teacher*, Vol. 31, No. 4 (April, 1969), pp. 252-56, by permission of author and publisher.

progress plan allows a student to progress through course work at his own rate. When a student finishes the reading of a unit of work and achieves well on an examination he then proceeds to the next section of the course. Under this plan a student may finish the course requirements in 4 or 5 months and then transfer to another course such as chemistry. In order for a student to do this, the entire science department and preferably school must be organized around the continuous progress plan.

Under the individualized unit plan, the student also is encouraged to go through the text and laboratory material at his own rate. However, once the student finishes the required material he does not progress to the next unit but does supplemental laboratory activities or other enrichments. He has opportunities to study in depth the topics covered in the unit.

The feasibility of the continuous progress plan was tested in the first phase (8 weeks) of the investigation and the individualized unit approach in the other two phases (16 weeks) of the study.

Two laboratory-school matched-heterogeneous biology classes of equal size (31) were established as the experimental and control groups for the purpose of the study. The students were matched according to Differential Aptitude test scores, science achievement, and IQ scores. During pretesting students at the laboratory school in biology scored 10 points above the national mean and 56 on the combined verbal reasoning and numerical ability sections of the Differential Aptitude Test. This placed the students average in the sixth stanine and above average as a group as indicated by Figures 15-1 and 15-2 below.

The BSCS Green Version materials were used by the students involved in this investigation. The only significance this version had for the purpose of the study is that it was the one used in the Laboratory School during the period of investigation.

In the first phase of the study, the control and experimental classes were divided into three tracks: slow, regular and fast. Students were placed in these groups according to scores on the verbal reasoning and numerical ability sections of the Differential Aptitude Test, class standing, I.Q. scores, and the Earth Science Curriculum Test scores they completed the previous year.

Three student syllabi were designed; one for each of the groups. The student syllabi outlined the directions the students should follow in moving through the course material at their own rate. Each syllabus contained three sections, listing Required, Suggested, and Enrichment activities. All students were to complete the required activities. These included mainly laboratory activities from the laboratory manual and readings from the text. The suggested activities involved additional supplemental laboratory exercises prepared mainly by the staff related to the work of the chapter. The enrichments included the following non-laboratory activities:

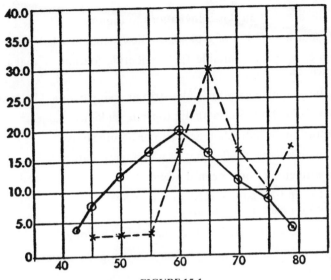

FIGURE 15-1

Stanine Summation: Graph of percent of pupils on National norms (solid line) and actual percent of males at College High (broken line) on the average (Verbal Reasoning plus Number Ability) of the Differential Aptitude Tests.

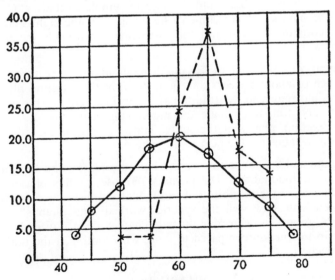

FIGURE 15-2

Stanine Summation: Graph of percent of pupils on National norms (solid line) and actual percent of females at College High (broken line) on the average (Verbal Reasoning plus Number Ability) of the Differential Aptitude Tests.

1. Read a BSCS pamphlet

2. Write a report on BSCS Invitations to Inquiry

3. Write a summation of a biological newspaper article

4. Write, in a style suitable for a scientific journal or magazine, an article on biology

5. Write a commentary on a film strip or a single topic film loop

6. Make a book report on an appropriate biological subject

7. Report on an individual field trip or nature study

8. Prepare scientific collections of a biological nature

9. Experiment at home or in the field

10. Watch and prepare a report on a special educational program on television concerning biology

11. Complete a programmed learning unit in biology

A sample page of how the syllabus was designed appears below (see Figure 15-3).

There are actually several pages similar to the one above for each unit. At the end of the unit several pages list the enrichment activities. The student records in the syllabus his progress by writing the date he began a required activity after "B___" and the date he completed it after "C___." He also lists the number of enrichments he finishes on the right margin. In this way, both the student and the instructor can quickly evaluate the amount of work done.

Initially it was planned to set up throughout the year three testing phases—each of about 8 weeks duration. Between these testing phases the students would return to the traditional group instruction. This was done in order to give time to evaluate and modify the instructional approaches for the succeeding phases of the study. Time was also needed to alter or redesign the syllabus for the next testing phase.

During the first 8-week testing period both the control and experimental groups were individualized. The primary purposes of this phase were as follows: determine the feasibility of individualized instruction for biology teaching; evaluate how well the syllabus worked; and establish a group (the control group) to determine attitude change when returned to traditional group instruction compared to those who continued the individualized approach.

PHASE I

Although the instructor and the syllabus outlined in detail for the students how the individualizing of the class should operate, students took

Chapter 2
Individuals and Populations

Required BSCS Laboratory I	Required and Suggested Activities II	Enrichments Date Completed III

2.1 Required

Note: Laboratory exercise 2.2 should be set up before doing other laboratory exercises in the chapter. Laboratory exercise 2.2 requires a period of 10 days for growth. It will be done as a class project.

1. Text reading pp 22-30

2. Answer text guide questions: 1, 2, 3, 4, 5, and 6 on pp 48-49

B_____2.1   3. "Population Growth, A Model"

4. Class will view the film: "Population Ecology." Encyclopedia Britannica Films

C_____2.1   5. Answer text problems #1 and 4 on page 49

1_____
2_____
3_____
4_____
5_____
6_____
7_____
8_____
9_____
10_____
11_____
12_____
13_____
14_____
15_____
16_____
17_____
18_____
19_____
20_____
21_____

2.1 Suggested

1. "For Further Investigation" choose No. 1, 2, or 3 on page 28 of your *Student's Manual.*

2. List and discuss at least three methods you might use in sampling bird populations in your neighborhood. Describe these methods in your data book.

3. By use of the library, make a comparative study of human population from 1000 B.C. to 1310 and from 1841 to the present. What has been the trend of human population on Earth? What factors have been responsible for this trend? Make graphs of your data to help explain your work.

FIGURE 15-3

about one week to adjust to the approach. Many students did not take advantage of their class time and there seemed to be considerable lack of direction. This, in part, may be explained by the fact that the students were not accustomed to self-direction and the instructor was unfamiliar as to what his role should be under this form of instruction. Many students, however, had little difficulty in adjusting to this style of classroom organization. After the adjustment phase was over, students moved through the syllabus with little trouble. Certain students, however, did require prodding by the instructor. These individuals also required similar attention when in traditional group instruction.

At the conclusion of the initial 8-week phase, it was decided to reject the use of three forms of a student syllabus. This rejection was based upon the fact that some students in the slow group, even though they were never told their group designation, resented being given a slow group syllabus. Then, too, some of the slow students actually achieved higher on the standardized BSCS unit test than did some of those in the fast group.

The continuous progress plan also was rejected in favor of the unit approach. The rationale for this was due to the fact that BSCS biology requires many live organisms, extensive preparations, and equipment. The logistic problems became complex when the students began to spread out in their work through the syllabus. It was the opinion of the staff that the continuous progress plan was, therefore, not feasible for use with a typical class and instructor. Since it was our fundamental aim to design a syllabus which could have utility for other BSCS teachers, this approach had to be rejected.

PHASE II

Phase II tested the feasibility of a single track syllabus for all groups designed around the enriched individualized unit approach. Following the completion of this Phase, the BSCS Achievement Test, No. 2, was given with the following results (see Table 15-1).

A test to determine the significance of the variations of the means of the two different approaches indicated no significant difference between

Table II
BSCS Achievement Test Number (2) Results

SEX	[2]BSCS National Norms		Individualized BSCS Scores	
	Mean	Standard Deviation	Mean	Standard Deviation
M	23.87	6.36	24.31	5.92
F	22.44	6.14	23.40	5.11
	Students 1513		Students 62	

TABLE 15-1

BSCS Achievement Test No. 2 Results[*]

*By permission of the BSCS from "Means and Standard Deviations of Scores on Pre-Tests, Post-Tests and Achievement Tests," *BSCS Newsletter,* No. 30, Jan. 1967.

the means at the 0.01 level of significance. Comparative results indicated achievement not significantly different from the national means for the BSCS Standardized Achievement Tests.

Student reaction to the Phase II approach was most positive. They appreciated not being grouped as in multi-track Phase I. The single track syllabus was more usable and caused little confusion among students.

PHASE III

In Phase III, the control class was returned to the non-individualized approach for the purpose of comparing it with the experimental group. The experimental group covered essentially the same material as the control group during eight weeks. They covered two week blocks followed by a teacher-prepared test devoted to the units for Chapters 14, 15, 16, and 17 of the Green Version. Both classes were taught by the same instructor as in the previous phases. Standardized BSCS Achievement Tests covering the material were given both groups at the conclusion of this phase with the following results (see Table 15-2).

A test to determine the significance of the variations of the means between groups indicated no significant difference between the means at the 0.01 level of significance.

TABLE 15-2

BSCS Achievement Test No. 3 Results *

Table III
BSCS Achievement Test Number (3) Results

SEX	BSCS Nat'l. Norms		Individualized BSCS Group		Control BSCS Group	
	Mean	Std. Dev.	Mean	Std. Dev.	Mean	Std. Dev.
M	21.06	6.06	19.88	5.27	19.08	2.79
F	20.07	5.67	19.20	3.49	18.73	4.30
	Students 1513		Students 31		Students 31	

*By permission of the BSCS from "Means and Standard Deviations of Scores on Pre-Tests, Post-Tests and Achievement Tests," *BSCS Newsletter,* No. 30, Jan. 1967.

STUDENT QUESTIONNAIRE

At the conclusion of the year, the students in both groups were given a questionnaire to determine their feelings toward individualization. The results of the objective part of the questionnaire are indicated below. Not all students answered all questions which explains the variations in the total number of responses (see Figure 15-4).

The questionnaire also asked the students to respond to five essay type questions. A number of students did not respond to all the questions. For this reason no statistical analysis of the answers were made. The type of responses, however, have been categorized and are listed below.

1.   What did you like most about the individualized approach?

The students liked the approach because they: had more freedom; could work at their own rate and were not held back; could do extra experiments; could use audio-visual aids; enjoyed the variety of things to do in class; worked harder.

2.   What did you like least about the individualized approach?

The students stated they did not like the approach because: there was not enough time, they were rushed, their grades dropped, everybody expected too much, they would rather work in groups, this tended to waste time; there was too much required work; and the directions in the syllabus were not clear.

3.   What should the instructor do to make you move through the course material at a faster rate?

The students said the instructor should: set dates for things due, have more class discussion, let a student progress at his own rate through the quarter; do nothing to speed up the class.

FIGURE 15-4

Individualized Study Questionnaire

	Poor	Fair	Good
1. I think the directions given before we started to use the individualized approach were	2	35	22
2. I think the directions to follow in the student syllabus are	Poor 8	Fair 32	Good 22
3. In the individualized approach how did your work compare to the traditional class approach?	Less 9	Same 19	Harder 31
4. I would rate the individualized approach compared to the traditional class approach	Poor 6	Fair 32	Good 22
5. The idea that all classes except P.E. should be individualized is	Poor 30	Fair 21	Good 9
6. The use of the BSCS individualized approach caused my grades in other subjects to	Drop 11	Same 33	Improve 12
7. The amount of lab work done in class should	Drop 13	Same 33	Improve 12
8. The number of possibilities for extra enriched activities should	Drop 16	Same 29	Improve 15

4. What should the instructor do to improve the individualized approach?

The students wrote that the instructor should: not count a lot on suggested and enrichment activities, not rush them, allow later dates to hand in work, require enrichments, have more outside reading, leave it the way it is because it is good.

5. List any other comments you wish to make below:

The comments made were: this is the best way to teach biology; some individuals can not move as fast as others and should not be expected to; the individualized approach was less boring; I liked it very much, at first I did not like it; I like it better; I hate it; I did not know how to budget my time; it is a good idea for part of the year but should not be used for the entire year.

CONCLUSIONS

The achievement scores and the questionnaire indicated biology classes could be individualized and students do achieve on standardized tests in individualized classes as well as those in non-individualized classes. The study also showed course materials not specifically designed for individualized instruction can be organized to meet this end. An analysis of student behavior showed students were able to follow an individualized student syllabus, tended to work harder in the course without affecting their other school grades, and generally preferred the approach to traditional group instruction.

IMPLICATIONS

After evaluating the study, it is our belief that the syllabus should be modified to include the suggested and enriched activities under one heading entitled "Suggested Activities." This is being done. A revised and modified syllabus is now in production and portions have been tested in our Laboratory School and by three instructors in Arapahoe High School, Littleton, Colorado. The instructors have found students have less difficulty in following the modified version. No further statistical analyses of the individualized biology project are presently planned for the Laboratory School. All biology classes, however, are now individualized and functioning smoothly. Our future energies shall be devoted to refining the syllabus by writing better suggested activities.

During the individualizing project some work was done to adapt the BSCS Invitations to Inquiry and inquiry film loops for the purposes of individualization. Although these materials were designed for group instruction, individuals in our classes using them have successfully achieved the objectives outlined for them by BSCS. Further investigation, however, is needed to determine how these materials can be best utilized in biology instruction. A study for this purpose is planned by members of our staff during the 1968-69 school year.

NOTES

[1] Paul Richard did the instructing of the individualizing of the biology course and Roger Bybee instructed the earth science individualizing project in the Laboratory School.

Chapter 16. PROGRAM EVALUATION BY CRITICAL APPLICATION OF A SCHOOL DISTRICT'S EDUCATIONAL MODEL

EVALUATION FOR A SMALL DISTRICT

Charles L. Jenks

The school should promote . . . intellectual training and a mastery of the academic curriculum to the extent of the individual's capacity. . . . The academic curriculum should be presented in such a way as to encourage the development of certain intellectual attitudes, skills, moral standards, self-confidence, and self-esteem. An inquiring mind; the ability to think creatively, imaginatively, and critically; the realization in the child that education is his chief responsibility; the techniques of problem-solving and the scientific method; leadership and initiative; a reasoned attitude toward acceptance of authority and the understanding of when and how to be a follower; responsibility for social behavior, respect for the rights, property, opinions,

SOURCE: Reprinted from *Educational Product Report*, Vol. 2, No. 5 (1969), pp. 8-17, by permission of author and publisher.

and feelings of others; and personal integrity, good moral standards and manners.

The above list comprises the goals toward which all staff in the Reed Union School District, Tiburon, California, are supposed to move. It is likely that most school districts have a similar set. But the similarity does not end with the nature of the list. It also extends to the difficulty of interpreting such lists into something that admits of clarity.

Our district has a student enrollment of approximately 2,000. For several years the district staff and community have made strong efforts to provide quality education. Low student-teacher ratios, a highly qualified staff, and support and implementation of educational innovations are characteristics of the instructional program. Another noteworthy achievement, resulting from the district's concern for educational progress, was the construction of the Granada Community School. Multi-age grouping, a variety of teaching styles, and a non-graded format are common practices at Granada and other schools within the district. Different ways to individualize the instructional program are constantly being tried.

After four years of operation at Granada, the Board of Trustees and staff agreed that evaluation of the educational program was in order. School districts around the country are increasingly being required to evaluate their programs. The demand for evaluation comes primarily from sources of financial aid—whether these be federal programs or local taxpayers. The demand itself does not seem unfair. What does prove troublesome is attempting to evaluate various educational programs in terms of a list of goals such as the one previously described. As the goals are written, disagreement is non-existent. It is only when these same goals are redefined into bite-size objectives that differences of opiniòn appear.

Education has long been accustomed to both formal and informal evaluation. Most reliance has probably been placed on the informal approach—the approach of casual observation, unclear goals, and subjective judgment. Because of the general lack of specificity, the results of informal evaluations have been highly varied and subject to numerous questions.

When formal evaluations have been accomplished by use of standardized tests, check lists, rating devices, or direct comparisons, results may be more objective and reliable, but there still remains a serious question. Does our information tell us what we need to know? Do the various scores we acquire truly reflect our educational objectives?

Further, even rigidly controlled experiments that are replicable do not necessarily tell us whether the measured change represents our educational intent. Before determining whether a technique, an innovation, or a new set of materials causes a desired change, we need first to address ourselves to the task of specifying the nature of the desired change.

Therefore, before gathering data from which judgments were going to be made, it was necessary for us to take some preliminary steps. First we needed to define, as explicitly as possible, our district goals: What do we mean when we state that our students should master the academic curriculum? What is meant by an inquiring mind? What behavior would we expect to see when a student is demonstrating responsibility for his learning? It was our opinion that these questions needed answers before an evaluation of our educational efforts could be informative and capable of giving direction.

It must be clarified that at no time was it assumed that all of the listed goals would ever be completely and satisfactorily defined. This is true because of the nebulous nature of the goals, the difficulty of measurement, and the likelihood of a strong causal relationship between attempts at specificity and disagreement among the specifiers. Nevertheless, a decision not to attempt definition of goals would leave evaluation, for us, where it was.

We assumed that the attainment of our stated goals by the students should become the final criteria by which we evaluated the educational program. Certain procedures were selected initially by which we hoped to arrive at (1) a more precise definition of the goals, (2) student behavior when the goals were in process of being attained, and (3) specific teaching strategies that would hopefully promote the desired student behavior. The expansion of goals into these categories were arrived at through joint efforts of school staff and the research specialist. Although not stated as such, the teaching strategies may be regarded as hypotheses. In other words, it was hypothesized that certain teacher behavior and techniques would result in certain "desirable" student behaviors. The testing of these, of course, remained.

Upon "completion" of these procedures, including behavioral description of students, teaching strategies, and the selection of measurement techniques, other steps can be taken. It is possible to view evaluation as a system-wide process, as a smaller, more actively oriented task, or both. For example, using a model proposed by Robert Stake (see Figure 16-1), it is possible to follow through with a teacher-student activity from its inception to an outcome and determine the following:

1. *The intent of the teacher* and student for the activity or task and whether the task represents probable growth toward one of the district goals.

2. *The intended transactions* between teacher and student for the activity and whether the transaction represents a desirable strategy.

3. *The intended outcome;* i.e., what the student will be doing as a result of the activity or task.

4. Whether the listed intents occurred as determined through observations.

5. Whether stated expectations with regard to time allowances, completion schedules, etc. actually occurred.

6. Whether stated expectations with regard to quality and type of teacher-student interactions actually occurred.

7. Whether expected terminal behavior for students actually occurred.

FIGURE 16-1

Intents	Observations		Standards	Judgments
		Antecedents		
		Transactions		
		Outcomes		
Description Matrix			Judgment Matrix	

In summary, based on terminal behavior and observations, judgments can be made with regard to the appropriateness of the intent, the worth of the transaction, and the outcomes as they reflect our operationally defined goals.

It will not be possible, or desirable, to evaluate every aspect of an educational system or to assess the value of every educational act. There are, fortunately, many inspirational, unplanned-for activities that defy premeditated evaluation in terms of our model. Evaluation of these will continue to be a teacher-pupil shared responsibility. However, it will be easier to assess outcomes of planned events, tasks, or materials as they relate to our goals.

We are also not suggesting that every teacher and student will be operationally aware of each of the hoped-for student behaviors and teacher strategies. Our operational goals are not admonitions. It is important that they not be for three reasons:

First, because teaching and learning styles in our district are at a high level, radical changes on the basis of our efforts should not be expected. We will be more able, however, to evaluate and adjust a program when needed on the basis of our mutually shared objectives.

Second, the success of the teaching and learning act depends heavily on a natural process of communication between teacher and learner. Over-emphasis on specific behavior which is not natural and spontaneous could create over-rigidity or inappropriate dependence.

Third, any attempt at assessing attainment of process goals requires defining non-cognitive behavior. This is an ambitious task. Therefore, even though our criteria may represent progress, they will not represent the end of the definition problem.

The implementation of our model dealing with district goals needs further clarification. It is important to say again that no classroom program can possibly reflect all goals at any moment in time. However, the use of our model will be more appropriate when our goals are more explicit. Most effective use of the model will be made by a teacher and a co-worker who wish to determine whether: (1) planned student-teacher transactions and hoped-for outcomes of a task do, in fact, occur; and (2) to what extent planned transactions and desired outcomes match behaviorally defined goals. Until we are able to implement such a procedure and begin to evaluate on the basis of our intents, research information will lack the full potential to assist us in making relevant decisions.

Our next step involved efforts on the part of the staff at Granada School and the research specialist to come to grips with the goals as stated. One of the most beneficial aspects of the effort was the process that resulted from the staff discussion. Differences and similarities of opinions were aired freely with the result that the staff felt that they had a better idea of each other's objectives. Communication did not start and stop with the meetings but continued at other times. From a research point of view, the discussions were helpful in devising a system of observation based on student behaviors that were specified in the staff discussions.

One of our goals states that the student should "develop the realization that education is his chief responsibility." There is no question that the acquisition of a "realization" is an internal occurrence. We cannot measure internal changes of this type in ways other than observable behavior. In order to be able to determine with some accuracy the extent to which a goal such as this is being achieved, the staff needed to build a list of behaviors that, for us, "stood for" the goals. Once this was done, teaching strategies could be specified as likely to promote the desired behaviors. Although it is possible to test the efficacy of the teacher techniques in promoting the desired behavior, we are unable to be entirely certain that the behaviors will stand the test of time. Do they really mean the same thing as the goal? We do not know. Nevertheless, as long as a staff is generally satisfied that the behaviors specified represent desirable ones, we can at least proceed.

The list below represents tentative efforts toward specification of one of our goals. The use of an observation system will assist us in measuring goal attainment.

Goal. To develop the realization in the student that education is his chief responsibility.

I.   *Procedures:* List observable behavior of a student who is demonstrating learning responsibility.

    A.   *General:* Students demonstrate the ability to plan individually and with others for needed learning.

       1. Specific behavior indicating growth toward objective

          a) The student is becoming proficient in evaluating self with regard to interests and styles of working.

          b) The student is becoming proficient in evaluating self with regard to skill development.

          c) The student is becoming proficient in long-range planning for skill development.

          d) . . . and other student behavior.

       2. Teaching strategies to promote specific behavior

          a) Curriculum organization and teaching styles need to allow for and promote student expression of interest.

          b) Curriculum organization and teaching styles need to promote a variety of input and output possibilities so that student and teachers can determine the student's most successful learning styles.

          c) Curriculum organization needs to be arranged so that the student can see the possibility of and be responsible for long-range planning based on his own needs and interests.

          d) . . . and other teaching strategies.

    B.   *General:* Students demonstrate the responsibility for tasks assigned by self or by teacher.

       1. Specific behavior indicating growth toward goal

          a) The student is satisfied only with careful work.

          b) The student is resourceful in figuring out solutions to problems.

      c) ... and other student behaviors.

   2. Teaching strategies to promote specific behavior

      a) The student is required to decide when work was carefully done—evaluation.

      b) The student is required to select careful work for display or folder.

      c) The teacher encourages best work of student.

      d) The teacher encourages students to persist.

      e) The teacher expresses confidence in ability of student.

      f) The teacher and student discuss limitations.

      g) ... and other teaching strategies.

  C. *General:* Students demonstrate the responsibility for evaluating work.

   1. Specific behavior indicating growth toward goal

      a) The student is proficient in self-evaluation of progress.

      b) The student participates in group evaluation.

      c) The student listens and reacts to suggestions of others in regard to performance.

   2. Teaching strategies to promote specific behaviors

      a) The students participate orally on 1:1 evaluation of work in progress and of assessment for possible change in procedures.

      b) The teacher schedules time for group evaluation of group project.

      c) The teacher schedules time for group to evaluate an individual project.

II. *Evaluation:* Develop instruments of measurement and testing and assess results of activities.

  A. Specific student behavior.

   1. Observational system, check lists, rating scales, etc., will be developed.

   2. Questionnaires will be created for students.

        3.   Student evaluation report forms are to be prepared for use by teachers and students to determine congruency.

   B.   Specified teacher strategies

        1.   Observational systems are to be developed to determine existence of strategies.

        2.   Student response to strategies from questionnaire, interview and observation will be analyzed.

   C.   Assessing change in student behavior

        1.   Cumulative observational records are to be kept.

        2.   Changes in student response to questionnaires are to be measured by pre- and posttesting.

        3.   Changes in congruency in teacher-student evaluation form are to be determined.

   D.   Conversion of techniques for teacher-student use.

After preliminary work on goal definition and the selection of measurement techniques, three general areas of the educational program were selected upon which to focus evaluation efforts.

I. Describing the Existing Program

This focus includes stated plans of a general nature, objectives, more specific teacher intents as to procedures and strategies, and desired student outcomes of the teaching staff. Generally, the teacher intents and desired outcomes in this area will be short-range, perhaps as brief as a series of one-day evaluations of teacher intent and observed student outcomes. Evaluation in this area should assist in developing individual teacher programs as well as providing descriptive information of the educational program.

II. Process Evaluation (Describing Conditions of Individualization)

Certain classroom conditions have been listed and defined as desirable for promoting individualization of instruction. An observational system, student response to conditions, and teacher narrative summaries will comprise the data for this section.

III. Student Evaluation

In order to determine the educational outcome of the program, the measurement of student growth in district goals that have been defined behaviorally will receive primary emphasis. Generally, results in student evaluation are long-range and more difficult to trace to specific teaching acts. Measurement in this area will be compared with a control group in some instances.

Below, each of the three listed evaluation areas are described in detail. The structure of the design is identical for each area, but the components are described in terms of the research needs of each. The outline used was adapted from a proposal by Daniel L. Stufflebeam of Ohio State University.

I. Describing the Existing Program

A. Focus of the Evaluation

1. Level of decision making—For purposes of this section, decisions are made by the staffs of each school for which descriptions are being prepared.

2. Types of decisions to be made

   a) Planning—Staff members will need to describe their planned programs in terms of their objectives, their procedures and strategies, the extent of diversification that they hope to accomplish, their plans as to the amount and kind of student-teacher interaction, and the amount of student involvement in activity selection.

   In addition to these general statements which resemble individual philosophies, a stratified sample of teachers will be asked to pre-state as clearly as possible with the researcher, their teaching objectives, intended procedures and strategies, and desired student outcomes of a brief instructional period of time (perhaps 1-3 days in duration). Following a joint effort by teacher and researcher, the instructional sequences described will be observed for determining the extent to which stated objectives, intents, and hoped-for student outcomes actually occur.

   b) In addition to *planning* decisions described under (2a), teachers will need to decide whether to *continue* the procedures and strategies planned with reference to observed student outcomes. Observed student outcomes need to be related to the original teacher-stated objectives.

3. Criteria to be used

   a) Planning—Criteria used in *planning* by teachers will largely consist of current knowledge and resources available to them.

     b)   Continuation—Criteria used in *continuation* decisions will be the stated teacher intents, teacher strategies and procedures, and the desired student outcomes. To the extent that observed student outcomes are different from hoped-for outcomes, then continuation decisions can be made in terms of either revised teacher intent (objectives, strategies, resources) or in terms of revised hoped-for student outcomes.

  4.   Evaluation policies

     a)   Evaluation under Section I will be limited to a stratified sample of staff members.

     b)   Because sufficient researcher-teacher time must be available, the number of such occurrences will be limited.

B.   Collection of Information

  1.   Source of information

     a)   Planning—information collected under planning decisions will be taken from participating teachers.

     b)   Continuation—information will be collected by observation of the teaching act and learner outcomes.

  2.   Instruments and methods of collecting information

     a)   Planning—teacher interviews will be scheduled for obtaining necessary objectives, procedures, and desired student outcomes.

     b)   Continuation—information obtained from teachers will be placed on a modified *"Stake's Matrix Model";* observation of student outcomes will complete the matrix for determination of the match between intents and outcomes (see Figure 16-1).

  3.   Sampling procedures—Selection of staff participation will be random. A sample of eight will be drawn from total list of 19 teachers on the Granada staff. A similar ratio will be used for the Middle School staff. It is assumed that the sample will be representative.

  4.   Schedule of information collection—For purposes of this phase, scheduling is left open. The nature of the decisions to be made, however, makes it necessary that data collection of both *planning* and *continuation* data be closely consecutive.

C. Organization of Information

    1.   Format of collected information

        a)   Data collected from teacher participants will be categorized under: (1) general objectives and (2) specific objectives (teacher intents and desired student outcomes).

        b)   Data collected from observations will consist of observed teacher procedures and observed student outcomes.

    2.   Status of collected information—Data from (1*a*) and (1*b*) above will be placed on a modified Stake matrix.

D. Analysis of Information.

    1.   General objectives as stated by teachers will be compiled into a descriptive summary.

    2.   Specific objectives (teacher intents and desired student outcomes) observations will be analyzed empirically on the following basis:

        a)   The match between teacher intents and observed procedures

        b)   The match between desired student outcomes and observed student outcomes

        c)   Listing of unanticipated student outcomes

        d)   Judgments made as to value of intended procedures for accomplishing hoped-for student outcomes

        e)   Recommendations.

E. Reporting of Information—Results of evaluation in the area of program description will be of most value to the teachers involved. In addition, a general description of the evaluation procedures and the results of individual unit evaluations, although anonymous, will be available for any interested staff member. It is assumed that the parents and the Board of Trustees will receive a summary report (1968-69) of the activities and results described.

F. Administration of the Evaluation

    1.   An activity chart of design components will be made to schedule the steps involved.

    2.   Staff and resource requirements for completion of this part of the total evaluation design are available. The number of teacher-researcher team efforts will partly depend on existing constraints.

3.   The potential value of Part I of the evaluation design lies in the domain of increasing teacher effectiveness in reaching stated objectives. There is no time limit on potential value; this phase could serve merely as a measure of success of specific teaching strategies or it *could serve a long-range purpose of program improvement.*

4.   This phase is dependent on the skills of the teacher-researcher team in stating clearly the specific objectives (teacher intents and desired student outcomes) and the precision of the observer. It is hoped that two persons will be available for observations.

II. *Process Evaluation*

The purpose of Part II of the research design is to determine to what degree the "signs" or "conditions" of a program of individualized instruction exist in the school program. The conditions of individualization are not necessarily descriptive of what is happening, but are based partly on experience and partly on research. They are conditions that are considered conducive to learning. They are such that if a school could describe their program as consisting of "these elements," we believe that this school deserves to use the term "individualized." No school program can presently boast of 100 percent individualized instruction, nor is it likely that this will ever be. Progress toward this state is the goal. Having the "desirable" conditions present in any given class is felt to be one important ingredient.

A. Focusing the Evaluation

1.   Level of decision making

a) Decisions concerning desirable conditions of individualization have been made partly by staff and partly by the researcher as based on experience and knowledge.

b) Decisions concerning actual classroom processes and procedures are made by the principal and teaching staff.

2.   Decision situations

a) The decisions to be made in Part II of the evaluation design are largely continuational and adoptive. On the basis of information collected, teachers will need to make decisions about their program.

b) The focus of Part II will be research oriented. Data collected is based on observed class situations without pre-specification of teacher intents. In this sense, it is n velopmental, although feedback to teachers in regaru the observations may cause change.

c) Alternatives—Pre-specified conditions are open to revision as the result of experience and student reaction.

3. Criteria

a) Results of observations on a scheduled basis will indicate the number of specified conditions that are present in the school program.

b) Student response to questions about specified conditions.

4. Policies of evaluation

All teachers involved in the Granada program will be involved in Part II of the evaluation design. Each staff member will have access to observation reports that pertain to him.

B. Collection of Information

1. Sources of information

a) Teacher and class observations with recorded presence or absence of specified conditions. Recording of observations will be accomplished with observation system developed and refined during previous year.

b) Student reaction to questionnaire items designed to elicit feelings about conditions of instruction.

2. Instruments

a) Observation system developed.

b) Questionnaire items locally devised to elicit student feelings.

3. Sampling procedures

a) Observation schedule—All teachers in Beta, Gamma, Delta and Omega schools.

b) Student questionnaire items—Granada-Omega Cluster.

4. Schedule of information collection

a) Observations to determine existence of conditions are to be conducted on a regular basis for the observer, but randomized by time of day and day of week. Two observations per day for two days per week at Granada. Accumulated observations should result in approximately 150 during the school year.

b)   The student questionnaire will be administered twice during the school year. Omega students at Granada will receive the test in October and again in May.

C. Organization of Information

1.   Information on observations to be recorded on report forms

2.   Information on student feelings about "conditions" will be summarized from questionnaire items with percentage response for items or categories.

D. Analysis of Information

1.   Presence or absence of conditions based on observation can result in either:

a)   Baseline data from which one phase of instructional program may be evaluated.

b)   Baseline data to determine change in existence of conditions following a change in program or procedure.

c)   Data by which other programs may be compared as to existence of specified conditions.

2.   Student response on two administrations can result in:

a)   Data by which program may react to student feelings.

b)   Baseline data by which change in student feelings may be traced to emphasis on "conditions" by teachers. In this regard tolerance, comfort, or support of students for the various conditions can aid in planning.

E. Reporting of Information

1.   Report of Part II of the evaluation design will be available for staff, parents, and Board of Trustees.

2.   Reporting will be available in written form, as well as an oral-visual presentation.

3.   Reports are intended to be ready for dissemination by the end of academic year 1968-69.

F. Administration of the Evaluation

    1. Activities under Part II of the evaluation design will take place during the school year 1968-69. It is believed that additional data from the various activities from subsequent years would increase the value of the evaluation. However, it is planned so that each school year represents a potential end of evaluation period.

    2. Present staff is assumed to be sufficient for completion of the activities, but unforeseen staff requirements may prevent the desired number of observations.

    3. The potential value of Part II of the evaluation design for teachers and students is one of being able to describe the instructional program in terms of appropriate and desirable conditions of individualization. Generally, the use of specified conditions of individualization will make it possible for our program to be described specifically, rather than in general terms.

    4. Annual updating of the design under Part II is felt to be indicated. Recommended action in regard to results of the evaluation will be a part of the evaluation report.

III. Student Evaluation

Parts I and II of the evaluation design have dealt primarily with the nature of the educational program. Unless a major effort is also made to assess the outcome of the program, we have stopped short of knowing what is needed. In this section, the design proposes to attend to student growth in skills, student growth in attitude toward learning, and parent feelings about the instructional program. It is important to remember that in addition to knowing how our students are "doing," we continue to obtain information that assists us in making new decisions. Assessing student growth in skills and attitudes toward learning is intended.

In Part II, the design will include both traditional methods of evaluation (standardized tests) and locally devised tests which attempt to measure criteria specified from our district goals.

A. Focusing the Evaluation

    1. Evaluation in Part III will provide information for decision making on the part of teaching staffs. Decisions to be made are largely continuative. As a result of measured outcomes, a staff will be able to decide on needed changes, if any, that will result in desired improvement. For purposes of this phase of the evaluation we had the following questions:

a) Do Granada students achieve as well as other students as compared with appropriate norms?

b) Does the Granada program cause a significant increase in critical thinking skills as compared with students of similar characteristics and who experience a more traditional program?

c) Do Granada students demonstrate significantly higher approach behavior toward subject matter areas as compared with students of similar characteristics and who experience a more traditional program?

d) ... and similar questions.

2. *Criteria*—The results of the educational program are being assessed in:

a) Academic achievement

b) Student response to subject areas

c) Student growth: Critical thinking skills

d) Student support or non-support of the instructional program

e) Student support or non-support of the teacher-student relationships that come about as a result of the program

f) Creativity

g) Teacher evaluation of program

h) Curiosity of student

i) Parent response to program.

B. Collection of Information

1. Sources of information include students and parents.

2. Instruments include:

a) Achievement—STEP

b) Critical thinking skills

(1) Ohio Thinking Check-up

(2) Selected tests from National Council of Social Studies

c) Student response

(1) To program and teacher strategies

(2) Evaluation of self and other students as a result of the program

(3) Approach-avoidance to subject areas

(4) Parent questionnaire (locally developed)

(5) Torrance Tests of Creativity

(6) Teacher evaluation (narrative summaries)

(7) Curiosity (Children's Reactive Curiosity test) Penney McCann.

3. Sampling Procedures—Samples will include both fifth and sixth graders. In addition, the samples will be stratified to obtain a range of ability levels. Samples will be limited to those students having a minimum of two years attendance in their respective programs.

   a) STEP test in achievement (baseline data for students being retested has been established from previous year).

   (1) Reading—grades 5 and 6; Math—grades 5 and 6; Social Studies—grade 6.

   b) Critical thinking skills

   (1) Granada—sample from Omega (60 students)

   (2) Control group ("X" district)—sample of 60 students

   c) Student response to program—questionnaires and rating scales

   (1) Program and teacher strategies

      (a) Granada-Omega—Samples of 60 students

      (b) Control group-"X" district—sample of 60 students

   (2) Evaluation of self and other students as a result of program

      (a) Granada-Omega—sample of 60 students

      (b) Control group-"X" district—sample 60 students

   (3) Student approach-avoidance to subject areas

      (a) Granada-Omega—sample of 60 students

      (b) Control group-"X" district—sample of 60 students

   (4) Parent questionnaire—total Granada parent population will be invited to participate

(5) Creativity

  (a) Granada-Omega—sample of 60 students

  (b) Control group-"X" district—sample of 60 students.

When there are so many areas to choose from, why did we select these criteria to measure the effects of an educational program? There were several reasons. Academic achievement is one of the goals listed. For this goal, standardized test batteries are used. Educators who have given serious thought to the question of evaluation realize, however, that once the area of standardized testing is put aside, evaluation becomes a bit cloudy.

Few would disagree with the importance of helping students become self-directing individuals who are capable of making decisions and judgments based on available data. As yet, however, techniques of assessing growth in the ability to make wise choices are limited.

To circumvent this problem, we are attempting to measure smaller, more discrete portions of the larger concept of critical thinking. Such areas as drawing comparisons, noting differences, judging whether statements are warranted, interpreting data, judging consistency and distinguishing between fact and opinion are some of the crucial skills we are hoping to assess.

Curiosity has been included even though it is not listed specifically as one of our goals. However, it does appear to be an ingredient or part of the makeup of children who are generally described as creative, who enjoy and profit from divergent thinking. According to Wallace and Ethel Maw, "Curiosity has long been considered an important attribute of many living organisms. In human beings, it seems to be a crucial element in creativity, learning, and problem solving. It is often discussed in connection with interest, set attention, and motivation."

The last and perhaps the most time-consuming part of the research design is that of collecting information dealing with reactions and responses to the educational program. Reactions or feelings are generated in parents, teachers, and most importantly in students. It is our contention that the attitudes of those who are served by an institution as well as those who operate the institution, may be the most important product.

With the staff, it is a fairly simple matter. When the school is open to ideas and is non-threatening to divergent opinions, it may be more difficult *not* to obtain honest opinions than the reverse.

Students are generally quite willing to cooperate in the matter of expressing themselves, and devising methods to assess their feelings are not too difficult. Our current efforts are centered on two questionnaires. The first one titled Approach-Avoidance, originated from a suggestion by Robert Mager in his very valuable booklet, *"Developing Attitudes Toward Learning."* An assessment of children's interest in certain subject areas on a 1-5 rating scale is obtained twice during the year. If the pre- and post-measures occur at the beginning and end of the school year, a "change increment" is obtained. A loss, an increase, or an unchanging differential score will indicate to some degree how the educational program has affected the student's interest in the subject area.

The second questionnaire attempts to measure a variety of school-oriented variables. In some instances students are asked to consider a class, themselves, and their teachers, in terms of lists of descriptive adjectives or phrases and rate these on a 1-5 scale. Also, the students are asked to select from lists of statements those which most typify their understanding of their teacher's expectations. Finally, students are asked to indicate agreement, disagreement, or no opinion on a series of statements that reflect many of our educational practices.

Both questionnaires can be used effectively to obtain information about student feelings. We feel strongly that how children feel about their school, their teachers, and themselves is a primary concern for anyone who wants to improve a program.

As was stated at the beginning of this description, evaluation is becoming increasingly demanded by sources of funding for our educational enterprises. In Reed Union School District, the community has strongly supported the educational program. Unless clear lines of communication remain open between the school and the parents, who supply the raw material as well as the economic means, support can gradually diminish. One method of determining parental attitudes is by asking them. To simplify the questioning, a questionnaire was developed.

As well as being asked to rate various programs, and the appropriateness of the program for their children, parents respond to a list of items describing techniques, teacher strategies in use, organizational patterns, and other descriptive statements. For purposes of obtaining differential scores, parents respond twice to the list. The first time their score is based on their understanding of the *current* emphasis being given to the various school tasks. The second time through, the score is based on parental opinion of what *should be* rather than what currently exists. The differential score may be used as an annual check of the degree to which an existing program corresponds to the community's wishes, or it may be used to focus in on areas of needed communication.

Although we will have difficulties with the design, we are satisfied that useful information will be obtained. Some of our criteria will be difficult to measure. There may not be a direct relationship between some of our measurement results and our program. Our conclusions therefore will necessarily be tentative.

REFERENCES

1. STAKE, ROBERT. "The Countenance of Educational Evaluation," *Teachers College Record,* Vol. 68, No. 7 (April 1967).

2. STUFFLEBEAM, DANIEL. "Toward a Science of Educational Evaluation," *Educational Technology,* Vol. VIII, No. 14 (July 30, 1968).

3. MAW, WALLACE H., and ETHEL W. "Establishing Criteria for Evaluating Measures of Curiosity," The American Documentation Institute, ERIC, ADI 6558.

4. MAGER, ROBERT. *Developing Attitudes toward Learning.* Palo Alto, Calif.: Fearon Publishers, Inc., 1968.

Part G.

The Teacher: A New Role

Introduction

Though the student is nearly always the central figure in an individualized learning environment even a casual classroom observer would be quick to note the numerous and important ways that the teacher facilitates the learning process. Whether she serves as diagnostician of learners' needs, as manager of the learning environment, as personal tutor, as developer of appropriate learning materials or as evaluator of the learner's progress, it is clear that a most challenging set of skills is required of this new kind of educator. All too often they are skills that were neither demonstrated nor taught during the teacher's own preservice education.

In Chapter 17, Horton Southworth lists the minimal competencies which are required of the educator in an individualized learning setting and organizes these competencies into an outline appropriate for use in both in-service and preservice teacher training. Each of the nine areas of competency is comprised of various tasks, which he states in behavioral terms. This suggests that attainment of the competencies (that is, performance of the behaviors) can be observed, evaluated, and systematically improved.

In Chapter 18, Donald Haefele gives a brief example of how some of these competencies might be initiated at the preservice teacher-training level. Haefele has suggested a quite simple format which, given appropriate circumstances, can provide the neophyte module developer with practice in diagnosing and prescribing for student need. At the same time, it can provide an end-product—a module of instruction which may be of direct value to those students for whom it is relevant.

Chapter 17. THE TEACHER-LEARNER RELATIONSHIPS

A MODEL OF TEACHER TRAINING FOR THE INDIVIDUALIZATION OF INSTRUCTION

Horton C. Southworth

DEFINITION

Individualized Instruction. The central theme in the elementary instructional programs for which the new model will train teachers is individualization. This term covers any arrangements and procedures that are employed to ensure that each pupil achieves the learning goals designated for him. The definition of individualization used in this model is as follows: *Individualized instruction consists of planning and conducting, with each pupil, programs of study and day-to-day lessons that are tailor-made to suit his learning requirements and his characteristics as a learner.* This definition focuses on instructional planning with and for each individual student before teaching him, then teaching him according to the plan. Most educators mistakenly define individualization in terms of the setting within

SOURCE: Adapted from *Final Report,* Project No. 8-9020, Contract No. OEC-0-8-089020-3309 (010), October, 1968, pp. 3, 14-24, by permission of the author.

which learning takes place, limiting it to tutorial instruction or independent study.

Group teaching can also be a part of individualized programs. Whenever two or more pupils are ready to study the same task in a like way through group presentation or discussion, it is proper for the teacher to assemble and teach them as a group. This is very different from most instruction today where plans are made for the group as a whole and where instruction pays limited attention to individual differences among pupils in the group.

MINIMAL TEACHER COMPETENCIES

A minimal competency means the ability of the teacher trainee to define and demonstrate successfully each specific task or function necessary for teacher certification.

The following nine competency areas are paramount for training teachers to individualize instruction for each child. Behaviors which are not currently within the capability of educators to observe or measure have not been included among these nine areas.

1. Specifying Learning Goals

Teachers will be prepared to specify learning goals in terms of observable competencies.

The teacher can:

1.01   Identify learning objectives of each type, independently of any one curricular area, or within a given area.

1.02   State learning objectives of each type within each (relevant) curricular area in terms of student behaviors.

The teacher can define:

1.021   Concepts, principles, facts

1.022   Skills

1.023   Inquiry competencies

1.024   Self-direction competencies

1.025   Interests, motives, and values

1.026   Competencies in self-analysis and self-evaluation

1.027   Personal development

1.028   Group process behaviors

1.03   Interpret learning outcomes in terms of acceptable criteria of performance.

1.04   Specify interrelationships among the various types of learning goals.

1.05   Specify interrelationships among learning goals from one curricular area to another.

1.06   Translate broad societal aims for schools into relevant learning goals.

1.07   Communicate learning objectives to pupils, teachers, parents, and others.

2. Assessing Pupil Achievement of Learning Goals

A detailed analysis of the initial capabilities of a learner in a curricular area provides the necessary baseline reference for the coming instruction. The teacher will be skillful in evaluating pupil accomplishments with regard to a variety of learning goals.

The teacher can:

2.01   Demonstrate competency in the use of rating methods, observational methods, interview methods, and situational tests in evaluating pupils' accomplishment of these types of learning goals; inquiry, self-direction, interests and motives, self-analysis and self-evaluation, personal development, cooperative behaviors, and group process.

2.02   Explain the relationships among placement tests, pretests, and posttests of a pupil's achievement in any curricular area.

2.03   Select appropriate placement tests for locating a pupil with a given curricular area.

2.04   Administer and score placement tests.

2.05   Interpret placement test results to locate pupil within a curricular area.

2.06   Identify a pupil's learning difficulties through analysis of test results.

2.07   Involve the pupil in evaluating and interpreting his test result.

2.08   Demonstrate competency in reporting test results to other staff members in numerical, graphic, or verbal form.

3. Diagnosing Learner Characteristics

The state of the learner is a dynamic phenomenon. Thus, teachers will need refined observational skills to recognize developing traits, synthesizing techniques to organize existing data, and supporting references to use in developing an improved appraisal of the learner.

The teacher will:

3.01 Appraise the intellectual capacities of the pupil.

  3.011 Report a pupil's general intellectual functioning as it is observed in a variety of learning activities.

  3.012 Summarize accumulated data pertaining to intellectual capacity, taking account of the pupil's background, developmental level, and reaction to testing.

  3.013 Identify appropriate tests which could be used to improve the appraisal of a pupil's general intellectual capacities.

3.02 Appraise the physical condition of the pupil.

  3.021 Report a pupil's sensory functioning, motor development, and general health as they are observed in a variety of learning activities.

  3.022 Summarize accumulated data pertaining to the pupil's sensory functioning, motor development and general health.

  3.023 Identify appropriate sources which could offer additional information to improve the appraisal of a pupil's physical condition.

3.03 Appraise the emotional condition of the pupil.

  3.031 Report a pupil's emotional condition as observed in a variety of learning activities.

  3.032 Summarize accumulated data pertaining to the pupil's emotional condition.

  3.033 Identify other sources and evaluative techniques which could be used to improve the appraisal of a pupil's emotional condition.

3.04 Appraise the social attitudes and behavior of the pupil.

  3.041 Report a pupil's social attitudes and behavior as observed in a variety of learning activities.

  3.042 Summarize accumulated data pertaining to the pupil's social attitudes and behaviors.

  3.043 Identify other sources and evaluative techniques which could be used to improve the appraisal of a pupil's social attitudes and behavior.

3.05 Describe the family and community background of the pupil.

3.06 Develop a summary description of a pupil's learner characteristics acknowledging the relationships among his intellectual, physical, emotional, and social traits.

4. *Planning Long-Term and Short-Term Learning Programs with Pupils*

Individualized learning places new responsibilities on the learner including planning, managing or organizing, directing, and evaluating. However, these endeavors are not pursued alone by the pupil. Rather a new partnership between the pupil and teacher is formed. This is a significant change from the prevalent authority base existent in too many classrooms.

The teacher, too, becomes a learner (i.e., about pupils, about objectives, about hypothesizing conditions). A new partnership WITH each child will manifest itself in true individualization.

With the pupil, the teacher will:

4.01   Integrate data on his over-all achievements and his learner characteristics into a long-term program that spells out the relative emphasis to be placed on different types of learning goals and on work within different curricular areas.

4.02   Utilize a pretest to specify what learning objectives a pupil will next undertake.

4.03   Utilize data on his characteristics as a learner in selecting the mode and setting and criterion for his individual learning.

4.04   Select materials and equipment that he will employ in the given learning task.

4.05   Select the instructional methods to be employed with his learning task.

4.06   Provide for him to take alternative routes toward the learning objectives.

4.07   Provide for him to employ self-direction in performing the learning task.

4.08   Provide for obtaining data on his performance of the learning task for use in assessing his progress and identifying his difficulties.

4.09   Estimate when he will complete the learning task.

4.10   Plan for interrelating his learning task in one curricular area with concurrent learning tasks in other areas.

4.11   Plan for his group learning situations.

4.12   Determine the means by which the pupil will request assistance or teacher will volunteer help.

5. Guiding Pupils in Their Learning Tasks

The role of the teacher in an individualized program includes several new dimensions. In a general sense, this image repeatedly illuminates the guidance function of teaching. It is visible when assistance is provided to the pupil who is experiencing difficulty. Other pupils are helped when provisions are made for equipment, materials, special-need groups, and alternative activities. Thus, regardless of the manifestation of this role by teachers, guiding behavior emerges from awareness of individual needs, knowledge of several procedures, and willingness and determination to assist the pupil.

The teacher can:

5.01   Diagnose nature of difficulty.

        5.011   Listen to pupil questions.

        5.012   Probe empathetically.

        5.013   Refer to appropriate records.

        5.014   Consult with colleagues.

5.02   Record the findings of the diagnosis in those situations revealing a significant pupil obstacle or inadequacy of curriculum materials.

5.03   Define the extent to which the pupil has utilized alternative approaches to the learning task.

5.04   Assisting the pupil immediately by examples, questions, prompting, hypothesizing, clarifying, organizing data, etc.

5.05   Provide the pupil with a peer tutor.

5.06   Convene special help groups around specific learning tasks.

5.07   Provide for pupils' working on an independent, pupil-team, or subgroup basis as called for in their individual learning plans.

5.08   Schedule the pupils in the class to provide them with access to the space, equipment, and learning materials they require.

5.09   Make provisions for safety, pupil mobility and volume control.

5.10   Orient pupils to the schedule for the learning plans, to any new materials or media they will be using, and to any guidelines they will be following.

5.11   Provide time for giving pupils posttests as needed, or to plan revised or new assignments for students requiring them.

5.12   Provide alternative activities for those pupils who complete learning tasks with difficulties such as spontaneous fun things using mechanical, artistic, musical, and spatial interests.

6. Directing Off-Task Pupil Behavior

The teacher and learner have developed a plan for learning which specifies the environmental components. Behavior of pupils which is not directly related to the learning task and specified environmental components is labeled off-task.

The prospective teacher will need a different orientation to pupil behavior because self-direction is a major outgrowth of individualized approaches. Since this ideal develops in many patterns with pupils, teachers also will need systematic and analytical approaches toward behavior control.

The teacher can:

6.01   Describe different approaches to behavior control.

6.02   Involve pupils in deciding on acceptable pupil conduct.

6.03   Reinforce acceptable behavior of pupil.

6.04   Identify sources of deviant behavior.

6.05   Intervene appropriately and consistently in cases of deviant behavior.

6.06   Initiate case studies when off-task behavior continually obstructs task completion.

6.07   Determine sources of inter-personal conflicts.

6.08   Assist in the resolution of inter-personal conflicts.

6.09   Distinguish between habitual and temporary deviant behavior and inter-personal conflict.

6.10   Involve pupils periodically in evaluation behavior control procedures.

6.11   Use consultation from colleagues and para-professionals in dealing with behavior direction.

7. Evaluating the Learner

Movement of pupils through the curricular areas is predicated on the process of evaluation. Pupils encounter each learning task on this basis. Posttest measures are used as the criteria for subsequent decisions regarding long-term and short-term plans.

The teacher can:

7.01   Administer, score, and interpret an appropriate pretest for determining a pupil's next learning task within a curricular area.

7.02   Administer, score, and interpret an appropriate posttest for determining mastery of a given learning task.

7.03   Develop and maintain records regarding pupil achievement, learning characteristics, off-task behavior.

7.04   Initiate depth studies of pupils as obstacles are noted to the successful completion of individual learning plans.

7.05   Organize all data generated by the system of individualization (Comp. 2.00 and 3.00) including both objective and subjective information.

8. Employing Teamwork with Colleagues

Effective participation on a team requires specific skills and attitudes. The general concepts of cooperation and leadership are analyzed so that specific skills can be developed. Teams also require a continuing concern for the process by which they operate. Thus, evaluative skills are equally important for effective team functioning.

The teacher will:

8.01   Define the organizational patterns of teams active in the operation of the school.

8.02   Define the differentiated roles present on each team active in the operation of the school.

8.03   Participate in team activity by:

   8.031   Revealing the way he sees things and does things.

   8.032   Bringing out the essential patterns, motives, and behavior in a situation in order to receive back clear and accurate information concerning the relevancy and effectiveness of his behavior.

   8.033   Trying out new patterns of thought and behavior in order to experience the process of change.

   8.034   Helping colleagues learn how to learn from the process of presentation-experimentation-feedback.

8.04   Evaluate team activity by

   8.041   Examining the nature of the discussion to determine the emphasis which is placed on content and process.

   8.042   Examining the patterns of communication in the team.

   8.043   Examining the decision-making procedures of the team.

   8.044   Observing the behavior of the team from the point of view of what its purpose or function seems to be.

   8.045   Identifying forces which disturb team work.

   8.046   Identifying consulting resources needed by team.

9. Enhancing Development

The teacher who recognizes those personal traits which appear to affect her learning process or her skills of interaction with pupils will relate to learners in a new fashion. This personal understanding also leads to an improved mental health status. Such developments represent major new emphases in the preparation of teachers, and are sometimes reflected in relationships with children.

The teacher can:

9.01   Participate in activities which will help reveal those personal traits which tend to limit his flexibility of behavior.

9.02   Analyze personal strengths and weaknesses which affect professional behavior.

9.03   Analyze values which affect professional behavior.

9.04   Analyze attitudes toward authority, supervision, learning which affect professional behavior.

9.05   Formulate a general plan for self-development to overcome limiting factors.

9.06   Modify personal behavior after interpreting evidence of performance.

9.07   Display self-acceptance by being attentive and responsive to pupils.

9.08   Display empathy and concern for children, including withdrawn, hostile, and non-productive children.

9.09   Display objectivity and rationality in dealing with each pupil's intellectual, personal, and social problems.

9.10   Evidence confidence and emotional control in responding to pressures and problems.

9.11   Demonstrate flexibility in personality by providing for differences to pupil ideas, wishes, actions and feelings.

9.12   Demonstrate flexibility by not becoming uneasy as children mention antisocial or asocial behavior.

9.13   Allow children to vent and express strong personal feelings.

9.14   Display skills for constructive intervention; and non-intervention.

9.15   Avoid wasting children's psychic energy by creating anxiety producing learning situations.

9.16   Listen to and view children's emotional behavior and irrational statements without becoming anxious and disorganized.

9.17 Control expressions of attitudes, feelings and emotional responses, and shifts of tone and voice and gestures.

9.18 Express enthusiasm for knowledge, for instruction, for furthering own learning, and for pupils' achievement and interest.

9.19 Exhibit friendly and cooperative behavior in relationship with other members of the school staff and parents.

9.20 Accept the impossibility of effectively relating with every child and adult in every circumstance.

Chapter 18. Teacher Development of Learning Modules

SELF-INSTRUCTION AND TEACHER EDUCATION

Donald L. Haefele

The University of Tennessee is developing and implementing an experimental Pilot Program in Teacher Education to test a new four-year professional education sequence. Two programs, the new one and the existing program, are presently operating, with the Pilot Program having been initiated in the fall of 1968. Sixty freshmen are enrolled in the new program.

An integral part of this program is the implementation and utilization of self-instructional modules. These modules will provide our preservice teachers with competencies which we feel are basic elements needed in the repertoire of every teacher. The following is a list of the modules thus far defined for our new program:

Behavioral Objectives
Evaluation of Learning

SOURCE: Reprinted from *Audiovisual Instruction*, Vol. 14, No. 1 (January, 1969), pp. 63-64, by permission of author and publisher.

Planning for Teaching
Organization for Instruction
Curriculum Development and Evaluation
Selection and Use of Audiovisual Materials
Operation of Audiovisual Equipment
Use of the Library
Research Literacy
Diagnosing of Learning Difficulties
Teaching the Disadvantaged

In my efforts to involve the College of Education's faculty members in the development of these modules, I have frequently found many of them interested, but not sure of how to go about developing self-instructional modules to incorporate this content. To provide them with a logical strategy for approaching the task, I have written a brief position paper for their use.

THE PREPARATION AND DESIGN OF A SELF-INSTRUCTIONAL MODULE

Some assumptions concerning our undergraduate students should be made at the outset. These assumptions are: Students learn at different rates and in varied ways; students are capable of being self-directed and self-propelling; and students can learn independently.

These assumptions support the efficacy of developing and implementing self-instruction oriented modules. A module is a format incorporating an instructional unit. Students may spend varying lengths of time working individually toward the achievement of the instructional objectives in the module.

With the above as a rationale, let's outline a logical sequence to use in designing a module.

1. Initially you should prepare a comprehensive list of your broad objectives. These objectives or terminal goals, should encompass the general concepts, understandings, knowledges, and appreciations you wish each student to possess. In most instances, this will not be a simple task. If you have taught the material to be presented in this module, it will be worthwhile to consider the intent of your examinations, and assigned papers or essays. Such broad areas of interest, as knowledge and problem solving you have stressed, will provide the framework for more specific objectives to be sought later. Again, try not to be too specific in this first stage of objectives delineation, but do attempt to identify these major short term goals.

2. Now that the broad objectives of the module are specified, establish "behavioral objectives" from the list of objectives you now have. A behavioral objective is a statement describing *what the student is expected to be able to do after instruction that he could not do before instruction.*

For each objective, you should specify what the student will be *doing* to demonstrate whether or not, and to what degree, he has achieved your objective(s). Do you want him to *answer* a certain number of questions correctly, *recognize* a correct or incorrect concept, or *state* a principle? These are examples of observable behaviors students can exhibit to demonstrate their achievement of your objectives. Objectives couched in terms of "to know," "to appreciate," and "to understand" are usually ambiguous to the student. He needs to know what behavior he must exhibit to demonstrate he has learned something. Therefore, if you want the student "to know" something, tell him what he must do to demonstrate he has this knowledge. Here is an example of a general goal: "The student will be able to communicate effectively in writing." If you are to teach such a skill and if the student is to know what performance level is expected of him, a more explicit objective is needed. If you and your students are going to end up at the same destination, direction should be provided at the outset. Many paths may lead to the goal and, as I see it, the choice of the particular path is irrelevant. What is critical is that you and your students have a congruent perception of the goal. Here are some examples of how the above goal could be stated as a behavioral objective: The student will write a theme of 500-1,000 words on an assigned subject,—or, the student will write a 300-500 word description of the basic functions a secondary mathematics teacher performs.

The action to be taken by the student is specified. In each case, he is giving evidence that he can communicate effectively in writing and, in each case, the nature of the communication is specified in advance.

Subsequent to this activity the careful specification of delimiting objectives should be undertaken. Thus, for each general objective written earlier, you should examine the prerequisite behaviors your students will need to attain each general objective.

For instance, what abilities are prerequisite to the student's writing a composition?

One could generate many subobjectives to support this ultimate goal and each one should be individually defined in behavioral terms. Presenting the student with a set of prerequisite tasks, or subobjectives, should aid him in acquiring the competencies you want him to exit with.

Here are a few examples of objectives designed to demonstrate abilities prerequisite to the task of writing an *essay*:

The student must be able to organize his thoughts:

Given seven sentences, the student will construct a logical paragraph.

The student will show awareness of proper titles for given written passages:

Given four short compositions and a list of eight titles, four of which are appropriate, the student will match the correct title to the respective composition.

Ambiguity is absent in these objectives. The student knows the intent of a module or course incorporating them. There is no mystical talent needed to write such specific goals. It takes time, thought, and persistent evaluation to produce a comprehensive list. Once it exists, you may only have to give it to the student and he will do the rest.

If you have progressed through these steps, you should have a list of broad behavioral objectives with a subordinate list of prerequisite behavioral objectives leading the student to the achievement of each of these broader objectives. Each objective, whether general or prerequisite to a general objective, should now be stated in terms of overt student behavior.

3. With the behavioral objectives delineated, the next task is to establish *performance standards*. This involves the examination and specification of criterion levels of behavior for each objective. For example, in establishing an objective such as "the student will plan a unit to teach children how to multiply two two-digit numbers," you would probably establish a number of performance standards. Some of these might be: "On a single type-written page, the students will outline the unit content, using two teaching methods and specifying at least three subobjectives of the lesson." The *"two"* prefacing *"teaching methods,"* and, the phrase *"at least three,"* are performance standards or criteria for evaluating how well the individual student has attained your objectives. Performance standards let the student know what minimal levels of competence you expect him to attain. They also aid you in evaluating the individual student's performance. These performance levels are behavioristic, but they are valuable in decreasing the ambiguity in the student's mind as to exactly what you want him to do and how well.

4. Next, the learning activities for mastering the objectives should be arranged. The methods and supporting media you select may be varied. One means of helping the student in areas where his knowledge or skill is insufficient could be the provision of guide or resource sheets for inquiry activities. The acquisition or development of learning materials to facilitate individualized study will no doubt be necessary. Resource staff members will be available as consultants in the developmental stage and at other levels to expedite the earliest implementation of the module. The accompanying chart can help you to organize the module:

Broad Objectives	Behavioralized Specific Objectives	Prerequisite Objectives or Tasks	Learning Activity	Performance (Evaluation) Criteria

This technique has been informally applied in the development of other components of our Pilot Program and I can confidently say, "It works!"

The involvement of the University of Tennessee College of Education faculty in this entire project is forcing us to examine our concept of what a teacher should be and focus our attention on how we can facilitate rather than inhibit the process of becoming.

Part H.

Learning Activities:
Individualized or Interactive?

Introduction

Those who are unfamiliar with individualized learning may naturally question the efficacy of any approach which seemingly limits the students' social interaction. They would find, upon analysis, that while this might have been true to a large degree in programmed instruction it is definitely not true of individualized learning as that term is generally used today.

Individualized learning does require the learner to take individual responsibility for attaining a level of proficiency in his performance but it provides a variety of settings in which this can occur. In some units of study the learner may work only with instructional materials while in other units he will also interact with other students, to share, discuss or otherwise explore their *different* views on subject matter content of *mutual* interest.

As individualized learning is practiced today, there is considerable variance from class to class, school to school, and even among the more sophisticated learning systems regarding the most appropriate justifications for bringing individual learners together to interact as part of a group.

At one end of the scale are those approaches which allow the learner to select courses of interest and which provide for individually adjusted amounts of study through *flexible scheduling*. However, they frequently rely on group-regulated behavior once the individual appears for class.

Some schools utilize individualized, small group, and large group learning situations as proportionately planned components of the instructional program. Sometimes termed the unit plan approach, this is a procedure which assumes that all students need certain "core" information, which can be disseminated *en masse,* followed by tutorial sessions where individual differences are meant to be accommodated.

Other schools provide individualized learning opportunities as an *adjunct* to regular classes and increase the ratio of independent study as particular students demonstrate responsibility for managing their own learning. This is sometimes termed a phase level program or a quest program.

Finally, there are comprehensive programs which are *predicated* on individualized learning as the process for achieving mastery of the basic subject matter disciplines. These systems (such as PLAN or IPI) use grouping practices *within* individualized modules whenever a particular learning activity calls for partners or teams, or when the teacher assists a group of learners who have common learning needs. However, the commonality of these needs is determined by measurement or by teacher-learner agreement rather than as the result of a predetermined administrative assignment. Historically, in a formal classroom it has been called "cheating" when one student obtains help from another. By contrast, collaborative help between students is encouraged in the newer systems, and in some of these participating schools the student-tutor has even been dubbed a "mini-teacher."

In addition to these *program* variations with respect to the ratio of individualized and social learning situations provided, there are certain *learning activities* which inherently offer *both* individualization and interaction. Educational games, for instance, are simulations of "real-life" experiences which often provide a chance for the learner to act in his *own* way within a *group* setting. Within the space constraints of this book, and as an illustration of one among the many alternative types of learning activities found in individualized learning settings, the two chapters which follow explain the use of educational games and their implications for the learner.

In Chapter 19, Thorwald Esbensen, a pioneer in individualized learning practices at Duluth, proposes the framework and operational rules for instituting a game of self-directed learning called BID. It should be appreciated by educators and students alike.

In Chapter 20, William McKay gives details of *The Sumerian Game,* a computer-directed game that builds a simulated environment (the ancient land of Sumer) which is then placed in the control of the student "ruler." Obviously, the learner must cope with the consequences of his decisions if the country is to "survive."

Chapter 19. A GAME FOR ENHANCING LEARNER RESPONSIBILITY

INDIVIDUALIZED INSTRUCTION AND SELF-DIRECTED LEARNING

Thorwald Esbensen

Across the country, there appears to be growing disenchantment with the practice of requiring students to pursue learning at the same pace, at the same time, and with the same instructional materials and activities. Increasingly, educators at all levels of formal instruction seem to be coming around to the idea that the goal of individualized instruction for all students may not be an impossible dream, that in *substantial* measure it may be accomplished over the next several years.

By individualized instruction is meant whatever arrangements make it possible for each student to be engaged at all times in learning those things that are of most value to himself, *as an individual.* As an absolute condition, this ideal can never be reached, of course. But progress can be made. This fact is what must ultimately inspire this imperfect venture.

SOURCE: Reprinted from Thorwald Esbensen in *Independent Study in Science* (Washington, D.C.: National Science Teachers Association, 1970), by permission of author and publisher.

In the long run, the basic thrust of individualized instruction is toward promoting the development of *self-directed* learning. In a democratic social order, every person is finally expected to be able to make up his own mind about things—not only with regard to society in general, but with particular reference to the means and ends of his own life as well. Teaching students to engage effectively in the process of *decision-making* should therefore be the central purpose of any instructional program that can properly call itself individualized.

However, this is not something that can happen all at once, without adequate preparation. At any given time, individual students will vary widely in their readiness to function as independent learners. This readiness is not inborn, but must be learned. And its development requires practice.

The time to begin is when the student first enters school. Regardless of whether the student is a kindergartner or a high school senior, he should have genuine options concerning various phases of the instructional process. Ordinarily, the sweep of this opportunity will be vastly greater for the high school student than it will be for the kindergartner. But in no case should the freedom of choice be reduced to zero.

Let us consider in more detail the relationship between individualized instruction and self-directed learning. An individualized program is one in which each student is encouraged to proceed according to his own personal inventory of abilities, needs, and interests. Self-directed learning is the long-range goal of this type of instruction *within a democratic society*. But because of different stages of readiness on the part of individual learners, the extent to which any student is engaged in the process of decision-making will depend upon what he is capable of deciding at any given point in time. What this means is that self-directed learning and individualized instruction are not one and the same thing, although an individualized program reaches fruition only when self-directed learning is finally achieved.

In order to clarify further the meaning of this relationship, it may be useful to examine the following matters:

- The Pace of Instruction
- The Materials of Instruction
- The Objectives of Instruction

Formal schooling, as most of us have known it, has generally functioned according to one fixed schedule of expectations for every member of the group. Whether the various parts of the instructional program have been called lessons, chapters, units, or something else, the idea of a single standard for all has dominated the classroom scene. Students have been forced to proceed together through each assignment. The rate of instruction, its techniques, and its goals have been the same for everyone.

Unfortunately for this system, the *results* of instruction have *not* been promising. Many students have simply failed to perform as instructed. Nevertheless, the system has carefully disclaimed any responsibility for this. Whatever inadequacies might exist have been attributed to the seemingly perverse determination of some students to avoid shaping up to the demands of instruction.

In recent years, however, educators have been compelled by the dropout problem, together with growing student unrest, to examine more critically the assumptions and practices of the old lockstep order. We are on the verge of witnessing far-reaching changes in the ways we operate our schools. In this context, the promise of individualized instruction has attracted the serious attention of a growing number of school people who see in it the possibility of at least a partial solution to some of our more pressing educational dilemmas.

Individualized instruction has more than one level of meaning. That is to say, student differences may be taken into account in one area and ignored in another.

Probably the most widespread form of individualization has to do with the *differentiated pacing* of instruction. In other words, the goals of instruction are the same and the materials are the same, but the students move along their common track at differing rates of speed depending on their various abilities.

A prime example of this approach is the programmed textbook (most notably when it has a linear format and when it is used as an entire course of study, say Algebra I). Basically, all pupils are expected to run the same race. Individualization occurs only insofar as each student is allowed to progress at his own *pace*.

On another level, individualization occurs when the *materials* of instruction vary according to the different needs or preferences of students. For instance, let us suppose that a youngster has serious reading difficulties. To deal with this problem, we set up a prescriptive program of remediation. Fair enough. However, within a traditional framework of schooling, what often happens is that while help is being given to the child in reading, in the other subject matter areas there is no adjustment whatever. In social studies, in science, it is business as usual. Our retarded reader is expected to grapple with printed matter that he has conclusively demonstrated he cannot read! The situation virtually guarantees failure for our hapless learner—not because he is stupid (he may be quite intelligent) but because the information he needs is being given to him in a mode he is not equipped to handle.

A sensible alternative would be to vary the format by which information is presented to the learner. In the case of our poor reader, for example, much of the needed information could be put on audio tape. What the student might not be able to grasp with his eyes, he might be able to acquire through his ears. The point is: the nature of the *materials* of instruction can be *varied* to suit the capabilities of the learner. In this manner, individualization of the program can take place at the level of the *mode* of instruction.

On a third level, individualization has to do with the *objectives* of instruction. Although it is reasonable to suppose that many of the basic skills we emphasize in school are appropriate for virtually all students, it is less evident that *all* of what we teach in the various subjects is necessary or best for all students. And it is not at all apparent that the *sequencing* of these objectives falls into a single pattern that is most desirable for every pupil. Individualizing the objectives of instruction, then, means *varying* the *goals* of learning for students, depending upon what seems to be needed in each case, and being able and willing to *vary* the *sequence* of instruction for these goals.

The three levels of individualization that we have mentioned (the pacing, the materials, the objectives) constitute one dimension of the problem. Another dimension that cuts across all three levels has to do with the question: Who makes what decisions? In other words, to what extent, if any, does the *student* determine how the instructional program shall be tailored to fit his individual needs, abilities, and interests? Generally speaking, programs that stress the benefits of *prescriptive* instruction will provide fewer opportunities for student decision-making than will programs that emphasize the importance of *self-directed* learning.

Below is a grid that represents the dimensions of individualized instruction mentioned thus far:

	Teacher Decides	Student Decides
Differentiated Pacing		
Differentiated Materials		
Differentiated Objectives		

An elaboration of this grid through the use of specific questions could provide one way of assessing the degree to which any given program was, or intended to be, individualized, and the extent to which its individualization provided for self-directed learning.

For example, under the heading of PACING, one might wish to pose the question: Is each student encouraged to learn at a rate commensurate with his own particular capabilities? An affirmative answer would be consistent with the goal of individualized instruction. Then the further question could be asked: Who decides what the pacing of instruction will be? Permitting the student to make this decision is consistent with the goal of self-directed learning.

The development of a program of individualized instruction designed to promote self-directed learning requires a system that will be largely self-regulating. Moreover, in the interests of effectiveness and efficiency, it should have the flavor of a *good game*.

The Game of School, as it currently exists in most classrooms, is not a good game. Obscure objectives, hidden agendas, and arbitrary changes in rules dominate much of the play—all of these being characteristics of *bad* games.

It may be helpful to describe in some detail a simple classroom game that could be used in any subject matter area to foster self-directed learning. Let us call it BID: A Game of Self-Directed Learning.

The major purposes of BID are (*a*) to give each player practice in trying to assess correctly his ability to accomplish designated learning tasks, and (*b*) to increase each player's motivation to accomplish the learning tasks.

The game of BID is played using the Record Sheet shown on the next page. The teacher keeps one Record Sheet for each student, and each student keeps one Record Sheet for himself.

Near the bottom of the Record Sheet are numbers listed in sequence. These numbers refer to learning tasks (i.e., instructional objectives) that are to be mastered by the students.

It is not intended that every objective should necessarily be achieved by every student. Ideally, the teacher should establish a certain range of tasks for each student. For example, tasks 25 through 50 might be suitable for one student, while tasks 50 through 75 might be appropriate for a somewhat better student.

These learning tasks are set forth in writing by the teacher on 8 1/2″ × 11″ sheets of paper housed in a three-ring binder that is available for inspection by each student playing the game.

Each task sheet contains three kinds of information for the student:

1.   A clear description of the objective to be achieved.

2.   An explanation or sample of the evaluation that will be undertaken to determine whether the student has accomplished the objective.

3.   A listing of the resources (i.e., materials and activities) that are available to help the student master the objective.

On page 275 is an example of such a task sheet.

The game may be played as follows by a given student:

First of all, within the range of tasks that the teacher has designated for a

Objective Number	BID	Date Due	COST	Evaluation	SCORE	Running Total

```
1    2    3    4    5    6    7    8    9    10   11   12   13   14   15   16   17   18
19   20   21   22   23   24   25   26   27   28   29   30   31   32   33   34
35   36   37   38   39   40   41   42   43   44   45   46   47   48   49   50
51   52   53   54   55   56   57   58   59   60   61   62   63   64   65   66
67   68   69   70   71   72   73   74   75   76   77   78   79   80   81   82
83   84   85   86   87   88   89   90   91   92   93   94   95   96   97   98
99   100
```

BID - COST = SCORE

RECORD SHEET

student, the student selects one that he would like to try to accomplish. This may be *any* one of the objectives within the *range* specified by the teacher.

It is important to note that the student is permitted to ignore (if he so chooses) the usual *sequence* of objectives within his assigned range. That is to say, if his band of appropriate tasks includes Objectives 13 through 30, he may begin with *any* of these. He does not need to start with Objective 13.

The point is: if the sequence the teacher thinks is necessary is *really* necessary, that conclusion will emerge as a result of the student's actual experience with choosing a pattern of tasks. As a matter of fact, there is a growing body of evidence suggesting that a teacher's predetermined notion of what constitutes an essential scope and sequence of objectives is sometimes mistaken (from the standpoint of what the student is able to achieve when he is able to establish his own *order* of things). In any case, the results will be instructive. If it turns out that the student can successfully circumvent the usual order in which objectives are achieved, that will be a useful thing to know. If it turns out, on the other hand, that violating the teacher's recommended sequence of learning is a hazardous enterprise at best, that will also be a useful thing to know. Either way, the student will learn something.

Of course, unless it is absolutely certain that Objective 15, for example, automatically requires those skills developed by Objectives 13 and 14, it will not be sufficient for the student simply to achieve Objective 15. He must also master the prior objectives. What our game permits, you see, is *not* the *skipping* of objectives, but a *re-ordering* of the *sequence* by which they may be accomplished.

For the purpose of explaining how the game is played, let us for the moment suppose that tasks 13 through 30 have been assigned to our hypothetical student. Let us further suppose that after due consideration, our student selects Objective 17 as his first undertaking. On both the Teacher Record Sheet and the Student Record Sheet (which are exactly the same), the numbers 13 through 30 are underlined (to show that this is the assigned band of suitable objectives), and the number 17 is first *circled* at the bottom of the page and then *written* inside the first space under the column called Objective Number.

On the next page is shown a Record Sheet with the first line entirely filled out for one round of bidding and its results. You may find it helpful to refer to this Record Sheet at different times as our explanation of the game of BID proceeds.

The next thing our student does is to make a BID on the objective he has chosen—in this case, Objective 17. He does so by allocating to this objective a certain number of points drawn from an initial Working Capital of 200 points he has been given in order to begin playing the game. Other things

Genetics - Contract # 5

Objective

Given the necessary basic items of information, you will be able to solve correctly any problem dealing with the probability of two or more independent chance events occurring simultaneously.

Sample Test Situation

In a kennel, there are 50 dogs. Of these, 10 are spotted red and white; 20 of them are long-eared; and 5 are bobtailed. If you picked 1 dog at random, what is the probability that it would be long-eared, spotted red and white, and bobtailed?

Resources

Coins to flip, counting the simultaneous occurrences of two heads (HH), two tails (TT), and one head-one tail (HT)

BSCS Blue (pp. 340-342)

Film on Probability

Practice Worksheet #5

Audio-tape #5

*The contents of this page were contributed by the Science Education Department of The Florida State University, Tallahassee, Florida.

TASK SHEET *

Objective Number	BID	Date Due	COST	Evaluation	SCORE	Running Total
17	90	March 25	30	Pass	+60	260

1   2   3   4   5   6   7   8   9   10   11   12   13   14   15   16   ⑰   18
19   20   21   22   23   24   25   26   27   28   29   30   31   32   33   34
35   36   37   38   39   40   41   42   43   44   45   46   47   48   49   50
51   52   53   54   55   56   57   58   59   60   61   62   63   64   65   66
67   68   69   70   71   72   73   74   75   76   77   78   79   80   81   82
83   84   85   86   87   88   89   90   91   92   93   94   95   96   97   98
99   100

BID — COST = SCORE

RECORD SHEET WITH FIRST LINE FILLED OUT

being relatively equal, the more confident he is about his ability to master the objective, the more points he will allocate for his BID.

The one constraint under which he is operating in this regard is that he *cannot* BID *more than half* of his Working Capital of points at any given time with respect to any objective. Inasmuch as he has 200 points at the outset, he may BID up to, but not more than, 100 points insofar as Objective 17 is concerned.

Let us say that, having surveyed the situation, he decides to BID 90 points on his ability to achieve Objective 17. These 90 points are now recorded inside the first space under the column called BID.

The next thing our student does is to establish a *due date* for accomplishing the objective. In order to encourage the student to make the optimum assessment of his ability to master the objective, there is a time COST of 10 points per day for every day that the student says he will need to achieve his chosen objective.

For example, let us suppose that our student has made the selection of Objective 17 on Thursday, March 20th. We have already said that his BID on this objective is 90 points. His next step is to set the due date for his achievement of the objective. Let us say that he decides it will take him three days to accomplish his learning task. Friday, March 21st, will be counted as the first day; Saturday and Sunday are not counted because they are not school days; Monday, March 24th, will be counted as the second day; and Tuesday, March 25th, will be counted as the third day, the day on which our student has said he will be able to demonstrate his mastery of Objective 17.

Inside the first space under the column called Date Due should be written *March 25th*. Because this is the third work day, and because there is a time COST of 10 points per day, inside the first space under the column called COST there should be written the numeral 30. It is important to remember that in establishing his own due date the student automatically sets his own time COST.

Once the due date and the time COST have been determined they cannot be changed for this particular round of bidding. This means that when March 25th arrives, the student *must* be *evaluated* on his accomplishment of Objective 17. Depending upon what the objective is, the evaluation might or might not be in the form of a paper and pencil test.

Regardless of this, the evaluation will reach one of two conclusions: The student will either PASS, or he will FAIL. That is to say, the student either will achieve the objective at the mastery level specified by the objective, or he will not. It is a GO/NO GO situation.

Let us say that when our student is evaluated on his accomplishment of Objective 17, it turns out that his performance in the test situation is satisfactory. Inside the first space under the column called Evaluation should be written the word PASS. (If the student does *not pass,* and if the word *fail* has too negative a connotation, some other word or symbol could be employed.)

We are now ready to obtain a SCORE with regard to Objective 17. The formula is simple, and it is given near the bottom of the Record Sheet. It is BID − COST = SCORE. *This will be true whether the student passes or fails the test.* The difference is that if the student passes the test, his SCORE will be a *plus* SCORE, while if he fails the test, his SCORE will be a *minus* SCORE.

In the case of Objective 17 for our hypothetical student, the BID was 90, the COST was 30, the student *passed* the test, and so (using the formula BID − COST = SCORE) the SCORE is +60. If our student had *failed* the test, his SCORE for Objective 17 would have been −60.

Depending upon whether it is plus or minus, the SCORE is then added to, or subtracted from, the student's Working Capital and the result is entered under the column called Running Total. For Objective 17, the SCORE of + 60 is added to the student's Working Capital of 200 points, and so his first Running Total becomes 260 points. (If our student had failed to achieve Objective 17, the resulting SCORE of −60 would have been subtracted from his Working Capital of 200 points, and his first Running Total would have been 140 points.) From now on, the student's Running Total is his Working Capital, and it will go up or down depending upon his performance on the various objectives.

We will now answer this question: What is the purpose of making points?

The student may *use* his points to *buy time* with which to *pursue other activities* in which he is *personally interested.* Again, the emphasis is on *student decision-making.* The choices are to be *curriculum-free* in the sense that they do not need to be related to the subject matter of formal schooling. For example, a student may have a hobby that he has been working on during his after-school hours. He might welcome the opportunity to continue his hobby activities during a portion of his in-school hours. Or he might wish to be excused from class in order to spend additional time in the library, or with other course work. At the elementary school level, particularly, a student might simply want to be able to play some games, just for fun. He could spend some of the points he has earned to buy time to do this.

How many points should buy how much time? One possibility is to say that 100 points will buy one class period of subject-free time. However, this is a matter that can best be settled on the basis of actual classroom experience, and the decision will presumably vary from one situation to another.

Other questions present themselves.

How many points can a student spend as a lump sum in order to buy curriculum-free time? He can spend any amount he pleases as long as he does not spend points *below* his initial Working Capital of 200 points. In other words, if he has accumulated a Running Total of 500 points, he may spend up to 300 points on curriculum-free time. In this connection, it should be noted that some students will perceive that it pays to *defer gratification.* That is to say, inasmuch as the points BID on each objective can be up to, but not more than, half of the Running Total at any given time, the student who is interested in making progressively larger BIDS will husband the points in his Running Total so that he can make such BIDS.

As a safeguard in the other direction, each player should know that his Running Total will not be allowed to sink below 100 points. What this means is that even though the player has lost points by failing to achieve certain objectives, he will never be penalized to such an extent that his Running Total will fall below 100 points. The reason for this is that it takes points to make points. Therefore, each player's Running Total must have a guaranteed minimum level at which it will be maintained. Otherwise, a player's situation could become so hopeless that there would be no reason for continuing the game. Each player must be assured of a certain critical mass of points that he can count on for making a comeback.

One important question has to do with the matter of work completion. We have said that once a player assigns himself a *due date* for a self-selected objective, he is responsible for meeting that date successfully. He is not (except for compelling reasons) allowed to extend his date. So let us consider this question: Is the player permitted to have himself checked out on his chosen objective *in advance of* his due date? The answer to this is yes, BUT the time COST to the player *remains the same.* This may seem unfair. However, if the time COST were reduced to fit the actual completion time instead of being maintained at the level of the due date that was self-assigned, there would be no reason for the student to attempt to assess his own capabilities correctly. For every objective, he would merely set a far-in-the-future *due date,* secure in the knowledge that he would eventually beat it and receive credit accordingly. Because the game of BID is designed to encourage each player to take stock of himself with respect to how well he may be able to organize resources (including time) in order to achieve specific learning tasks, it is very important to base the time COST on the player's own selected due date. Essential to the game of BID is each player's *bidding!* (The fringe benefit of being checked out early on an objective would simply be the player's opportunity to start bidding immediately on a new objective.)

An especially interesting feature of BID concerns the use of Student Experts as an integral part of the game. Here is how this might work: Every student who has *mastered* an objective may, if he wishes, have himself listed as an Expert for that particular objective. Any student who *chooses* an objective may, if he wishes, go to one of the students who is listed as an

Expert for that objective and ask this Expert to take him on as a Client for the objective in question.

The Expert may, if he wishes, accept as his Client the student who is asking for help. The Expert and his Client now cooperatively decide what the BID and the Date Due will be for the Client. The Expert then supervises (perhaps through direct tutoring) the instructional strategy for this objective. Finally, when the Client is evaluated on his accomplishment of the objective, the Expert's own Running Total will (to the same extent as his Client's Running Total) go up or down depending upon whether his Client achieves the objective! In other words, the Expert's own stake in the matter is the same as his Client's!

(The fact that an Expert is helping a Client does *not* release the Expert from his continuing responsibilities as a player to be achieving his *own* objectives. Every player, except when he has purchased time, must always be working on an objective of his own choosing, even though he may also be serving as an Expert to one or more other players.)

We have discussed the general procedures for playing BID. Some final comments are in order. First, some cautionary advice.

Although it has been played successfully as far down as the third grade level, the game of BID is nevertheless sufficiently complicated to require careful explanation and preparation before it is undertaken in the classroom. And even under the best of circumstances, the teacher can expect a certain amount of initial confusion before his students get the feel of the game and settle down to playing it efficiently.

In this connection, it is important to point out that some students will begin by making unrealistic bids. That is to say, they will choose objectives carelessly, and then greatly underestimate the time they will need to master their chosen learning tasks. The teacher should be on the lookout for this sort of thing and take corrective action before such students become frustrated by their lack of success and stop trying altogether.

Here is a possible rule to follow: If a student fails two times consecutively, then his next objective, his BID, and his Date Due, must be decided as a result of direct consultation with the teacher. The teacher should probably also arrange to supervise rather closely the study materials, time, and procedures used by the student. As a further step, the teacher may find it necessary to undertake some individual or small group tutoring (depending upon which students are working with which objectives).

In any case, the essential point is this: *The teacher must employ whatever practices may be needed to ensure that every student is experiencing reasonable success in playing the game.* All other considerations must yield to this. Student motivation is the key to self-directed learning.

One more observation will close this discussion. Educational shop talk these days is full of references to something called *learning style*. Each student, we like to say, has his own personal style of learning.

This is an important idea, but it is not very clear. Until we can provide some operational descriptions of meaning, we shall not be able to improve matters much in this area.

The game of BID may help us look at one aspect of the problem. What is meant here is that a student's style of learning presumably includes, among other things, his propensity for taking *risks*. The game of BID is structured in such a way that the *difference* between a student's BID and his time COST is a measure of the *risk* he is willing to assume with respect to his ability to achieve a designated objective. The higher the BID and the lower the time COST, the greater the risk. For example, our student who BID 90 points and assigned himself a time COST of 30 points was risking 60 points. Over a given run of objectives (in relation to an evolving pattern of success and failure), it should be possible to compare the risk-taking behavior of students—one dimension, presumably, of a style of learning. Other points of measurement will no doubt suggest themselves as the game is studied from various points of view.

Chapter 20. LEARNER CONTROLLED ENVIRONMENTAL SIMULATION

COMPUTER-DIRECTED INSTRUCTIONAL GAMES

William McKay

A combined course in economic theory and social studies may sound as though it belongs in a college curriculum, but sixth graders have taken just such a course in the form of a computer-assisted instructional game. Sitting at typewriter-like computer terminals, the students entered a simulated environment where each became the ruler of a city-state in the ancient land of Sumer. Cast in a dramatic story role, the student "rulers" sought to feed their people in the face of catastrophes like floods, through technological advances like fertilizer, and the introduction of foreign trade.

The experiment was carried on under the direction of Richard L. Wing of the Northern Westchester (New York) Board of Cooperative Educational Services, with the participation of the Advanced Systems Development Division of International Business Machines Corporation. The original idea for such a game-playing use of computers was suggested by Bruse Moncrieff who coined the term *simulated environment* used in much the same sense as

SOURCE: Reprinted from *Audiovisual Instruction,* Vol. 14, No. 4 (April, 1969), pp. 37-40, by permission of the author and publisher.

the more popular term *game*. The Sumerian Game was written by ɪ̠ᵣ.
Mabel Addis, a teacher at the Katonah Elementary School, Katonah, New
York.

A similar game based on the economy of modern-day Sierra Leone was
tested at the same time. Here, the student's role was that of an American
economic advisor to a newly emerging nation. (A modified IBM 7090
computing system was used. It has since been dismantled. Parts of the games
were reprogramed for other systems and have been used experimentally and
in demonstrations since 1966.)

Students play the games by interacting via the typewriter terminal.
Messages from the computer are printed on the typewriter, and students use
the terminal keyboard to make responses. The keyboard is normally locked,
and is unlocked only following a message requesting the student to respond.
At that point, a green "proceed" light flashes on and the computer-
programed game waits for the response. When the student completes his
response, by striking a special end-of-message key, the game continues. A
prerequisite, of course, is that the student know how to use the typewriter-
like keyboard and be able to understand the messages sent to him. In actual
operation, the terminals are brought to a ready-to-play state by the teacher-
monitor.

A preliminary lecture, delivered via a conventional tape recorder driving a
slide projector, introduces the subject matter and suggests the learning
method. This takes about 20 minutes. The student is then seated at a terminal
keyboard and told to begin the programed play.

The first messages introduce the proper use of the terminal and acquaint
the player with his game objectives. After this, the student receives a first
seasonal population and harvest report (Figure 20-1), providing facts about
population, acres of land for planting grain, number of farm workers, grain
recently harvested, and grain remaining in inventory from previous
harvests. The last part of the report asks the student to allocate his resources
(grain harvested plus grain in inventory) to meet three requirements: food
for the people, seed for next season's planting, and inventory for future
needs. Such seasonal reports (a sample is shown in Figure 20-2) with their
related allocation decisions comprise the basis of play of the entire game.

The passage of time is signified by successive reportings. Good play is
identified by an increase in population and harvests, poor play by a decrease.

The method of computing a change in population from one report to the
next is illustrated in Figure 20-3, which shows that the best amount of grain
to use for food is 18 bushels per person. The formulas used to compute the
harvest (Table 20-1) do not show the effects of disasters or other temporary
variations in harvest. Also, the numbers in the formulas do not remain fixed
through a complete play of the game; for example, the formula for the

Initial Economic Report Made to the New Ruler of Lagash by his Humble
Steward:

Total population now	500
Total farm land under cultivation, acres	600
Total grain in inventory, bushels	900
one season old	900
two seasons old	0
three seasons old	0
Total grain just harvested, bushels	13000
Total resources, harvest and inventory	22000

You must now decide how to use your resources.

How many bushels of grain do you wish to feed your people?

How many bushels of grain do you want planted for the next crop?

This means that .... bushels must be placed in storage. Is this all
right? Do you wish to (1) let your decisions stand, or (2) revise them?

Resulting inventory   ....
The steward will execute the royal commands and return in 6 months.

FIGURE 20-1

THE INITIAL SEASONAL REPORT

harvest, H = 4S (Item 1), becomes H = 5S after the use of fertilizer is
introduced.

In the text of a typical seasonal report, the comment, "The quantity of
food the people received last season was _____," is modified to read
"far too little," "too little," "satisfactory," "too much," or "far too much."
The rules for insertion of the ratings are shown in Table 20-2.

Occasionally, brief reports of events that alter conditions in the city-state
follow the season report. The most persistent happenings are natural
disasters—floods and fires that kill people and ruin the harvests. These
natural disasters point up the need for maintaining a well-stocked inventory.
Both the occasion and severity of the disasters are determined by a pseudo
random computation procedure known as the Monte Carlo Method.

Another frequent report concerns the rotting of grain left in inventory.
The comment, "Sir, I am sorry to report that _____ bushels of grain have
rotted or been eaten by rats this past season," is given if the amount of rotted grain is not zero. The calculation of the amounts is given in Table 20-3.

Economic report of the ruler's steward for the fall season in the year 14 of Luduga 1.

Population at previous report	514
Change in population	12
Total population now	526

The quantity of food the people received last season was satisfactory.

Harvest last season	15829
Harvest this season	15829
Previous inventory	2620
Change in inventory	−456
Present inventory	2164
Total resources, harvest + inventory	17993

You must now decide how to use your resources.
How many bushels of grain do you wish to feed your people?
9500
How many bushels of grain do you want planted for the next crop?
4500
This means that 1829 bushels must be placed in storage. Is this all right? Do you wish to (1) let your decisions stand, or (2) revise them?
1

Resulting inventory	3993

The steward will execute the royal commands and return in 6 months.

FIGURE 20-2 A TYPICAL SEASONAL REPORT

TABLE 20-1 FORMULAS RELATING HARVEST TO SEED PLANTED, LAND CULTIVATED AND NUMBER OF FARMERS

Symbol Definition:

Let H = the number of bushels in the harvest
S = the number of bushels of seed planted
L = the number of acres of land cultivated
W = the number of workers on the farm lands

Formulas:

1. If too much seed has not been planted
$$S \leqslant 6L$$
and if there are enough farmers
$$W \geqslant L/4$$
then
$$H = 4S$$

2. If too much seed has not been planted
$$S \leqslant 6L$$
but there are too few farmers
$$W < L/4$$
then
$$H = (4W/L)\,4S$$

3. If too much seed has been planted
$$S > 6L$$
and if there are enough farmers
$$W \geqslant L/4$$
then
$$H = 24L$$

4. If too much seed has been planted
$$S > 6L$$
and there are too few farmers
$$W < L/4$$
then
$$H = 96W$$

FIGURE 20-3 GRAPH RELATING POPULATION CHANGE TO FOOD CONSUMPTION

Let P = the population
ΔP = the change in population over one season
F = the number of bushels of grain set aside as food for one season
X = food per person in one season

then $X = F/P$
and the ratio $\Delta P/P$ is given in the graph below:

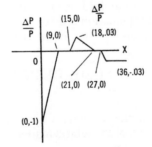

Example: If P = 600 and F = 10,200
then X = 17, $\Delta P/P = .02$
and $\Delta P = 12$
The next population figure would then be 612.

The economic condition of the city-state may improve in two ways: through good management of the basic grain allocation and by accepting with some good judgment a sequence of innovations presented in special end-of-season reports. Improvements of the second kind show themselves dramatically—a harvest productivity parameter is increased by 25 percent, the rate of rotting is cut by 50 percent, or perhaps the number of farmers required per acre of land is reduced by 50 percent. Progress through the game can be measured in terms of the number of special reports reviewed by the students. These reports normally follow a strict sequence in which no report can be given before a specific predecessor. Some of the reports are not offered until the student has exhibited sóme "good" judgment, e.g., has fed his people satisfactorily for two consecutive seasons. The student is often required to respond to questions during the reporting and any of the state-of-the-nation variables may have its value altered in the process. Such alterations invariably show themselves in subsequent population and harvest reports.

All of the state-of-the-nation variables used in the Sumerian Game are described in Table 20-4. For one group of variables, values are maintained over four seasonal report times. This "brief history" provides information for judging the "goodness" of play. Another group of variables is for current play-time only.

The Sumerian Game is played in three successive parts corresponding to the reigns of three rulers, Luduga I, II, and III. In addition to contributing to the story line of the game, this organization of the game makes plausible the resetting of the state-of-the-nation variables. That is, no matter how a student has directed the city-state through his reign as Luduga I or Luduga II (he may, for example, have increased his population by 20 percent or decreased it by 30 percent), he would start his play in the role of Luduga II or III with a standard set of values, for the state-of-the-nation variables. The story line explanation is that a period of time elapses between the completion of one part and the start of the next.

SOME DESIGN CONSIDERATIONS

Some of the techniques used in the design of the Sumerian Game are independent of the subject matter and, perhaps, usable in a broad context.

To enable rapid differentiation between student and computer information, the following design rule was selected: computer type-outs (the larger volume of material) will appear in black; student type-ins in red.

The design of a student response syntax is a more involved problem. In responding to questions printed by the computer, the student must express himself in a form anticipated by the game designers. In specific sections of the games, responses might be acceptable if, for example, they are only single-digit or single-word type-ins. This kind of constraint is determined by the game authors depending upon the context of the response. A more basic set of syntactical rules applicable to *all* responses is listed below:

• A response is made up of a sequence of typewriter keystrokes, the last, a special one signaling an end-of-message.

• Words and numbers may be constructed using a special alphabet; the normal alphabet a to z, the digits 0 to 9, and the special characters @ # $, . + − and /.

• The distinction between upper and lower case letters is ignored.

• Either space or tab keystroke indicates a separation between words or numbers.

• A backspace keystroke in a response indicates that the preceding non-backspace keystroke is to be deleted.

• Other keystrokes not explicitly mentioned above are simply ignored.

• A sequence of characters starting with a digit, a decimal point, a plus or minus sign, and extending to a non-digital character other than a period or comma, will be treated as a number. Acceptable forms are:

$$1234 \quad\quad 1{,}234{,}000 \quad\quad 1.234$$
$$.0034 \quad\quad +4.5 \quad\quad -67.8$$

The Sumerian Game also demonstrated the technical feasibility of incorporating an evaluation of student response and a printout of a report card. A general report-card form (Figure 20-4) was established to accept a recording of a grade (A, B, C, or D) in each of four categories of questions: impossible, hard, easy, other. The format also includes recordings of time-of-response in the same four categories. The instructor may request a report at any time, but normally it is printed at the terminal immediately after a student has finished a section of his play. The report card data in Figure 20-4 shows that a total of 40 questions were put to the student, the average time of response was 11.4 seconds, 2 answers earned a grade of D, 9 a C, 8 a B, and 21 a grade of A. The overall grade was 88 based on weighting the scores: 50 for a D, 70 for a C, 85 for a B, and 100 for an A. In the experiment, the report card was not used to measure a student's play except in scattered instances for demonstration.

Procedures were designed to handle two exceptional conditions that might be detected by the computing system. If, during the time the green "proceed" light is on, no key is struck within a period of approximately 30 seconds, the keyboard is locked and the light is turned off. The procedure for handling this is to return the carriage, advance the paper, and reinitiate the ready by turning the green "proceed" light on again. If during a transmission of information to or from the terminal a bit of information is either lost or picked up from some noise source, the transmission is terminated and the normal sequence interrupted. If this condition is encountered while sending a message to the terminal, the carriage is returned, "Machine Error" is printed in red, and the carriage is returned again and the last printed unit of information is reprinted. If the condition is encountered while composing a message at the terminal, the carriage is returned, "Please retype reply" is printed, the carriage returns again, and the "proceed" light turns on.

A complete play of the game spanned a number of days. Picking up a play of a game was very simply done by selecting from a system memory device a copy of the previous day's program. This "saved" program contained records identifying the student, his place in the play of the game, and a summary of the effects of his past decisions.

While some design problems are technical ones, not especially related to methods of teaching, the simulated environment mode does require a unique organization of the subject matter.

Many aspects must be planned in the development of such games: the script, the rules which control the sequencing through the script, the model governing the computations of report content, and the overall programing problems of making the computer "understand" the above specifications.

A team for developing a computer-controlled game might include: a subject matter specialist or teacher to interpret the overall educational objectives and write the script; a human-factors specialist to advise on the best manner of interaction between student and terminals; a mathematical model builder to create computational schemes which embody the desired theoretical behaviors; and a computer programing specialist to translate the specifications into computer programs. This last specialty may become unnecessary in view of the present trend among computer manufacturers to make application-oriented programing languages available to equipment users.

The principal output of an instructional game development project would be the computer programs and perhaps other media such as recorded sound passages, recorded TV picture sequences, photographic film images, and print materials. The computer programs would contain both the conversational control procedure (*what* message is shown to the student *when*) and the conversational material to be printed (the script). Also desirable is a comprehensive description of the game, with the complete script, a list of other informational units such as pictures, and a description of the control mechanisms. Control can best be described by charts showing lines of flow of control and branch points at which a description of the

Category	N	T-Ave.	D	C	B	A	GRADE
Hard	10	10.65	0	3	1	6	89
Easy	5	9.69	0	1	0	4	94
Other	23	12.78	2	4	7	10	86
All	40	11.40	2	9	8	21	88

FIGURE 20-4 REPORT CARD

TABLE 20-2 MESSAGE INSERTS

Let the comment "The quantity of food the people received last season was _____" have a variable insertion, to be specified below:

Let $X =$ food per person in one season (see Figure 1); then

If $X < 9$ the insert is "far too little."

If $9 \leqslant X \leqslant 15$ the insert is "too little."

If $15 < X < 21$ the insert is "satisfactory."

If $21 \leqslant X < 27$ the insert is "too much."

If $27 \leqslant X$ the insert is "far too much."

TABLE 20-3 THE GRAIN ROTTING COMPUTATIONS

Let $I_0 =$ grain put into inventory this past season

$I_1 =$ grain put into inventory one season back

$I_2 =$ grain put into inventory two seasons back

$I_3 =$ grain put into inventory three seasons back

$\Delta I =$ the change in inventory due to rotting

There are four rates of rotting. The applicable rate is determined by other factors, e.g. the extent of the use of clay pots, rather than baskets, for the storage of grain.

(1) $\Delta I = .1 \, I_0 + .25 I_1 + .75 I_2 + I_3$

(2) $\Delta I = .75 I_2 + I_3$

(3) $\Delta I = I_3$

(4) $\Delta I = .5 I_3$

TABLE 20-4 STATE-OF-THE-NATION VARIABLES

FOUR TIME PERIODS

The first group of variables have values maintained as of 4 distinct points in time (simulated play time). They are the current seasonal report, seasonal report time 1 season ago, seasonal report time 2 seasons ago and seasonal report time 3 seasons ago.

$P =$ the population
$F =$ the amount of grain allocated for food
$H =$ the amount of the harvest
$S =$ the amount of seed planted
$L =$ the number of acres of land under cultivation
$W =$ the number of workers in farming
$I_0 =$ the amount of grain in inventory zero seasons old
$I_1 =$ the amount of grain in inventory one season old
$I_2 =$ the amount of grain in inventory two seasons old
$I_3 =$ the amount of grain in inventory three seasons old

CURRENT PLAY TIME ONLY

Values of the following group of variables are maintained only for the current-play time.

$R_0 =$ the normal rate of return—harvest to seed planted
$R_1 =$ the maximum ratio of seed planted to land cultivated for normal harvests
$R_3 =$ the minimum ratio of farm workers to land cultivated for normal harvests
$R_4 =$ the ratio of farm workers to total population
$Y =$ the number of seasons played

conditions for branching is included. The parts of the script corresponding to unbroken conversational phrases should be uniquely labeled and referred to at the appropriate places on the flow chart. Similarly, the other informational units should be labeled and referenced.

In designing the Sumerian game, a most crucial design decision was the degree of freedom to allow a student in constructing responses. The student's role always seems too passive in that he is always strictly led by the program. A more positive role could be assumed if the student had some sort of command language available to him in which he could type, for example, "Stop the play. What was the ratio of grain harvested to grain planted for the past three seasons?"

Why not a command language then? On the one hand, to attempt to translate student commands expressed in natural language is foolhardy on two accounts: the domain of conversational interest in a game is, and should be, immensely restricted compared to the domain of possible conversation; and the problems of machine translation of natural language are so great that present efforts in this direction have only limited objectives.

The possibility of inventing artificial language exists, but here, the other side of the problem enters—the need for the student to know the language. One sensible approach is to introduce the student to the game playing material by way of a course in understanding and expressing ideas in a man-machine communication language. The more such an artificial language could be made standard across many computer-controlled courses, the greater the usefulness of the language.

Characteristic of the makeup of a game is the simulated situation—the dramatization of a changing situation which embodies the knowledge to be taught. It is not a presentation of abstract theories followed by examples illustrating the value of the theories. Rather it is the creation of an exemplary situation that exposes the student to an experience in which he can be involved and from which he can extract the underlying theory.

Also characteristic of this approach is the necessity of repetition. Multiple exposures are more or less needed by the players depending upon the abstractness of the theories relative to the situations embodying them.

The Sumerian Game is an interesting new use of modern technology in education. The novelty of the educational ideas embodied in the game (other than simply using EDP equipment) lies in the degree to which they are now being employed. Game-like situations have been used in the past to present knowledge in an especially palatable form. The notion, too, of displaying knowledge in unrefined form with a natural amount of "noise" surrounding it is not in itself new. What is new is the technology which gives a new freedom to employing the instructional games methods.

Part I.
The Learning Environment: Instructional Technology

Introduction

Technology is a force of significance in most aspects of modern civilization and it is no less significant in the field of education. Instructional technology does not simply mean machines in the classroom, however, it means much more than that. Charles F. Hoban, in Chapter 21, defines it as the management of ideas, procedures, money, machines and people in the instructional process. He further suggests five criteria which "justify" the use of instructional technology, including one that is enabling of individualized learning as a process that would otherwise be too difficult to achieve.

Educational media are crucial to the individual learner because they represent an alternative means of his accessing relevant information in the absence of a traditional teacher/lecturer. In the general sense, educational media include texts, workbooks, programmed books and other print materials; tapes, records and other audio materials; filmstrips, motion pictures, study prints and other photographic materials; games, realia, apparatus and a number of other manipulative materials; charts, signs, maps, and other graphic materials; dioramas, bulletin boards, felt boards and other displays; as well as a variety of other cue-organizing resources which serve as the carriers of messages. Many of these media-based messages are accessed by the individual learner in his classroom, others are obtained in a school resource center, and still others must be obtained from remote locations.

Television, dial access systems, shared-time computers, and the telephone are all techniques for accessing remote educational material. The relationship of telecommunications to individualized learning is discussed by C. R. Carpenter in Chapter 22.

It is *not* necessary to have sophisticated technology in order to individualize learning and many "audio-visual" resources currently in use are quite well suited to this application. In Chapter 23, Robert A. Weisgerber compares the appropriateness of selected media, considers facility design, and discusses certain management and logistic considerations.

Finally, recognizing that the term technology refers as much to a *process* as to a set of hardware and media alternatives, it is useful to examine how the process of technology may alter the man-machine relationship in the days and years to come. In Chapter 24, John W. Loughary forecasts the ways in which a *systematic* application of technology could greatly improve our educational capabilities. The focus of his reasoning suggests the use of information-processing technologies to develop a school data base comprised of curriculum files and student-descriptive files. Then, through the analysis of school management needs, evaluative research needs, and instructional needs it should be possible to reallocate those functions which technology can appropriately perform, freeing professional educators to provide more personalized attention to individual students. A model of a System for Individualized Instruction Management shows how this might work.

Chapter 21. A DEFINITION AND
RATIONALE FOR
TECHNOLOGY

MAN, RITUAL, THE ESTABLISHMENT AND
INSTRUCTIONAL TECHNOLOGY

Charles F. Hoban

Appointment of a national Commission on Instructional Technology under the Public Broadcasting Act points up the need for broad participation in defining agreeable boundaries of the field, locating the problem within its human, social, and institutional contexts, and considering priorities of emphasis and action.

The Commission's assignment is complicated by a posture of pessimism in a new power structure of instructional technology, or "learning systems," particularly among those involved in adapting computers to instruction. This posture appears to be based on the partial truth that instructional technological *devices* have failed to live up to *overstated* performance promises when adopted by the schools. Consequently, all technological innovations, including those in various stages of R.&D., are viewed as

SOURCE: Reprinted from *Educational Technology*, Vol. 8, No. 20 (October 30, 1968), pp. 5-11. Englewood Cliffs, N.J., by permission of author and publisher.

vulnerable to the dreadful disclosure of fraud when submitted to the pragmatic test of trial and adoption in actual instructional situations. The fact that many schools and colleges are virtually without funds intensifies the new pessimism toward instructional technology.

FACTORS UNDERLYING PESSIMISM

Underlying this pessimism or defeatism are several identifiable factors which lie deep in the educational system as sources of many problems of instruction. The salience of these factors is well known to those who have *(a)* participated directly in technological innovation in public school systems, colleges, and mass military training; *(b)* done both contextual and evaluation research on what hitherto have been known as "new media in education"; and *(c)* tried to develop viable theories dealing with the "new media in instruction." Among these factors are the following:

1.   An overexpectation of effects from any given gadget or process, simple or complex, adapted to instruction from some other area, such as entertainment (motion pictures, television) and automated industrial processes and commercial transactions (computers).

2.   "Measurement of effects" (evaluation) of the "new media" by instruments and techniques which are non-metric in the mathematical sense of measurement and insensitive to dimensions of human response that may be of much greater importance than the "behavioral objectives" they are designed to "measure."

3.   A "scientific" outlook among learning theorists, instructional systems analysts and designers, programmed instruction developers, etc., which *(a)* ignores the importance and operation of intuition in classroom interaction, and *(b)* prescribes narrow behavioral objectives and their criterial "measures."

4.   An inertial property of educational and adjunct institutions which makes them resistant to change, slow to innovate, and methodologically non-adaptive when innovation is tried.

5.   An irrelevance of much of learning theory to classroom teaching situations as they exist in reality, rather than in psychology laboratories.

6.   A curriculum which is frequently misphased, overintellectualized, and irrelevant to the individual needs and social milieu of large numbers of students, and consequently operative at best among bright and/or docile students responsive to pressures for compliance from both parents and teachers.

7.   An overextended period of compulsory or socially prescribed education which induces boredom and maintains the status quo in a seller's market in formal education, and an underdeveloped program of continuing

education which is particularly receptive and adaptive to instructional technology.

8. A narrow exclusiveness in the Educational Establishment, including the U.S. Office of Education and professional educational organizations, which equates education and instruction with public (and private) school systems and colleges, and ignores the educational and training programs of business, industry, the military services, etc.

The list of factors may be easily extended. The eight listed above are sufficient to indicate that *many problems of instructional technology are embedded in the broader and more universal problems of institutionalized instruction.*

A CONCEPT OF INSTRUCTIONAL TECHNOLOGY

It seems the better part of valor in the present state of things to adopt a moderate view of the scope of *instructional* technology. Otherwise, we will become involved in a range of concerns from team teaching to underground, windowless schools.

Essentially, instructional technology, in its modern usage, involves the *management* of ideas, procedures, money, machines, and people in the instructional process. As such, it involves:

1. A physical device(s) which mediates information transmission;

2. A system of instruction of which this device(s) is one of several components; and

3. A range of mediating options involving progression in *(a)* requirements for physical alteration of the "classroom"; *(b)* remoteness in time and space between the tutor-planner and the student; *(c)* sophistication of design of programmed information exchange between "tutor" and student; *(d)* complexity and cost of hardware; *(e)* level of technical skills required for equipment construction, installation, "de-bugging," operation, and maintenance; *(f)* independence from classroom teacher control or continuous monitoring in the operation of the device centered "teaching"; *(g)* additional manpower required by way of paraprofessional personnel for use of the instructional technology; and *(h)* role changes and new skills required of "classroom" teachers in (1) management of the technology, and (2) other and/or new non-structured, non-mediated teaching activities essential to personality development, humanistic growth, and cultivation of values, all of which lie outside the present and foreseeable potential of instructional technology as herein considered.

While the progression in technological devices indicated above is not deliberately sequenced in order of increasing administrator and teacher resistance to technological innovations in education, such a heuristic resistance sequence is implicit.

CLASSROOM TEACHER RITUAL

The current and historical role of the classroom teacher is highly ritualized. Any major change in ritual is likely to be resisted as an invasion of the sanctuary by the barbarians.

Ritualization in teaching is flexible enough to permit idiosyncrasies of personal style, arrangement of the daily schedule, police methods, pacing, etc., but *major characteristics of ritual tend to be invariant.*

Two of these invariants are (1) teacher control (within institutional limits of courses of study, textbooks, films, etc.) of the teaching-testing-grading-reward-punishment processes, and (2) face-to-face interaction with students. These two variants in rituals of teaching are likely to be important determinants in the trial and adoption of technological innovation and in its effectiveness in either event at the classroom level.

Any *sudden* or *substantial reduction* of dominance status and/or domain of activities of the classroom teacher, any *major* change in the interpersonal teacher-student communication situation, or any *systematic* attempt to scientize and rationalize the intuitively determined interaction patterns of the teacher is likely to elicit at least some teacher hostility and resistance.

The attitude of the classroom teacher toward any instructional innovation—technological or otherwise—is of paramount importance. While trial or adoption of innovation may be formalized at the federal, state, or community levels of control, it is in the individual school and individual classroom that the transaction occurs functionally (or dysfunctionally).

Indeed, it may be that the more or less generally accepted theory of instructional innovation as *(a)* originating from the outside (the supra system), and *(b)* proceeding from the top down in the hierarchical structure, carries within it the seeds of its own failures or imperfections by omitting participation of classroom teachers in adaptation and adoption decisions at the local policy making and implementation level.

Some remarkable research findings with direct bearing on the effects of teacher attitudes on student behavior are currently being spelled out by Robert Rosenthal and his associates using the concept of communication of expectancy.

In studies of the introduction of programmed instruction in Denver, Colorado, it was reported that students performed better under teachers favorable to programmed instruction *even when the sole function of the teacher was to maintain order.* Put another way, better results were obtained from students under programmed instruction when the expectancy of teachers was in a favorable direction, and this expectance effect occurred independently of the participational activity role of the teachers in the instructional process.

Apparently, human beings are highly sensitive to both intended and unintended expectancy cuing behavior of other human beings in dominant roles. Rosenthal reports that in an experiment on perception of people through photographs, subjects were asked to rate the experimenters on the "honesty" variable. This variable could be operative only *after* the experiment, and could occur in tabulating and summing the results. Errors in tabulation could be random or in the direction of confirming the hypothesis held by the experimenter, and tabulation and computational errors could be large or small.

Both tabulation and computational errors occurred. Among those who erred in the direction of the expectancy of their hypotheses, tabulation errors were larger. Mean ratings on an honesty scale by the experimental subjects were significantly lower for those experimenters who made errors in the direction of their hypothesis, i.e., experimenter expectancy. This suggests that subjects in the experiment were able to detect some cues in the behavior of experimenters which predicted beyond chance the subsequent errors in experimental data processing.

This apparent sensitivity of subjects (mostly students) to unintentional and perhaps non-formally coded cues to expectancy of results manifested by authority figures in an authority-structured social situation can be related to teacher influence on student performance in the direction of their expectancy hypothesis in the Denver trials of programmed instruction—especially when monitoring teachers exercised only the police function of preserving order in the classroom.

Even more remarkable results of teacher expectance on student development of competencies are reported by Robert Rosenthal and Lenore Jacobson in their recent book *Pygmalion in the Classroom.* Teachers in a San Francisco Bay Area school were told that about 20 percent of the students in each class included in the experiment had been identified through extensive testing as having unusual potential for intellectual gains. No such extensive testing had been done. The names of the 20 percent identified as having this unusual potential were selected randomly.

In this experiment no special programs, tutoring activities, or enrichment activities were involved. The only new element was that of favorable teacher expectation—teacher attitude toward the "unusual" pupils—and presumably consequent verbal and non-verbal expression by the teachers of this attitude toward these students.

To oversimplify interesting results, "unusual" students made significantly greater gains in IQ than the non-unusuals. The implications of these findings are difficult to overestimate. They suggest that *(a)* teacher expectancy, often operating at the unintentional level, is a variable of major importance in the instructional and developmental processes; and *(b)* students are highly sensitive and responsive to teacher expectancy along previously unsuspected dimensions of perception and growth.

It is reasonable to assume teacher expectance operates negatively as well as positively, as suggested by the Denver findings. That is, negative teacher expectancy may have a depressing, or leveling, or inhibiting, or hostility-arousing effect on student development. Yet, as far as I know, teacher selection and certification procedures do not ordinarily include the criterion of the *true believer* in the "unusual" growth potential of students.

It may be hypothesized that all innovators and agents of change tend to be what Eric Hoffer calls "true believers," oriented toward a better future of mankind, an improvement of the human condition of everyone; and that one of the most important aspects of instructional technology is the inherent expectancy of educational improvement shared by its advocates. The corollary is that instructional technology fails or disappoints when its implementation falls into the hands of skeptics and infidels whose habituated classroom rituals have attained doctrinal significance, and consequently whose expectancy of ritualistic change is negative.

CRYSTALLIZATION OF THE ARGUMENT

To crystallize the argument, it should be borne in mind that:

1. Many of the troublesome problems of instructional technology are essentially further manifestations of the troublesome problems and properties of instruction in the American educational system.

2. The fashionable attitude of pessimism and "pooh-pooh" toward instructional technology is particularly evident among an elite of the supra Educational Establishment for whom the world of instructional technology originated last year or the year before and consists largely of promised but undelivered computer regulation of the process of individualized, multi-tracked instructional programs, task assignments, and performance monitoring.

3. At least some, if not many, of the significant variables of in-school growth and development of students lie beyond the cognizance of learning theory, and the consequences of these variables escape the narrowly prescribed "first order," behaviorally operationalized objectives of instruction and their criterial "measures."

4. The process of innovation has been studied on the normative rather than the explanatory, i.e., theoretical, level and consequently the literature on innovation provides few cues for acceleration and adoption of desirable changes in the system of instruction.

5. The classroom teacher is by training and institutional control a prisoner of the orthodox ritualization of the educational system, negatively disposed to automation, and perhaps less effective as a gatekeeper than as a positive or negative expectancy reflector.

It follows that substantial, difficult, and not-clearly-defined changes must be made in the educational system both for its own effective survival and in order to accelerate the rate of development, adoption, and optimum use of instructional technology, assuming that instructional technology can be justified in the first place.

JUSTIFICATION OF INSTRUCTIONAL TECHNOLOGY

Instructional technology is more justified by its own logic than by empirical studies of its effectiveness in facilitating "learning." Empirical (evaluative) studies often ignore critical variables, and typically "measure" only those results which are easiest to operationalize within the state of the art of criterial specification and educational testing. The notion of "unobtrusive measures" has scarcely penetrated educational research, and at least some of the vigorously promoted techniques of multivariate analysis are too often used as substitutes for thinking. This is not to say that empirical research has no place in uncovering important relationships or evaluating procedures and progress in instruction, but only that too often it is overburdened by techniques and designed with impoverished insight and imagination.

The development, use, and improvement of instructional technology, as defined in this article, is justified in general by the fact that American schools operate as a formative institution of a highly technological society and should therefore incorporate, as appropriate, this characteristic of the larger society as well as other idealized values. In a sense, this principle of justification is aesthetic and can rest at that without decisive challenge.

However, since aesthetics generates much subjectivity and little objectivity, stimulates lofty dialogue at the philosophical level and restless, insistent controversy in relation to specific events, it is desirable to get down to tangible criteria in justifying instructional technology.

It may be said reflectively that instructional technology is justified if and when it:

a) makes available a mode or multimodes of representation on any of several levels of reality (culturally recognizable as such), without constraints of geography or of real time, and hitherto not available for instruction;

b) provides a model of behavior otherwise unavailable, in scarce supply, or lacking authenticity or correctness of definition, and preferably when it provides opportunity for the student to compare his imitative behavior with that of the model;

c)   sequences and, within reasonable limits and without undue restraints, manages stimulus inputs and response outputs on a desirable individualized and structured basis otherwise difficult or impossible to achieve;

d)   stores, retrieves, and rapidly processes a large amount of important and useful information not otherwise readily available, or, if available, too time-consuming to process manually;

e)   involves desirable latent functions of a critical nature in the instructional process or system which, because they are not immediately related to improved and "measured" student progress, may escape proper assessment or even official observation.

None of these five criteria is necessarily independent of the other four. All can be combined in instructional systems involving simple or complex hardware, or electronic components. Also, it goes without saying that this brief list of criteria is not intended to be either definitive or exhaustive.

MINIMIZING CONTINGENCIES OF INSTRUCTIONAL TECHNOLOGY

For what it is worth, it may be said reflectively, and with some empirical evidence, that the effectiveness of instructional technology will be less than optimum if and when it:

a)   incorporates the format of other modes of instruction known to be relatively inefficient and ineffective instructionally, i.e., when McLuhan's "rearview mirror" effect occurs;

b)   fails to challenge or slows down the natural pace of progression of students and thus induces student boredom and/or resentment;

c)   rapidly reaches a point of diminishing returns and thus becomes monotonous and unrewarding;

d)   severely and continuously reduces the social process of education, i.e., face-to-face interpersonal interactions, group participation, etc.;

e)   requires logistical support beyond the capacity of the system to provide in proper time-phase and matching characteristics, and without heavy encumbrance of hardware, additional personnel, or hard-to-find dollars.

PRIORITIES AND EMPHASES

It may be reasonably expected that all of us will sooner or later come to some decisions on priorities. A set of questions such as the following deserve consideration and allocation of priorities:

1.1 Should motion pictures, filmstrips, radio, and other media, currently not considered as technological innovations but as adoptions, be taken for granted, or should they be re-examined, for: currency of content, state of the art such as employment of more involving and perhaps less isomorphic symbolism, extent of adoption, logistical adequacy, etc.?

1.2 Should emphasis now placed on the newer technologies, such as ITV and PTV, individually prescribed instruction, computer regulated instruction, etc., be intensified, or should they undergo more extensive feasibility, operational suitability, and effectiveness testing, bearing in mind the kinds of variables already discussed, and the present limitations and necessary modifications of research procedures and techniques?

2.1 Should efforts to diffuse instructional technology and increase its effectiveness be time-phased from the elementary school, which is more open to innovation, and progressively to the high school and college which are more conservative and less open to changes in teacher role and ritual?

2.2 Should the efforts to diffuse instructional technology and increase its effectiveness be more emphasized among formally certified "systems" of education, such as public schools and colleges, which often defy systems analysis simply because they are *systematically chaotic,* or should they be more emphasized on the para-formal educational institutions of industry, commerce, and the military services which are better systematized and more definitively goal oriented?

3.1 Within the formally structured and certified educational "systems," should emphasis on the employment of instructional technology be directed to use among those schools serving the "culturally deprived" student population, or should it be directed to use among those schools serving the family reinforced, docile, compliant and thus more "teachable" student population?

3.2 Again within the formally structured and certified educational "systems," should emphasis on instructional technology be placed on the full-time day student population, or on the continuing education population among whom the struggle is greater, the need more acute, and the motivation possibly more intense?

4.1 What changes are required in teaching rituals and functions in order to increase allocations of time to *learning* activities of students directly related to "new media," and in teachers' expectancy images of students so they are perceived as human beings with primordial capacities to learn, "turn on," and develop on higher levels?

4.2 What balances and directions are required in the development of the newer more complex technologies of instruction and/or their employment, for *both* the essential individualizing and the essential socializing processes of education?

The list of questions is not exhaustive, and their formulation does not exclude the middle ground from consideration. Omitted from the list are questions dealing with the important issues of teacher education, strategies of innovation, and research methodologies. Such questions are implicit in various foregoing sections. Also omitted are questions of use of technology in public relations, class scheduling, library controls, etc., not because they are unimportant but because they attenuate the problems of *instructional* technology. However, we will all be in error if we ignore these areas of application.

THE SYSTEMS APPROACH

Throughout the above discussion, the systems concept is embedded in various points. Like cost effectiveness, operations research, the cognitive and affective domains, and other terms on current display in the best company, the systems concept is being scourged mercilessly in educational discourse; nevertheless it is imperative that instructional technology be approached within a central concept of instruction as a system, and not as the installation of appliances, or the design of school buildings in the round. *A system is no more or no less than an arrangement in which everything is related to everything else so that the malfunctioning of any part affects the system output or outcome.*

The systems concept is not fully explicated or articulated in its educational applications and implications but its seminal ideas are clear and simple and need not await the master blueprint to be accepted and acted upon.

Perhaps those neat, big or little flow charts with boxes, circles, and arrows that appear so elegantly professional and slightly awesome in the new educational literature are a necessary and useful step in beginning to take a fresh look at instructional technology.

Chapter 22. ACCESS TO
REMOTE LEARNING
MATERIALS

TELEINSTRUCTION AND INDIVIDUALIZED LEARNING

C. R. Carpenter

APPROACHES TO THE SUBJECT

The purpose of this paper is to contribute to the tasks of clarifying and extending design strategies and practices for effectively using available and emerging telecommunication technologies for instigating the formal learning of college students.

SOURCE: Reprinted from a mimeographed report *Using Educational Media to Individualize Instruction.* Lewisburg, Pennsylvania: Bucknell University, November 1967, p. 24, by permission of author and publisher.

This paper was originally prepared for a Faculty Seminar on Educational Media sponsored jointly by Bucknell University and the U.S. Office of Education under provisions of Title VI-Part B of the Higher Education Act of 1965. This seminar was held at Bucknell University on December 7 and 8, 1967.

The new cryptic term, *teleinstruction,* conveys the concept of the use of equipment, processes and procedures which provide instruction or the stimulation of learning at a distance from the original source of the stimulus materials. The operations can be simultaneous or sequential and involve recordings and time schedules.

THE MULTI-MEDIA APPROACH

Closed-circuit television (CCTV) is only one type of a very wide array of equipment, apparatus, instrumentation and procedures for providing communications for the instruction of individuals at remote points. Radio and broadcast television, on-line and shared-time computer arrangements, dial access materials and telephones can be used for purposes of teleinstruction. This extended concept should make a useful contribution to this important seminar on *Using Educational Media to Individualize Instruction* and to the design and use of instructional systems.

The problem that confronts us, and which we shall attempt to resolve, is to show how the so-called "mass media" and other associated and complemental technologies can be used in new patterns and varied configurations to provide some of the required conditions for formal instruction and the educational development of college students.

Rapidly advancing thinking holds that the designing of optimum conditions and general systems of information for learning by students in colleges and universities requires the use of planned and tested *combinations of media.* The correct instructional uses of closed-circuit television, for example, currently may require books and periodicals, audio communication, tutorials, seminars and direct lectures, laboratory "experiments" and field experiences. This list does not exhaust the possible means and methods that may be needed for designing the complex requirements for optimally stimulating academic learning.

The multi-media system of instruction is widely accepted, and wise knowledgeable people have long since ceased to display the pathological syndrome of *single medium fixation* which was so characteristic of educational media innovators of the 1940's, 1950's and the early 1960's. Nevertheless there are still at this late hour fashions of media. The current one can probably be labeled "computer aided instruction" (CAI). Programed instruction and teaching machines were CAI's immediate predecessors, and closed-circuit and broadcast television were previous fashions. We are becoming rapidly more perceptive than formerly about media fads and fashions, and we calmly understand as each medium is proposed as the solution to learning strategies that "this, too, shall pass away."

REDEFINITION OF THE PROBLEM

There is an advance also of conceptual thinking about the media. They are carriers of information. They are empty channels and raw tapes, films and paper. The basic complex problem is to select the most *appropriate modes of communication* for learning strategies and put these into combinations. What kinds and proportions of modes are most effective for insuring specified learning results and performance changes for specified content units and for learners with known characteristics? When and where do we use print, spoken language (directly or recorded), graphic modes of communications, animation, art forms, and photography (both still and motion)? What kinds of print, and in what formats, best fit the requirements for optimizing the learning conditions? The same question can be asked about the other modes of communication. How do we use combinations of these modes in both simultaneous or sequential configurations? For what reasons or learning objectives should different modes and *combinations of modes* be used to provide high quality instruction? When do different modes summate, extend learning, increase generalization, and when do different modes produce interference with learning?

When we become more specific in the task of design strategies, the problem becomes that of selecting modes and mode configurations which summate, reinforce and strengthen the stimulus impact on students and which shape their conceptual skills and intellectual competencies. Those media and modes should be selected and used to *broaden* and *vary* stimulus conditions, to enhance the interests of students and to increase the possibilities for the retention and generalization of learned performances. It is most difficult to select mode combinations which do not have internal interferences or do not overload the neuro-sensory channels with information or exceed the optimum rate of stimulus presentations.

What are the relations of all of these questions to the problem of individualizing instruction?

This line of thinking points to some of the most fundamental problems of instructional communications, and indeed of the nature of knowledge, its origin and order, its growth and organization.

INDIVIDUALIZED AND SOCIALIZED LEARNING

Teleinstruction and individualized learning would seem to pose a dilemma, a clash of ideas and a conflict of concepts—How can the media and modes of modern technology be appropriately employed in learning strategies?

Education has many shrines where educators worship, and one of these modern shrines is *individualized instruction*. There is no inter-individual nerve net. Let us agree once and for all time that only individuals learn.

Classes, groups, seminars, families, audiences and populations do *not* l
Individuals alone learn, but most frequently they learn *in* classes, gr
seminars, families, audiences and populations. These groupings constitute
important if not essential *conditions* which affect in many ways the learning
of individuals.

Furthermore, it should be observed that there are factors in social
conditions that affect learning positively by reinforcing the learning, and
there are other factors that affect learning negatively by interfering with or
inhibiting learning.

Surely individuals do talk audibly or subvocally with themselves to good
effect; they think, solve problems, test for better words or phrases, imagine
new concept structures, create art objects and dream about the future. Surely,
too, individuals do listen to others and learn; they engage in intensive and
revealing dialogues, contend in debate and try their wings of logic in
disputations. They observe models of intellectual performances and reject
them or emulate them. In brief, learning is individualized and socialized.
Only individuals learn but social factors provide positive and negative
conditions which importantly affect the kind and rate of learning.

FOUR USEFUL GUIDELINES

There are four practical guidelines that may be useful in the planning and
execution of learning strategies.

First, design and provide varied and balanced patterns of conditions for
learning. Vary sizes and composition of learning groups. Vary schedules.
Balance study in splendid isolation for depth with discussions in groups for
brightness and interest.

Second, design and provide conditions for learning which are like or
which simulate the future conditions under which the individuals will
continue to learn during their whole life cycle. There is, pertinent to our topic
of *teleinstruction,* little prospect that the radio, the telephone, television, and
motion-picture films will disappear as sources of information, instruction
and entertainment.

Third, whatever the conditions of learning and learning technology,
students need training in the strategies and skills for learning under the
special conditions arranged or provided for formal learning. This proposition
applies especially to individualizing learning and to planning for students to
study independently.

Fourth, students should be taught in ways which lead them to become
autonomous learners who are weaned both from their parents and teachers.
The autonomous learner is freed from school requirements and restraints.
He sets his own learning tasks, selects his own materials and methods, he
achieves his own goals and reaps his own rewards.

TELEINSTRUCTION—APPARATUS

With these approaches now made explicit, let us turn directly to the question of how to use *teleinstruction media* and how at the same time to individualize optimally the learning conditions. The question could be stated to read: How are we to individualize learning optimally while using teleinstructional principles, means and methods?

Let us be very clear about the kinds of equipment, methods and content or messages that we are discussing and from which we can select patterns and combinations. The roll call is as follows: printed materials; recordings on film or tape, both audio and video; live transmissions ranging from telephone lines to multi-channel cables and from on-line computer to laser beams; and broadcast diffusions ranging from radio to continent-spanning communication satellites. It is proposed, furthermore, that many patterns of these *phenotypically different* but functionally similar media can be used to solve the design problems of maximizing the efficacy of instruction for learning. The design may include the special case of precisely adapted instruction for individualized learning.

ANALYSIS OF THE PROBLEM OF INDIVIDUALIZATION OF LEARNING

Essentially the general problem is to arrange for and adapt mediated instruction and conditions of media-mode uses to accommodate within the *tolerance limits* of individual differences which are essential and integral to learning. We are not to be concerned here with individual differences which are not highly contingent to learning operations. We are especially concerned with those adaptations and sets of conditions which affect learning to a degree of *practical significance* as well as *statistical significance*.

Ideally and theoretically we should include the *settings* or conditions for learning as well as the displays of materials for learning whether mediated by a teacher or through technologies. Individual requirements for learning are not unlimited. Tolerance limits can be found, it is assumed, and levels of difficulty, pacing rates and progression rates can be adjusted within these limits.

MANAGING INSTRUCTION

In addition to individual differences of students, there are other major components of the problem of individualized learning. Some of these are the following:

1. Arranging for optimized interactions of instructional materials with the personalized goals, values, interests and activated motives of students.

2. Determining the general and specific educational competency levels of students and adjusting the levels of possible interactions with the right *kinds* and *levels* of instructional materials and methods.

3. Designing and arranging the *places* where learning interactions are to occur between students and the stimulus materials, students and teachers, and students with students.

4. Scheduling, programing and pacing the patterns of interactions with the selected and designed instructional materials.

5. Programing the gradual transition from external control to self-regulated learning activities.

The regulation of interactions over time involves two main operations; scheduling or programing and timing or pacing. Programing a student through a curriculum or course is a gross operation extending over years, months, days and hours. Pacing is the rate at which an individual processes information provided by the instruction; the rate of perceiving, speed of reading, the rates of learning and understanding stimulus materials are processes that are included in pacing or fine timing. Pacing requires fine timing which may have an optimum rate range extending from microseconds for some kinds of foreign language learning, which involves matching and modeling phrases and sentences, to minutes for some kinds of problem solving or the mastery of complex concepts. Furthermore, pacing like scheduling can be self-regulated or externally controlled.

LEARNER ADAPTATIONS

The designing of instructional strategies includes another problem; namely, apportioning the kinds and amounts of adaptation demands or requirements between the *instructional materials and associated media* on the one hand and *the student* on the other hand. Effective instruction involves, among many other things, making appropriate and increasing demands on the student for increasing efforts to learn. When this is done, the student has many options of his own for accommodating to these demands. He can accept, reject or accommodate to them. Involved here are many styles of gamesmanship that are both understood and misunderstood by teachers and students. Students are not merely response mechanisms; they are persons who take action.

There is a problem here that we believe we discovered at Penn State. We had been mystified over and over again by the finding that, regardless of the attempts to improve the instruction of courses, at least by greatly increasing the instructional energy input and by elaborating the instructional materials and methods, grades and test scores remained relatively constant. The results were reflected both in measurements of means and variances.

A condition that prevailed in our experiments was that we usually attempted to develop only one, and never more than two, of the four or five semester courses of the students' full course load.

It is known that students establish for themselves levels of performance expectancies, and these same expectancies are established for grades. Serious students also differentiate grade level expectancies for different courses in relation to the importance of a particular course to them. It is more important for students to achieve good grades, for example, in their majors than in their elective courses.

There is an additional set of factors which seems to be operating. *Poor instruction may be compensated for by good learning.* A condition for this to occur is strong interest on the part of students for a subject.

Now we are ready for the paradox and hypothesis: when instruction is importantly improved in one of a set of courses and learning is made easier for the student, the demands on the student are reduced in that course and the grade level expectancy can be achieved with less effort; then, the student channels his energies into the other courses of his total program. Consequently grades and test measures in the improved experimental course remain as they were before the course was developed.

The most important conclusion that can be formulated, assuming that the hypothesis is correct, is that good experimentation in an operational educational context requires that the *total demand system* which operates on students be brought under control or included in the experimental design strategies.

It is interesting to observe that our definition of an adequate sampling of content has changed from lesson or instructional units in 1948 to full courses in 1958 and now the entire work load of students in 1968!

PATTERNS OF USE OF TELEINSTRUCTION

The patterns of use of telecommunications equipment and technology for instruction in colleges and universities are only part of the full strategies of instruction. From 1954 to 1964 we at Penn State planned, developed, used and generally evaluated about twenty-five permutations and variations of patterns of use of telecommunications.

These studies have been reported in four major reports and a sound motion picture.[1] I propose to review some of the main developments and suggest how some of these patterns can be used to accommodate to the goals and interests of students and their individual differences and also used to provide flexibility of instruction. Other patterns of use require adaptations that students themselves can make. There are patterns of production and patterns of use that cannot be recommended. There are those that remain to be developed, perfected and accepted by educators.

Initially we used the basic and primitive method of originating instruction from a large classroom with fixed cameras connected by means of cable to a series of small and moderate-sized classrooms. The instructors lectured, performed demonstrations, asked and answered questions and otherwise conducted the class as they would have done before the introduction of television. The television equipment and operating personnel were intentionally made inconspicuous and unobtrusive.

This basic feasibility study which was done for the Fund for the Advancement of Education provided comparisons between (1) *direct instruction* in a class of several hundred students with fixed cameras and (2) transmitted and cathode-tube displayed instruction in classes ranging in size from about thirty-five to sixty students.

The classes with television receivers were monitored first by faculty members, then by graduate students and later by undergraduate proctors. Finally, monitoring in classrooms was reduced in most courses and discontinued entirely in some courses. We made every effort to encourage students to *accept increasing amounts of responsibility for managing their own learning and for other classroom behavior.*

Otherwise there was no more or less individualization of learning for students than in traditional college courses of instruction even though the students were one TV cable length removed from the instructor. Here a teacherless classroom was a new learning condition for many students. They needed to adjust to this condition.

It was clear from these early experiments that the fields of perception and information displays were importantly selected by the camera operations. Objects and processes were enlarged or magnified, and the view of the instructor and what he displayed, including blackboard work, was improved for students conventionally seated from the center to the back of large classrooms. Thus, demands on students to select and react to instructional elements may have been reduced while viewing conditions were improved. Interferences of the large classes were reduced in the classrooms with television receivers.

The next set of variations which we introduced was renovating a classroom and remodeling it to serve as a place where instruction could be originated. In this "origination room" or studio there were several variations which differed from the pattern just described. The instructor could have with him in the studio small groups of students *who could give immediate reactions* to his lecture or questions, or raise representative questions which might have been asked in larger sections or by students not in the origination room. In another variation the instructor could lecture in the studio without students but direct his instruction to the movable cameras and the camera operators. This pattern made it possible to have more and better instructional materials such as charts, titles and graphics, as a result of more space and maneuverability of the television cameras. Later when slide and film chains were added to our equipment, these media could be used also by the instructor.

On the reception side we used a wide range of classroom sizes and solved many problems of arrangements of television receivers and speakers in classrooms that were not designed for the uses of "new" media. The objective was to have good viewing and listening conditions in all of the varied classrooms. Television was used as a justification for renovating old classrooms.

It was in developing a third set of conditions of learning that we gave the most attention to providing for adaptations and *variations of conditions* for student learning. The first step was to determine that the whole course of instruction need not be channeled over television and that the academic *time-credit accounting system could and should be changed.* Scheduling of segments of some courses was changed to provide time for lectures, both straight verbal and illustrated; lecture-demonstrations; proctor-led discussions; practicum sessions (e.g., in accounting); and regular and special laboratory work in sciences. In addition, of course, there were the regular assignments of text materials, reference sources, library work and other study. What we began to realize at this stage was that closed-circuit television could be made flexible and varied across courses and curriculums and within a course of study.

Flexibility and variations of instructional technology, methods and even goals and levels of attainment are very important even if they are not ideal conditions for *individualized* learning.

The instructors in originating studios without students expressed the need for means of talking with students. Realizing the problem of *passivity of television viewing* and the need for active responses and "feedback" to the instructors, we developed the "Telequest" means for studio-classroom and classroom-studio intercommunication. With the "Telequest" sub-system, either the instructor or a student in any of the classrooms (and there could be fourteen of these) could initiate a question. The question or comment could be heard by students in all fourteen interconnected classrooms. Then, there could follow a discussion between the instructor and an individual student or several students in any of the classrooms.

The "Telequest" arrangement provided a means for the instructor to query individual students, and thus to introduce an element into his instruction which increased the alertness of students in television classrooms. This had a beneficial effect on class attendance even when rolls were not checked.

Some instructors provided times when students could seem them, but the students infrequently used these periods set aside for them. This problem raises a cluster of questions about how "feedback" on learning can be provided and used to improve instruction and the conditions for student learning.

Stephens College has very successfully adapted the telephone for mediating the "Telelecture." We tested this method at Penn State for reaching out long distances for information that is current and for outstanding people who could not have been otherwise brought to students in formal class instruction. Thus, two further developments followed.

The closed-circuit television and "Telequest" systems were interconnected with the telephone systems so that up to 400 or 500 students located in fourteen classrooms could listen to conversations and discussions by leaders in relevant fields and by specialists in subjects of interest. Students on signals could query the remote guest telelecturer. Conference telephone arrangements made available to students in a course in economics the opportunity to hear management and labor leaders at a state capitol in a strike situation and in a legislative debate on proposals for new labor laws. In political science, leaders of contesting parties were invited into the closed-circuit course by means of telelecture discussions.

The second major development during the early stages of experimentation was on the distribution side of the television operation. We reasoned that if it was practical to transmit instruction from one campus building to another then why couldn't we reach out to the expanding number of Commonwealth campuses. This we did as a test case by installing a microwave link between University Park and the Altoona campus.

In the pre-videotape era we also experimented with kinescopic recordings of instruction. We undertook to produce two core-of-course sets of instruction for the Air Force. We helped the Dage Bell (now Raytheon) Company perfect an inexpensive kinescopic recorder and used a strategy that opened up television instruction to many and varied patterns of use and flexibility for individualized learning or study in small groups. The strategy is that of recording the *central* and most *important parts* of *courses,* those parts that are appropriate for the medium, and those that have the "longest half-life" or slowest rate of antiquation, along with the greatest consensus of experts about both the content and methods.

The recorded core-of-course development provides flexibility of scheduling and actually requires planned supplementary work on the parts of students and teachers in the learning situations.

The effects of the developments can be to provide specified places and roles for both students and teachers. Thus, the *displacement effects* of the televised "master teacher" can be greatly reduced or perhaps entirely eliminated.

The next development which became possible by linkage of classrooms at University Park with Channel 10 Altoona was to simultaneously broadcast courses of instruction while the same instruction was being given to formally organized classes at University Park and at the Altoona campus. Here we challenged the course-credit-fee structure of higher education. Courses in philosophy, sociology, economics, history and meteorology were distributed by both closed-circuit arrangements and by broadcast methods.

We determined by a well-conducted telephone survey of population of people of the broadcast area that about 35,000 people viewed and listened fairly regularly to the course in sociology. However, less than 25 persons were interested in credit for the course. Most of the 35,000 were *individual* viewers. Thus, we opened up the formal classrooms of the University and invited the public to see and learn what transpires at the very heart of the University's instructional program. Sensitive administrators viewed as public relations issues instruction in such subjects as comparisons of religions, political issues, comparative economic systems, and instruction of the physiology of reproduction. Actually there was less than one-tenth of one percent of negative comments. The economics professor received almost a thousand letters of appreciation.

Agreements were proposed to the colleges in the broadcast area in Central Pennsylvania that they use the teleinstruction without cost during the experiment and keep records of the results. There were few professors who would accept instruction originated by another in another university. This reaction deserves further discussion and constitutes one of the main barriers to the development of levels of utilization that justify the costs of producing high quality programs of instruction.

What did this development show? That we could move instruction of some kinds to people rather than transport people to already crowded campuses. It showed that a very small percentage of the adult population is interested in courses for *credit*. Finally, it showed that it is difficult to share or exchange instruction among institutions.

There is much to be done and much promise in instructional broadcasting that can lead to individualized learning. Neither management strategies for instructional broadcasts nor those for use in homes have been as fully developed as they might be. There are needs for an instrument development for the home which will do the following: provide the means for informing viewers *immediately* of the correctness or incorrectness of their responses to questions, problems and issues; make permanent records of the learners' responses which can be transmitted to the place of origination of the instruction; make, on a pre-scheduled timing, a record of a unit of instruction that can be studied when it is best and most practical for the learner.

In addition, there need to be developments in producing and testing printed materials for coordinated study with televised instruction. There are no real technical barriers to the use of telephones for feedback from home-viewed instruction to points of origination. And finally, radio and television can be harnessed together. This could be modeled after the successful demonstrations of two-way radio made by the Albany Medical School, that an adaptation could also involve television components.

We at Penn State demonstrated two other adaptations of televised instruction before attempting to apply programing procedures to courses for use over the media. First, we developed a variation of the Pyramid Plan for use with large television-instructed sections in sociology. This involved the organization of several hundred students in a closed-circuit television course into small groups of twelve to fifteen individuals. The groups' discussions were led by selected and coached *under-graduate* students. The focus of the groups' dialogues was on the issues and problems raised by the professor over television and on those that were of interest to students themselves.

The other adaptation of television during this phase was to install receivers in dormitories. This method of use was at a later date tested thoroughly at the University of Illinois and found to be acceptable. The next step, obviously, is to provide television sets for student dormitory rooms which make some of the best carrel spaces available on university campuses. Further advances in dormitory design using individual rooms in the same manner as is now done in modern hospitals, will make it possible to individualize learning by having in the living-study room arrays of equipment which include sound systems, small television receivers and dial access capabilities for sound tape and film clips. In the building but not in the individual rooms, there could be on-line terminals for accesses to Computer Regulated Instruction (CRI).

In summary, we have in this section traced one exploratory development of *teleinstruction,* and thus we have described how technology has progressively become more varied and flexible, and therefore, more useful in *individualizing instruction.* By developing patterns of distribution of instruction over space, by scheduling and time-sequencing, by creating new patterns of course arrangements, the instruction has become more pliable and adaptable for both instructors and students. What remains is to deal with advances in providing pacing rates that are optimized for the differences in learning rates of individuals and to demonstrate how branching and differential leveling may be accomplished.

PACING RATES OF MEDIA

There is a pervasive belief in educational circles that pacing rates should be adjusted to each individual learner. When it is said that the student should be allowed to proceed at his own rate, two very different conditions may be involved: (1) the rate or schedule at which a student progresses through a course in terms of hours, weeks or months, and (2) the rate of learning which may include speeds of perceiving, reading, conceptualizing, choosing, solving problems and responding.

The independent study plan at Bucknell University releases the student from regular class attendance and permits him to regulate his own rate of progression through the course. The more microscopic pacing rate is not controlled. The Bucknell condition provides, however, possibilities of great economies. The problem would seem to be that of preparing students for accepting the unusual responsibilities for managing their own study time. It should be observed that after instructional materials are prepared and made available the students may need to make little demand on their instructors for their time and help.

We at Penn State have conducted research and development work in an attempt to apply programing principles with the "new" media, including closed-circuit television (CCTV). The critical problem to be solved was that of the rate of presentation and the rate of development of the instructional materials, lessons and courses. We solved this problem by determining the normal rate of work of samples of the target audience of students using preliminary versions of programed instruction in algebra and grammar. After these empirical tests, pacing was adjusted to the several formats used in the project. Experiments were conducted with different pacing rates, both slower and faster than the learner based norms. Students adjusted their work rates to the controlled rates. There were no significant differences in test scores among the $-80, -90, 100 + 110$ rates.

Two concepts resulted from these studies. First, it became doubtful whether or not the self-pacing rates of students are the optimum rates. Second, pacing that is slightly faster than an individual's normal rate over a whole course may favorably increase the perceptual cognitive response speeds of learning.

Results of the studies and analyses of pacing rates of instructional displays gave us confidence to proceed with programing materials for filmstrips, motion-picture films, film loops and for closed-circuit television.

Programed instruction was originated "live" in television studios by especially planned mirror techniques, precisely paced on the basis of information collected from sample groups of students and distributed to classrooms where experimental groups, randomly assigned, observed and responded to the frame-by-frame materials. Student responses were made on "response schedule sheets" which paralleled the televised instruction. Reinforcement was given in either the written or the verbal mode at a time estimated to be after students had made their responses. Thus administered, the test scores for students who were instructed over closed-circuit television were not significantly different from the scores made by students who were instructed by the programed book, filmstrip and teacher-presented versions of the course.

There was an incidental finding which relates to individualized instruction. It is generally known that some programed books may not maintain the interest and motivation of students. This was found to be true with the Penn State programed grammar course. Student assistants and observers proctored the evening sessions, and the students complained about the lack of availability of instructors and the dullness or absence of appeal of the course material. Reacting to these opinions and attitudes, we *paired students* randomly and required each pair to use the same programed booklet and to complete one answer sheet. The pairs of students were asked to agree about the responses to frames or answers to problems and to accept the same unit test score. Complaints about the lack of attention from instructors ceased, as did complaints about dullness of rather finely programed material.

It will be observed that programed courses administered by media permitted the instruction of classes and multi-sectioned courses. Also, it is proposed that these feasibility demonstrations present the very real possibility that the procedures can be adapted and developed for uses with the broadcast media and further adaptations made for individualizing instruction.

INDIVIDUALIZED INSTRUCTION BY MULTI-VERSIONS OF INSTRUCTIONAL MATERIALS

Instructional film research led to the development of production procedures for making multiple film versions. The experimental films differed with respect to defined variables either in the commentary and sound or in pictorial characteristics. All materials for the versions were "shot" or processed on a planned schedule and then edited together to meet the requirements of experimental designs.

This development demonstrated a means for producing instructional units for target audiences of trainees and students who differed in significant learning characteristics. Versions could be produced at low, medium and high levels of difficulty or in rates of context development. Thus, it was suggested that instructional film units could be adapted so as to accommodate to limited ranges of individual differences.

An extension of this methodology involves the production and use of "single concept" films, either 8mm or 16mm, which present usually in silent form the core-of-a-unit or the core-of-a-course of instruction. This method then provides varied opportunities for individualized adaptations to be made in the situations of use. This arrangement has the advantage at some levels of instruction of schools and colleges of providing essential and defined roles for teachers and instructors. They are not as clearly displaced with core-of-unit or core-of-course materials as they are by full courses of media-presented instruction.

Dial access tapes and films are yet other adaptations of mediated instruction for different individuals. It should be observed that pacing rates are fixed in most dial access materials but that the rate of progression through a course of study, the selection of what units to study when and the amount of repetition and review are under the control and judgment of individual students.

In conclusion, the theme that has been developed is (1) that individualized instruction has both limitations and advantages, (2) that the varied characteristics of individualized instruction such as pacing rates and rates of progression through courses of study, or the levels of relative difficulty, need to be defined, and (3) that many adaptations can be made in media programs to provide new and significant means for *teleinstruction and individualized learning.*

NOTES

[1] First closed-circuit TV report, The Pennsylvania State University. C. R. Carpenter, L. P. Greenhill, *Project Number One: An Investigation of Closed-Circuit Television for Teaching University Courses,* July 1955. C. R. Carpenter, L. P. Greenhill, *An Investigation of Closed-Circuit Television for Teaching University Courses, Report Number Two.* C. R. Carpenter, L. P. Greenhill, *Comparative Research on Methods and Media for Presenting Programed Courses in Mathematics and English,* NDEA-VIIA-567 (ED003178). U. S. Office of Education, *Instructional TV at the Pennsylvania State University:* 1954-1963. A documentary sound film 38 min., 16mm.

Chapter 23. FACTORS TO CONSIDER WHEN USING MEDIA TO INDIVIDUALIZE LEARNING

MEDIA, FACILITIES AND LEARNER OPTIONS

Robert A. Weisgerber

It has often been suggested that learning is *always* a singular act, even when the setting for learning is not private. The plausible argument can be made that even in a group setting where all learners receive the "same" stimulus material, say a 16-mm. motion-picture film, each of the learners will gain something different from the experience. In part this is because each learner is unique in the readiness he brings to the experience, e.g., his maturation, and prior educational development. It is also evident that ethnic, cultural or socioeconomic backgrounds, physiological impairments, and emotional disorders will have important effects upon his learning ability. The diverse effects of personality traits, motivation, attitude, and self-image will also differentially influence each of the learners. Lastly, and rather obviously, sheer environmental or situational differences are important, e.g., some learners may be sitting near the projector noise, or in a corner with a poor angle of vision, or too near a heater or ventilator. Any of these many factors can radically alter the perceptual and cognitive capacities of each learner in the group.

Education has traditionally recognized these differences among individuals in the group and has evolved a grading system to reflect these differences. Through normative grading it establishes an acceptable level for the "average" child and then reminds the slower learner of how poorly he is doing by giving him low marks. If such a child does not soon become convinced of his incompetence and "turn off" it is little short of miraculous (Bloom, 1968). Instruction, to the extent possible, should be geared to the individual rather than the group.

What can media do? Properly used, and within the information transmission parameters suggested by Travers (1964), the media can be adaptive to the needs of the different learners and can, through their multisensory nature, provide a broader communication base line. Potentially, a wider variety of learners can benefit from the intended instruction (Twyford, 1969).

Just as the use of media may facilitate communication in the *group instruction mode,* it is also clear that media can have a similar function where communication takes place in the *individual learning mode* (Allen, 1969). Indeed, individualization *cannot* be accomplished unless there are more sources of information (message origination points) than the teacher in the classroom. Media, with their reproducibility and enduring nature, can carry a large portion of the instructional load.

It must be recognized that existing types of media vary in their appropriateness for use in group or individualized situations. This chapter takes the position that to the extent possible, within cost constraints and local administrative limitations, media should be selected for their flexibility and applicability to specific learner needs and not to meet the needs of hypothetical "average" learners in the group (Torkelson and Driscoll, 1968).

GROUP-PROCESS MEDIA[1]

To set a base line or reference point for comparison, four of the media which seem particularly suited to the advancement of *instructional* goals are described in Table 23-1. (It should be noted that the messages carried by any of these media are here *presumed* to be a valid use of the learner's time and that the messages generally facilitate his grasp of the content when contrasted with oral or written methods.)

TABLE 23-1
FOUR MEDIA ESPECIALLY SUITED TO GROUP INSTRUCTION

1.   Television (Broadcast, 2,500 Megahertz, and closed circuit)

   a)   Key Instructional Benefits:

   Increases the potential teacher/student ratio. Allows a greater audience to share an immediate "live" event. Permits a proportionately greater amount of time to be spent by the instructor in preparing and rehearsing his presentation. Allows special effects and other unusual instructional "assists" to be carried in a single communication channel. Encourages bridging of great distances, which enables expertise to be brought to remote locations. Can be recorded and played back repeatedly to amortize the cost of the original production.

b)   Limitation for Individualization:

Cost of the system precludes its operation to meet an individual need. (Video tape recorders and video-active carrels are variants of television which may become economically viable for individualized learning in the context of self-performance evaluation.)

2.   16-mm. Motion Pictures

a)   Key Instructional Benefits:

Permits unique control (through photographic, animation and editing techniques) over the spatial and temporal aspects of the message, and this is equally true with both the picture and sound tracks. Can be readily projected to physical dimensions proportionate to group size. Can be used interchangeably on many machines, often negating the need to transport the equipment from place to place. Can be repeatedly interrupted or replayed as judged necessary by the instructor. Represents a wealth of "ready-made" topics to enrich instructional presentations.

b)   Limitations for Individualization:

Acquisition and maintenance costs for equipment and film (particularly multiple amounts of each) are prohibitive for broad— based individualization applications. Difficulty in the operation of equipment and limited access to the films currently preclude much use by young learners.

3.   Overhead Projection

a)   Key Instructional Benefits:

Instructor is given extraordinary variety of control over the rate and form of stimulus presentation. Permits alteration of sequence, partial disclosure, and a number of other "ideal" instructional techniques. Focuses learner attention to a high degree while room lights are on. Permits continuous instructor—student eye contact. Is well suited to local development of instructional material. Enlarges the image readily without consuming much room space. Is "affordable" for every classroom.

b)   Limitations for Individualization:

The projectuals (projected materials) can almost always be viewed directly by an individual *without* the need of a machine. Excepting the multicell transparencies, most images could be reproduced more cheaply in paper form and still be effective for individuals.

4.   Group Response System (Edex, etc.)

   a)   Key Instructional Benefits:

   Provides the instructor with immediate feedback. The proportion of the group that "got the message" is known and not surmised. The presentation can be multimedia, and rather complex, and yet be preprogrammed for automatic display. Personalized and immediate scoring, as well as the accumulation of scores over time, is facilitated.

   b)   Limitations for Individualization:

   In some manufacturers' versions no provision is made in the equipment to give the learner feedback on the correctness of his answer. Some other manufacturers' versions provide such feedback to the student but lack the automatic control features for preprogramming of multimedia presentation. Cost of the equipment is quite high and programming is too complex to encourage message development for direct use by an individual.

To review the general point indicated above, certain media may be highly appropriate to group instruction but have drawbacks for facilitating individualization. This does not negate their value or suggest that their use be discontinued in appropriate situations.

As one rather obvious example of a "quality" message which had important learning value to heterogeneous groups (with little reference to their individual differences) one can cite the initial moon landing. The television medium reached a group of watchers as diverse as can be conceived, *all of whom "learned" but not all of whom learned the same thing.* In other words, though the event was a "constant" it was viewed differently by scientists, first graders, the astronauts' parents, and so on. In this instance, there was little to be gained by deliberately "individualizing" the experience in order to meet the special interests of the various viewers, simply because the immediacy (and the suspense) of the event was paramount for all.

A particular message, such as the moon landing cited above, need not be *exclusively* group oriented, however, even though that was its original intent. For instance, videotape replays of the landing or the astronauts' movements would yield considerable additional data to a lunar scientist who quite likely missed important details in his first viewing.

MEDIA FOR INDIVIDUALIZED LEARNING

When we consider the special requirements imposed on media (and implicitly on the messages carried by them) by emphasizing the meeting of an *individual* learner's needs we introduce a number of considerations which have historically been by-passed in the development of school audio visual collections.

Table 23-2 gives four examples of media which are probably better used in individualized contexts than group contexts. *These are given only as illustrations and in no sense are the only media that are well suited in this regard.*

TABLE 23-2

FOUR MEDIA APPROPRIATE FOR INDIVIDUALIZED LEARNING

1. Computer-Based Learning

    a) Key Benefits to Facilitate Individualized Learning:

    The medium has the inherent characteristic of giving the learner a sense of dynamic interaction and of *controlling* his learning to a larger degree. It has a high potential for enhancing a self-competitive spirit in the learner. It allows a high degree of sophistication in the selection of appropriate "next steps" in the learning material by taking full advantage of the principles developed for use in programmed learning. In particular, the programs can be made adaptive through the computer's ability to "generate" instructional material according to complex decision rules which take into account the learner's previous responses *as well as* his present one. The computer makes feasible the precise and simultaneous measurement of learner progress along any of a number of continuums, such as time taken to respond, adequacy of response, etc.

    b) Limitations for Individualization:

    At the present time, computer terminals cannot be considered economically feasible as learning stations for the vast numbers of individual learners in the schools today. Rather, for the foreseeable future, the computer will be used to *support* individualized learning and will not be in the classroom. It will be used primarily for its prescriptive and evaluative functions but it will not be used to present materials and interact (via terminals) with the learner.

2. 8-mm. Motion Pictures (Hand-held and Table-top)

    a) Key Benefits to Facilitate Individualized Learning:

    Control over cues on a temporal basis (motion) is a crucial ingredient to the learning of certain concepts and processes, and the 8-mm. motion picture represents the most economical means for facilitating these types of learning. A wide variety of 16-mm. films can be adapted (edited) and reproduced for use in the less expensive 8-mm. format. In addition, however, certain types of projectors provide the learner with control over *stopping* the film for the study of individual frames, or the opportunity to control the *rate* of viewing and listening. Since many 8-mm. projectors accept cartridges or provide automatic rewinding, operation of the equipment as well as storage and handling of the films is simplified. The 8-mm. motion-picture medium presents a unique opportunity for local production by teachers, thus enhancing the relevance of the curriculum to the children's own lives. Finally, the children can find in the 8-mm. motion-picture medium a creative outlet for self-expression.

b)   Limitations for Individualization:

Relative to the *duration* of their use (typically two or three minutes) commercially available 8-mm. films are costly. (Locally produced 8-mm. films tend to be somewhat less costly, provided the camera original film is used and prints are not required.) To realistically appraise their initial cost, it is also necessary to consider the *longevity* 8-mm. films will have, provided students use them with reasonable care, and to think in terms of amortized cost over their useful life. A further consideration is their impact value, since two minutes of viewing film that is unusual and memorable can be a rich educational experience.

3.   Audio Card Readers

a)   Key Benefits to Facilitate Individualized Learning:

Increments of instruction contained on each card are usually quite short, lasting only a few seconds. Each card is separately inserted and played, facilitating repeated use by a learner. The sound is reinforced by visual material imprinted on the card. Learners can sequence the cards to suit themselves and few learners in the classroom listen to each of the cards to the same extent. Blank cards can be recorded to meet local (or individual) instructional needs.

b)   Limitations for Individualization:

Most versions of the card player are far too expensive (i.e., $200 or more). This is unfortunate since not only are they mechanically simple but they typically do not produce sound of high fidelity quality. A cost approaching $30 per unit would enable a greater number of machines, and hence cards, to be shared among the children. The method could then become a mainstay of individualized learning at the primary grades rather than an adjunct.

4.   Electric Boards

a)   Key Benefits to Facilitate Individualized Learning:

The electric board is a self-check device which allows presentation of information, asks questions, calls for the matching of the correct response to each question, and gives immediate feedback on the correctness of the response. In a sense, it is a battery operated, audio-visual version of the matching question format used on some tests. As such, it invariably generates considerable interest on the part of learners. They view it as fun and also as a way to demonstrate their mastery of the content. The electric board lends itself *only* to manipulation by one learner at a time. However, others can watch, thereby participating vicariously. It is readily adaptable, as a technique, across subject matters and grade levels.

b)   Limitations for Individualization:

Electric board devices are typically set up as a semi-permanent display, available to learners as a kind of informal adjunct to instruction. Often they are relatively large (poster-sized) and are affixed to walls. In order for the technique to be integrated into the mainstream of learning it is desirable that (1) the electrical connections between question and answer be easily and frequently varied to ensure that the content rather than the wiring pattern is learned, (2) items included should be organized and interrelated so that the self-test becomes informative to the learner in a diagnostic way, and (3) results of the students' self-checks are accumulated so that the electric board (like other materials for self-instruction) can be modified and improved in a systematic way.

Acquisition Considerations

In the past, the purchase of equipment and materials has generally been predicted on amortization and maintenance schedules which assume occasional *teacher* use. This assumption is wholly inappropriate to individualization. As alluded to previously, individualization of a school program will almost certainly require a *different pattern* in the types and amounts of equipment and materials that are made available. Since it is implicit that the students will be operating the equipment, it is a virtual certainty that some items need to be in greater supply than currently are available in most schools that are group oriented. Of course, the initial capital outlay for equipment and materials can be lessened if equipment and materials can be reassigned from existing school resources. It should *never* occur that the introduction of individualization should be expected to succeed by using *only* the existing school resources. This would certainly be a case of "the tail wagging the dog."

As individualization is introduced to a school it very often begins with one class, under one teacher, or it may begin with several classes at a particular developmental (grade) level. In the next year a second developmental level or more is added, until eventually the phasing from experiment to adoption is accomplished and the whole school is operational with the new educational approach. When adoption is in its early phases, the provision of equipment and materials must be predicated on the notion of essentially self-contained rooms. Later, when levels and classes begin to lose much of their identity because of the different rates at which the students in the school are progressing, it is no longer economic to duplicate resources in each room. It is better to develop a readily accessible resource room and/or learning center within the school with only the more frequently used items remaining in the separate rooms.

Let us assume, for purposes of illustration, that a student-teacher ratio of 30 to 1 exists in a classroom and that an individualized program which allows self-pacing, and which is both print and nonprint (multimedia) in nature, is introduced to the room on a "pilot" basis for the school. It is a virtual certainty that by the end of the first few weeks the 30 students will be well dispersed along a continuum of study. At any given point in time they will be requiring different instructional materials as well as various types of equipment. How, then, can one establish the *number* of items that must be purchased in order to allow continuous study? The answer is not easily obtained. One answer is to "overbuy" amounts and then introduce them into the learning environment *as needed*. Unfortunately, this iterative approach to the problem is rather costly and not too practical to implement.

Another way of answering the problem is to estimate the need as a function of five variables: [2]

Variable 1: *Estimate the number of students that might be using the same type of equipment at any given moment according to chance.* In our example of a multimedia program a child may be using texts, work sheets, audio cassettes, filmstrips, motion pictures, manipulative objects, records, and educational simulation games, plus some kind of learning guide which prescribes the objectives and relevant activities. Thus if the 30 students were equally dispersed (by chance) among these 10 alternatives then only 3 of the 30 students would need to work with cassettes and cassette recorders at a given time.

Variable 2: *Estimate the proportion of the overall curriculum which is distributed or carried by the different media.* Most often the print materials are the prime medium by which the learner masters concepts and nonprint materials are used less frequently. If, in our example, the print materials were used predominantly then the chance-based estimate that three cassette recorders were required could be reduced proportionately, and perhaps only two would be needed.

Variable 3: *Estimate the typical duration of time that each type of item will be in use by a student before he releases it to the next student.* Continuing with the example of cassettes, it may be established that the average playing time for cassettes in the classroom collection is 15 minutes. If allowance is made for setup time and/or rewind time, another 5 minutes might elapse for a total "in use time" of 20 minutes. In this classroom, where two machines are planned, the average waiting time would be about 10 minutes, even if they were being run steadily throughout the school day. The question to be answered, then, is whether a delay of 10 minutes is tolerable for a learner who is ready for the lesson material provided by a cassette but finds the two machines are busy. In most cases, it isn't likely that a 10-minute delay would seriously hamper the child's progress, but other considerations may contradict that assumption. For instance, materials may have been specified in *sequence* for important pedagogical reasons and he might not be able to continue study while he waits. If such were the case and the student was forced to wait *without* staying busy, then his idleness may lead to some form of classroom disruption or simply to a general loss of initiative and sensitivity to the specified learning tasks. In this case, let's assume that our learners are quite young and impatient; we consider this factor to be important enough that we would want no more than a 5-minute wait. Four cassette recorders would now seem to be required.

Variable 4:   *Estimate whether coincidence of need for a given item actually requires more units of that material or whether a single copy can be shared when several students simultaneously require it.* The same equipment or materials may be needed by several students at the same time, even though the students have advanced to different levels in the curriculum. Or, as is more commonly the case, several students may reach the same point in their studies at the same time. If coincidence of need is expected to occur when cassettes are the medium being used for learning then the availability of a listening post with multiple earphone jacks is preferable to either the use of the cassette loudspeaker or the purchase of additional machines. Therefore, we might decide to lower our estimate from four cassette machines to three, but acquire at least one listening post.

By contrast, if coincidence occurs when texts are the medium for learning there is clearly a need for the purchase of more copies. In another example, work sheets would probably not need to be increased in quantity because these are likely to be consumed on a one-for-one basis and it is immaterial whether this consumption occurred simultaneously or not. Other items, such as large study prints, may simply be viewed by more people at the same time and no additional purchases would be required.

Variable 5:   *Beyond the basic complement of materials and equipment judged necessary (variables 1-4 above) there is a requirement for additional "spares."* Spares are necessary to assure progress when loss or breakdown of the basic items occurs. These backup items need not be in the classroom but should be in the school since they need to be available on short notice. Generally, spare items should be acquired in proportion to the number of basic items that have been purchased, except in the case of particularly "destruct-proof" materials. At least one of each type of equipment item should be obtained for backup purposes and more than one if that type of equipment is heavily used.

Also, since machines which are appropriate for individualization are often small and portable it is not unusual that students will want to borrow them, along with the cassettes or other materials, for home study. Because this practice is to be encouraged, enough additional machines should be purchased to ensure that the regular school program is not impaired when some are inadvertently left at home. Certain items, such as a highly portable cassette recorder, are susceptible to theft because of their general desirability and some loss should be anticipated.

As compared to the implementation of individualization in a single classroom, there are operational advantages and savings which accrue when a schoolwide individualization takes place. For one thing, the number of "spare" items required does not rise appreciably by adding more rooms of students. For another, the pooling of less frequently used equipment and instructional materials in the school learning center enables a much fuller utilization of them than if the same items were duplicated in a number of separate rooms. For this economy to be realizable, however, it is essential that maximum student mobility and self-responsibility be encouraged and that browsing as well as formal study be permitted.

GENERAL CONSIDERATIONS IN EQUIPMENT SELECTION

While curiosity may be harmless in its intent, it is not always harmless in its effect. At the middle and upper grade levels some damage can be caused by students who loosen screws or otherwise disassemble the equipment in order to see how it works. Machines that discourage disassembly (with hidden screws, etc.) are to be preferred. Considerable care should be exercised that the equipment will not present a hazard during its operating life. To minimize the chances for accidental fire or electrical shocks to exploring fingers, only UL approved equipment should be purchased. It is evident that the students should be taught how to operate the equipment rather than being left to their own ingenuity in discovering how it works. Damage to equipment is *not* typically a result of youthfulness per se. More often it is a result of carelessness or a lack of understanding of proper operating procedures. To prevent inadvertent breakage, purchasers should avoid equipment having delicate plastic knobs or switches that are mounted in an elevated or unprotected position.

As implied above, students of all school ages (including first graders) can be taught to operate equipment. Naturally, the simpler and the more clearly marked are the controls, the easier and quicker this training can be accomplished. Fortunately, simplicity in equipment is often a concomitant of inexpensiveness. For example, cassette tape recorders are preferable to open-reel recorders not only because they are easier to manipulate but also because they tend to be less expensive.

A Note about Cost versus Quality

A major consideration in equipment selection is its cost per unit. In that regard, established (audio-visual) buying patterns for group instruction are simply inappropriate for individualization. Traditionally, school district and college audio-visual centers have stockpiled expensive, heavy duty equipment which they then loan out on a daily basis to teachers. They expect to absorb this high initial cost by amortizing it over a 7- to 10-year period. To make these machines last for 10 years, however, they must receive regular maintenance and "overhauls" in addition to any short-term repair to correct unexpected malfunctions.

An alternative to this approach is the purchase of lower cost, shorter life equipment. This course of action may well be dictated by sheer economic realities in instances where many machines must be acquired in one school year in order to implement a new program of individualization.

A realistic appraisal of the costs required to maintain a technical service staff should be taken into account, since all school districts should have their own staff of technicians. It is quite possible that warranty coverage provided at the time of purchase may be adequate to cover defective merchandise for the first year. Leasing, with an option to buy, can be a further way of ensuring against mechanical "lemons." The lower cost of some machines lessens the inevitability of major maintenance overhauls since these may require man-hours of effort disproportionate to the costs of a replacement item. If a $40 piece of equipment is at the end of its fourth year of use and is showing wear, it may possibly be regarded as "disposable" rather than invest four or five hours of a technician's time in a major overhaul. (Incidentally, "disposable" equipment items need not be thrown away. They can be used for parts, or, in the upper grades, many students have an interest in repairing them for their own use or in stripping them for components to be used for other projects in which they are engaged.)

In selecting low cost equipment for purchase some concessions *may* have to be made. It does *not* follow that quality standards (for picture and sound) should be ignored, but rather that they should be applied selectively according to the context; e.g., learning needs. For instance, one should ask whether:

1. The message (materials) cannot be effectively understood (used) unless *high* fidelity is present,

2. The equipment has the operating features necessary to meet *specific* educational requirements, for example, an instant stop button on a record player can allow time for notetaking,

3. There is evidence of faulty *workmanship* in creation of the product such that damage or wear might be disproportionate to the amount of use.

To reiterate, simplicity is one way to lower costs, but this does not necessarily imply a reduction of standards for quality. For instance, filmstrip previewers at about $17 each are perfectly adequate for individual viewing and represent only a small fraction of the cost for the much more complex filmstrip projectors that are intended for group use.

The general desirability of learner control over the form and rate of message presentation leads to certain engineering options, which may be cost beneficial. As an example, an 8-mm., sound, motion-picture device has recently been developed in the form of a battery-operated, hand-held viewer. The device uses a variable speed motor (to compensate for loss of battery power) which has the beneficial effect of giving the learner control over the *rate* at which he views the films. This feature makes possible more flexibility and variety of use than is present in current 8-mm. desk-top projectors and does so at less cost.

STUDENT ACCESS TO RESOURCE MATERIALS

It is quite likely to be the case that students' enthusiasm and success in individualized learning will be directly related to the ease (or frustration) with which they obtain and use learning materials. As a general rule materials should be located where they will be most readily and frequently used. New technology has introduced the possibility for materials to be *remotely* stored and accessed, but for most schools individualization can be accomplished by a reorganization of materials in open stock for *direct* student access.

Open-Stock Materials

Book materials should be on open shelving and tapes, films and other nonprint materials seem best stored in cupboards. The materials should be filed according to type of media, with labels readily discernible to help the student match the material to identifying code numbers as specified in his learning guide. Color-coded stripes laid diagonally across the edges of materials enable quick checks for completeness of the collection at the end of a school day and facilitate the proper return of the materials by students.

A considerable amount of time is usually consumed in preparing and cataloging these open-stock materials collections. Since the teacher should avoid becoming a stock clerk, she may seek the assistance of librarians, teacher-aides, parents, or students in setting up the collection. Further, she should develop an attitude of participant-citizenship among her students in order to maintain the collection, for the materials are quite literally each learner's key to academic success.

Remote Resources

The idea of remote access materials was first exemplified in the schools with the concept of the language laboratory, intended for the learning of second languages. It soon became apparent that a *learning* laboratory would be a more appropriate term since a number of content areas could be contained in the laboratory's tape collection. Later, lockstep listening (from a master tape deck) was replaced by a dial-demand capability (from a bank of tape recorders). It should be noted that then, and only then, did individualization begin to replace the group process because each learner could be served separately. The dial-access approach has subsequently proliferated and has reached new levels of complexity. Presently some versions offer the student direct control over television channels as well as audio channels. By an automatic process of accessing and dubbing of computer stored "instruction" at ultrahigh speeds, the individual learner can "call up" a particular segment of material and in seconds be studying from his own personal copy. Thus, if another individual "calls up" the same segment he is not forced to listen in on a partly elapsed presentation, as was true in the earlier laboratories, but starts at the beginning, being delayed no more than the minute or so it would take him to open his printed study materials and settle down to business.

The use of student terminals which are on-line to computers extends the technological continuum beyond the dial-access resource system just described. While many differences exist, just three will be noted here. First, the computer terminal often offers more student-input options. For instance, it may use a keyboard, touch-panel, or light-pen controls. Second, the range of data-base information available to the learner is extraordinary, since the decision rules programmed into the computer cause messages to be *composed* for the learner based on his response pattern. Thus, two learners who start with a particular computerized instructional segment are almost certainly *not* going to be receiving the same material throughout their study period because their different responses have helped to formulate subsequent computer-generated messages. Third, the capability for computer control over remote display devices at the student station, such as motion-picture cartridges, slide projectors, etc., increases the variety of communication channels which may be used to inform the learner.

The dial systems and computer networks both represent a heavy capital outlay for "hardware" *and* for the "software" (materials) which are to be remotely accessed. High operating costs and maintenance costs can be expected as well. It is probable that further improvements in technique and lower costs for terminals, lines, and central processing units will be achieved in the next decade. However, we are not likely to see widespread adoption of either approach in the *typical* classroom across the country unless per student costs are kept in reasonable relationship to the present operating costs of group-oriented instruction.

As can be seen in the preceding paragraphs, a dependence on sophisticated hardware as a means of introducing individualization is likely to be costly. For the near term, an alternative is to use existing types of audio-visual hardware (or slight modifications of it) in new ways. To the extent that costs can be kept low, then individualization will be affordable on a "normal" school tax base and replication of successful programs will be facilitated. The present challenge, then, is to introduce individualization by way of a plan which uses equipment and materials functionally and with economic feasibility.

Updating the Materials Inventory

The process of keeping learning materials updated and relevant represents a difficult and complex problem. No simple techniques can be suggested which will prevail across the many present forms of individualized learning that exist in the schools, but at least one principle warrants mention.

New editions of printed materials typically represent either a change in pagination or format, or they may be a rewrite, deletion, or addition of content. If the school chooses to save its old editions *and* purchase some new ones (and use of both editions appears likely), the learner should be directed only to those specific learning activities that are appropriate to his edition. This may seem obvious to the point of absurdity but it is nevertheless quite crucial. Inefficiency of teaching will arise from having to make minor corrections in instructional references (to page numbers, etc.) during classtime and inefficiency of learning will arise if the child cannot quickly find the information he needs.

Facilities Design and Centralized Learning Centers

Any school can individualize its educational program *without* the benefit of new buildings, unusual floor plans, centralized learning centers, or private study carrels. On the other hand, the presence of these features in the learning environment can facilitate individualization to a great degree.

Obviously, the learner requires space for carrying out his learning activities. Upon occasion he may need privacy (for instance, in test taking) and access to a carrel is quite helpful. On other occasions he may need table space in order to experiment with science apparatus or to use audio-visual equipment. On still other occasions he may want to interact with classmates and a large carpeted area could provide an ideal learning space. Facilities should be designed for maximum flexibility of use from the *learner's* point of view.

As has been alluded to earlier, the school which commits to individualized learning should not try to make all the classrooms fully self-contained in terms of materials or equipment. This would not only be too costly but it would also inhibit the resourcefulness of those students whose learning patterns are characterized by divergent thinking and high activity levels. A more practical approach is to designate a centrally located portion of the school as the learning center, make it functional in design for ease of access to equipment and materials, and encourage its use by the students. The learning center *can* be a focus not only for student activity but for adult learning as well. If this is the case in a given school, it could be advantageous to make it accessible from the outside when the remainder of the school is closed. The concept of keying facilities design to learning rather than to teaching is equally relevant to the renovation of old school buildings and to the building of new ones.

Three factors should be kept in mind when locating a learning center in the school. First, the notion of centrality may be considered either in terms of nearness to most classrooms or in terms of proximity to the heaviest point of student traffic. Both approaches have merit but probably the former has more application in elementary schools while the latter has more application for secondary schools and colleges where students may "move" to science labs or other departmental facilities.

Second, the learning center should be designed and/or located in a way that will permit its economical enlargement as growth needs occur. All too often where growth was not anticipated the costs of major remodeling will be so great that it is "easier" to compromise the educational program, with the inevitable result that the "tail has once again wagged the dog."

Third, the utilization-oriented learning center should be bordered by ancillary rooms where teachers and students can prepare instructional materials such as displays, models, and recorded tapes. Production supplies (film, card stock, inks, etc.) and production equipment (dry mount press, thermal or diazo copy machine, lettering aids, etc.) should be available at all times.

Ideally, the learning center should be designed to give a feeling of openness, comfort, and aesthetic appeal. Carpeting, non-glare lighting and the nesting of study spaces, book shelves and other furniture will do much to enhance this effect.

Through proper design, classrooms can also be given a feeling of openness. One way is to group them in sets of four or six, equip them with folding partitions (typically kept in the folded, pushed-back position) and locate them around a commonly shared area (i.e., floor space) in which materials and equipment are accessible to all. Carpeting and proper lighting in the classrooms will have a salutary effect on the students' attention to their learning tasks and their feelings about the school.

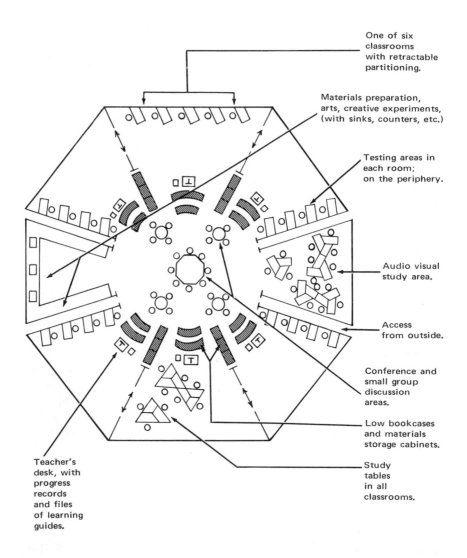

One of six
classrooms
with retractable
partitioning.

Materials preparation,
arts, creative experiments,
(with sinks, counters, etc.)

Testing areas in
each room;
on the periphery.

Audio visual
study area.

Access
from outside.

Conference and
small group
discussion
areas.

Low bookcases
and materials
storage cabinets.

Study
tables
in all
classrooms.

Teacher's
desk, with
progress
records
and files
of learning
guides.

FIGURE 23-1

An elementary school design for six classes, each with access to a central discussion area, an audio-visual study area, and an area for experiments and materials preparation. Each class has easy access to its own low bookcases and materials storage cabinets. Each class also has an area set aside for testing. Design—R. Weisgerber

Learning Stations and Furniture Arrangements

Individualized learning is characterized by the behavior of students and not by the physical appearance of any *particular* type of learning station or precise arrangement of furniture in the classroom. This is not to suggest that the nature of the learning station or furniture arrangement makes no difference, but rather suggests that these factors can vary considerably according to program goals and budgetary constraints, yet still provide an effective setting for learning.

Individual study carrels have been adopted fairly widely at the college and high school level, and especially in courses for which the content can be precisely defined and articulated into an orderly series of preplanned exercises. "Built-in" carrels (i.e., where standard desk-top equipment is built in for ease of use and to enhance security) may be located as convenient in the room or school. Dial access and computer systems also use carrels but rely on installed wiring and are necessarily in a more permanent room arrangement.

Small tables, often having the shape of a triangle or trapezoid, with detached chairs, have been adopted rather widely at the elementary and middle school grade levels. The tables can be thought of as modular units, permitting the addition of components such as dividers and book shelves. The shape of the tables encourages their use for various individual and small group situations and allows great flexibility in room arrangement. Testing can be occurring in one part of a room with the tables drawn apart; elsewhere the tables might be nested to provide a larger work space where students can "spread out," and still elsewhere they could be clustered to constitute a "media" corner where audio and visual devices are readily available. Typically these audio-visual clusters will be located around the periphery of the room to meet the need for proximity to electrical current: Any long power cords stretched across aisles to reach wall plugs represent a hazard both to the youngsters and to the equipment. A second reason for peripheral placement of equipment is to minimize any distraction resulting from operating noise. (See Figures 23-2 and 23-3.)

MEDIA AS A MEANS FOR PROVIDING LEARNER OPTIONS

While researchers are working on the problem (Briggs, 1967; Gagné, 1965) they have not, as yet, been able to establish highly generalizable or functional ground rules for matching the different media to individual learning styles. Nevertheless, there are few educators who would deny that "true" individualized learning should permit some student control over the form of the instructional material as well as its content. As indicated previously in Table 23-2, by four selected examples, various media appear to have logical applicability to individualized learning. In the future,

Exploded view.

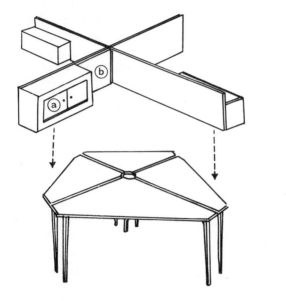

Low dividers with
book or equipment
storage case (a) and
small recessed matte white
screen (b) for each table.
(component # 2)

Four clustered tables. Any
equipment must be placed on
table tops. Power cords
go down to floor or to the
wall baseboard through
the center opening in
the cluster.
(component # 1)

(a)   Cassette player with
        earphones

(b)   Filmstrip
        previewer

(c)   8 mm. projector

Basic equipment.

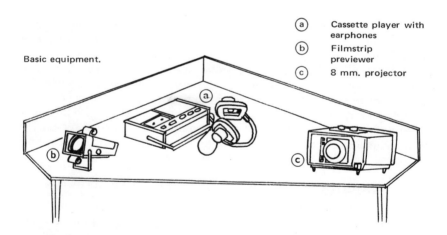

FIGURE 23-2

Study carrels can be both simple and flexible. The requirements imposed by various curricula
and school budgets can be met by beginning with small inexpensive tables and adding
components as needed. Design—R. Weisgerber. (Adapted from J. Beynon, *Study Carrels:
Designs for Independent Study Space* [New York: Educational Facilities Laboratories, Inc.,
1964]).

Learning station arrangements

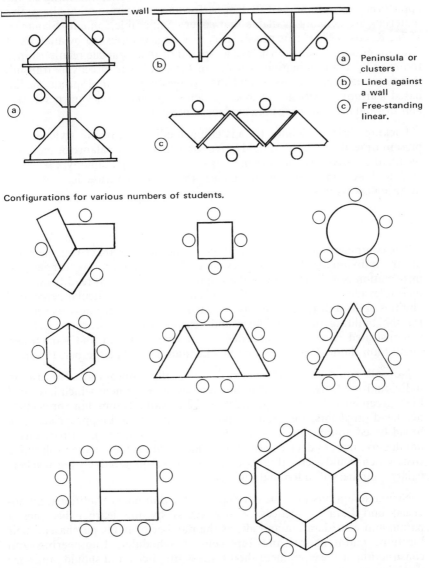

(a) Peninsula or clusters

(b) Lined against a wall

(c) Free-standing linear.

Configurations for various numbers of students.

FIGURE 23-3

Carrels and tables can be clustered in ways that encourage individual study or small discussions of various sizes. The configurations shown here are only suggestive of the possible variations that might be adopted, depending on the table shapes. (Adapted from R. E. Ellsworth and H. D. Wagener, *The School Library: Facilities for Independent Study in the Secondary School* [New York: Educational Facilities Laboratories, Inc., 1963]).

accumulation of empirical evidence may enable a better matching of the appropriate medium to past student performance, assuming that alternative materials are actually available that cover comparable content (Flanagan, 1970; Rhetts, 1970). This process may well be accomplished by analysis of relevant message characteristics (e.g., spatial or temporal cue relationships), followed by a determination of which of the media can effectively transmit these message characteristics, and then suggesting the appropriate media-based learning experience to those students for whom relevant perceptual abilities and interests have been evidenced previously.

Lacking clear guidelines for matching media to learning styles at the present time, the educator should strive for a reasonable balance of method/media alternatives. He must be alert against excessive parsimony, that could lead to boredom, and overabundance, that could confuse learners with meaningless choices.

In Summary

The equipment and materials that the learner utilizes are critical elements in an individualized learning system. Their function as carriers of information is well established, their motivational nature is readily evident, their relevance to the needs of different learners having particular perceptual abilities or disabilities is generally accepted, and their usefulness as vehicles for the building of self-reliance and responsibility in learners is being demonstrated currently at all educational levels (Hoban and Van Ormer, 1950; Lumsdaine, 1963; Reid and MacLennan, 1967; Weisgerber, 1968).

Not all equipment and material is equally appropriate for use in individualized learning contexts. Some types of equipment which have had high acceptance for group instruction (television, 16mm film projectors, overhead projectors, and group response systems) seem inappropriate for a broad-based approach to individualized learning. For the most part this is not due to inherent deficiencies in these media but rather to the prohibitive costs which would accrue if their *use* was shifted from relatively few teachers to large numbers of individual students.

New assumptions must be developed regarding many traditional audio-visual and library practices. Ready access by the learner becomes a paramount consideration and affects the number of items purchased, their location, maintenance, and replacement schedules. Engineering and construction of the equipment should stress simplicity and should minimize the opportunities for student operators to disassemble or damage the machines through natural curiosity or deliberate tampering.

Configurations of study spaces within the school and classroom vary considerably depending upon such factors as the proportion of the school engaged in the individualization process and the opportunities available for planning of school learning centers, classrooms without permanent walls, and other flexible design characteristics. Resources for learning should be located in both the learning center and the classroom. Quite often they are clustered in particular study areas within these settings in order to localize machine or audio noise, to permit the items to be left in a "ready to use" status, and to facilitate supervision and assistance by the teacher.

Finally, learning should involve the learner in some control not only over *what* he studies but *how* he studies it. Ample provision should be made in the school program so that the mastery of objectives can be accomplished in alternative ways, accommodating diverse perceptual abilities, interests, and needs. One obvious way to provide alternative learning methods is through the use of various media. It is reasonable to expect that the process of matching learners with appropriate media and materials can increasingly take into account the students' preferences as a result of the empiric evidence which continues to accumulate in various national projects, such as Project PLAN, which are focused on individualized learning.

NOTES

[1] For purposes of this paper, group process refers primarily to situations in which a number of persons are exposed to essentially the same stimulus material, at the same time, irrespective of whether the persons are physically proximate to each other or are interactive in any way.

[2] The example given here is used only to illustrate the variables and is not intended as a formula. Program needs will vary and should be examined in their specific context.

REFERENCES

ALLEN, W. H.   "Technology: Roles for Men and Machines." *Britannica Review of American Education,* Vol. 1 (1969), pp. 139-157.

BLOOM, B. S.   "Learning for Mastery," *Evaluation Comment.* University of California, Los Angeles, Center for the Study of Evaluation of Instructional Programs. May 1968.

BRIGGS, L. J., CAMPEAU, P. L., GAGNÉ, R. M., and MAY, M. A.   *Instructional Media: A procedure for the design of multi-media instruction, a critical review of research, and suggestions for future research.* Monograph No. 2. Palo Alto: American Institutes for Research. 1967.

FLANAGAN, J. C.   "Individualizing Education." *Education,* Vol. 90 (1970), pp. 191-206.

GAGNÉ, R. M.   *Conditions of Learning.* New York: Holt, Rinehart and Winston, Inc., 1965, 308 pp.

HOBAN, C. F., JR., and VAN ORMER, E. B.   *Instructional Film Research, 1918-1950.* Technical Report No. SDC 269-7-19, Instructional Film Research Program,

Pennsylvania State University, Port Washington, N.Y.: U.S. Naval Special Devices Center, December, 1950. 180 pp.

LUMSDAINE, A. A.   "Instruments and Media of Instruction," in N. L. Gage (ed.), *Handbook of Research on Teaching.* Chicago: Rand McNally and Co., 1963, pp. 583-682.

REID, J. C., and MACLENNAN, D. W.   *Research in Instructional Television and Film.* U.S. Office of Education, No. OE-34041. Washington, D.C.: U.S. Government Printing Office, 1967. 216 pp.

RHETTS, J. E.   "The Impact of Student Learning Style on Curriculum Assignment and Performance in the PLAN Program of Individualized Instruction," *Education,* Vol. 90 (1970), pp. 248-251.

TORKELSON, G. M., and DRISCOLL, J. P.   "Utilization and Management of Learning Resources," *Review of Educational Research,* Vol. 38 (April, 1968), pp. 129-159.

TRAVERS, R. M. W. (ed.)   *Research and Theory Related to Audio-visual Information Transmission.* Interim Report. U.S. Office of Education Contract No. 3-20-003. Salt Lake City: University of Utah, July, 1964.

TWYFORD, L. C., JR.   "Educational Communications Media," in R. L. Ebel (ed.), *Encyclopedia of Educational Research.* 4th ed. American Educational Research Association. London: The Macmillan Co., 1969, pp. 367-379.

WEISGERBER, R. A. (ed.).   *Instructional Process and Media Innovation.* Chicago: Rand McNally and Co., 1968. 569 pp.

Chapter 24. **A LOOK AT
TECHNOLOGY'S
FUTURE ROLE**

THE CHANGING CAPABILITIES IN EDUCATION

John W. Loughary

In this chapter I will discuss some of the general kinds of changes in educational capabilities that should result from the effective utilization of appropriate technologies, and will suggest their implications, especially for future planning.

FORECASTING AND FORECASTS

If there is value in the proposed approach (and I am increasingly convinced that there is) it arises from the uncertainty which surrounds specific technological developments. These are in part determined by the present state of the art, which can be assessed. They are also affected by a variety of other factors which are difficult to identify with any reliability, except to know that they are always potentially important. Economic

---

SOURCE: Reprinted from *Planning for Effective Utilization of Technology in Education,* by permission of author and publisher. Copyright © 1969 by Scholastic Magazines, Inc.

conditions, congressional fads, rediscovering the poor, changes in the Department of Defense structure and concerns, modifications in corporate goals and teacher-student revolutions are illustrations of such variables. They can have surprising and unpredictable effects on advances in education. World War II, in every sense, probably did as much indirectly to refine education as any other single phenomenon. The training demands of the massive military mobilization overwhelmed educational capabilities. The need for greater capabilities was extremely critical, and new capabilities were created almost overnight. But we cannot conclude that critical periods of national defense necessarily encourage the development of new educational capabilities. Conditions change. In the last few years, funds for increasing educational capabilities have been made available—this time, to the educational community itself. However, the continuing war has been a direct cause of reducing this support.

There are other illustrations of the problems involved in forecasting specific developments and capabilities. It appeared obvious to many in 1960, for example, that programmed instruction was well on its way to becoming commonplace in classrooms throughout the country. Dozens of firms began marketing—or at least advertising—hardware and software; professional associations and publications devoted to programmed instruction were formed; and a few colleges began to offer course work in programming procedures. What happened? Several explanations have been offered, but my point is that what appeared to be an obviously valid forecast did not materialize. Will the same be true, for example, of computer-assisted-instruction? We hear much talk and promise about the impact of CAI in the near future. But many of my school district friends are asking: Where is the necessary software? Will it be developed, and when, and by whom?

One of the more important problems in attempting forecasts about technological developments in education, it seems to me, is that, as a result of our excitement about hoped-for improvements, we have tended to be premature, and often have been careless in judging the readiness of a given technological development for use in schools. Many of us, in our enthusiasm, describe an idea to the practicing educator but fail to note the state of the concept in the research and development process. We tend to get our tenses mixed. We often say *is* when we mean *will*, or even worse, *could*, or the most unpardonable *might*. The problem is that in all phases of the research and development process we have learned more not only about the technology, but also about what we should be seeking to do in education. The communication process being what it is, many of us operate in blissful ignorance of more recent findings and, more important, about revised decisions and plans.

The resolution of this problem can be expensive. For example, a pilot friend who is responsible for navigation training for a major air line was directed to mount a "crash" program for training flying officers in the use of a revolutionary new navigation system which was in its final test stage. The system manufacturer gave assurances that it was reliable, extremely accurate, and permitted a San Francisco to Honolulu runway-to-runway trip without the necessity for any human calculations except perhaps for some minor adjustments in the course plotted by the system. By turning dials and flicking switches, the captain and crew could obtain displays of all pertinent navigation information. In addition, the computer was prepared to effect, automatically, changes in aircraft performance indicated by the data. In effect, the system eliminated the second officer navigation function. It was "fail safe"—the probabilities of the dual system malfunctioning were equal to those of the captain and the first officer dying of heart attacks on the same trip. Midway into a tremendously expensive training program designed to teach all cockpit personnel to use the system, the impossible happened. Both the captain's and the first officer's systems failed on a training flight over the Pacific. All went well due to a trusty compass and dead reckoning. The educational implications, however, were serious. The air line had counted on the system and had *planned* on using it. Based on an assumed validity of the technological development, the company mounted a significant, far reaching, and expensive training program which had to be abandoned. In this situation considerable savings could have been effected had the forecasting been more accurate.

This little drama, admittedly, has implications only for a relatively short range forecast regarding educational plans based on technological developments. While planning for a ten to twenty-year time span can be much more general, and thus more flexible and amenable to changes because of revised technological forecasts, there is still a point at which educational leaders must make a commitment. We cannot wait until the technology has proven itself before deciding to go along with it—that is, to gear up our institutions to accept a capability. To do so would be to engage in a never ending waiting game involving those who are primarily concerned with developing technology, and those who are mainly interested in using it.

It is appropriate to complete this perspective for forecasting changes in educational capabilities resulting from technology with the addition of one more concept: The nature of technology being what it is, we should not rule out anything! Timing of course is important and affects the relevancy of what to consider and for what to plan. As suggested above, if the task is to decide, plan, and implement, then a relatively conservative forecast is appropriate. But when the task is to begin developing strategy for the next two decades, I would argue that we should not rule out any kind of potential educational capability.

With all of these challenges and cautions in mind, I want to suggest several kinds of educational capabilities that will be changed as a result of using emerging technology, and which we should explore carefully within the immediate future. Such an exploration, I believe, will lead to more specific and valid forecasts.

What follows should be qualified by "it could be possible." What takes place—that is, the capabilities that actually evolve—will depend in part upon what we and many others like us do about existing technology.

I have the vague feeling that we are really only in the mechanical phase of the technological revolution in education. Nearly all of the man-machine systems in education which are now being operated are, in a relative sense, clumsy. Admittedly, they are exciting, but so was the Model T as compared with what it replaced—that is, brute force. Computer applications in education to date are actually quite cumbersome. They seldom work as well as predicted; they cause many inconveniences; and they usually require a fairly constant application of technological bailing wire. As a number of users have commented, for example, the only trouble with flexible scheduling is that it is highly inflexible. If its goal is to make possible individualized instruction, then flexible scheduling will have succeeded on the day that we no longer need to schedule students.

COMPUTER BASED DATA SYSTEMS

Perhaps the most obvious increased capability is that of storing, retrieving and manipulating large amounts of data about students. Computer technology should result in the development of large and flexible learning data systems. These will have two main functions: (1) instructional management, and (2) educational research. The first is absolutely essential for individualized instruction which requires constant monitoring and analysis of student learning behavior. The second offers one of the greatest opportunities for making substantial improvement in the teaching-learning process. It should be helpful to describe in some detail at least, the components of such a system. Several are under development, including one at the American Institutes for Research and another by the Portland, Oregon, schools. The one with which I am most familiar is called System for Individualized Instruction Management (SIIM).

This system includes two basic computer files: a curriculum file and a student file. The system can have one or several input/output modes. Figure 24-1 shows the kind of reports that can be generated, as well as the research and evaluation activities that can be undertaken by using the system. Probable types of output from an initial version include:

- Student appraisal reports;
- Student status reports;
- Warning messages for students not meeting expectations;
- Suggestions for instructor-directed presentation groupings;

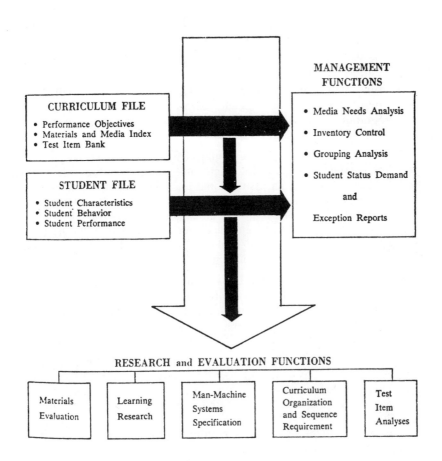

FIGURE 24-1

SYSTEM FOR INDIVIDUALIZED INSTRUCTION MANAGEMENT

- Individualized instructional materials list;
- Instructional materials inventory lists; and
- Indications of special interest groups.

Research generated by the system would include:

- Evaluation of specific materials to various kinds of pupils;
- Studies of objective sequence patterns;
- Studies of teacher and student use in reactions to various input/ output formats and modes;
- Studies of information volume and space limitations and instruction; and
- Studies of comparative instructional systems and procedures.

There is a master curriculum file (map) for each course unit, as well as an individual curriculum map for each student. The master file contains performance objectives, an instructional materials index, a test item bank, sequence dependencies, and classifications of intellectual activity. All test items and instructional materials are indexed to the performance objectives. The curriculum file serves as a unique driver for the system that permits the development of generalized program design, applicable in different subject-matter areas and different environments.

The student file contains the individual curriculum map; characteristics such as age, aptitude, and interest; behavior records (materials and activities involved in the student's work); and his performance record (test scores).

Given the initial curriculum map and student file, daily or weekly recommended changes for the map are based on updated performance objectives. An analysis is made of the student's subject matter strengths and weaknesses, as well as of his intellectual activity. Recommendations might include: a change in the sequence of performance objectives; substitution for an objective where unexpected strength has been revealed; or the addition or repetition of an objective to overcome an indicated weakness. (A print-out of this record would be provided at regular intervals as requested, or when changes are to be recommended.)

An analysis also is made of the instructional materials used; this is based on recorded data and student performance. The analysis indicates materials best suited for a particular individual, as well as a broader evaluation of the effectiveness of the materials in instruction.

The test item bank assembles tests, and incorporates review items based on objectives already attained. Students concurrently working on the same objective could receive different test items, depending on analysis results. Extensive item analysis procedures would be completed, including the determination of difficulty and discrimination indexes for test items. An instructor might begin the day by studying a report summarizing student status. He would note those who need special attention, organize instructor-directed presentations, determine special instruction materials requirements for the day, and determine the points of emphasis of the group's study. Instructor-aide assignments would be made, and anticipated tests ordered and printed. He would make inputs on student behavior and performance during the day. If appropriate, he might receive warning messages regarding students having difficulty with their contracted objectives. Toward the close of the day, the instructor would input requests for data and materials needed for the next day. The administrator, counselor, and other support personnel would monitor the instructional program daily as a basis for guiding their own efforts. The system should be available to both students and staff, on demand, as well as on an exception report basis.

Consider the research function of such a system. Imagine that we have 50,000 pupils in several districts, all served by the system. Each pupil has a file in the system. The file contains data about personal and social characteristics, specific research of past achievement, and measures of interest and personality. As each pupil pursues an educational objective (defined in operational terms) the following are input to the system: (1) descriptions of the material and procedures he uses; (2) his reactions to these; (3) teacher observations; and (4) the student's actual terminal behavior. We also have definitive descriptions of the materials and procedures.

An important capability would be that of providing answers to research questions of several levels and kinds. Relatively simple analyses of alternate materials designed or proclaimed to teach similar objectives could be made. For example, a sample of students could be drawn, each of whom had been pursuing similar objectives, but with different instructional materials—for example, using three different texts. One could easily compare the learning achievement of each of the groups. A more sophisticated analysis would be a comparison of different sequence patterns. My guess is that instead of a single sequence, we would discover a number of ways of sequencing instructional material, and that these would vary in effectiveness with students who manifest different characteristics. Most of us, I assume, have reacted—after reading a book, listening to a lecture, or viewing a film—with a comment such as "If he had said that earlier I would not have been confused all this time," and at the same time, being aware that the fellow in the next seat—no more or no less bright—*had* understood—that is, the sequence of instruction was totally adequate for him.

The capability of a research based instructional system could, if we would use it, revolutionize education as it now exists. The capability obviously would not be limited to instruction per se, but should be applied to staffing and any other aspect of education.

SATELLITE SUPPORTED INSTRUCTION

One of the more exciting capabilities will be that of providing what might be termed *real time instruction* rather than historical instruction, by increased use of television, and especially by the use of worldwide satellite systems. Given increased technological facilities and personnel, students at all age levels—even in the smallest and most remote schools—should be able to observe and view events as they occur throughout the world. Whether it is a riot in Chicago, a debate in the British Parliament, or a ten-week series of half hour programs on experimental farming in Arabia, the capability will exist for pupils to observe what is taking place *at the time it takes place*. This worldwide communication facility has many obvious advantages for education. Not the least among them is the elimination of much of the provincialism characteristic of elementary education. I am not suggesting that there is no value in acquainting students with a local and regional history. I am convinced that there is. Perhaps such study is becoming even more important as a way of assisting young people to gain an appreciation for and learn the benefits that can be derived from understanding the cultural micro-environment in which they live, and which, at least on a day to day basis, is the arena in which they work, play, love, and exert a personal influence on their fellow men.

At the same time, it is clear that we must become more cognizant of a world society. Traditional schools have attempted something like this through the study of either ancient civilization or of a regional history. In the case of my own region, for example, elementary children spend what seems to me an unreasonable amount of time examining the living habits of Northwest Indians, in part—according to curriculum guides—as a means of studying primitive and developing countries such as those in Africa. Meanwhile, the new nations of Africa queue up until grade nine when they finally receive some systematic study. One reason that this is done, of course, is that materials exist on the Northwest Indians, while they are much more difficult to find on the emerging African nations. The problem has been—and to some extent still is—one of educational capability. Movies are expensive and, in the area of social studies, they are frequently out of date before they are available for classroom use. Video tapes are relatively inexpensive, and the lag between recording and use is practically insignificant.

Grant then, if you will, the future existence of a rather tremendous worldwide satellite assisted audio-video network capability for education. It is clear, I believe, that some such system will develop, even though the specific characteristics will be unpredictable at this time. Educators should therefore begin thinking about how they can make the best use of the capabilities. There are a number of serious problems and difficult tasks which lay between the existence of the capability and its effective use in education. One problem is especially critical. It involves the level of inference of presentations and displays of the subject matter, whether it is by lecture, book, film, tour or some other medium.

A certain amount of abstracting or selecting takes place in the preparation of content for presentation. Usually this is done with some degree of purpose by the teacher or preparer of materials which, of course, implies that control of time is important. While there may be considerable and significant disagreement among us regarding the substance of the editing and abstracting process, there is undoubtedly agreement that this function is important. The learner's time is too valuable to waste on irrelevant and needlessly repetitious materials.

Given the real time nature of an audio-visual worldwide communications capability, we must deal with two kinds of questions: How can we be selective, given the short time frame? What shall we select, or more to the point, what shall we use as selective criteria? The first problem apparently can be solved reasonably satisfactorily. In general, representatives from television suggest buffer systems in which "raw" information is temporarily stored, analyzed, edited, rearranged, merged, or whatever is appropriate, and then displayed to the learner. They are quick to point out that the real problem relates to what is selected. It is not so much a technological capability problem—that is, a machine problem—but rather is a criterion problem—the human problem—which is basic. This is the problem which has been part of the whole technological revolution in education. The machines exist in some usable form, but before they can be useful, one has to know the purposes or objectives of the educator. The issue itself, particularly in a world oriented educational enterprise, can be deceptively complex. It is even more complex when the educational vehicle has the real time characteristic noted above.

A good part of the deception results from the problem of omission because of unawareness. The current concern over whether or not history texts give adequate attention to Negro history and its contribution to the development of America is illustrative. It is apparent that the critics are correct. And while it could be that the omission was willful in the case of some small number of authors and publishers, the important reason for the omission of research in writing is really insensitivity, or middle class cultural blindness. The Negro was not maliciously left out of history books (he was, however, maliciously left out of history); he was simply seldom seen. Apparently in the eyes of many writers he did not exist in spite of the long time frame available to them for study. How can we avoid the same kind of error in using an audio-visual technology capability?

The immediate interpretation of an event may be revised significantly with the perspective of time. When the publication lag no longer exists and serves as a tempering mechanism, how can we guard against teaching concepts which may soon need to be "untaught"?

PUBLISHING CAPABILITIES

Another capability resulting from computer technology and increased audio-visual reproduction devices will have great impact on the primary medium of instruction, namely books. This capability can destroy the basic one book-one course educational model. It will be possible to go from author manuscript to indexing to magnetic storage, to generating hard copies of such things as CBI (Computer Based Instruction) programs in response to specifications provided by teachers. Authors will not be contracted to write or revise texts, as is now the case, but rather to update data banks and materials. Ideally, a teacher—or "instructional team leader" will indicate the learning objectives for one or more students, and the computer will search its files and produce a combination of materials best suited to the objectives. The chief problem, as always, will involve the issue of stating objectives. Whether we call them performance criteria or behavioral objectives, *this kind of capability will make a significant contribution only after learning objectives are stated in precise terms.* Our experience to date has taught us that this is an extremely difficult task. Until we achieve it, however, what is done, essentially, is to index the subsections of books, and treat these as entities. This, in itself, offers at least certain economic advantages and somewhat greater flexibility, but falls short of individualized or prescribed instruction which is truly responsive to the needs of pupils.

INSTRUCTION THAT IS INDEPENDENT OF TEACHERS

The technology . . . can be viewed from another perspective: that is, the changed role and function of the teacher and student in the educational process. Much has been written about the impact of technology on the role of teachers, but I would suggest that *more attention should be given to the changed role and responsibilities of the student.* We really cannot appreciate the importance of technology for the teacher's role without considering what will happen to students.

It appears obvious to many that the application of sophisticated technology in education will reduce the need for the teacher "interface" function between instructional materials (content or substance) and the learner. In other words, *the capability for teacher-independent instruction will be increased.*

The teacher's function as a presenter of information could easily be eliminated entirely. He will continue to interpret, synthesize, and clarify information displayed in another mode. The question as to whether the predicted amount of time which the teacher and student will spend together will be decreased has caused concern among some educators. They ask if this will dehumanize education. It could lead in this direction, but I doubt that it will, due to the quality of much of the student-teacher interaction. The term "interaction" is probably an inaccurate designation of what actually takes place in the lecture hall. *A reduction in the traditional kind of student-teacher relationship, and a concomitant increase in task or problem oriented student-teacher interaction may in fact increase the humaneness of instruction.*

A more important outcome of the teacher independent instructional capability for students is, by definition, the increase in responsibility which students must assume for their own learning behavior. I am not sure what this means, but it is such a radical change from the tight control teachers have maintained over students in the past that the role of the student will certainly change. The freedom to explore and to set his own pace, plus a comprehensive in-depth instructional capability to support independent learning behavior, should lead to the development of a new breed of students. Their perceptions of "school" will be very different from that of counterparts of today, and they will in turn be perceived differently by teachers. The burden, it can be added, will be on educators, for the "newness" will be limited to their experiences. Students, having nothing for contrast, will accept the new as if it were always so.

TECHNOLOGY AND THE ROLE OF TEACHERS

Increased technological capabilities will obviously have an impact on the role of teachers. Technology will both provide new educational tools directly, and thus cause changes in what teachers do in the teaching process, and in a less direct manner, cause teachers to become involved in new kinds of educational functions. Most of what has been said so far has been about the first kind of educational capability. A few comments regarding the second kind of capability—namely changes in educational personnel capabilities—are appropriate at this point.[1]

The Teacher

Traditionally, a teacher has had to build his own teaching methods and materials (for example, charts, pictures, audio-visual presentations, and so on). The economics of time provides strong support for the concept of staying with a few tested teaching procedures, with tested instructional materials, and perhaps to an extent greater than commonly recognized, with the same subject matter. However, *when the teacher's role and responsibilities change* from those of the generalist who must be responsible for the total teaching process (including the development of many instructional materials) *to those of the professional specialist responsible for designing instructional programs for individual pupils, the emphasis shifts to decision making and planning.* While still involved in implementing the plan, the teacher focuses more than before on defining the needs of individual pupils, synthesizing these, and communicating them to others who then make the appropriate resources available to the pupil in the most appropriate teaching mode.

The Non-Teaching Specialist's Team

One hesitates at this point to apply labels to the new kinds of personnel in education, because it is far from clear what particular combinations of competencies will be most desirable. If we keep in mind that the labels are merely suggestive, *it is reasonable to assume that at least four areas of non-teaching specialists will emerge in regard to man-machine systems in education.* They are: (1) content research specialists, (2) media specialists, (3) educational systems specialists, and (4) educational engineers. People in these four areas of specialty will serve as a kind of support team to teachers.

It should be helpful to speculate briefly on the competencies in the four areas of specialization suggested, since they will constitute increased educational capabilities. *The team concept is critical and the maximum contribution by each area cannot be made independently of the others.* Perhaps the most effective way to describe the function of each is to illustrate how they might operate in a school employing new capabilities.

The teacher's first responsibility would be to determine the learning objectives for pupils and to communicate these to the supporting team of specialists. Before members of the team can function, they must know what the teacher-leader wants to achieve. Precisely what behaviors of his students does he think should be modified, promoted, or eliminated? This is not an easy task, but given a statement of objectives and information about the pupils to be taught, the content researcher, media specialist, and systems specialist could assist the teacher to develop appropriate instructional systems.

Content Research Specialists. The content researcher would have the responsibility of identifying and synthesizing subject matter relevant to the particular objectives. In part a librarian, he would have at his disposal an information-retrieval system much more sophisticated and sensitive than traditional manual classification systems. The task would be to identify the most appropriate materials for the instructional objectives stated—those which are maximally sensitive to the characteristics of the learners. In order to accomplish this, of course, he must have the capability to analyze great amounts of materials in terms of both content and learning criteria.

Media Specialists. Given the learning goals, learners' characteristics, and a pool of material from which to work, the media specialist will have to determine the most effective modes of presentation and then assemble and construct instructional materials. While libraries of materials and collections of equipment should certainly continue to be available, an equally important resource would be a media laboratory and production shop. Media specialists will include artists, audio-visual production specialists, material programmers, and so on.

Educational Systems Specialists. In regard to new personnel, the educational systems specialist represents the greatest innovation entailed in man-machine systems in education. While the extent of assistance from resource materials and media entailed in man-machine systems in education represents a radical change, the concept of providing this kind of support for teachers is certainly not new. In the past, however, it has been the instructor's responsibility to integrate these resources into his own classroom procedures. Man-machine systems in education entail a level of complexity and coordination and a knowledge of machines which the teacher, as defined above, cannot reasonably be expected to master. The systems specialist has responsibility for putting the various resources together and designing a control procedure which will enable the teacher to exercise and maintain maximum surveillance and control over the teaching and learning processes. The basic goal of man-machine systems in education is to achieve the ultimate in individualized instruction, and the closer one comes toward achieving this goal, the more complex the systems will become. The potential for chaos—the failure to instruct anybody in much of anything—also increases. All of the "what happens if" and "what should be done when this takes place" questions must be anticipated and thought through, with solutions provided and built into the system. This is the task of the systems specialist, to assemble piece by piece the components of instruction constructed by the resource and material specialists according to the specifications determined by the teacher. In a more sophisticated systems, the educational systems area undoubtedly will require the skills of computer programers.

Educational Engineers.   In larger schools and colleges the efficient use, maintenance, and modification of complex man-machine educational systems will require a staff of engineers familiar with the school or college and with education in general.

BIO-ELECTRONIC LEARNING

Only a few of the many kinds of possible new educational capabilities have been discussed here. However, I would not want to leave this brief exercise in forecasting, without at least mentioning a kind of future capability which represents a new dimension, rather than an extension, of education. The capabilities discussed to this point are, in a sense, refinements of educational psychology—centered especially on perceptual problems and issues. In a word, they are all "outside" of the individual—that is, they stop short of making direct changes in the organism. Rather, they attempt to make it easier for the organism to change itself.

We will soon see, I believe, the clear emergence of capabilities for making direct changes in the organism for learning purposes. Such things as laser beam technology, advances in endocrinology, bio-chemical control of genetics, and pre-conscious cognition techniques will provide both an exciting and somewhat frightening educational capability. They will be exciting because of the tremendous potential for enhancing learning—and frightening because they entail moral, ethical, and philosophical problems with which we have not had to deal. Admittedly, while not as immediate as other kinds of emerging technology, educational planning which does not give them at least some serious consideration, is short sighted.

IN SUMMARY

The main obstacle to the development and use of sophisticated data banks and information systems, I suspect, is not the technology itself, but the threat posed to the educational establishment. American education operates on a set of myths which have evolved from the time that only a few had access to stored knowledge (print on pages) and thereby had the power to influence tremendously who should learn what. The educational elite—that is, "the establishment"—guarded its capability closely, and carefully handed it down to each new generation. More recently the professors of administration largely decided what the practicing administrator should know. The administrator in turn decided what teachers could know and do, and the teachers (which is only fair, of course) decided what materials the pupils should learn. Somewhere in the shuffle professors of teacher education tended to get bumped aside. But the bastion around educational capabilities is crumbling, and capabilities are cropping up in other places. The old restrictions on classroom content are made ineffective by information available through such sources as movies, television, and greater freedom in the printing and distribution of materials.

The point is simply that new and powerful educational capabilities exist outside the school, and out of control of the educational establishment. This emerging trend will continue, and educators will either "get with it" or find learners increasingly dissatisfied with their offering and teachers who are unable to hold their attention. This is happening now on college campuses in the form of student initiated courses. The most significant aspect of the student revolt is not their questioning of the appropriateness of subject matter or content. It is, instead, their increasing rejection of traditional educational procedures. They are asking—perhaps demanding—"When are you going to use your new educational capabilities?", and when they hear no satisfactory response, they set out to try to use them independently.

NOTES

[1] The remainder of this section has in large part been excerpted from an earlier book by the author: John W. Loughary (ed.), *Man Machine Systems in Education* (New York: Harper and Row, 1966).

Part J.
**Computers And The
Individualization Of Learning:
Today and Tomorrow**

Introduction

Perhaps one of the best publicized trends in education in recent years has been the rush to experiment with computers. Computers are already widely used for business or scientific purposes in the colleges and larger school districts. Records are maintained by them, research is conducted through them, courses are taught via them, and in some places, clubs are formed to utilize them. There have been some expensive experiments and some "shoestring" ones, but as yet there is no answer to the question of how they can economically fit into the educational mainstream. They can only do so if their purchase and operating costs can be kept within the modest tax base that is characteristic of most school districts.

It is certainly true that in the business world computers *are* efficient tools in certain types of tasks, and there are parallels to many of these tasks in the field of education. For instance, computers are unparalleled at keeping track of continuously changing inventories. In the business world these inventories might be bank accounts, people on payroll, location of freight cars, etc. In the educational enterprise these changing inventories might be collections of current learning materials, lists of off-site resource people, or learners' personal progress files.

Another prominent kind of computer application is that which relates several components of a system. For instance, computers are used to regulate the flow of chemicals being mixed, or to adjust prices of products according to changes in raw materials costs. In education, by comparison, certain computer managed programs "blend together" learning materials, instructors and learners—with varying degrees of efficiency and cost effectiveness.

Hopefully, the oversimplified examples above have made it clear that the optimum use of computers in education is not yet fully defined, although there are numerous (and competing) alternatives.

In Chapter 25, Robert F. Bundy reviews the state-of-the-art (up to 1968) and reports in succinct form some major conclusions of selected research in computer-assisted instruction as well as some recommendations for future research.

In Chapter 26, James Rogers extends this analysis of computer functions. He develops a framework or paradigm for computer use that describes the input, function, and output characteristics for each of six computer applications.

In Chapter 27, Patrick Suppes describes certain functions which he believes the computer can serve in education. He argues that the use of the computer can, contrary to widespread opinion, *personalize* education.

Numerous other projects use computers as a means of individualizing learning in addition to those mentioned in these few chapters. Both IPI and Project PLAN, described in *Developmental Efforts in Individualized Learning,* use the computer, though not to the same degree. Other projects in which the computer serves a managing function include AIMS (Automated Instructional Management System—developed by the New York Institute of Technology), CAM (Comprehensive Achievement Monitoring—a Stanford University/University of Massachusetts project), and TAG (Teacher's Automated Guide—a project in the Portland School System, Portland, Oregon).

A number of universities and colleges are active in the context of CAI. Among these are the University of Illinois, Florida State University, Harvard University, and the University of California—Irvine, to name a few.

The computer has also been used rather extensively in various developmental projects intended to enhance guidance and vocational counseling programs in the public schools. These computer-oriented guidance projects will possibly have a potent impact on future individualized learning practices, for they enable the learner to perceive that many career options are open to him and they provide him with a way to seek more detailed information as his goals become refined and more specific. Large-scale learning systems, such as PLAN and IPI, typically integrate the guidance function into their systems design.

Chapter 25. THE STATE-OF-THE-ART IN COMPUTER-ASSISTED INSTRUCTION

COMPUTER-ASSISTED INSTRUCTION — WHERE ARE WE?

Robert F. Bundy

> More than ever before, we are concerned with the nature of the educational process, with the goals of education, with the impact of change—and, . . . with the techniques and devices that can be used in improving the educational enterprise. . . . Indeed, to the outside observer it must seem as if we were preparing to embark upon a permanent revolution in education.

Jerome Bruner[1] made the above observations in 1962. There can be little doubt that we are now writing the early chapters of this "permanent revolution" in education. To date, we are not sufficiently experienced to be able to define adequately its nature and scope, but one fact stands out clearly: Technology will play a major role.

SOURCE: Reprinted from *Phi Delta Kappan*, Vol. 59, No. 8 (April 1968), pp. 424-29, by permission of author and publisher.

Robert Hutchins, writing in 1967. sees the possibility that changes brought by technology ". . . may go so far as to dissolve the institutions we have known, or make them largely unrecognizable."[2] The real danger, however, warns Hutchins, is that the technology of education may come to determine the methods and aims of education itself.

Perhaps these issues are nowhere more evident than in the current research and discussions on the use of the computer in the instructional process, most frequently referred to as computer-assisted instruction (CAI) or computer-based learning.[2a]

Since the early sixties research money appropriated for the development of CAI and documents probing the boundaries of this technology have swelled enormously. Educational institutions and business corporations have begun or are making plans to begin extensive CAI projects. And in the midst of all this activity we are continually being reminded that CAI will bring about dramatic and far-reaching changes at every level of education.

To many on the sidelines, this must present a confusing, if not a bewildering situation. Where in fact do we stand with CAI? What do we know? What are the advantages? Where lie the dangers? On what timetable are we to prepare for the changes this technology will bring? These and many more questions are being asked today in both professional and lay circles.

Unfortunately, there are few references that deal with these questions in a comprehensive and constructive manner. Most assuredly, CAI technology must be given time to grow and mature, but in the meanwhile there is urgent need for continuing professional assessment and evaluation.

In the following pages, an attempt will be made to take a look at CAI from several vantage points. First, what results are being reported about CAI research? Second, what is being said about the kinds of research needed? Third, what generalizations can be made about CAI research reported to date? Fourth, what trends in CAI seem to be evolving at this time? And fifth, what overall conclusions can be drawn about CAI based on our current understanding of this technology?

The information presented for the first three objectives derives from some recent work during which a large number of documents dealing with CAI were analyzed and evaluated. Objectives four and five will be primarily personal value judgments, although they are based in part on discussions with teachers and researchers currently involved with CAI.

For additional background information about CAI and for some different points of view, a number of sources are available.[3]

RESULTS FROM CAI RESEARCH

Summarized below are research conclusions concerning CAI as reported in a fairly broad sampling of journals and institutional reports. Actually, only a relatively small number of research reports were found to be readily available. This is understandable, however, for as Hansen points out: "The vast majority of CAI projects have expended tremendous energy in the development of curriculum materials; consequently, this development phase has limited the availability of research findings."[4]

The references cited refer either to research reports or to sources where the investigators have commented on research they or others have conducted. It was not possible in every instance to separate carefully controlled research from anecdotal accounts or general observations.

The conclusions listed would probably be considered tentative by most of the researchers and lack broad generalization at this time. In any event, taken as a whole, they would seem to represent a reasonable picture of the current state of the art of CAI as reflected in the literature.

1.   Students seem to learn at least as well with CAI as with conventional classroom instruction. Most of the researchers report this conclusion for various short courses. Some researchers indicate that greater learning and retention can occur with CAI.[5-9] In addition, Coulson[10] has reported an example of raising the performance of lower aptitude students to that of higher aptitude students.

2.   CAI can provide learning and retention at least equivalent to conventional techniques in the same amount of time. Some report significant reduction in time required.[11-14]

3.   The computer learning program can make logical decisions and adjust to individual student differences with regard to learning sequence, depth and mode of material, and rate of progress.[15-25]

4.   The computer can record and manipulate a wide variety of learning data about the student during instruction. For example, sequence of learning steps, response time, number of errors, cumulative performance, etc. All researchers report this conclusion as being well within the capability of the present technology. However, in view of the quantity of information that can be collected, it is difficult to select only that information which can be permanently recorded.[26]

5.   The computer can reduce certain kinds of tedious work usually required of the student. For example, in mathematical logic.[27]

6.   The computer program can integrate and control a wide variety of audio-visual aids in the learning program, for enrichment and motivation. The computer can also provide dynamic real time displays of mathematical and physical relationships, and relieve the students of a large number of routine calculations.[28-34] However, computer-controlled slide presentations are not necessarily better than visual materials presented in booklet form.[35]

7. Time sharing (a number of students using the same computer simultaneously, and perhaps at remote distances from the computer) is within the capabilities of present technology.[36, 37]

8. A broad range of courses can be programmed for CAI. No known limits have been reported as yet to the kinds of subject matter or conceptual level that can be programmed. Well-structured subjects can, in particular, be easily handled by CAI tutorial systems.[38]

9. Students are generally interested in and like the CAI form of instruction.

> Student attitude toward CAI generally relates directly to personal performance.[39]

> Appropriate pacing of materials presented and time-out limits can keep the concentration of even very young children at a relatively high level in a CAI system.[40]

> However, students often feel the need for shorter sessions with more discussion and teacher interaction.[41-43]

10. Learning time and learning effectiveness with CAI depend on a number of factors.

With respect to learning time:

> The major determinant of time to complete the computer program is the number of student responses required to meet internal course criteria established by the author-teacher.[44]

> Employment of optional delays in the learning program, plus the opportunity for review and remedial work, would provide help for some students.[45]

> There is great variability in how long children will work at the computer instructional terminal when free to decide.[46]

> Deterioration in learning performance has been noted in grade school children when sessions run longer than 20-30 minutes.[47]

With respect to learning effectiveness, we need to examine the factors of learning style, instructional sequencing, and learning performance:

> The cognitive style of a student appears to be related to his ability and his approach to and utilization of the computer system.[48]

> Visual learners respond more favorably to sequences of graphically or pictorially laid-out instructional items, and have been brought to a level of superior performance on achievement tests.[49]

Student errors during instruction and responses to self-evaluation questions provide effective criteria for branching the student to different instructional sequences.[50]

Branching methods can provide more efficient instruction than fixed-sequence presentations.[51]

Allowing students to determine their own sequence of instruction does not work as well with younger children as with older children.[52]

Having too many "help" sequences available could encourage students to rely on this as the easier and faster way of getting an answer.[53]

A sophisticated latency criterion of performance can be easily applied in a computer-based laboratory.[54]

When poor typists are permitted to score their own implicit responses rather than type them out, their performance is markedly better.[55]

Auto-instruction can be effective in helping mentally retarded young children to read.[56]

Student responses entered in wrong form (where only one form of an answer is permitted) tend to interfere seriously with student learning.[57]

Some students get flustered by the machinery and need, therefore, a good orientation to this form of instruction.[58]

Students become confused in a time-sharing system, if the computer does not respond immediately to their commands.[59]

A large proportion of the teacher's current responsibility for imparting facts, basic skills, and concepts, as well as his responsibility for providing routine drill, can be handled more efficiently and effectively by the machine.[60]

11.   Already existing curriculum materials can be readily used in development of computer courses.[61, 62]

12.   The computer has been shown to provide an excellent opportunity for an experimental research lab to study learning.[64–69]

13.   Computer-simulated laboratories can be helpful for:

teaching lab procedures;[70]

exposing students to a variety of analytical problems and physical processes in considerably less time than actual lab analysis;[71, 72]

providing an excellent adjunct to conventional instruction;[73]

reducing student stress in learning by allowing freedom to manipulate objects normally not permitted, e.g., in clinical nursing.[74]

14. The beginnings of a versatile computer programming logic has been developed that permits:

easy changes from one subject matter to another;[75, 76]
a syntax for the student to use in communicating with the computer;[77]
some ease and flexibility in preparing programs;[78, 79]
substantial possibilities for constructed student responses.[80]

15. Time for qualified personnel to write, de-bug, and validate one hour of CAI instruction may be from 75 to 150 man-hours. Total cost, including machine time, may be several thousand dollars. (These are private guesses based on conversations with people involved in programmed instruction and CAI. Actually, there are so many variables involved, such as quality of instructional materials, level of instruction, and extent of validation, that rules of thumb such as the above are not very helpful. The literature is almost completely silent on cost-benefit analysis.)

Most of the above findings have resulted from very short courses conducted with small numbers of students. Long-term CAI data involving sizeable numbers of students have not yet been collected.

RECOMMENDED RESEARCH AREAS

Many searching questions have been raised about CAI in the literature. It is difficult to categorize these questions neatly because they probe far-ranging pedagogical and technological issues. However, the following will perhaps give a brief picture of those questions considered most important and most frequently recommended for further research:

First, there are some strictly pedagogical issues. Questions related to the *effectiveness* of CAI have drawn a great deal of attention. How effective can CAI be in providing individualized learning opportunities, separate from or integrated with conventional forms of instruction? What is the best way to divide a student's involvement with CAI among remedial, review, drill and practice, tutorial, and interactive learning experiences? To what extent can creative and original thinking be encouraged in a CAI environment? What kinds of information are important for developing meaningful student learning profiles? How should this mass of information be organized and presented to teachers so that they can further prescribe and work with students on an individual basis?

Underlying these questions, researchers realize, are more basic concerns to which research attention must be given. For example, extensive consideration must be given to modes of presentation, program structure, and types of learning reinforcement. Ways must be found to design computer programs which will be able, in a sophisticated way, to analyze and act on student background, ability, and progress. This in itself implies a systematic classification of individual difference variables and their interaction with instructional materials and modes of presentation.

The *effects* of CAI present another area of intriguing questions for further research. For example, what are the psychological and physiological effects on students after long-term or intensive short-term use of CAI? What are the sociological implications? What will be the effect of CAI on the teacher's training and school role? What additional skill roles will be necessary? What effects will CAI have on school systems design, allocation of resources, and administration? In short, what jobs are best handled by machines and what jobs by humans?

A wide variety of questions probing technological issues have also been presented in the literature. Typical examples would be the following:

What requirements should CAI input-output devices have in order to be easy and natural for the student to use and as little distractive as possible from the learning process? What requirements should CAI languages have to allow teacher-authors not familiar with the operation of the computer to use its full power and capability effectively in developing learning programs and collecting student data? What are the requirements for the student to be able to use his own natural spoken or written language in carrying on an extended dialogue with the computer learning program?

While preliminary research efforts have been directed toward some of the above questions, the extent of our knowledge is sketchy and tentative at this time. Many of the questions raised have much broader implications than just CAI, and some will not be researchable for a number of years. In order of importance, the most critical research needs at this time reside in the pedagogical questions raised.

GENERALIZATIONS ABOUT RESEARCH

Several major criticisms (perhaps limitations is the better word) can be made which apply generally to CAI research methodology. Attention has been drawn to some of the factors affecting the validity of the research designs.[81]

Very little effort is made, in most instances, to *consider other pertinent research studies* (not necessarily CAI), and to show how the current research fits into the broader picture. As Krathwohl[82] has pointed out, no research starts *de novo:* it is part of a continuum, and such studies should, over the course of time, deepen and broaden our understanding.

There are *biases of selection*. The methods of selecting students for CAI studies generally prohibit any generalizations of results beyond the subjects themselves in the particular situation they were exposed to, at the time they were exposed to it. A number of replications of the studies, plus the application of random selection techniques, would have to be made before any meaningful generalizations could be derived. (Usually, the researchers themselves express reluctance to extend their conclusions very far from the specific situations tested.)

There are *maturation effects*. It is probable that the student's behavior is affected by his interaction with the computer during the instruction. For example, being bothered or upset by the machinery can too easily introduce changes which are confused with the effect of the experimental variable. In addition, many of the experiments are short. And with the small populations used, individual influences on the student can become extremely exaggerated, e.g., sickness, time of the year.

Also, there are *reactive arrangements*. Frequently, the artificiality of the experimental setting seems to militate against the external validity of the research design. To take students out of class, to have them meet at special times and places, and to introduce them to a special setting where they will work with the computer inevitably influences the students, particularly over short periods of time. Is the student pleased because he is getting special treatment? Is he impressed with the equipment? Does he feel he must do better because he is being observed or knows he is a part of an experiment? Thus we must ask, "Are student performance differences really attributable to the experimental variables under study?" In short, reactive arrangements (and similarly, selection biases and maturation effects) confound our understanding of what the real change-producing events are and leave the research results open to question.

A final observation is that there appears to be a feeling or urgency among some researchers to make in-depth comparisons between CAI and other forms of conventional instruction. This is regrettable, in that it tends to force artificial designs on the research and places undue emphasis on proving or disproving CAI as a way of individualizing instruction.

The approach that does seem warranted at this time is to use CAI as a way of *learning about learning*. The powerful data collection and data reduction capabilities of the computer offer immense possibilities for studying and controlling the variables of learning. This, in turn, should lead to the development of thoroughly tested and validated instructional materials and teaching strategies, and ultimately to a theory of instruction itself.[83]

The appropriate question to be asked, therefore, is not "How much better is CAI than the ways we have been trying to teach?" but "How can CAI assist us to understand and control learning itself?"

CURRENT TRENDS IN CAI

Recent history has shown that substantial sums of money are available for CAI development. This trend will undoubtedly continue, perhaps dramatically, during the next several years. The money will come from business corporations, federal and private funding agencies, and the military, and will be directed toward the research and development of curriculum materials and CAI programming languages. The number of educational institutions, manufacturers, and publishing houses announcing or expanding their commitment to CAI development will increase at a similar pace. We can also expect a greater dispersion of research at all levels of education rather than concentration at the elementary and secondary levels. Hopefully, we will also see experts from a variety of disciplines giving their attention to CAI research. Some evidence of this is already apparent.

We should also expect that some institutions will be attracted to CAI for reasons of prestige or misguided enthusiasm. Bushnell,[84] in reviewing Title III proposals for computer technology, shows this is already beginning to occur. Schools which take this approach run a high risk of being quickly disillusioned when they discover the dearth of off-the-shelf CAI programs available, and the time, personnel, and cost required to develop instructional materials and operate a CAI system. Perhaps education's difficult experience with teaching machines a few years ago will offset this trend.

One of the few centers where significant research with CAI is being conducted is the Stanford-Brentwood Computer-Assisted Instruction Laboratory.[85-87] In 1964, the U.S. Office of Education granted a contract to the Institute of Mathematical Studies in the Social Sciences at Stanford to set up a computer-based laboratory at a public elementary school. The purpose was to investigate CAI over an extended period of time. Brentwood Elementary School in East Palo Alto, California, was selected as the site for this experiment.

The project is directed by Patrick Suppes and Richard C. Atkinson, senior members of the Institute for Mathematical Studies. Other personnel on the project include about 50 teachers, psychologists, linguists, mathematicians, curriculum and reading experts, writers, artists, and computer programmers.

After two years of planning and preparation, instruction in mathematics and reading was started in September, 1966, with 100 first-grade children at Brentwood. The program includes both drill and practice and tutorial instruction, and the students are allowed to progress at their own rate. In addition, the sequence of material presented to a student is a function of his prior history of responses. Thus at any particular time each student working with the system can be going through a completely different set of materials from any other student. An extensive history of responses is being collected on all the participants as they proceed through the programs.

An IBM 1500 system with 16 student terminals is being used as the instructional system. Each terminal includes an audio system, a CRT display with light-pen, a picture projector, and a typewriter keyboard. The system is housed in a special building on the grounds of the elementary school.

This project deserves special mention for several reasons. It is the first project of its kind for bringing about an in-depth integration of CAI into an elementary school curriculum. It is the first project of its kind for collecting and analyzing long-term data with CAI, with a sizeable number of students involved. The project illustrates the kind of effort required to plan, develop, operate, and maintain a live CAI system in an elementary school setting. It also illustrates the costs involved. Direct costs have been estimated to be about one-half million dollars for the hardware and building and one-half million for curriculum development. These figures do not include the costs of previous research and curriculum development.

In time, this type of project can result in thoroughly tested and validated instructional materials which other schools could use at considerably less cost. A great deal of important and useful information should also be forthcoming, particularly with regard to curriculum design, instructional strategies, and basic information related to learning models. (For results to date, see the article by Suppes which follows as Chapter 27.)

CONCLUSIONS

The following conclusions seem warranted at this time as we survey what we know about CAI.

1. It is important in evaluating CAI to keep clearly in mind the distinction between pedagogical and technological issues. The computer is a powerful tool for gathering and manipulating data, but by itself it tells us nothing about learning or how learning occurs. "The research and curriculum work done thus far as a result of the current interest in teaching machines and programmed instruction show clearly that technology alone is not going to produce any fundamental or long-lasting changes in the curriculum. Only if its applications are guided by appropriate psychological principles and subject-matter insight will such changes be brought about." [88]

2. CAI would appear to offer significant potential in providing individualized instruction. However, we have barely begun the exploration and necessary development. "The problem now is the hard one of finding the critical data that will make such a technological capability truly effective." [89]

3. For some time in the future, then, one of the most critical and important applications for CAI will be as a school laboratory to learn about learning and perhaps ultimately to build a theory of instruction. Education has never had such a unique facility available to perform this task.

4. We can expect for some years to come that CAI will have to be heavily subsidized, because of its high costs and the lack of thoroughly tested and high quality instructional programs.

5. One of the current dangers is that schools will erroneously attempt an involvement with CAI based only on faddism or a sincere but naive understanding of what is involved.

6. Legitimate research with CAI should be strongly encouraged, but schools should be realistically aware of the kinds of skills required, the kinds of commitment needed from personnel, and the costs that will be incurred.

7. Critical needs exist, therefore, for well-designed and well-executed research extending over long periods of time, coupled with well-planned dissemination of research results. Also vital are periodic professional assessments of the research to maintain a balanced perspective of this emerging technology.

History may well bear out Suppes' observation that:

> . . . it is fair to forecast that in the next 10 years the impact of computer-assisted instruction will be felt in a very large number of school systems in this country. The technology alone is not important. What is important is that by the use of computers we can realize the goals of individualized instruction that have been discussed in American education since the beginning of this century. And we can take another significant step toward realizing the full learning potential of our children.[90]

But in the last analysis, it would seem that we should also heed Hutchins' concern that " . . . we may come to desire the kind of education that is easiest for the computer to provide." [91] Our final, most difficult decision, therefore, may be whether "The safest course will be to turn over to the machines the task of training and informing, thus relieving teachers for the work of education." [92]

NOTES

[1] Jerome Bruner, "The New Educational Technology" in *Revolution in Teaching.* New York: Bantam Books, 1962, p. 1.

[2] Robert Hutchins, "The Machines Run Education." Sunday Punch Section, *San Francisco Sunday Examiner & Chronicle,* August 6, 1967.

[2a] Essentially, this technology seeks to provide an individualized learning environment for each student. Instructional programs are stored in the computer and the student interacts with these programs by means of electronic interface devices. The instructional programs may include a broad range of subject matter content and extend across a spectrum from simple drill and practice routines to complex tutorial-type learning experiences.

[3] See Robert Bundy, "Computer-Assisted Instruction: Now and for the Future," *Audiovisual Instruction*, April, 1967, pp. 244-48; Walter Dick, "The Development and Current Status of Computer-Based Instruction," *American Educational Research Journal*, January, 1965, pp. 41-55; Ronald J. Gentile, "The First Generation of Computer-Assisted Instruction Systems: An Evaluative Review," in *CAI Laboratory Report* (University Park, Pa.: The Pennsylvania State University, 1965); Gerald T. Gleason, "Computer Assisted Instruction—Prospects and Problems," *Educational Technology*, November 15, 1967, pp. 1-8; Duncan N. Hansen, "Computer Assistance with the Educational Process," *Review of Educational Research*, December, 1966, pp. 588-603; Albert E. Hickey and John M. Newton, "Computer-Assisted Instruction, A Survey of the Literature" (Newburyport, Mass.: Entelek, Inc.) (Prepared under Office of Naval Research Contract Nonr 4757(00): updated semiannually); Gloria M. Silvern and Leonard C. Silvern, "Computer-Assisted Instruction: Specification of Attributes for CAI Programs and Programmers," *Proceedings of 21st National ACM Conference*, 1966; Patrick Suppes, "The Uses of Computers in Education," *Scientific American*, September, 1966, pp. 207-20; Karl L. Zinn, "Computer Assistance for Instruction, a Review of Systems and Projects," in E. Goodman (ed.), *Automated Education Handbook* (Detroit: Automated Education Center, 1965), pp. 1-45.

[4] Duncan Hansen, *op. cit.* (footnote 3), p. 595.

[5] Maryann Bitzer, "Self-Directed Inquiry in Clinical Nursing Instruction by Means of the Plato Simulated Laboratory," in *University of Illinois Coordinated Science Laboratory Report R-184, 1963.*

[6] Ralph E. Grubb and Lenore D. Selfridge, "Computer Tutoring in Statistics," in *Computers and Automation*, 1964, pp. 20-26.

[7] John Henry Martin, *Freeport Public School Experiment on Early Reading Using the Edison Responsive Environment Instrument* (New York: Responsive Environments Corporation, 1964), as cited by Richard L. Wing, *Use of Technical Media for Simulating Environments to Provide Individualized Instruction.* (Westchester County, N.Y.: Cooperative Research Project No. 1948), I, p. 20.

[8] John J. Schurdak, "An Approach to the Use of Computers in the Instructional Process and an Evaluation," in Yorktown Heights, *I.B.M. Research Report RC-1432,* 1965.

[9] Suppes, *op. cit.* (footnote 3)

[10] John E. Coulson, *et al.,* "Effects of Branching in a Computer Controlled Autoinstructional Device," *Journal of Applied Psychology,* June, 1962, pp. 389-92.

[11] Bitzer, *op. cit.* (footnote 5)

[12] Grubb and Selfridge, *op. cit.* (footnote 6)

[13] William R. Uttal, "On Conversational Interaction," in John E. Coulson (ed.), *Programmed Learning and Computer Based Instruction* (New York: John Wiley & Sons, Inc., 1962), pp. 171-90.

[14] Wing, *op. cit.* (footnote 7)

[15] E. N. Adams, "Roles of the Electronic Computer in University Education." Yorktown Heights: *I.B.M. Research Report RC-1530,* 1965.

[16] Richard C. Atkinson and Duncan N. Hansen, "Computer-Assisted Instruction in Initial Reading: The Stanford Project," *Reading Research Quarterly,* Summer, 1966, pp. 5-25.

[17] Donald L. Bitzer and J. A. Easley, Jr., "Plato: A Computer-Controlled Teaching System," in Margo A. Sass (ed.), *Computer Augmentation of Human Reasoning* (Washington, D.C.: Spartan Books, Inc., 1965), pp. 89-103.

[18] Robert L. Chapman and Janeth T. Carpenter, "Computer Techniques in Instruction," in John E. Coulson (ed.), *Programmed Learning and Computer Based Instruction* (New York: John Wiley & Sons, Inc., 1962), pp. 240-53.

[19] Coulson *et al., op. cit.* (footnote 10)

[20] Schurdak, *op. cit.* (footnote 8)

[21] Lawrence M. Stolurow, "Some Educational Problems and Prospects of a Systems Approach to Instruction." Paper prepared for a conference on "New Dimensions for Research in Educational Media" at Syracuse University, April, 1964.

[22] Suppes, *op. cit.* (footnote 3)

[23] Uttal, *op. cit.* (footnote 13)

[24] Wing, *op. cit.* (footnote 7)

[25] Zinn, *op. cit.* (footnote 3)

[26] Suppes, *op. cit.* (footnote 3)

[27] Patrick Suppes, "Modern Learning Theory and the Elementary-School Curriculum," *American Educational Research Journal,* March, 1964, pp. 79-93.

[28] Donald L. Bitzer *et al.,* "Plato II: A Multiple-Student Computer-Controlled Automatic Teaching Device," in Coulson, *op. cit.* (footnote 18)

[29] Coulson, *op. cit.* (footnote 10)

[30] J. C. R. Licklider, "Preliminary Experiments in Computer-Aided Teaching," in Coulson, *op. cit.* (footnote 18)

[31] Harold E. Mitzel and Kenneth H. Wodke, "The Development and Presentation of Four Different College Courses by Computer Teleprocessing." University Park, Pa.: *CAI Laboratory Interim Report,* 1965.

[32] Donald L. Shirer, "Computers and Physics Teaching. Part I: Digital Computers," *American Journal of Physics,* 1965, pp. 575-83.

[33] Suppes, *op. cit.* (footnote 3)

[34] Wing, *op. cit.* (footnote 7)

[35] Lloyd A. Lewis, Jr., "A Comparison of Two Modes of Visual Display in a Computer Assisted Instruction Situation." Graduate Thesis, Florida State University, December, 1965.

[36] Bitzer and Easley, *op. cit.* (footnote 17)

[37] Jeremy Main, "Computer Time-Sharing—Everyman at the Console," *Fortune,* August, 1967, pp. 88-91, 187-90.

[38] Suppes, *op. cit.* (footnote 3)

[39] Mitzel and Wodke, *op. cit.* (footnote 31)

[40] H. A. Wilson, "Computer-Assisted Instruction: A Tool for Teaching and Research." (Discussion of Stanford-Brentwood CAI Project, no date)

[41] Bitzer, *op. cit.* (footnote 5)

[42] Schurdak, *op. cit.* (footnote 8)

[43] Wing, *op. cit.* (footnote 7)

[44] Schurdak, *op. cit.* (footnote 8)

[45] Mitzel and Wodke, *op. cit.* (footnote 31)

[46] E. M. Quinn, "A CAI Reading Program—Preliminary Field Test." Yorktown Heights: *I.B.M. Research Report NC 576,* 1966.

[47] *Ibid.*

[48] Bitzer, *op. cit.* (footnote 5)

[49] Donald D. Bushnell, "Computer Mediated Instruction—A Survey of New Developments," *Computers and Automation,* March, 1965, pp. 18-20.

[50] Coulson, *op. cit.* (footnote 10)

[51] *Ibid.*

[52] Launor Carter and Harry Silberman, "The Systems Approach, Technology and the School." Santa Monica: *System Development Corporation Report SP-2025,* 1965.

[53] Bitzer, *op. cit.* (footnote 5)

[54] Suppes, *op. cit.* (footnote 27)

[55] Dick, *op. cit.* (footnote 3)

[56] Martin, *op. cit.* (footnote 7)

[57] Mitzel and Wodke, *op. cit.* (footnote 31)

[58] *Ibid.*

[59] Bitzer and Easley, *op. cit.* (footnote 28)

[60] Wilson, *op. cit.* (footnote 40)

[61] Schurdak, *op. cit.* (footnote 8)

[62] E. M. Quinn, "One Way to Get More Economical CAI Materials." Yorktown Heights: *I.B.M. Research Report NC 535,* 1965.

[63] Atkinson and Hansen, *op. cit.* (footnote 16)

[64] Bushnell, *op. cit.* (footnote 49)

[65] John E. Coulson, "A Computer-Based Laboratory for Research and Development in Education," in John E. Coulson (ed.), *Programmed Learning and Computer Based Instruction* (New York: John Wiley & Sons, Inc., 1962), pp. 191-204.

[66] Stolurow, *op. cit.* (footnote 21)

[67] Lawrence M. Stolurow, "A Computer-Assisted Instructional System in Theory and Research." From *Aspects of Educational Technology,* proceedings of a programmed learning conference held at Loughborough, April, 1966. London: Methuen, pp. 257-72.

[68] Patrick Suppes, "Arithmetic Drills and Review on a Computer-Based Teletype," *The Arithmetic Teacher,* April, 1966, pp. 303-09.

[69] Zinn, *op. cit.* (footnote 3)

[70] Wing, *op. cit.* (footnote 7)

[71] Adams, *op. cit.* (footnote 15)

[72] Wing, *op. cit.* (footnote 7)

[73] Bitzer, *op. cit.* (footnote 5)

[74] *Ibid.*

[75] Bitzer *et al., op. cit.* (footnote 28)

[76] Uttal, *op. cit.* (footnote 13)

[77] Bitzer and Easley, *op. cit.* (footnote 17)

[78] Silvern and Silvern, *op. cit.* (footnote 3)

[79] Zinn, *op. cit.* (footnote 3)

[80] Suppes, *op. cit.* (footnote 27)

[81] Donald T. Campbell and Julian C. Stanley, "Experimental and Quasi-Experimental Designs for Research in Teaching" in N. L. Gage (ed.), *Handbook of Research on Teaching* (Chicago: Rand McNally & Co., 1963), pp. 171-246.

[82] David R. Krathwohl, *How to Prepare a Research Proposal* (Syracuse, N.Y.: Syracuse University Press, 1965), 50 pp.

[83] Jerome S. Bruner, *Toward a Theory of Instruction* (Cambridge, Mass.: Belknap Press, 1966).

[84] Donald D. Bushnell, "Computer Technology," in *Catalyst for Change: A National Study of ESEA Title III,* prepared for the Subcommittee on Education of the Committee on Labor and Public Welfare (Washington, D.C.: U.S. Government Printing Office, 1967), pp. 353-55.

[85] Atkinson and Hansen, *op. cit.* (footnote 16)

[86] Wilson, *op. cit.* (footnote 40)

[87] Stanford-Brentwood Computer-Assisted Instruction Laboratory (Stanford-Brentwood CAI Laboratory visitors handout), March, 1967, 10 pp.

[88] Suppes, *op. cit.,* p. 79 (footnote 27)

[89] Stolurow, *op. cit.,* p. 272 (footnote 67)

[90] Patrick Suppes, "The Computer and Excellence," *Saturday Review,* January 14, 1967, p. 50.

[91] Hutchins, *op. cit.* (footnote 2)

[92] *Ibid.*

Chapter 26. EDUCATIONAL FUNCTIONS FOR COMPUTERS

CURRENT PROBLEMS IN CAI

James L. Rogers

Even the reader who only casually keeps up with developments in the data processing field, or in education and training, is aware that computers are being used in elementary and secondary schools, higher education, business, industry, and government agencies to assist in the process of instruction. There are many different points of view from which these activities can be described—one could list the existing installations, or discuss the different applications, or describe the various hardware systems or languages being used, and so forth.

The aim of this article is to consider the progress in CAI to date, identifying some of the difficulties that have been encountered, and suggesting changes needed if matters are to improve. Accordingly, we will describe CAI developments under the following headings:

SOURCE: Reprinted with permission from ® *Datamation*, September, 1968, pp. 28-33. Published and copyrighted 1968 by F. D. Thompson, Inc., 35 Mason St., Greenwich, Conn. 06830. Reprinted by permission of the author and publisher.

1. Ways in which computers are used to assist instruction—a list and brief description of six different kinds of computer applications in instruction;

2. Issues and problems—a discussion of some results of implementing CAI;

3. Suggestions for future developments—a discussion of efforts which are needed to help resolve some of the current issues and problems.

WAYS COMPUTERS ASSIST INSTRUCTION

In this article, we will limit our discussion to those applications in which the computer output produces some readily identifiable effect upon the instructional interaction. Six different categories of such applications are often included in discussions of CAI, and these are shown in Table 26.1.

In the last category—Interactive Instruction—the computer is used as one agent in the instructional interaction itself, and its effect is direct and immediate. In other categories, the effect of the computer's output may take place through an intermediary, or may be delayed in time. For example, where the learner has access to a computer which he uses as a computational

APPLICATION CATEGORY	INPUTS TO THE SYSTEM	SYSTEM FUNCTIONS	SYSTEM OUTPUT
COMPUTATIONAL AID	Values of variables Data from observations	Solves the formula Carries out the analysis	Solutions to the problem (results of the calculation, statistical analysis, etc.)
SIMULATION	Responses to instruction or data in the learning environment (decisions in games, procedures for operating on-line terminals, test cases in laboratories, maneuvers in aircraft, spacecraft, or naval vessel crew training, etc.)	Uses learner inputs to solve a mathematical model of the process (physical, social, organizational, economic, etc.) being simulated	Outcomes of the learner's decisions, sometimes expressed as changes in the computer-controlled parts of the learner's environment.
LESSON MATERIAL STORAGE AND RETRIEVAL	Information which identifies the learner's area of interest (subject, period, area, etc.) or the learner's progress in a particular course of instruction.	Matches identifiers with those of stored lesson or supplementary material.	Lesson (or supplementary) material requested by the learner (language exercises, classroom or homework assignments, etc.)
LESSON PRESCRIPTION	Learner's performance on test administered following last assignment (may be entered by teacher, teacher's aide, etc.)	Matches learner's performance on last test with characteristics of alternative instructional units for next topic.	Assignment of next instructional unit for use in classroom or laboratory, or for homework, outside reading, etc.
TESTING	Answers to drill and review problems	Grades learner's answers (right or wrong); adjusts difficulty level of next problem set; collects data on all students by problem set.	To learner—right or wrong on each problems; % for set. To teacher—summaries of learner performance
INTERACTIVE INSTRUCTION	Responses to questions asked by the system	Analyzes learner's response, and selects next item to be presented to learner.	To learner—for correct answers, indication of correctness, plus next item; for incorrect answers, some dialogue exploring the correct answer. To course designers—error data by item

TABLE 26-1

FEATURES OF SOME CAI APPLICATIONS

aid, the most readily identifiable effect upon the instructional process may be that the teacher can assign work in areas which simply could not be covered otherwise.

By considering only those cases in which the computer affects the instructional process, we will ignore the many computer applications in education and training which affect other processes. For example, we will not consider the uses of computers to assist school administration (such as class scheduling, staff payroll, test grading, or materials inventory), guidance and placement (such as matching job requirements to student characteristics), nor research (such as item analysis for the purpose of test validation).

The purpose of presenting these categories of CAI applications is not to define CAI, but simply to direct attention to those characteristics of CAI which are most fruitful for the discussion which follows.

Of the many issues and problems—foreseen and not—which have resulted from the different attempts to implement CAI in educational, commercial, and governmental environments, I want to discuss three, chosen because their resolution is necessary if CAI is to evolve into a useful tool.

GAPS IN THE INSTRUCTIONAL PROCESS

Perhaps the most widely known applications of computers in education are those which use the drill-and-review materials developed over the last few years at Stanford University. At last count, the system, feeding a PDP-1/PDP-8 combination at the Stanford University Computation Center, included approximately 83 Teletype terminals located in elementary schools in California, Mississippi, and Kentucky. A similar system of 192 terminals, connected to an RCA Spectra 70, is being installed in 16 elementary schools in New York City. These installations deserve careful examination because they involve large numbers of students in widely separated parts of the country, and represent an enormous investment of public research funds. Furthermore, RCA's very active marketing of the drill-and-review approach may pressure other manufacturers into announcing competitive systems.

The problem which such applications raises can best be appreciated by describing how the system is supposed to work. During each meeting of a 7th grade algebra class, for example, each student leaves the classroom in order to spend approximately 5 to 10 minutes at a Teletype terminal. When the student signs on, the computer presents him with approximately 20 drill-and-review questions appropriate to that day's lesson. The exercises are arranged into five tracks according to "level of difficulty," and the computer selects the track from which this student's exercise is taken based upon his performance on the previous exercise. The computer then prepares a daily performance summary for the teacher of each class.

The most important problem raised by this approach is the lack of any direct interaction between the system and those classroom practices which result in learning. In effect, the computer is being used to test the students, and to prepare test performance statistics for the teacher, and that is all. The teacher is given the responsibility both of interpreting the test data, and of altering his classroom practices to compensate for whatever instructional deficiencies are revealed by the test data.

What happens when the computer dumps all the performance data on the teachers? Perhaps we can infer from Suppes' remark ". . . there are so many questions about performance that can be asked and that the computer can answer that teachers, administrators and supervisors are in danger of being swamped by more summary information than they can possibly digest." [1] If the teachers cannot possibly digest the information, one wonders how they can use the information to advantage in the classroom.

One researcher on the Stanford project remarked "The only reason the teachers like the system is because it takes attendance for them." But in all fairness, it should be realized that unless the teacher has been specifically trained to do so, he will not know where to start in using the data to improve his classroom practices. Under the circumstances, the teacher may be very well justified in feeling that the computer's only tangible contribution to events in the classroom *is* the taking of attendance.

The current drill-and-review applications, then, point up the difficulties encountered when a computer system is installed to do part of the job, and the responsibility to do the rest of the job is left up to teachers who are less than adequately prepared to apply the computer's results to their everyday classroom practices. It would be difficult to find a clearer example of the problem Skinner refers to when he describes efforts which concentrate upon ". . . measuring the results of teaching while neglecting teaching itself." [2]

LIMITATIONS IMPOSED BY SYSTEMS

The characteristics of any CAI system can impose severe limitations upon both the kinds of materials which can be presented to the learner, and the kinds of responses the learner can be required to make. In choosing one CAI system from among those available, and in deciding whether or not to use a given CAI system for a particular instruction task, it is important for the potential user to ask: "What limitations does this system impose upon the material I need to present, and upon the responses I must elicit?" (Again, because our main concern in this article is the instructional interaction, we will not describe the limitations which a CAI system may impose upon other aspects of education or training. CAI system characteristics cannot help but affect the administration of instruction: for example, the system's storage capacity limits the amount of instructional material that can be handled at any one time; the terminals may have to be located within a given number of feet of the central processor, requiring that learners from outlying schools in the district, or offices in the company, would have to be transported to use the system.) Unfortunately, there are few generalizations which are useful in answering this question. It is not useful, for example, to describe the suitability of a CAI system in terms of subject areas, because the limitations imposed by any system affect the teaching interaction at the stimulus-response level, and therefore cut across subject areas. To make matters worse, there are no characteristics common to CAI hardware, nor to CAI software, nor to the kinds of teaching materials used with CAI systems, which can support generalizations about CAI systems with respect to proposed applications.

While a mismatch between system limitations and use requirements cannot be avoided by trusting to generalities, it can be avoided by an analysis which includes a description of the input-output capabilities of the system, and a description of the instructional objectives in terms of the stimuli and responses required.

To show what might be involved in such an analysis, let us consider some representative examples of the kinds of materials we may wish to display to the learner, and of the kinds of responses we may want the learner to make.

1. *Kinds of material to be displayed to the learner.*

   a)   Text: in teaching foreign languages, we may wish to display text including special alphabetic characters; in teaching mathematics, chemistry, and logic, we require special symbols, signs, subscripts, etc., for displaying equations, formulas and expressions.

   b)   Audio: we may want to play back recordings of spoken messages in teaching communication skills, languages or basal reading; and recordings of instruments in teaching music appreciation.

   c)   Graphics: we may wish to display maps in teaching history; motion pictures in engineering or science; still photographs in medicine or art; circuit diagrams in electricity; graphs in mathematics or statistics; engineering drawings in blueprint reading; cardiograms in medical diagnosis; and so forth.

At the present time, no operating CAI system (known to this author) is capable of presenting all of the above materials to a learner. Most CAI systems use a typewriter as their interface with the learner, and are not designed to handle *any* of the teaching materials mentioned above. Strum and Ward describe the problems they encountered in using typewriter terminals.[3] The difficulties are even greater, of course, if one wishes to prepare hard copy of any of these materials for use and retention by the learner. The ability to present to the learner each different kind of material usually requires a different kind of presentation device, together with instructions in the computer language to operate the device—in other words, each different kind of display capability may involve its own peculiar hardware and software problems.

2. *Kinds of responses to be required of the learner.* The terminal behavior specifications (i.e., the teaching objectives of the course, stated in terms of observable changes in the learner's behavior) for courses in various subjects might include the following items:

a) State the expression for the area under the curve.

b) Translate the above sentence into Russian.

c) Fill in the missing parts of the following table.

d) Point to the antibodies in the microphotograph.

e) Outline the temperate zone on the map.

f) Complete the circuit diagram.

g) Describe a relationship.

h) Define a concept.

i) Explain how something works.

j) Summarize the speaker's remarks orally.

There are two major sources of difficulty in using a CAI system to teach anything: the system may not have the *hardware* capability to allow the student to make the response, and it may not provide a *language* in which the instructor can specify how to analyze and evaluate the student's response.

Item *(a)* in the above list requires a keyboard equipped with special mathematical symbols. Item *(b)* requires a keyboard with a complete Cyrillic alphabet. Item *(c)* can be handled easily on a system which includes *crt* display, but a system which provides only a typewriter interface requires that the learner reverse line feed until he positions the proper line of typing with the print element. Items *(d), (e),* and *(f)* each require special equipment, some of which is now in the prototype stage of development.

Items *(g), (h),* and *(i)* pose difficulties of another sort. Using even the simplest available alphabetic keyboard, the student can easily type in his description, definition, explanation, or whatever the question requires him to enter. The problem is that there are no methods for deciding the semantic equivalence of what Spolsky[4] modestly describes as ". . . a very large number . . . " of sentences. As a result, we cannot, at present, tell the computer how to process a learner's input to decide whether or not his response *means the same* as the model answer we have stored for that response. Instead, we force the learner to respond within the constraints of an artificial language, thus allowing no ambiguity. Or, we allow natural language responses, but we restrict the length of the response to that which rules out the most probable sources of ambiguity. At best, we rely upon features of the response other than its meaning (the presence of specified key words, the order in which they appear, etc.) to determine its match to our "answer" (right or wrong). In all such cases, we allow the tail to wag the dog: it is the specification of the learner's terminal behavior which should determine the characteristics of the response, not our inability to handle problems of meaning, and whenever we modify the requirements for the response in a way that settles for something less than the terminal behavior specification, to that extent we degrade the quality of the instruction.

In everyday practice, this problem is aggravated by the fact that some of the CAI languages which the instructor must use to specify his requirements for acceptable responses do not allow even the primitive level of analysis represented by such procedures as scanning for key words, editing out punctuation, allowing certain flexibility in spelling, etc.

Item *(j)* presents both hardware and software problems. We do not yet know how to translate spoken words into written words, that is, we cannot speak into one end of a device, and have the text of our spoken words print out at the other end. So we lack this kind of student interface in available CAI systems. But even if such a device were available, we would be just as far from being able to analyze its output as we are from analyzing any other free-form response. Recognition of the meaning of speech therefore involves both a hardware problem which is unique and a software problem which it shares with other kinds of responses.

One revealing question to ask is, "If available CAI systems impose such restrictions as these, how are they being applied to teaching applications?" In other words, how are researchers overcoming the inherent limitations of the CAI systems they are stuck with? Several approaches are being tried, and are worth considering:

a)   Add outside components to perform the functions which the CAI system cannot—for example, if your CAI system cannot present photographs to students, have the photographs reproduced in advance, packaged, and distributed to each student; then at least your course can direct the student's attention to the information, and ask questions based upon the "supplementary" material.

b)   Modify the system—for example, the Slavic linguistics department at Stanford has installed Teletypewriters with Cyrillic keyboards in their introductory Russian course.

c)   Modify your teaching objectives to fit within the capabilities of the system—for example, one of your course objectives may be to teach the student to list the characteristics of something (a chemical compound, a period of a nation's history, a style of poetry, etc.); if your CAI system language will not accept alphabetic inputs, then abandon your original course objective, and substitute another one which can be handled by your computational language—instead of teaching the student to *produce* the list of characteristics, produce each item for him, and ask him to enter numbers which indicate whether or not he *recognizes* that it belongs in the list (your course outline will look the same to anyone who is curious as to what you are teaching).

d) Conclude that CAI is not a fruitful approach, and continue to teach the way you used to.

None of these approaches is very satisfactory: Adding outside components may pose complicated distribution and inventory problems. Modifying the system can be expensive. Modifying one's teaching objectives to fit the hardware capabilities usually results in a deterioration of the good qualities of the instruction. Concluding that CAI is not a fruitful approach is foolish, unless you have investigated all existing systems, and unless you know that future technological developments will never change the situation.

PRODUCTION OF CAI TEACHING MATERIALS

Since the earliest experiments with CAI systems, it has been recognized that a major obstacle to the successful application of CAI is the lack of quality course materials. As we will see later on, the shortage of qualified people to produce such materials is an important factor here. This lack is not a great problem for industry, business, or government. Each company or agency tends to develop much of its own instructional materials since course content usually concerns facts about products, services, policies, or procedures which are relevant only to a particular organization.

In contrast, the formal educational establishment tends to produce a smaller portion of the instructional materials it consumes, and relies instead for the bulk of its needs upon the textbook publishers, and upon the manufacturers of supplementary materials (audio-visual aids, kits, laboratory equipment, and so forth). As a result, the availability of CAI curriculum materials for use in formal education is a critical matter, and the means employed to meet this need will have far-reaching effects upon the quality of the instruction, and hence upon the acceptability of the concept of CAI itself. The discouraging example of the unimaginative use of educational television should stand as a warning that the availability of hardware with powerful functional characteristics is not enough to result in improvement of education. Today we face the very real danger that the challenge of applying CAI will be avoided, and that this opportunity for educational improvement will be lost. This danger will persist as long as CAI is regarded primarily as a means of extending traditional classroom practices, or as long as educators remain enchanted by visions of using a CAI system because it allows them to "orchestrate" the presentation of multi-media materials. Students do not learn simply because they know they'll be tested, nor because material is presented to them in four colors, nor because they are bombarded with multi-media presentations.

The computer is the most effective tool yet devised for arranging the stimulus-response-reinforcement contingencies which constitute the learning interaction. How CAI course material is designed will determine whether the potential of the computer will be wasted in simulating traditional practices. There is already some evidence of the bad results which can be expected when CAI users systematically disregard even the most general prescriptions of behavioral technology.[5]

From time to time, with emphasis depending on the source, it has been suggested that CAI course materials will be produced by computer manufacturers, school teachers, textbook publishers, and independent companies specializing in curriculum development for CAI. We will briefly examine each of these suggestions.

The suggestions that CAI system manufacturers would produce curriculum materials have died out, mainly because no computer manufacturer (with one exception to be discussed next) has the appropriate resources to attempt the time-consuming and expensive developmental and marketing efforts involved. The one manufacturer having a recognized and respected in-house curriculum development capability is IBM, which bought Science Research Associates, Inc., in 1964. When the IBM 1500 CAI System was announced two years later, the press release stated that course and supplementary materials in nine subject areas were being developed by SRA.[6] Since then, however, SRA has not published any CAI courses, and it is not now clear when, or if, such materials will be available as standard products to educators. In retrospect, then, it has turned out that computer manufacturers have not been an important supplier of curriculum materials.

An alternative suggestion—that teachers produce their own CAI materials—has enjoyed much greater favor. In fact, faced with the current lack of available programs, there is scarcely any other path open to the would-be CAI user. But there are difficulties in this approach which should be recognized.

First, the time required to produce CAI materials exceeds the time which teachers can reasonably be expected to spend. The accumulated experience in producing programmed instructional materials shows that approximately 100 hours of analysis, programming, and editing effort are required to produce material which occupies the student for one hour.

To this must be added the time required to put the instructional program into CAI form. Strum and Ward [7] summarize their experience as follows: "It has been estimated that the writing of a programmed book absorbs one to two orders of magnitude more effort than is required to write a conventional text on the same subject. The present authors estimate that *another* one or two orders of magnitude separate the computer program from the programmed text." Reynolds states that ". . . fairly careful records we have kept in course development in CAI at Texas Christian University (and other sources as well) indicates a minimum of 300 man-hours per hour of instruction . . . " [8] But even if we assume a conservative 100-to-1 hour ratio, where is the average school teacher or college professor going to get the time to produce CAI material covering any significant portion of a course?

The second difficulty is that there are few people—teachers included—who possess the diverse skills required to prepare self-instructional materials. Such courses are usually produced by a team, combining the skills of:

1. Subject matter experts, who specify content and objectives;

2. Behavior analysts, who apply learning principles to specified knowledge and skills;

3. Programmers, who convert the behavioral analysis into appropriate instructional interactions; and

4. Program editors, who revise and refine the instructional sequences in the light of performance data.

In addition, test subjects, typists, draftsmen, and illustrators may be needed from time to time in the production process.

If we consider the teacher or professor developing material for use in a CAI system, we can probably assume that he will be his own subject matter expert. Furthermore, he probably can use his own students as test subjects. And he may be able to use keypunch operators at his institution's *edp* center instead of the typists we have listed. But even with these simplifying assumptions, the central problem remains: few people have the skills required to produce instructional material with predictable performance characteristics. Quality CAI material is not produced by simply using the computer to emulate classroom practice, yet many teachers have little else to guide them when they begin trying to use CAI systems.

THE MANUFACTURERS' CONTRIBUTION

Ironically, the manufacturers of CAI systems have little help to offer. (One example of this deficiency occurred when the Philadelphia City Schools were installing a Philco-Ford 16-terminal CAI system, and had to hire an independent consultant to discuss with teachers the strategies of organizing course material for computer input.) All of the CAI system manuals I have seen assume that the user has already solved the problems of behavioral design and testing, that is, they begin at the point at which the user is ready to express his instructional sequences in a particular CAI language. Even SDC's PLANIT, which guides the program writer by reminding him of the choices available during his on-line program construction and entry, actually assumes that all of the important pedagogical decisions have been made before the program writer makes his entries.

The user's plight is not helped by the style of CAI systems manuals—all of those I have examined start off as if the reader were thoroughly familiar with *edp* concepts, terminology, and procedures. There is no evidence that the authors took into account the background that teachers, curriculum writers, training specialists, and others would bring to the task of using CAI systems.

In summary, then, the lack of available CAI course materials, together with the shortage of people with relevant production skills, have forced many teachers into preparing their own CAI materials. The difficulties they have faced in so doing include their own lack of the specialized skills required to produce self-instructional materials, the restraints on the amount of time they can devote to such work and the lack of any effective help from the CAI systems manufacturers.

A third source of CAI course materials is the textbook publishers. To review some of the developments in this area, we must go back to RCA's entry into the CAI field. At the opening of the RCA Instructional Systems offices in March of 1967, the president of Random House, Inc. (an RCA subsidiary) stated, in discussing the new venture, "Our specific assignment is the provision of the instructional materials themselves." [9] Subsequently, it was revealed that the L. W. Singer Division of Random House is adapting *Spelling-Diagnostic Paragraphs* for CAI. In May of 1967, RCA announced an agreement with Harcourt, Brace & World, Inc., under which the publisher would adapt its *Language and Daily Use* series in grades 4, 5 and 6 for use with RCA computer equipment. Later in 1967, Harper & Row also reached agreement with RCA to produce supplementary material for use with their widely used *Today's Basic Science* series.

THE PUBLISHERS' ACTIVITIES

In a relatively short time, RCA has formed a network of alliances with major textbook publishers which may have far-reaching effects on CAI curriculum development. Such a move is potentially of great benefit to each of the participants. It enables the computer manufacturer to avoid the costly, unfamiliar job of curriculum development, and yet he can assure his potential customers that reputable publishers are busy producing learning materials for use with his system. The publisher also stands to gain: his textbook salesmen have a distinct marketing advantage when dealing with any school which uses (or intends to use) that manufacturer's CAI system. Such schools will be under heavy pressure to show tangible results from their adventures in CAI, and will find it difficult to turn away a textbook salesman who offers a ready-to-go package of computer-based material which supplements an established text series. If the school is already using that textbook series, the argument will be even stronger.

However, the publisher in such an alliance takes a risk to the extent that he invests in developing programs for a system which may not be well received, or which may become obsolete before he regains his investment. As more different CAI systems are introduced to the market, it will become decreasingly attractive for the publisher to develop materials for any one of them, and increasingly expensive for him to develop materials for all of them. These problems raise the whole issue of a CAI common language, and do so with an urgency which is unique in the development of computer applications. It would not be surprising to find textbook publishers in the vanguard of efforts to establish standards for a common CAI language.

While only secondarily aimed at curriculum material production, several related projects are underway at McGraw-Hill: collaboration with the University of Texas CAI Laboratory in the development of remedial English materials for college freshmen; support of exploratory work at the University of Pittsburgh Learning Research and Development Center relating to innovations in spelling teaching; and collaboration with a major urban school district in preparing curriculum packages in areas yet to be specified. The primary aim of these efforts is to help establish the appropriate roles of authors, editors, and consultants in the CAI production process, and to investigate different modes of a publisher's interaction with teachers, CAI programmers, researchers, etc.

The fourth and last possibility we shall consider is that CAI courses will become available from organizations formed for the specific purpose of producing such materials. The largest and apparently most successful of these companies is Computer Curriculum Corp. (formed by Suppes, Atkinson, and Wilson) which started operations in October, 1967. Their major curriculum contract is with Harcourt, Brace and World to produce drill-and-practice materials for use with Harcourt's *Language and Daily Use* text series, but generalized so that they can be used with other language arts texts. Computer Curriculum Corp. employs about 25 writers, editors, and computer programmers, organized into project teams.

It is far too soon to evaluate the impact of these CAI materials production houses. They face the same shortage of qualified people which their competitors do. They have several potential advantages going for them—for example, compared to the efforts of individual teachers, professors, or consultants, they can presumably apply to any given project a greater variety of the skills which are needed to assure the quality of self-instructional materials.

In summary, the CAI material houses are a development worth watching. Their activities are aimed at filling an obvious need, and their activities may have an important impact upon the application of CAI systems.

SUGGESTIONS FOR FUTURE DEVELOPMENTS

In the previous section, we examined three problems which have arisen in connection with the current CAI applications. Several of our suggestions for future developments will, then, deal with the problems we have already mentioned.

1. Some of the funds available to schools for the purchase of the hardware used in drill-and-review systems should be spent instead to study what it takes for the teacher to apply the summarized test data to classroom practice, and to develop a vehicle for appropriate teacher training. The emphasis in drill-and-review systems should be shifted, at least temporarily, from the problem of gathering the data to the problem of understanding and applying the data.

2. Much more work needs to be done aimed at overcoming what Spolsky identifies as "... the present inadequacy or incompleteness of linguistic theory." [10] Ideally, the person writing an instructional program should be able to state a question to be asked of the learner, provide an answer to the question, and then specify that any response of the learner's which means the same is to be treated in the same way by the program. Although we may never attain this ideal goal, any approximation to it will have a significant beneficial effect upon CAI applications.

3. In his article in this issue, Zinn points out that the "... benefits unique to computer presentation and control have not yet been demonstrated ... few lesson designers have made use of capabilities beyond those which can be accomplished with the printed format." One reason this is the case is that most lesson designers are using CAI systems to prepare specific course material, and the exigencies of such work—deadlines, funding arrangements, contract commitments, available time on the system, etc.—preclude the investigation of untried techniques. To correct this situation, projects should be initiated for the primary purpose of making the computer do that which the text—programmed or otherwise—cannot do.

4. While recognizing the dangers of too-hasty standardization, efforts aimed at specifying a common CAI language should continue. This work will be most difficult, since it will require reconciling the conflicting interests of such diverse parties as hardware manufacturers; educators (teachers, school administrators, curriculum specialists); textbook publishers; trainers in business, industry and government; and research specialists representing linguistics, behavioral technology, man-machine communications, etc.

5. The obvious hardware improvements are needed in CAI as well as in other computer application areas: more reliable, less expensive components. Significant advances which promise to improve the performance and to reduce the cost of terminal displays have been

demonstrated by the Plasma Display Group at the University of Illinois Coordinated Science Laboratory, and more recently by RCA. Work is also needed to provide CAI system hard copy output devices for graphic as well as alphanumeric information, under both learner and program control.

Clearly there is much work to be done. One can only hope that those involved in the work will heed Oettinger's articulate warning, "Whatever the setting for educational experimentation, it is vital in our still profound ignorance to shy away from rigid prescriptions of either goal or technique. There is too much rigidity even in the present innovation fad which, ironically, diverts human and financial resources from both basic research and sustained application and evaluation efforts into the most visible quickie approaches that can sustain the illusion of progress." [11]

NOTES

[1] P. Suppes, "The Uses of Computers in Education," *Scientific American,* Vol. 215, No. 3 (September, 1966) p. 217.

[2] B. F. Skinner, *The Technology of Teaching,* New York: Appleton-Century-Crofts, 1968, p. 94.

[3] R. D. Strum and J. R. Ward, "Some Comments on Computer-Assisted Instruction in Engineering Education," *IEEE. Transactions on Education,* E-10, Vol. 1 (March, 1967) pp. 1-3.

[4] B. Spolsky, "Some Problems of Computer-Based Instruction," *Computers in Behavioral Science,* Vol. 11, No. 6 (November, 1966) pp. 487-96.

[5] C. A. Riedesel and M. N. Suydam, "Computer-Assisted Instruction: Implications for Teacher Education," *The Arithmetic Teacher,* Vol. 14, No. 1 (January, 1967) pp. 24-29.

[6] "Preliminary versions of course materials that educators may use with the new instructional system are being developed by Science Research Associates, Inc., an IBM subsidiary. Course materials are in algebra, computer science, German, and statistics. SRA is also developing supplementary materials that allow the student to use the system to solve problems and perform simulated experiments in the study of physics, chemistry, biology, general science and the social sciences." From IBM Processing Div. press release of March 31, 1966, p. 2.

[7] *Op. cit.,* p. 3.

[8] D. Reynolds, "CAI Within a Systems Approach to Instruction," paper presented to the convention of the Association for Educational Data Systems, May 3, 1968, Fort Worth, Texas, p. 14.

[9] Remarks by Robert Bernstein, President, Random House, Inc., RCA Instructional Systems Conference, March 13, 1967, p. 1.

[10] *Op. cit.,* p. 495.

[11] A. G. Oettinger, "The Myths of Educational Technology," *Saturday Review,* Vol. 51, No. 20 (May 18, 1968), p. 91.

Chapter 27. **PERSONALIZING EDUCATION THROUGH COMPUTERS**

COMPUTER TECHNOLOGY AND THE FUTURE OF EDUCATION

Patrick Suppes

Current applications of computers and related information-processing techniques run the gamut in our society from the automatic control of factories to the scrutiny of tax returns. I have not seen any recent data, but we are certainly reaching the point at which a high percentage of regular employees in this country are paid by computerized payroll systems. As another example, every kind of complex experiment is beginning to be subject to computer assistance either in terms of the actual experimentation or in terms of extensive computations integral to the analysis of the experiment. These applications range from bubble-chamber data on elementary particles to the crystallography of protein molecules.

As yet, the use of computer technology in administration and management on the one hand, and scientific and engineering applications on the other, far exceed direct applications in education. However, if potentials are properly

SOURCE: Reprinted from *Phi Delta Kappan,* Vol. 49, No. 8 (April, 1968), pp. 420-23, by permission of author and publisher.

realized, the character and nature of education during the course of our lifetimes will be radically changed. Perhaps the most important aspect of computerized instructional devices is that the kind of individualized instruction once possible for only a few members of the aristocracy can be made available to all students at all levels of abilities.

Because some may not be familiar with how computers can be used to provide individualized instruction, let me briefly review the mode of operation. In the first place, because of its great speed of operation, a computer can handle simultaneously a large number of students—for instance, 200 or more, and each of the 200 can be at a different point in the curriculum. In the simplest mode of operation, the terminal device at which the student sits is something like an electric typewriter. Messages can be typed out by the computer and the student in turn can enter his responses on the keyboard. The first and most important feature to add is the delivery of audio messages under computer control to the student. Not only children, but students of all ages learn by ear as much as by eye, and for tutorial ventures in individualized instruction it is essential that the computer system be able to talk to the student.

A simple example may make this idea more concrete. Practically no one learns mathematics simply by reading a book, except at a relatively advanced level. Hearing lectures and listening to someone else's talk seem to be almost psychologically essential to learning complex subjects, at least as far as ordinary learners are concerned. In addition to the typewriter and the earphones for audio messages, the next desirable feature is that graphical and pictorial displays be available under computer control. Such displays can be provided in a variety of formats. The simplest mode is to have color slides that may be selected by computer control. More flexible, and therefore more desirable, devices are cathode-ray tubes that look very much like television sets. The beauty of cathode-ray tubes is that a graphical display may be shown to the student and then his own response, entered on a keyboard, can be made an integral part of the display itself.

This is not the place to review these matters in detail; but I mean to convey a visual image of a student sitting at a variety of terminal gear—as it is called in the computer world. These terminals are used to provide the student with individualized instruction. He receives information from audio messages, from typewritten messages, and also from visual displays ranging from graphics to complex photographs. In turn, he may respond to the system and give his own answers by using the keyboard on the typewriter. Other devices for student response are also available, but I shall not go into them now.

So, with such devices available, individualized instruction in a wide variety of subject matters may be offered students of all ages. The technology is already available, although it will continue to be improved. There are two main factors standing in our way. One is that currently it is expensive to prepare an individualized curriculum. The second factor, and even more important, is that as yet we have little operational experience in precisely how this should best be done. For some time to come, individualized instruction will have to depend on a basis of practical judgment and pedagogical intuition of the sort now used in constructing textbook materials for ordinary courses. One of the exciting potentialities of computer-assisted instruction is that for the first time we shall be able to get hard data to use as a basis for a more serious scientific investigation and evaluation of any given instructional program.

To give a more concrete sense of the possibilities of individualized instruction, I would like to describe briefly three possible levels of interaction between the student and computer program. Following a current usage, I shall refer to each of the instructional programs as a particular system of instruction. At the simplest level there are *individualized drill-and-practice systems*, which are meant to supplement the regular curriculum taught by the teacher. The introduction of concepts and new ideas is handled in conventional fashion by the teacher. The role of the computer is to provide regular review and practice on basic concepts and skills. In the case of elementary mathematics, for example, each student would receive daily a certain number of exercises, which would be automatically presented, evaluated, and scored by the computer program without any effort by the classroom teacher. Moreover, these exercises can be presented on an individualized basis, with the brighter students receiving exercises that are harder than the average, and the slower students receiving easier problems.

One important aspect of this kind of individualization should be emphasized. In using a computer in this fashion, it is not necessary to decide at the beginning of the school year in which track a student should be placed; for example, a student need not be classified as a slow student for the entire year. Individualized drill-and-practice work is suitable to all the elementary subjects which occupy a good part of the curriculum. Elementary mathematics, elementary science, and the beginning work in foreign language are typical parts of the curriculum which benefit from standardized and regularly presented drill-and-practice exercises. A large computer with 200 terminals can handle as many as 6,000 students on a daily basis in this instructional mode. In all likelihood, it will soon be feasible to increase these numbers to a thousand terminals and 30,000 students. Operational details of our 1965-66 drill-and-practice program at Stanford are to be found in the forthcoming book by Suppes, Jerman, and Brian.[1]

At the second and deeper level of interaction between student and computer program there are *tutorial systems*, which take over the main responsibility both for presenting a concept and for developing skill in its use. The intention is to approximate the interaction a patient tutor would have with an individual student. An important aspect of the tutorial programs in reading and elementary mathematics with which we have been concerned at Stanford in the past three years is that every effort is made to avoid an initial experience of failure on the part of the slower children. On the other hand, the program has enough flexibility to avoid boring the brighter children with endlessly repetitive exercises. As soon as the student manifests a clear understanding of a concept on the basis of his handling of a number of exercises, he is moved on to a new concept and new exercises. (A detailed evaluation of the Stanford reading program, which is under the direction of Richard C. Atkinson, may be found in the report by Wilson and Atkinson.[2] A report on the tutorial mathematics program will soon be available. The data show that the computer-based curriculum was particularly beneficial for the slower students.)

At the third and deepest level of interaction there are *dialogue systems* aimed at permitting the student to conduct a genuine dialogue with the computer. The dialogue systems at the present time exist primarily at the conceptual rather than the operational level, and I do want to emphasize that in the case of dialogue systems a number of difficult technical problems must first be solved. One problem is that of recognizing spoken speech. Especially in the case of young children, we would like the child to be able simply to ask the computer program a question. To permit this interaction, we must be able to recognize the spoken speech of the child and also to recognize the meaning of the question he is asking. The problem of recognizing meaning is at least as difficult as that of recognizing the spoken speech. It will be some time before we will be able to do either one of these things with any efficiency and economy.

I would predict that within the next decade many children will use individualized drill-and-practice systems in elementary school; and by the time they reach high school, tutorial systems will be available on a broad basis. Their children may use dialogue systems throughout their school experience.

If these predictions are even approximately correct, they have far-reaching implications for education and society. As has been pointed out repeatedly by many people in many different ways, the role of education in our society is not simply the transmission of knowledge but also the transmission of culture, including the entire range of individual, political, and social values. Some recent studies—for example, the Coleman report—have attempted to show that the schools are not as effective in transmitting this culture as we might hope; but still there is little doubt that the schools play a major role, and the directions they take have serious implications for the character of our society in the future. Now I hope it is evident from the very brief descriptions I have given that the widespread use of computer technology in education has an enormous potential for improving the quality of education, because the possibility of individualizing instruction at ever deeper levels of interaction can be realized in an economically feasible fashion. I take it that this potentiality is evident enough, and I would like to examine some of the problems it raises, problems now beginning to be widely discussed.

Three rather closely related issues are particularly prominent in this discussion. The first centers around the claim that the deep use of technology, especially computer technology, will impose a rigid regime of impersonalized teaching. In considering such a claim, it is important to say at once that indeed this is a possibility. Computer technology could be used this way, and in some instances it probably will. This is no different from saying that there are many kinds of teaching, some good and some bad. The important point to insist upon, however, is that it is certainly not a *necessary* aspect of the use of the technology. In fact, contrary to the expectations sometimes expressed in the popular press, I would claim that one of the computer's most important potentials is in making learning and teaching more personalized, rather than less so. Students will be subject to less regimentation and lockstepping, because computer systems will be able to offer highly individualized instruction. The routine that occupies a good part of the teacher's day can be taken over by the computer.

It is worth noting in this connection that the amount of paper work required of teachers is very much on the increase. The computer seems to offer the only possibility of decreasing the time spent in administrative routine by ordinary teachers. Let us examine briefly one or two aspects of instruction ranging from the elementary school to the college. At the elementary level, no one anticipates that students will spend most of their time at computer consoles. Only 20 to 30 percent of the student's time would be spent in this fashion. Teachers would be able to work with classes reduced in size. Also, they could work more intensely with individual students, because some of the students will be at the console and, more importantly, because routine aspects of teaching will be handled by the computer system.

At the college level, the situation is somewhat different. At most colleges and universities, students do not now receive a great deal of individual attention from instructors. I think we can all recognize that the degree of personal attention is certainly not less in a computer program designed to accommodate itself to the individual student's progress than in the lecture course that has more than 200 students in daily attendance. (In our tutorial Russian program at Stanford, under the direction of Joseph Van Campen, all regular classroom instruction has been eliminated. Students receive 50 minutes daily of individualized instruction at a computer terminal consisting of a teletype with Cyrillic keyboard and earphones; the audio tapes are controlled by the computer.)

A second common claim is that the widespread use of computer technology will lead to excessive standardization of education. Again, it is important to admit at once that this is indeed a possibility. The sterility of standardization and what it implies for teaching used to be illustrated by a story about the French educational system. It was claimed that the French minister of education could look at his watch at any time of the school day and say at once what subject was being taught at each grade level throughout the country. The claim was not true, but such a situation could be brought about in the organization of computer-based instruction. It would technically be possible for a state department of education, for example, to require every fifth-grader at 11:03 in the morning to be subtracting one-fifth from three-tenths, or for every senior in high school to be reciting the virtues of a democratic society. The danger of the technology is that edicts can be enforced as well as issued, and many persons are rightly concerned at the spectre of the rigid standardization that could be imposed.

On the other hand, there is another meaning of standardization that holds great potential. This is the imposition of educational standards on schools and colleges throughout the land. Let me give one example of what I mean. A couple of years ago I consulted with one of the large city school systems in this country in connection with its mathematics program. The curriculum outline of the mathematics program running from kindergarten to high school was excellent. The curriculum as specified in the outline was about as good as any in the country. The real source of difficulty was the magnitude of the discrepancy between the actual performance of the students and the specified curriculum. At almost every grade level, students were performing far below the standard set in the curriculum guide. I do not mean to suggest that computer technology will, in one fell stroke, provide a solution to the difficult and complicated problems of raising the educational standards that now obtain among the poor and culturally deprived. I do say that the technology will provide us with unparalleled insight into the actual performance of students.

Yet I do not mean to suggest that this problem of standardization is not serious. It is, and it will take much wisdom to avoid its grosser aspects. But the point I would like to emphasize is that the wide use of computers permits the introduction of an almost unlimited diversity of curriculum and teaching. The very opposite of standardization *can* be achieved. I think we would all agree that the ever-increasing use of books from the sixteenth century to the present has deepened the varieties of educational and intellectual experience generally available. There is every reason to believe that the appropriate development of instructional programs for computer systems will increase rather than decrease this variety of intellectual experience. The potential is there.

The real problem is that as yet we do not understand very well how to take advantage of this potential. If we examine the teaching of any subject in the curriculum, ranging from elementary mathematics to ancient history, what is striking is the great similarity between teachers and between textbooks dealing with the same subject, not the vast differences between them. It can even be argued that it is a subtle philosophical question of social policy to determine the extent to which we want to emphasize diversity in our teaching of standard subjects. Do we want a "cool" presentation of American history for some students and a fervent one for others? Do we want to emphasize geometric and perceptual aspects of mathematics more for some students, and symbolic and algebraic aspects more for others? Do we want to make the learning of language more oriented toward the ear for some students and more toward the eye for those who have a poor sense of auditory discrimination? These are issues that have as yet scarcely been explored in educational philosophy or in discussions of educational policy. With the advent of the new technology they will become practical questions of considerable moment.

The third and final issue I wish to discuss is the place of individuality and human freedom in the modern technology. The crudest form of opposition to widespread use of technology in education and in other parts of our society is to claim that we face the real danger of men becoming slaves of machines. I feel strongly that the threat to human individuality and freedom in our society does not come from technology at all, but from another source that was well described by John Stuart Mill more than a hundred years ago. In discussing precisely this matter in his famous essay *On Liberty*, he said,

> the greatest difficulty to be encountered does not lie in the appreciation of means towards an acknowledged end, but in the indifference of persons in general to the end itself. If it were felt that the free development of individuality is one of the leading essentials of well-being; that it is not only a co-ordinate element with all that is designated by the terms civilization, instruction, education, culture, but is itself a necessary part and condition of all those things; there would be no danger that liberty should be undervalued, and the adjustment of the boundaries between it and social control would present no extraordinary difficulty.

Just as books freed serious students from the tyranny of overly simple methods of oral recitation, so computers can free students from the drudgery of doing exactly similar tasks unadjusted and untailored to their individual needs. As in the case of other parts of our society, our new and wondrous technology is there for beneficial use. It is our problem to learn how to use it well. When a child of six begins to learn in school under the direction of a teacher, he hardly has a concept of a free intelligence able to reach objective knowledge of the world. He depends heavily upon every word and gesture of the teacher to guide his own reactions and responses. This intellectual weaning of children is a complicated process that we do not yet manage or understand very well. There are too many adults among us who are not able to express their own feelings or to reach their own judgments. I would claim that the wise use of technology and science, particularly in education, presents a major opportunity and challenge. I do not want to claim that we know very much yet about how to realize the full potential of human beings; but I do not doubt that we can use our modern instruments to reduce the personal tyranny of one individual over another, wherever that tyranny depends upon ignorance.

NOTES

[1] P. Suppes, M. Jerman, and D. Brian, *Computer-assisted Instruction at Stanford: The 1965-66 Arithmetic Drill-and-Practice Program* (New York: Academic Press, Inc., 1968).

[2] H. A. Wilson and R. C. Atkinson, *Computer-based Instruction in Initial Reading: A Progress Report on the Stanford Project.* Technical Report No. 119, August 25, 1967, Institute for Mathematical Studies in the Social Sciences, Stanford University.

Name Index

Subject Index